# Spain: *The Rise of the First World Power*

Mediterranean Europe Series I

# Spain: *The Rise of the First World Power*

### John Fraser Ramsey

Published for the

**Office for
International Studies and Programs**

by

**The University of Alabama Press**
University, Alabama

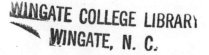

*To Brooks, Harriet,*
*and Michele Thompson*

# Contents

# FOREWORD

OF THE THREE GREAT IMPERIAL EXPERIMENTS OF WESTERN CIVILI-
zation—the Roman, the Spanish, and the British—the Spanish is the
most intriguing and in many ways the most remarkable. The Roman
was the most compact and enjoyed the unifying factor of Mediterranean
geography. Distances, while great, were not impossible to conquer,
and much of the empire could be reached by overland journeys or
relatively short sea voyages. The British empire, reaching its greatest
growth during the era of the revolution in transportation and communications, was able to conquer its problems of time and space with
the assistance of train and steamship, telephone, telegraph, and cable.

It was the unique achievement of the Spanish peoples to establish
a world empire with industrial and technical equipment not much
advanced beyond that of the Romans, but covering an area many times
greater. In spite of the proud claim of the British, it was the Spanish
empire of the sixteenth century on which the sun never set and which
may be truly called the first world power. The events which enabled
a small collection of Iberian states to achieve a larger unity and, under
a German dynasty, to become the dominant European power of the
sixteenth century have always constituted a certain challenge to historians. How was it possible that Castile, torn by feudal anarchy in
the fifteenth century, or Aragon, about to experience the throes of
social revolution, could have established the foundations of empire,
both within and without Europe by the century's end? Indeed, the
internal history of the two principal Iberian states in the fourteenth
and fifteenth centuries seemed to make such a development highly
unlikely.

But the obvious is not a trustworthy guide, in history as in much
else in life. Powerful forces were at work in Aragon and especially
in Castile that were going to constitute an excellent apprenticeship
to empire. And once two wise rulers were able to put down anarchy
and coordinate their efforts, the outburst of energy that resulted was
to astonish the world. Defining and describing these forces is the
purpose of this study.

Writing a history of the rise of the first world power is not quite
the same thing as writing a history of Spain. The focus is different:
some events are dramatically emphasized; others are pushed into the
background. It is a history of a process that is being written, rather
than the history of a geographical area. The political events are them-

selves well enough known and need little elaboration; they cannot be ignored, but other factors—intellectual, social, economic, religious —are more significant in explaining the rise of Spain. Viewed from the vantage point of several centuries later, the roots of Spanish world power were in the process of growth from early medieval times. The climax—Spain under the Habsburgs—was anything but an accident.

Several people made generous contributions of their time and energy in helping the author prepare this book for publication and he is grateful for their assistance. Mr. Carl J. Mora read the manuscript in its entirety and made valuable suggestions. Professor Edward H. Moseley, of the Department of History, The University of Alabama, read a portion of the manuscript to its great improvement. Thanks are also due to the University Research Grants Committee, who made it possible for the writer to spend a summer at the Library of Congress; and to the University administration, which granted a sabbatical leave at a crucial moment. The demanding task of typing the manuscript was efficiently carried out by Mrs. Brooks Thompson; my appreciation for her and her family has already been indicated. Mr. James Garcia Russell, Mrs. Carolyn Sassaman, and Mr. Boyd Childress all worked faithfully on various parts of the index, and my special thanks go to Mr. Terry J. Guthrie for laboring diligently with me on proofreading, as well as preparing and typing the index material. The maps are the work of Dr. Walter Koch of The University of Alabama Department of Geography.

Tuscaloosa, Alabama                                          John F. Ramsey

# PART I
## Introduction

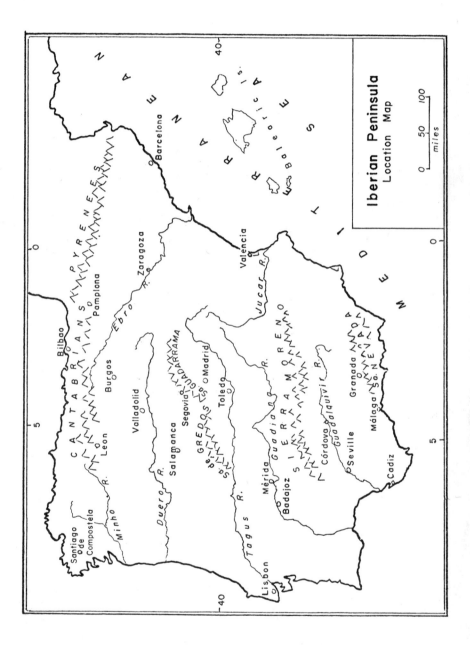

Iberian Peninsula
Location Map

# CHAPTER I

# The Genesis of a People

# and a Nation

THE HISTORY OF SPAIN IS NOT THE HISTORY OF A HIGHLY unified area, nor of a racially pure people. In its geography, Spain presents a wide diversity of topography and climate: low coastal areas quickly give place to high interior semi-arid plateaus cut by deep river basins, or broken up into isolated valleys by transverse ranges of mountains. The diversity of topography is matched by contrasts of climate, as the words hot, dry, cold, wet, warm, and humid, all of which can be applied, indicate. The connection with Europe is narrow and mountainous. Seven-eighths of Spain's border is sea coast, and the remaining eighth, which forms the connection with the rest of the continent, is occupied by the second highest range of mountains in Europe. The Pyrenees have always been more of a barrier than the Strait of Gibraltar, which Spanish zoology and botany show as clearly as history. Europe, according to an old saying, begins (or ends) at the Pyrenees.

To geographical diversity, one must add a diversity of peoples and, within historical times, nations. God, nature, and history all seem to have intended that this land should be many Spains rather than one. It is true that as early as the seventh century A.D. St. Isidore salutes his country in resounding Latin as *O sacra semperque felix, mater Hispania*, but history was to prove this mainly rhetoric for many centuries to come. The earliest accounts (Greek writings probably derived from older Phoenician sources) refer to separate groups under such names as Tartessians, Mastienians, and Iberians.

Concerning the earliest inhabitants, very little is known.[1] Some

1. Earlier assumptions that the prehistoric peoples of Iberia came mainly from north Africa are now being questioned. The younger prehistorians tend

scholars refer to them as Ligurians, but almost any name would do. Around 15,000 B.C. their descendants or later invaders had developed a high prehistoric culture. We should probably give them the credit for one of the outstanding achievements of the human spirit, namely, painting—as the incredible drawings of the Altamira Caves attest. Other, and quite different, cave paintings found along the eastern coast from Lérida to Granada seem to indicate the existence of several distinct stone-age cultures even at this very remote time. It is significant to point out that while these paintings are, for the period, unique in Europe, somewhat similar drawings have been found in the Sahara. Eventually, as the ruins and artifacts show, this era, which prehistorians call the Upper Paleolithic, came to an end and was succeeded by the Neolithic with its polished stone implements, its agriculture, its domestication of animals, and its massive stone monuments. The earliest metal implements are made of copper, which seems to have been first worked in Andalusia sometime between 2800–2500 B.C. With the ending of the prehistoric period, usually associated with the appearance of metals, we find ourselves on slightly less shaky ground with regard to folk movements and time periods.

2

Within roughly historical times, Spain has been visited, invaded, colonized—almost any term is appropriate—by Phoenicians, Greeks, Carthaginians, Romans, Celts, and Iberians. For convenience sake, I think we might classify them as invaders from the east, and migrations from the north and south. Of the peoples listed, the first four obviously came from the east and mainly by sea, while the last two were probably overland migrations from Europe and Africa.

The Iberians are a definite people and various ancient writers have described them, yet it is not known whence they came or precisely when. They are supposed, by some scholars, to have come from Mesopotamia and possibly by way of north Africa, or southern Europe. One writer notes a possible connection between them and the pre-Celtic population of Ireland, chiefly because of certain burial customs.

to emphasize the importance of the European or Mediterranean element in these early peoples. In view of the lack of concrete evidence, probably all final judgments should be withheld. As Jaime Vicens Vives so aptly has pointed out, "A simple calculation suffices to show that the deposits of stone artifacts cover barely one-thousandth of the time and space needed to formulate a theory that would have any chance of being successfully defended. One glance at the archaeological map is enough to demonstrate that the distribution of these deposits has much more to do with their proximity to a university center, or to a government-supported archaelogical team than with the possible diffusion of a culture." Jaime Vicens Vives, *Approaches to the History of Spain.* Translated and edited by Joan Connelly Ullman, with a foreword by José Ferrater Mora (Berkeley: University of California Press, 1967), pp. 151–52.

What is certain is that around the middle of the first millennium B.C. they were living in central and eastern Spain and had even penetrated southeastern France. Later, the Celts may have pushed them into central Portugal. Their name survives in the *Ebro* River and other place names, although it must be remembered that the word itself is a Greek term and we do not know what they called themselves in their own tongue.

The Celts had already occupied considerable parts of central and western Europe when they came into Spain through the eastern Pyrenees sometime between 1000–700 B.C. Modern Spanish place names ending in *briga* are supposed to be survivals of Celtish names. They seem to have been somewhat lower in civilization than the Iberians whom they fought and probably expelled from large areas of the center and northwest. At least two, and possibly more, waves of Celts invaded the peninsula. They brought with them the use of iron and great skill in metal working as well as the custom of building fortified cities and forts. Ancient Spain seems to have been fairly well divided between Iberians and Celts and in some zones a fusion may have taken place, as the word Celtiberian, used by some writers ancient and modern, suggests. Again the evidence is far too scanty to permit any kind of dogmatic assertion about these peoples from the dawn of Spanish history.

3

While the Celts were perhaps entering Spain for the first time through the Pyrenean passes, the far south of the peninsula was being visited by that busy and ubiquitous Mediterranean people, the Phoenicians. Perhaps, like the Spaniards in America some 2500 years later, they were attracted by the fame of a mysterious and wealthy city, in this case Tartessos, somewhere near the south Atlantic coast. They found in this region many things of value, particularly minerals, and soon they began to establish trading posts, one of which, Agadir (near the modern Cádiz), became a center of considerable splendor. Another important center was constructed on the site of modern Málaga. The Phoenicians seem to have been so stimulated by their travels that they wrote about them, thus introducing to the world the first literature of discovery and exploration. Unfortunately, these accounts survive only in references by other ancient writers who had read them; the originals vanished millennia ago.

The Phoenicians brought to Spain the art of mining, their own superior metallurgy, all sorts of *objets d'arts*, sculpture, and, for the first time, writing. This writing was apparently taken up by the early inhabitants of southwestern Spain and later spread to the eastern regions. Unfortunately, it still cannot be deciphered.

Presumably the news of Spain and its products was spread eastward through the Mediterranean by the Phoenicians. Since the Greek world was already well into its age of expansion and colonization, we may easily assume that contacts with the Phoenicians led the Greeks to Spain. Certainly, they were the next of the eastern peoples to come there and the contacts they established were many and important, although mainly restricted to the east coast.

The Greeks constructed several cities in Spain, of which the most important was Emporion (modern Ampurias) whose name—market place—indicates its *raison d'être*. This city seems to have been the first we know of that possessed a "native quarter," since the Greeks permitted the local Iberians to live in a section of the city surrounded by their own wall. This situation, which obviously dated from the early days of the colony, must have disappeared in time for eventually Emporion became one city rather than two, ruled by "Greek law and native custom."[2]

The Greeks brought to Spain all the great achievements of Greek civilization, and their centers in Spain appear to have been equipped with all the material splendors of a typical Greek city of the great age—spacious temples, theatres, monumental sculpture. To what extent the less material aspects of Greek culture influenced the native inhabitants can never be known, but at least in the field of the plastic arts a real native style, strongly marked by Greek influence, made its appearance.

The last of the eastern invaders, and the only ones before the Romans who attempted an actual conquest, were the Carthaginians. There are the usual stories of a direct invitation from the Phoenicians of Agadir, inviting the Carthaginians to come to their aid when hard pressed by the natives. Whether true or not, certainly by the end of the sixth century the newcomers were firmly settled along the eastern coast from the Strait of Gibraltar to the modern Catalonia. Until the founding of Barcelona during the third century, the center of Carthaginian rule was the city of New Carthage (modern Cartagena), one of the most important commercial and military locations in Spain. Strongly fortified and served by a good harbor, its foreign trade was one of its sources of strength. The development that most strongly impressed the Romans, when they later took the city, was the vast mining operations carried on in the area; during the Roman period some 40,000 men were used to work them.[3]

It should be pointed out that the first effort by a foreign power to establish anything like a centralized rule in Spain was undertaken

2. Rafael Altamira, *A History of Spain from the Beginnings to the Present Day*, translated by Muna Lee (New York, 1949), p. 22.
3. Altamira, p. 29.

not by the Romans but by Carthage, although the Carthaginians were able only to make a start in the direction of unification, which was carried to a successful conclusion by the Romans. After its losses in Sicily, Carthage was led by the famous Barca family to seek compensation in Spain. It was then that a real attempt was made to expand into the interior and turn the isolated trading centers of the coast into something more substantial. Hamilcar Barca and other members of the family largely rebuilt New Carthage in 228–227 B.C. and presumably some member of the family founded Barcelona which represented the extreme northern limits of the Carthaginian power. At the same time Carthaginian arms penetrated as far west as the central plateau, but here their holdings were so quickly terminated by the Second Punic War that they left no permanent organization of the territory.

4

The appearance of Roman power in Spain was an accident of the Second Punic War (218–202 B.C.). As is known to all students of Roman history, the northward advance of the Carthaginians brought them into conflict with the town of Saguntum, a Roman ally. When Hannibal besieged the city in 219 B.C. it appealed to Rome for aid and this precipitated the second great conflict between the two main powers of the western Mediterranean. Before the Romans learned of Hannibal's appearance south of the Alps, a Roman army under Consul Publius Scipio had already started for Marseilles with the intention of attacking the Carthaginians in Spain. When these forces reached the mouth of the Rhone, they learned of the deadly menace of the Carthaginians in Italy itself, and the consul immediately returned to Italy. However, he sent the troops on to Spain under his brother Cnaeus and these landed at Emporion late in the summer of 218. Their successors were to remain in Spain some 600 years.

After a few years of Roman victories, disaster struck in 212 and 211. In a series of reverses both Scipios were killed and the legions were forced back to the Ebro River. However, the growing weakness of the Punic forces in Italy enabled the Romans to send another army to Spain under the command of their best general, the younger Scipio, later known as Africanus. He once more brought victory to the Romans by a bold *coup de main* against the great Carthaginian arsenal of New Carthage, which fell in a bloody assault in 209. With this strong place in their control, the Romans went on the offensive. Although they were unable to prevent a Punic army under Hasdrubal, younger brother of Hannibal, from leaving Spain to come to Italy, this army was later destroyed near Sinigaglia in 208. Meanwhile, the Carthaginian forces remaining in Spain were finally brought to battle near the modern Seville in 207, where Scipio destroyed them. By 206 the war in Spain was at an end, and when the Second Punic War ended in 202, Rome somewhat slowly and hesitantly took over the work of Carthage in the peninsula.

The Roman occupation, pacification, and colonization of Spain was an enormous task that strained to the utmost the resources of the Republic, already burdened with heavy commitments in Greece and Asia Minor. They had to bring together into some kind of hitherto unknown political unity a few Greek coastal settlements, a handful of Phoenician and Carthaginian towns, a narrow hinterland of barely Hellenized natives, and finally a vast stretch of rugged and largely unknown interior. Perhaps no one has summarized it as neatly as Bouchier when he wrote:

> The task which lay before the Republic was to complete the conquest of the peninsula: in the south to add the idea of a state to that of a number of isolated towns by providing common magistrates, an official religion, priesthood, language and code of laws; in the center to develop the natural resources of a not very productive district; in the north to bring down the fierce highland clans to the plains, to overawe them with military colonies and encourage them to pursue the peaceful occupations of mining and agriculture, or else to take service as legionaries or auxiliaries.[4]

It is not surprising, then, that the actual occupation was slow and filled with years of fighting.

After the Second Punic War, the occupation proceeded without too much difficulty until 181 B.C. when native resistance became more determined. In 153 the first Roman efforts were made against the stronghold of Numantia, a name destined for immortality. As the Numantian War was just beginning, a native chieftain succeeded in organizing successful resistance against the Romans on a grand scale. This was the celebrated Viriathus. Taking advantage of the growing hatred of Roman cruelty and deception, he was able to bring under his authority several entire tribes of central and southern Spain. For several years he repeatedly defeated the Roman armies and even forced them back toward the north. However, Viriathus was finally murdered through Roman instigation in 138 and after his death organized resistance began to collapse. Only Numantia, among the cities, maintained a heroic resistance. First attacked about 153 and under almost constant siege after 143, the city did not fall until Scipio Aemilianus undertook operations against it (134–133), and then all that the Romans got was a few acres of smoking ruins. The city was excavated by Adolf Schulten between 1905 and 1912, revealing extensive foundations.

4. E. S. Bouchier, *Spain Under the Roman Empire* (Oxford, 1914), p. 16.

Between 133 and 83 B.C. Spain was at peace internally and the progress of Romanization continued steadily. Spanish troops now began to appear with the legions, and the first provincial organization began to be set up, although it is probable that the actual number of Roman citizens in Spain was still small. The extreme northwest (northern Portugal, Léon, Galicia, Asturias) was probably unoccupied. In 123 B.C. the Romans occupied the Balearic Islands in order to check the activities of pirates who used these islands as a base of operations. The islanders were famous in ancient times as slingers, and soon after the occupation the Balearic slingers became a formidable corps in the Roman army.

The Sertorian War (83—72 B.C.) marks the beginning of a new phase in the relations of the Republic and its Spanish colony. For the first time, and by no means the last, a Roman now used Spain as a base for operations against the Republic. Quintus Sertorius had supported Marius and the Popular Party in the Roman civil wars and as a result had been forced out of the tribuneship by Marius' great opponent Sulla. Going to Spain in 83, he soon came out openly against the Sullan dictatorship and eventually, by 80, was the leader of a major Spanish revolt against Rome. He seems to have had remarkable qualities of leadership, and many Roman deserters joined his forces. In addition to defeating Roman armies repeatedly, he attempted to set up a government on the Roman model (there was even a Senate of 300 members) including the best of both Roman and Spanish elements. Toward the last, his ambitions apparently grew for he was conducting negotiations with the Mediterranean pirates, insurgent slaves in Italy, and Mithridates of Pontus, when the Romans, utterly failing to defeat him in the field, had him assassinated at a banquet in 72.

During the wars between Caesar and Pompey, Spain again provided troops for both sides and important battles were fought there. Caesar's connection with Spain began early in his career when he seems to have procured an amnesty for the supporters of Sertorius after the latter's assassination. In 69–68 he served in the peninsula as a quaestor. When the Pompeian wars broke out, both forces battled in Spain without decision until Caesar intervened in person, securing a decisive victory in 49. Two years later, fighting again flared up in the peninsula, where Pompey's sons continued the struggle after the death of their father. Again Caesar had to be present in person, and the last phase of the Pompeian War finally ended in Spain and for the Roman world as a whole when Caesar won the battle of Munda on March 17, 45 B.C.

In the last upheavals that attended the death of the Republic and the birth of the Principate, the East was more important than the

West and consequently Spain was virtually a spectator. A brief revolt
in 26 brought Augustus to Spain for two years in a final suppression
of the northwest tribes. More important was the new provincial reorganization that the great emperor established. Until 49 Spain had
been divided into two provinces known as Hither and Farther Spain
(Hispania Citerior and Ulterior). Pompey had tried a threefold division,
but the civil wars had prevented a permanent reorganization. After
a geographical survey by Agrippa, Augustus returned to Pompey's
idea of the threefold division. Southern Spain became the province
of Baetica; a new province was set up to the north consisting of Portugal
to the Duero River and part of Extremadura, and known as Lusitania;
and the rest of the peninsula kept the old name of Hither Spain,
or, more commonly, Tarraconensis. This arrangement was generally
adhered to for the next three centuries.

The Augustan Peace was as important for Spain as for the other
areas of the empire. It was a period of much commercial activity and
the building of roads and cities. The *Via Augusta* was constructed
from the eastern Pyrenees along the coast as far southwest as Cádiz,
and twenty-three Roman *coloniae* were established. Important as
always for its minerals, Spain was the center of extensive mining
operations which the Romans conducted on the basis of slave labor.
At the same time, wine and olive oil production was tremendously
important during the period of the Republic and the Empire. Some
classical writers maintained that the olive oil from Baetica was the
best in the empire while others held it to be second only to the best
Greek and Italian oil; in any event, it was of high quality and was
exported all over the Roman world. It is possible that Lyons may
have had a guild of wholesale importers of Spanish oil. For the first
three centuries of the Roman occupation, Spain exported more oil
than any other province.[5] Wine was also important although the quality
of Spanish wine was admittedly not equal to the Spanish olive oil.
The wine industry may have declined during the third century; at
least, it does not appear in Diocletian's famous edict for regulating
prices.[6] Raw wool and corn played an important part in Spain's export
trade, and since much of this commerce filtered through Cádiz it
became an important business center in the early empire.

A further sign of Spain's close identification with all major developments was the appearance of the imperial cult; soon temples to the
deities Roma and Augustus began to appear. Under the later Flavians,
there was an increase in the products of the mines and agriculture,
and Vespasian signalized the increasing importance of the three provinces by extending in 74 A.D. the Latin Right to Spaniards who were

5. Louis Caulton West, *Imperial Roman Spain, The Objects of Trade* (Oxford, 1929), pp. 14–20.
6. Ibid.

not yet Roman citizens. In the opinion of a leading Spanish authority, "by the beginning of the Christian era, a considerable part of the ancient native peoples of Spain had been Romanized."[7]

### 5

Any description of Spain under the Empire obviously involves the introduction of Christianity. There is a tradition that Paul visited Spain and preached there, but this is very uncertain. There are vague references in contemporary writings to Christian churches between 180 and 200 A.D., but no specific names are given. During the persecutions of Decius (249–51) and Valerius (257–59) the references become more specific, and from the reign of the Emperor Diocletian (284–305) the names of some fifty martyrs have been preserved.

That the Diocletian persecutions did not seriously hurt the Spanish Church is shown by the fact that the Council of Elvira was held in 306 in the midst of the persecutions, and was attended by nineteen bishops. It is also clear that the Church was now moving into the upper classes since one of the Canons of Elvira deals with the problems of a Christian serving as a magistrate.[8] It is also interesting to note that this council first formally established the rule of clerical celibacy in Spain and also prohibited the marriage of Christians and pagans. These Church councils were held more frequently in Spain than in any other part of the Christian world; three of them (306, 380, and 406 A.D.) were held during the Roman period, and later, under the Visigoths, they came close to approximating a national assembly.

The two most famous Hispano-Roman emperors, Trajan and Hadrian, did much for their native land, and Hadrian traveled there in 120. But there is some evidence that the economic prosperity of Spain was drawing to a close. Marcus Aurelius (161–180) reduced the taxes — not a sign of prosperity but of the opposite. Evidently the provinces simply could not furnish the required amount. Caracalla in 211–212 bestowed full Roman citizenship on all the empire and this, of course, included Spain. The same emperor also split off Galicia from Lusitania and made it a separate province. Diocletian continued the process and divided Tarraconensis in two, calling the new southern province Carthageniensis. Of more interest is the fact that Diocletian included Mauretania in the Spanish provinces, thus intensifying the connection with North Africa that was to have such fateful consequences in Spanish history.

Spain was remote enough from the barbarian pressure areas to escape

---

7. Altamira, p. 49. It should be added that Romanization was probably limited to urban areas. In the countryside the native element must have been overwhelmingly predominant.

8. Stephen McKenna, *Paganism and Pagan Survivals in Spain up to the Fall of the Visigothic Kingdom* (Washington, D.C., 1938), p. 38.

the Germanic raids until the sixth decade of the third century, when the frontiers of the empire were repeatedly penetrated. Recent investigations have shown that a mixture of Franks and other Germanic peoples crossed the Pyrenees about 262. They destroyed Tarragona, and did much damage in the Levant and in Baetica. A second raid around 275 seems to have reached the interior of the Meseta. All this contributed to a general economic decline, and more specifically to the downfall of the urban classes.[9] Aside from these attacks, the third century was relatively peaceful in Spain, and the number of ruins standing today which date after 200 A.D. suggests that even in decline the Spanish provinces managed to sustain a relatively high culture and standard of living, at least for the upper classes.

6

The presence of Roman arms and Roman institutions for almost six hundred years in Spain has obviously raised important questions for Spanish historians. Just what was the role of Rome in Iberia? Was it a force for unification? Did it help to create modern Spain, or Spanish national consciousness? Can *hispanidad* be understood without taking into account the Roman element? In their answers to these and other questions, Spanish historians have frequently disagreed with one another. Américo Castro in *The Structure of Spanish History* sees no connection between Roman ideals and the Spain of the Reconquest. Ramon Menéndez Pidal, in his various works, believes that there is such a connection, and Vicens Vives and Claudio Sánchez Albornoz seem to vacillate between the two extremes. Perhaps the questions raised have become overly intellectualized. Common sense would certainly indicate that some six hundred years of a foreign occupation would leave strong traces in the historical development of a people, initial resistance notwithstanding. As has been shown, there was such a resistance to the process of Romanization during the first two centuries of the occupation. Nor did the old languages and customs die out at once. The inscriptions of the first two centuries show that in some areas the native tongues had a stubborn persistence. But in the end the new Latin prevailed over all and modern Spanish shows no trace of the pre-Roman languages.[10] Indeed, a linguistic unity is one of the most important results of the Roman rule; not only did the native dialects disappear, but they were replaced

9. Jaime Vicens Vives, *An Economic History of Spain*. With the collaboration of Jorge Nadal Oller. Translated by Frances M. López-Morillas (Princeton: Princeton University Press, 1969), p. 81. Henceforth cited as *Economic History*.

10. Of course, one pre-Roman language is still spoken today in the Basque country, but aside from a few place names taken over into Spanish, it has exercised practically no influence on modern Spanish.

not by others, but *by one*—a fact of great importance. In addition, the imposition of Roman law added another facet of unity, namely, juridical unification. And finally, the establishment of one central authority emanating from Rome, replacing the multitude of tribal governments, brought about a political unity to the peninsula which, above all, was the great achievement and gift of the Romans.

Needless to say, such an achievement was not wrought with kindness and gentle methods. The Romans did not hesitate ruthlessly to destroy cities and uproot whole peoples. The Lusitanians were transferred from an area north of the Tagus to another south of it; the Cantabrians and other tribes were forced to abandon their native mountains and settle in the flat lands far to the south—a part of a general Roman policy of getting the tribes out of the mountains (where the natural defenses favored them) and into the plains. The new Roman cities were also a means of disseminating Roman culture and language. Many of them, such as Augusta Emerita (Mérida), Caesar Augusta (Saragossa), Tarraco (Tarragona), Asturica (Astorga), Hispalis (Seville), Legio Septima (Leon) and Lucus Augusti (Lugo), are flourishing today while Cádiz, Cartagena, Málaga, and Barcelona date from the pre-Roman era, although continuing to be important as leading urban centers throughout the Roman period.

Roman building operations were carried on constantly and extensively throughout the peninsula. All the characteristic achievements of Roman architecture and engineering, such as baths, roads, temples, walls, aqueducts, bridges, and arches are widely distributed; some of them, such as the aqueduct at Segovia or the bridge at Alcantara, are in excellent condition and have been famous for centuries. The contributions, of course, run both ways. Spaniards, both during the Roman period and centuries later in the days of imperial Spain of the sixteenth century, were tremendously proud of contributions made to Roman literature, government, and religion by Hispano-Romans. Here the citations are impressive. Both the Senecas, father and son, were from Córdoba. Lucan also hailed from Córdoba and Martial, the famous poet and epigrammatist, was born near the modern Calatayud. Quintilian came from Calahorra. Among the emperors, some of the greatest were Spanish born, or descended from Roman families long resident in Spain; such were Trajan, Hadrian, Marcus Aurelius, and Theodosius the Great. Thus, as the Spaniards later boasted, when other regions sent tribute to Rome, Spain sent emperors.

In the field of religious activities, Bishop Hosius of Córdoba (256–337) was for a time religious advisor to Constantine the Great, and Saint Damasus, the first Spanish pope (d. 384), entrusted to Saint Jerome the revision of the Latin text of the Bible. Among the early

Christian literary figures should be mentioned the name of Prudentius (348–405?), Orosius (d. ca. 412), who wrote the famous *Seven Books of History against the Pagans* at the instigation of Saint Augustine; and, above all, Saint Isidore of Seville (ca. 570–636) whose encyclopedic writings were a major source of information (and misinformation) on almost every subject during the early Middle Ages.[11]

Thus by the end of the Roman period Spain had achieved, in addition to an artistic and literary tradition, a basic unity of religion, language, law, custom, and government. It does not seem too strong a statement to say that by the opening of the fifth century there were brief stirrings of national feeling. Certainly Saint Isidore's reference to *"mater Hispania"*, cited earlier, seems to imply this. What stands out clearly is that Spaniards of a later day never forgot this close connection between their country and the imperial tradition; when greatness returned to Spain in the sixteenth century, the tradition was very close and fresh to their minds. Sepúlveda, the chronicler of Charles V, saw in his master a figure very similar to Trajan, the expander of empire; J. P. Martir Rizo, writing in 1627, expressed the same idea.[12] A few years later, a Benedictine monk, Benito de Peñalosa, regarded the Spanish conquest of the Indians as an event similar to the expansion of Rome, especially since he felt the Spanish empire had been achieved not by valor alone, but by much patience and wisdom.[13] Juan Blazquez Mayoralgo, an apologist for Ferdinand II, thought the king could be suitably compared with Augustus because both of them were victorious in civil wars.[14] To fully understand the apparent aptitude the later Spaniards had for empire, one must remember that to them it was, in part, the repetition of a role they had already played with some distinction.

11. Pierre Bernadou, *Le Génie de l'Espagne. Études historiques et litteraires*, 3rd ed. (Geneva, 1943), pp. 17–19.

12. Ricardo del Arco, *La idea de imperio en la política y la literatura española*, Madrid, 1944, p. 17 et seq.

13. Ibid.

14. Ibid., p. 22.

# CHAPTER II

# The Visigothic Occupation

EARLY IN THE FIFTH CENTURY, SPAIN WAS INVADED BY SEVERAL German tribes and, although a fiction of Roman rule was maintained by various expedients, it was actually doomed from the moment the invasions occurred. To understand the process by which the Visigoths finally ousted or absorbed the other Germanic peoples and eventually became sole rulers of the peninsula, three developments must be considered: 1) the early history and migrations of the Visigothic people; 2) the origins of the first Hispano-Gallic Visigothic state; and 3) the development of the purely Spanish Visigothic kingdom and its institutions.

The original home of the Germanic tribes seems to have been the Scandinavian peninsula and the shores of the Baltic Sea. Some centuries before Christ (it is impossible to be more precise) they began to move southward, pushing other peoples ahead of them south and west. By the first century B.C. considerable pressure had been built up against the eastern frontier of the Roman Empire, and a few German raids into Illyria, Gaul, and northern Italy had already occurred. Caesar was perhaps the first Roman political figure who had to deal with what might be called "the German problem," and he and his successors for the next century were engaged in establishing a permanent defensive frontier along the Rhine and Danube Rivers. This was carried out with considerable success. Nonetheless, a kind of pacific penetration of the empire by the Germans was going on, in a limited way, throughout this period. Many of them were brought in as prisoners of war and made slaves since the Romans greatly esteemed them for their size, physical strength, and fighting qualities. Some were enrolled in the legions and Caligula prided himself on a personal bodyguard of Germans who were devoted to him; many of them also fought in the arena as gladiators. Later the imperial government permitted them to come in as allies and settled thousands on vacant lands within the empire. In the fifth and sixth centuries when the greatest mass migrations took place, the Germans undoubtedly did a great deal of damage, but it would be wrong to place too much emphasis on this phase of the movement. The word commonly used to describe the German intrusion—invasion—connotating prolonged warfare, contributes to our misconception of what really occurred, and that is why it is preferable to call them "migrations" rather than invasions. As the historian, James Westfall Thompson, used to remark in his lectures, "After all, the Roman Empire was not an enemy to the barbarians; it was a career."

That part of the German peoples who called themselves Goths appear in history about the first century A.D., living in the middle Vistula basin. They believed that they had come from lands farther north and it seems likely that they had some connection with the Baltic island which still bears their name, namely Gotland. Their first contacts with the Romans were violent. In 251 they killed the emperor Decius and defeated his army; and during the next twenty years they ravaged parts of the eastern empire and finally forced the imperial government to abandon the province of Dacia, north of the Danube.

Eventually the Goths split into two groups: the East Goths, also called Ostrogoths, settled north and east of the Black Sea, and do not really belong to this history. The West Goths, or Visigoths, occupied the great plains north of the Danube and were relatively quiet until the overwhelming advent of the Huns, an event which undoubtedly changed the course of European history.

Some time about the middle of the fourth century the Huns, a Mongolian people from central Asia, arrived at the area inhabited by the Goths. The initial impact appears to have been devastating. The Ostrogoths were overwhelmed; certainly for a time they disappear from history. The Visigoths, striving frantically to avoid the fate of their kindred, appeared on the Danube frontier in 376 and asked for shelter within the empire. The rest, of course, is well known to history. How they were miserably cheated and bullied by imperial agents sent to deal with them, how they rebelled, and how they utterly defeated a Roman army and killed the emperor Valens in a great battle near Adrianople in 378, is not really pertinent here. What is significant is the fact that for many years thereafter the Visigoths were loose in the empire, and however difficult this made life for the Romans, it contributed greatly to the development and education of the Visigothic people. In essence, it was training for their rule in

Spain. Shortly after the catastrophe of Adrianople, the government made peace with them and accepted them as *foederati*, or imperial allies. In 395 they chose Alaric for their first king and from then on were an independent people under a primitive government. They had already accepted the Arian form of Christianity; now through countless dealings with Roman officials from emperors on down, they learned something of statecraft and of what the empire meant in the ancient world. In short, an intense process of Romanization began. Athanaric, a Gothic chief, was received with ceremonial honors when he visited Constantinople in 381 and was given a state funeral by the Byzantines when he died. Alaric's celebrated sack of Rome in 410 does not mark the end of cooperation with the empire; rather, it appears as an episode, an unfortunate aberration in a period marked by a considerable degree of harmony. At least, it can be said that Ataulf, Alaric's successor, seems to have had some idea of what Roman-Visigothic cooperation might be able to achieve. His marriage with Galla Placidia, daughter of Theodosius the Great, might have marked the beginning of a real working alliance, but unfortunately his murder at Barcelona in 415 ended such a possibility. However, the great Hunnish crisis of the mid-fifth century produced one final and outstanding example of Roman-Visigothic joint action. When Attila, assisted by his subject Ostrogoths, invaded Gaul, he was defeated by the Roman Aetius commanding an army made up of Roman troops and Visigothic warriors (Châlons, 451); it was in this battle that the Visigothic king Theodoric I (419—451) was killed. By this time the Visigoths were permanently established around Toulouse, had already invaded Spain, and were about to do so again—this time permanently.

It has seemed worthwhile to examine in some detail this early period of Visigothic history because it is necessary to stress the fact that when they came into Spain they were probably more civilized, and certainly more experienced, than the other Germanic tribes in contact with the empire. This fact helps to explain why, for all the bloodshed and violence of its internal development, the Visigothic kingdom of Spain was to be the most advanced Germanic state for the next two centuries. Now, after this lengthy digression, we may return to things more specifically Spanish.

2

During the night of January 1, 406 A.D., a horde of Vandals, Suevi, and Alans crossed the frozen Rhine and permanently breached the frontier defenses in the north. After ravaging in Gaul and doing great damage, they reached the Pyrenees and passed through into Spain in 409. Despairing of getting them out, the weak government of the western emperor Honorius made them *foederati* of the empire in 411 and assigned them parts of Spain in permanent occupation: the

Asding Vandals and the Suevi got Galicia; another Vandal branch, the Silingians, got Baetica; and the Alans, numerically the largest group, received Lusitania and Carthaginiensis. However, before they could consolidate these holdings, the Visigoths enter the story.

After the marriage of Galla Placidia, Ataulf and his brother-in-law, Honorius, had quarreled and the emperor cut off the food and supplies promised to Ataulf. In 415 the latter, in retaliation, invaded Spain only to be assassinated the same year in Barcelona. Eventually Wallia, the new king, returned to the previous understanding with the imperial government, and in return for supplies of grain agreed to subdue the other Germanic tribes in Spain. Ferocious attacks on the Silingian Vandals in Baetica practically exterminated them, and the Alans were greatly weakened. The Asding Vandals migrated from Galicia to Baetica and although time proved that they could not hold it, they did succeed in changing its name from Baetica to Vandalusia, later Andalusia. In 428 or 429 they were apparently invited into the Roman province of north Africa by Count Bonifacius, who had fallen out with the western imperial government that was now located at Ravenna. By this time the Vandals were under the leadership of the redoubtable Gaiseric, destined to be the scourge of Rome and the Mediterranean for the next fifty years. Assembling his tribe, about 80,000 males, on the shores of Andalusia in the spring of 429, he led them to north Africa in ships provided by the traitor Count Bonifacius. Thus the Vandals pass out of Spanish history forever.

By this time the Visigoths were well established in the Roman province of *Aquitania Secunda* or, as it is more commonly called, the Visigothic kingdom of Toulouse, as that city was its capital. In 454 they entered Spain again as *foederati* to put down a revolt in the Roman area and then, at the request of the emperor Avitus, they attacked the Suevi, the only tribe of the original invasion still holding out. A long period of warfare followed. Much damage was done and the issue was still in doubt at the succession of the Visigothic king Euric (466–485).

Coming in between the ages of Gaiseric and Clovis, Euric is the outstanding leader of the Germanic world. Altamira describes him as "not only a great warrior, but also a man of culture with talent and ability for governing."[1] In addition, he was fortunate in being able to escape the assassin's dagger, usually the normal ending of a Visigothic reign, and thus had a much longer time to develop his policies. Euric was able to extend his authority throughout all of Spain except the extreme northwest, where the Suevi still held out. In 475 the emperor Nepos recognized the independence of the Kingdom

1. Altamira, p. 76.

of Toulouse and ceded Auvergne to it. The next year the western imperial line ended with the dethronement of Romulus Augustulus, leaving the Visigothic state as the largest and, superficially at least, the most imposing political structure west of the Rhine.

It must be noted that this state had not yet assumed its exclusive Spanish form. Visigothic territories north of the Pyrenees were extensive, ranging from south of the Loire to west of the Rhone, and were evidently considered by the Visigoths as the most important part of their realm since the royal residence was usually located at Bordeaux, Toulouse, or Narbonne, and never south of the Pyrenees until after 507. The king's subjects included such diverse peoples as Gallo-Romans, Hispano-Romans, Jews, and various fragments of Germanic tribes in addition to the Visigothic aristocracy. Yet this state had serious weaknesses. Given the increasing insecurity of communications in the west at this time, it was much too large to be easily held together. Furthermore, in the revived eastern Roman Empire and in the newly formed kingdom of the Franks, it had enemies who were exceedingly dangerous. Serious religious divisions also constituted another element of weakness. The ruling Visigoths were Arians, while the great majority of the native Hispano-Roman population were Catholics. Early in the sixth century, the Franks, who were by now Catholics, found these religious differences of great advantage to them when they moved south to attack Visigothic Gaul.

By the end of the fifth century, Clovis, King of the Franks, had occupied the northern third of Gaul and established the rudiments of a state, somewhat crudely modeled after Rome. Coming into the empire as a pagan, he had the great good fortune to be converted directly to Catholicism without passing through an intervening period of Arianism. Consequently there were no serious religious differences with the Gallo-Roman population, and he enjoyed the great advantage of the whole-hearted support of the Catholic hierarchy in Gaul. Orthodox Catholics in Arian Burgundy and the Visigothic kingdom looked to him as a future liberator. Clovis did not succeed in the case of Burgundy, which later fell to his sons, but he did better with the Visigoths. Some efforts were made to prevent a break between the leading German states of the west. When Syagrius, a Roman general defeated by Clovis, fled to Spain, Alaric II handed him back to the Franks. However, this did not save Alaric in the end. In spite of attempts by Theodoric, king of the Ostrogoths, to prevent the war, Clovis attacked Alaric II in 507 and personally slew him at the Battle of Vouillé near Poitiers. There is considerable evidence that the campaign was aided by the activities of Catholic bishops in southern France who, because of their common Catholicism, attempted to facilitate the Frankish conquest.

After the disaster of Vouillé, the Visigothic rule north of the Pyrenees collapsed, never to be reestablished. Spain, heretofore rather secondary, now became all-important to the Visigoths. During the remainder of the sixth century, something like a Visigothic migration seems to have taken place from southern France into Spain, with the majority settling in what is today the province of Segovia and some spilling over into Burgos, Soria, Guadalajara, Madrid, Toledo, Valladolid, and Palencia.[2] Demographically speaking, then, the nucleus of the Visigothic state in Spain consisted of some 200,000 Visigoths and perhaps about 100,000 Suevi located in what later would be Old Castile and comprising about ten percent of the total land area of the peninsula.[3] Whether or not one accepts Vicens Vives' figures of some five or six million Hispano-Romans living in Spain during the sixth century, it is clear that in comparison with the native element, the number of Germans then settling in Spain was very small. It should also be noted that the invaders confined themselves largely to the central plateau region and the mountains immediately to the north and stayed out of the periphery especially in the east and south; these regions were still in close contact with the Mediterranean world and retained their late Roman culture relatively intact.[4]

With the loss of Toulouse, it was necessary to find a new center south of the Pyrenees, and Toledo was eventually chosen. This was logical because it was not only an important city during Roman times, but it lay within the central plateau where the Visigoths were settling; henceforth, it was to be one of the most important cities in Spain.

In the middle of the sixth century, Spain became briefly involved in the attempt of the emperor Justinian to revive the western empire. If we are to believe the legends, quarrels among members of the Visigothic royal family led to an appeal by Athanagild to the eastern emperor for military assistance. Whether the stories are true or not, it is clear that Byzantine expansion to the far west of the Mediterranean world was in keeping with Justinian's policies. Consequently a Byzantine expedition succeeded in occupying the southeastern coastal area in 554. Politically, this development was not very important since the Byzantine beachhead was eliminated early in the next century, but culturally it brought new life to the remains of the old Hispano-Roman civilization and strengthened its natural superiority over Germanic influences and tendencies. Byzantine influences in the art and architecture of the period can now be observed. However, the internal exhaustion of the empire after 565, and the growing crisis with Persia, prevented any further extension of these Spanish holdings.

2. Vicens Vives, *Economic History.* p.p. 83–84.
3. Ibid., p. 25, pp. 83–84.
4. See also his *Approaches to the History of Spain*, pp. 22–23.

In spite of the potential danger from Byzantium, the remainder of the sixth century shows a steady advance and consolidation of the Visigothic kingdom of Spain. The loss of the trans-Pyrenean realm appears as a blessing in disguise since the kings could now devote themselves exclusively to the reduction of the last centers of resistance in the Iberian peninsula. By 585, King Leovigild (568–586), the last Arian king and the conqueror of the Suevi, could call himself master of all the peninsula except the Byzantine holdings along the coast,[5] and these were eliminated by King Swinthila (629–31). The formative period of the Spanish Visigothic kingdom was now over.

3

The state set up by these Germanic invaders of Roman Spain might be described as a Visigothic veneer over a solid Roman base. The Roman administrative units were taken over, almost without change, from the largest unit, the province, down to the smallest, the *civitas*. The Roman municipal apparatus in the *civitas* still remained intact although the Visigoths did impose some of their own officials, such as the *thiufadus*—who led 1,000 men in war and also acted as a kind of municipal judge. Bishops were very important, especially since to control the refractory nobility the king "had to throw himself into the arms of the church."[6]

Although the Visigoths were more civilized than the Franks or the Suevi and had been in permanent contact with the Roman world much earlier than the other German tribes, it is significant to note the persistence of some German habits among them. They clung to their Germanic law, and for some time avoided mixing with the Hispano-Roman population. This was fairly easy since they settled mainly in the country and until the time of Leovigild mixed marriages were prohibited by law. As late as 467 the Visigothic king wore his hair long and had a bodyguard clothed in animal skins.[7] On the other hand, the victory of the Latin language, in its late form, was complete. At one time Gothic was probably widely spoken, yet it appears to have disappeared rapidly. Certainly in Spain it had ceased to be used even at court before the Mohammedan invasion.

In actual numbers, the ruling Visigoths continued to be a small minority. In the time of Wallia, the tribe claimed 100,000 warriors; even allowing for a considerable increase in the next century, this would still make them a handful among the much larger numbers

5. A good account of these developments can be found in the opening pages of Ziegler, Aloysius Kieran, *Church and State in Visigothic Spain* (Washington, D.C., 1930), p. 13.
6. Ibid., p. 22.
7. Ibid., p. 17.

of Hispano-Romans living in the peninsula.[8] When it came to land division, the Visigoths fared very well. Except pastures and woodland, which were undivided, estates were broken up on the basis of two-thirds to the invaders and one-third for the native inhabitants; according to Ziegler, the small as well as the large estates were divided.[9] Large holdings soon made their appearance among the Visigoths, and were cultivated by slave labor. Both the *commendatio* and the *precarium* are mentioned in the *Lex Visigothorum* as well as in the fragments that have been preserved of Euric's law code. The king received the private estates of the emperor for his own use, and also the imperial fisc; in later years, probably a good deal of the royal domain passed into the hands of the turbulent nobility.

Unlike the later feudal concepts, in theory at least, the Visigoths held that the monarchy was national and indivisible; this accorded fairly well with both Roman and ecclesiastical concepts. For this reason, because it was not regarded as the personal possession of a family, the crown tended to retain an elective aspect. In theory the ruler was supreme, but the Visigoths did not take kindly to extreme assertions of personal authority among their kings. Those who tried it usually came quickly to an untimely end, as the large number of royal assassinations in the sixth century clearly shows. As the crown became weaker in the later Visigothic period, the rulers lived longer.

The religious history of the post-Roman era naturally falls into two divisions: 1) the Arian supremacy to 589; and 2) the Catholic period, 589–711. As has been pointed out, the Visigoths were Arians when they entered the peninsula. This created a serious division between the new rulers and the masses of the Roman Catholic population, especially since some of the kings were persecutors; Leovigild, one of the outstanding rulers of his time, certainly considered the Catholics to be heretics and tried to force a religious unity based on Arianism.

It was during the reign of this same Leovigild that the religious division of Spain produced a major crisis. One of his sons, Hermenegild, had married a Frankish princess who was, of course, a Catholic. With the aid of Saint Leander of Seville, this lady succeeded in converting her husband to her faith. The result of this conversion seems to have been a general uprising of Catholics in Andalusia to depose Leovigild and place Hermenegild on the throne.[10] After several

8. Ibid., pp. 13–16.
9. Ibid.
10. Here it seems desirable to cite the views of Vicens Vives who, as usual with this scholar, views the quarrel between father and son as considerably more complex than would first appear. Although his terminology is probably more sophisticated than the events warrant, there does seem to be considerable merit to his theory that Leovigild was making a final attempt to assert Visigothic

years of fighting, the rebellion was suppressed and Hermenegild was taken prisoner. The year before his father's death he was executed, although whether at royal command is not known. As a result of this revolt, the strength of the Catholic party throughout the kingdom must have made a powerful impression on Reccared, the new king. In 589, he and most of the nation were received into the Catholic Church at the Third Council of Toledo. Henceforth, the religious unity of the peninsula was gradually established, and the Visigothic Catholic Church began to play an important role in the political life of the nation.

Perhaps the most unique institution of this Church was the Councils of Toledo, of which eighteen were held between 589 and 701. Although nominally Church councils, most of them came close to being national assemblies of the Visigothic state. In addition to passing on a great many religious problems, they also served as a mild check on royal authority and performed important civil functions as well. Matters of internal administration, not specifically religious, were frequently considered.

The councils were usually convoked by the king, and the majority who attended were bishops; however, local documents contain references to abbots, priests, deacons, and even members of the lay nobility so that we may assume the gatherings represented a fairly good cross-section of the upper classes in the monarchy. Later, the presence of laymen must have occasioned some embarrassment, especially when the scandals of the clergy were being aired. At the seventeenth council (694), it was decided that matters of faith and morals of the clergy would be taken up during the first three days, at which time laymen were to be excluded; doubtless this was much safer. The king opened the councils in person; the records show that only the sixth and the seventh were opened with the king being *in absentia*. At later councils, the king retired after an opening statement and his wishes, stated in a formal document, were debated by the gathering in his absence.

---

supremacy (both in religion and government) over the masses of Hispano-Romans. He notes that this king was the first Visigoth to assume Roman royal insignia and that he made a determined attempt to assert his political authority over Andalusia. Here he met a determined resistance which even reached his own family when Hermenegild led a southern revolt against him. Although Leovigild succeeded in suppressing this uprising, his effort to bring the native element to acknowledge Visigothic supremacy was unsuccessful as was shown by Reccared's conversion to Catholicism almost immediately after his succession. Vicens Vives sees this as a victory for the Hispano-Roman culture. Henceforth, he has stated, although the Visigoths exercised a declining political power over the country, the Hispano-Romans kept it going, and exercised the dominant influence on legislation, economics, and spiritual life. Vicens Vives, *Approaches to the History of Spain*, p. 24.

At the end of each council, decisions both spiritual and temporal were ratified by the sovereign in a formal decree. There is no other medieval institution at this time that exactly compares with the Spanish Councils of Toledo. While not a full parliament, they were far more than an advisory, or purely religious, body. It might be noted, however, that they had no taxing power.[11]

Relations between the Visigothic Church and the Holy See were rather slight. Spain was far away and communications during the sixth and seventh centuries were always uncertain at best. For political reasons, Rome was much more concerned with the development of the Frankish state. In fact, between 604 and 711 only eight papal letters appear to have passed from Rome to Spain. This relative isolation may have helped to develop the independence and self-sufficiency of the Visigothic Church to an unhealthy degree, as Ziegler seems to think.

> The comparative isolation of Spain from the rest of the Christian world, the peculiar union of Church and State, and the mixing of spiritual and civil matters, the acknowledged powers of the king in the sphere of religion, the participation of the bishops in secular and civil affairs, the magnified importance of the national councils and of the metropolitan See of Toledo, all served to give the Visigothic Church a character self-contained and self-sufficient to a degree not found elsewhere. There was a trend in the Spanish Church that might be called Hispanism. It did not forbode good.[12]

We shall meet most of these characteristics again in the Spanish Church of the imperial age.

Perhaps the greatest intellectual achievement of the Visigoths, if we except the delightfully inaccurate works of that mine of misinformation, Saint Isidore, was their legal codes. No other German people produced anything comparable at such an early period. There are fragments of a code issued by King Euric about 475 which is largely taken from Roman models. The next king, the unfortunate Alaric II, issued in 506 the Lex Romana Visigothorum for his Roman subjects, perhaps hoping to win their support on the eve of his great struggle with Clovis. Leovigild revised the code and expanded it. Later rulers tended to ignore the differences between Roman and Visigothic law and finally in 654 Recceswinth promulgated the famous Liber Iudiciorum which fused both systems into one, intended for all subjects. It was later modified, mainly against the Jews or to add additional curbs to the power of the nobles. Centuries after, in the thirteenth

11. For an excellent discussion of these councils, see Ziegler, Chapter II, *passim*.

12. Ibid., pp. 52–53.

century, it was translated into medieval Castilian as the *Fuero Juzgo* and had a wide influence. It is interesting to note that the *Liber* is based on the idea of territorial rather than personal law, a fact which greatly appealed to Gibbon, who dealt with it in a characteristic passage: "I dislike the style; I detest the superstition; but I shall presume to think that the civil jurisprudence displays a more civilized and enlightened state of society than that of the Burgundians or even of the Lombards."[13]

Like the other parts of the Roman Empire, the larger cities of Spain contained Jewish minorities, although the actual numbers will never be known. In view of the fact that some writers believe this minority facilitated the Mohammedan invasion, it is worthwhile to consider briefly the policy of the Visigothic Church and the state toward this people. The first anti-Jewish canons go back to the Council of Elvira about 306. Alaric II introduced anti-Jewish legislation into his Code, but Jews were still able to carry on their worship. Probably an unfortunate result of the conversion of Reccared was an increase of restrictions, and Sisebut (612–621) actually carried on some persecutions of the Jews. It seems evident that by the seventh century both church and state were in full accord on a policy of persecution, and this must be considered as one of the chief stains on the record of the Visigothic Church. In 654 Jewish worship was forbidden under penalty of death. During the reign of Egica (687–702), Jews lost all their economic rights, being forbidden to trade with Christians or retain any property purchased from Christians. In fact, the Seventeenth Council of Toledo was specifically called in 694 to deal with the Jewish situation. In view of all this, did Jews then assist the Arab invasion? It will have to be stated that there is no historical evidence for an answer either way. However, human nature being what it is, and the provocation being great, it seems very likely that they might have cooperated with the Moslems.

## 4

The later history of the Visigothic monarchy shows that it was beginning to be affected by that blight that seemed to strike most of the Germanic kingdoms of the west. No one, of course, accepts today the old legend derived from Tacitus of the corrupt Romans revivified and an empire revitalized by the pure children of the forests. The Germans had their vices and, once within the empire, showed a remarkable ability to adopt the more sophisticated sins of the Romans.

13. Edward Gibbon. *The History of the Decline and Fall of the Roman Empire*, edited by J. B. Burn, 2nd ed. 7 vol. (London, 1901), IV, 144, fn. 132.

Political history shows the same tendency. From the third century A.D., the empire had shown a tendency to break up into smaller units. In spite of the heroic efforts of a Diocletian or a Constantine, the tendency grew stronger rather than weaker. The new German states set up in the western empire soon were infected by these trends that corresponded to deep-seated historical realities too strong to be denied. These realities simply dictated that no large political structure could long survive, conditions in the sixth and seventh centuries being what they were. As the history of the German states shows, they seem almost fated, as it were, to break up from internal conflicts or from outside invasions, and frequently both. Thus, the Vandal kingdom of north Africa was destroyed by civil war and the troops of Justinian, England was at this time dissolving into the tiny states of the heptarchy, the Ostrogothic kingdom of northern Italy was gone, and neither the Byzantine Empire nor the Lombards had been able to put anything as stable in its place. France under the late Merovingians, the *rois fainéants*, seemed headed for the same fate, and was only saved by the remarkable political genius of Pepin of Heristal and his descendants.

The last half century of Visigothic rule in the peninsula shows all these tendencies. Although the records grow increasingly scanty—itself a sign of increasing insecurity and confusion—from what is available one senses a steady deterioration of the body politic. The nobles are constantly in rebellion, the crown is worn by weak kings (Wamba, 672–680, is the last ruler who shows any ability), and there were frequent disputes over the succession. Wamba, who had to face the first probings of the Mohammedans, did what he could to strengthen the institutions of the state, especially the army, but what happened in 711 suggests that he was not very successful.

## 5

A great deal of revising is being done by Spanish historians on the Visigothic period of their history. Older theories are being discarded, yet much more research needs to be done before a clearer picture of Visigothic Spain can emerge. Generally speaking, the trend today is toward downgrading the importance of the period between 409 and 711, and many earlier judgments are now being questioned. One thinks of the distinguished historian Ramón Menéndez Pidal (1869–1969) who has emphasized, in many and various works, the continuity of Roman and Visigothic institutions into the later history of Spain.[14] His theories are now sharply challenged, especially by

14. See especially his *España y su historia* (Madrid, 1957), and *La España del Cid*, 5th edition, 2 vols. (Madrid, 1956).

América Castro, who holds that the Visigothic state was in no way Spanish nor was there any connection between the Visigoths and the later Spanish *personalidad*.[15] Furthermore, one would hesitate today to assert, as does Claudio Sánchez-Albornoz, that Germanic pre-feudal institutions such as the comitatus, later prolonged into the *Gardingato* of the Visigothic kings or the patrocinium, helped to develop in the rural north of Spain after 711 a love of freedom and personal independence.[16] Or to follow this last historian in his theory of a dynamic fusion of Visigothic, Basque, and Cantabrian peoples which helped to launch the Reconquest in Castile.[17] Today, historians are more likely to emphasize the relative insignificance of the *numbers* of the Germanic invaders of Iberia, their dependence on the preexisting Roman structure, the lack of any real assimilation of the invading minority by the native majority, and the delicate balance of the political structure which collapsed "amid general indifference" at the first miniscule probe from without.[18]

Yet it would seem that in denying any continuity between Spain before 711 and the Spain that developed thereafter, América Castro has gone too far. The compartments of history are not that watertight. Inevitably there is always some carry-over across the discontinuities of history and such might be the case here. However, for the purposes of this study, the question of Visigothic survivals might be posed in an even more severe form than that raised by Castro, Sánchez-Albornoz, Vicens Vives, and others. Was there anything in the history of the Visigothic monarchy, a state relatively similar to the other German states of the west, which contributed in any special way, directly

15. América Castro, *The Structure of Spanish History*. Translated by Edmund L. King (Princeton: Princeton University Press, 1954). pp. 120–21. Since Castro largely revised his text for the English translation, and since this revision represents his latest ideas, I have used the translation instead of the original Spanish edition. In pursuit of his theory, Castro has noted that no Christian kingdom ever used Visigoth as an adjective in its name nor ever called itself Gothia. He has an interesting suggestion that the title of "emperor" sometimes assumed by the kings of Leon was not a throwback to the days of Visigothic unity, but an attempt to correspond to the pretensions of the archbishop of Santiago de Compostela.

16. Claudio Sánchez-Albornoz, *España, un enigma histórico*. 2 vols., (Buenos Aires, 1956), I, 136–137.

17. Ibid., I, 138–39. For a contrary view, see Vicens Vives, *Approaches to the History of Spain*, pp. 158–59.

18. "A fragile edifice, Visigothic royalty was unable to overcome its own contradictions—economic, social, ethnic, and religious—when confronted by even the slightest threat from abroad. In 711, amid general indifference, it collapsed. The Gothic oligarchy capitulated in many areas. Some survivors of the old administration found refuge in the Cantabrian north. The Visigothic masses who had settled in Castile were, after the lapse of a century, moved to Galicia." Vicens Vives, *Approaches to the History of Spain*, p. 27.

or indirectly, to the rise of imperial Spain of the sixteenth century? Directly, probably not; but indirectly, in at least two instances, the answer must be an affirmative, referring specifically to 1) the maintenance of Iberian unity, and 2) the establishment of a strongly individualistic Church, closely involved with the states. It must be remembered that the Visigothic tribe was only one of a number that entered Spain in the fifth century. It might have happened that none could have subdued the others, and the history of Castile, Leon, Aragon, and the rest might have begun at this point. The skill, luck, in any event the success of the Visigoths in imposing their dominion on the peninsula, their good fortune in being deprived of their trans-Pyrenean holdings by the Franks, enabled them to give Spain another two centuries of territorial unity. This, added to Roman rule, gave the Spaniards a certain tradition of homogeneity that centuries of Mohammedan rule in the south and the confusion of feudal principalities in the north could not completely efface. The Visigothic state, so often denigrated, did, in this, make a contribution to Saint Isidore's concept of *Mater Hispania,* and facilitated the later task of Ferdinand and Isabella.

As Ziegler has suggested, the Visigothic Church, well isolated from other important centers of Catholicism in the early Middle Ages, developed along its own lines. First forced to endure a longer period of subjection to an Arian administration than any other Catholic group in the west, it is not surprising that it emerged from its struggle with a strong sense of independence and national dedication. Its close connection with the state, especially in that remarkable institution, the Councils of Toledo, gave it great power and helped to erase the line between things secular and religious, ever an aspect of religion in the Iberian peninsula. The Visigothic Church was only one foundation of Spanish Catholicism, but it was a foundation particularly fitted to sustain the vast institution of a Church militant in a world power, the Catholic Church of the Inquisition, the *Autos da Fe,* and the far-flung missionary activities.

# CHAPTER III

# Mohammedan Spain

MEDIEVAL SPAIN WAS CHARACTERIZED BY TWO VERY IMPORTANT DE-velopments: 1) the occupation early in the eighth century of most of the peninsula by various peoples of the Mohammedan faith; and 2) the long wars, known as the *Reconquista*, waged by the Christian states of the north often as much to acquire new lands as to expel the aliens of a different culture and faith. As to the first, which will concern us in this chapter, it lasted for over seven hundred years and profoundly affected every phase of Spanish life. With the possible exceptions of Russia and Ireland, no other country in Europe experienced a foreign occupation for such a long period, and many of the unique aspects of the Spanish character and Spanish history derive from it. In the next chapter it will be shown how deeply marked were the Christian kingdoms by their various efforts to drive out the invaders. Before that, however, it is first necessary to describe the early expansion of the Arabs, and other peoples who accepted Islam,[1] the occupation of the Iberian peninsula, and lastly the nature and culture of the regime established.

The prophet Mohammed, who founded the faith officially known as *Islam* (i.e., submission to the will of God), was probably born at Mecca about 570 A.D. and died in the same place in 632. Between these two dates he founded one of the great religions of the world. Based on extensive borrowings from both Jewish and Christian sources, his teachings were marked by their simplicity, practicality,

---

1. Throughout this study, Islamic, Moslem, and Mohammedan will be used interchangeably.

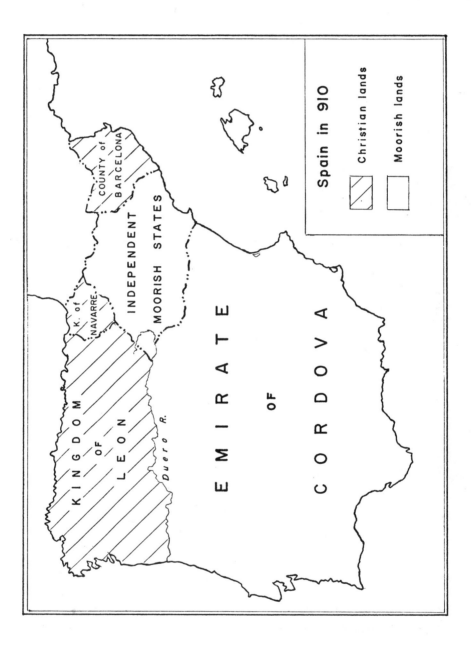

Spain in 910

Christian lands

Moorish lands

COUNTY of BARCELONA

K. of NAVARRE

INDEPENDENT MOORISH STATES

KINGDOM OF LEON

Duero R.

EMIRATE OF CORDOVA

devotion to monotheism; and graced frequently by dramatic poetry of a very high order. Since doctrinal subtleties, such as had been and were to be the curse of Christianity, were happily absent, the faith made a ready appeal to the simple tribesmen of the Arabian desert, and had already begun to spread widely by the time of the prophet's death.

Because the appearance of Islam coincided with an amazing expansion of the desert tribes into more fertile areas to the east and west, earlier historians were convinced that the new faith was the obvious explanation and cause. The historians of the mid-twentieth century are much less sure of this; and, being aware that these violent descents of desert nomads upon the more fertile areas have been going on since the earliest Egyptian and Babylonian times, they prefer to think in terms of climate, food supply, and population pressure rather than the supposed aggressive tendencies of Mohammedanism. In any event, shortly after the death of Mohammed, the Arabs literally exploded out of the peninsula and, finding both Persia and the Byzantine Empire exhausted from years of mutual warfare, proceeded to move into their territory. In a short time Persia, Syria, Palestine, and Egypt were occupied and used as bases for further expansion. After the second capture of Alexandria in 646, the Arabs now had the beginnings of a first class naval base in the eastern Mediterranean, and a springboard for further advances along the north African littoral. This rapid extension toward the west was paralleled by a similar movement at the center of gravity within Arabia itself. In 661 the second caliphate was founded by Muawiyah the Ommayyad with its capital far to the northwest of Mecca at Damascus. The new dynasty thus established marked the growing importance of the Syrian Arabs over their less civilized kin of the south (Mecca and Yemen). It also marked the beginnings of an imperial regime, closely copied after Byzantine and Persian models, in which the purely Arab contributions were limited to religion and language.

Soon after the subjection of Egypt, raids began to be carried on into the west or, as the Moslems called it, Ifriqiyah. But lack of an advance base, and strong opposition from Byzantium and the Berbers, slowed the advance down for some years. The Berbers were a segment of the Hamitic speaking caucasoids who had been distributed along the north African coast since earliest historical times. Owing to the strong influences of those grim African Church fathers, Tertullian, Saint Cyprian, and Saint Augustine, they had been converted to Christianity long before the advent of the Mohammedans. Their apparently rapid conversion to Islam is surprising and somewhat difficult to explain, unless one remembers that they were a non-urban people and the Romanization of north Africa was apparently confined to the towns; and this was also probably true of Christian and Byzantine influence. Evidently the countryside had not changed greatly in thousands of years. Traces of the ancient Punic tongue were still in existence not long before the Moslem conquest, and it obviously proved not too difficult to turn the Berbers from things Roman and Christian to Islam.[2]

With the establishment of Kairouan in 670 as a center of operations against the Berbers, events began to move more rapidly. Under the governorship of Hassan (693–699), Carthage was taken and both Byzantine and Berber resistance broken. Hassan was succeeded by the more famous Musa ibn Nusayr, who later sponsored the first invasion of Spain. Musa, acting directly under orders of the Ommayyad caliph at Damascus, extended the frontiers of his dominion as far west as Tangier, thus reaching the African side of the famous straits by the beginning of the eighth century. Although still less than a century old, Islam was ready to undertake the invasion of Spain.

2

Several factors in the early eighth century favored the continuance of this expansion. A new imperialistic caliph, Walid, succeeded at Damascus in 705; an able and ambitious governor was present in north Africa; the newly converted Berbers provided an ample supply of tough soldiers. Finally, since it was necessary to reward them, the obvious divisions of the Visigothic monarchy made the prospect of raids and booty exceedingly tempting. Curiously enough, conquest does not seem to have been considered; it is incredible but true that the entire structure of the Visigothic monarchy collapsed before the initial thrust of a *razzia*, a border raid.

A brief feeler took place in 710. Musa sent a local chief named Tarif and about five hundred men in a small raid across the strait to the little peninsula thereafter named Tarifa. Local resistance was light and it was decided to mount a raid in force the following year. This time Musa gave the command to his Berber freedman, Tariq. In July of 711 he crossed the strait with some seven thousand Berbers, and landed close to the rock which still bears his name, Jabal Tariq, or Gibraltar. After a short march inland, he came upon King Rodrigo and a Visigothic army near the lake of La Janda. Contemporary information is extremely vague about the battle which was fought there on or about July 25–26. Although evidently greatly outnumbered, Tariq appears to have won a decisive victory. Rodrigo may have been killed; he simply vanishes after the engagement and is never heard

2. Philip K. Hitti, *History of the Arabs*, 3rd. ed. rev. (London, 1943), p. 214.

from again. At this point, Tariq probably violated his instructions.[3] The expedition had not intended to be more than a large raid in search of booty and slaves; from this moment on it became territorial conquest.

Musa was probably asked to send more troops (he came over himself with reinforcements the next year), while Tariq continued north. Apparently he avoided strong places such as Seville, which were too large for his small force to handle. A second Visigothic army barred his way at Écija, between Seville and Córdoba, and here, after the fiercest struggle of the campaign, Tariq was victorious again. Musa sent the needed troops, and then arrived himself in 712 with an army of ten thousand, for the first time containing many Syrian and Arab units. He attacked the strong places avoided by Tariq but was held up almost a year by Seville, which fell in June, 713. Both Musa and Tariq combined forces to takeToledo and then, together, subjugated northern Spain from Saragossa to Navarre. Musa returned to Africa the following year, and in February 715 he staged a solemn entry into Damascus with thousands of Christian captives and enormous amounts of booty. It was an event that Islam long remembered and was undoubtedly the apogee of the Ommayyad dynasty.

However legendary the quarrel between Musa and Tariq, it is clear that there was not much harmony among the chief commanders of the early operations. Unfortunately, things were soon to become far worse. The Berbers complained that in the distribution of lands they were slighted by the Arab minority; they were particularly offended when they received lands in the barren north while the Arabs enjoyed sunny Andalusia.[4] The Pyrenees were reached in 717 or 718 and were crossed by Al Hurr, who made the first attack on southern France. However, the rebellious Berbers made an agreement with Eudo, the Frankish count of Aquitaine; and a further advance was temporarily checked by a Moslem defeat before the walls of Toulouse.

When Hisham (724–743) became caliph, expansion in all directions was resumed. To put an end to Arab-Berber feuds in the peninsula, he sent out a new emir, Abd-ar-Rahman, the first to bear a name destined to be illustrious in Spanish Moslem history. Abd-ar-Rahman

---

3. There is a legend that when Tariq first met Musa after the beginning of the conquest the Berber commander was whipped for disobeying orders by carrying the advance beyond what had been intended. There is also a tale that Musa fell from favor shortly after his reception in Damascus, and died in disgrace.

4. So impressed were the Moslems by the beauties and wealth of Andalusia that they gave the name of Al-Andalus to the part of Spain that they held. The part in Christian control was usually known as Ishbaniya, although sometimes Al-Andalus was applied to that area also.

crossed the Pyrenees, defeated the rebellious Berbers and their ally Count Eudo, and proceeded to pursue the Franks northward in the direction of the Loire. At this point the redoubtable Charles Martel, Austrasian mayor of the palace, decided to intervene. The Frankish army under his command met the Mohammedans on an October Saturday in 732, roughly between Tours and Poitiers. In spite of repeated attacks, the heavy masses of Frankish infantry stood firm, and the light-armed Mohammedan cavalry was cut to pieces against them. Abd-ar-Rahman was killed in the battle and during the night the Moslems made their escape to the south. It was the farthest northern advance of the Crescent.

The Battle of Tours (or Poitiers) is one of those engagements that assumes tremendous proportions in retrospect. While Charles Martel won great acclaim for his victory, it cannot have seemed especially decisive for contemporaries. It did not mark the immediate withdrawal of the Moslems from southern France. In 734 they seized Avignon, pillaged Lyons in 743, and did not give up Narbonne (taken in 720) until 759. It is said that Christendom was saved at Tours; it is far more likely that it was saved in 718 by the successful resistance of Constantinople to the biggest Arab attack yet staged. Furthermore, while no one can detract from the heroism of Charles Martel and his warriors, it is probable that the great Berber revolt in north Africa about this time had more to do with checking the northern advance of Islam than anything else.

3

The years between the invasion of Tariq and the arrival of Abd-ar-Rahman I (711–755) have a certain grim consistency. They were principally years of civil war, bitter feuds among the conquerors, sporadic resistance of the natives, and violent shifts among the high command. Aside from the fact that at this period the Moslems were still relatively uncivilized peoples, much bloodshed and violence from certain rather significant, and often ignored, factors attended the early conquest.

In the first place, the whole Tariq-Musa operation was accomplished too easily. The reasons for the astonishing collapse of the Visigothic regime are still something of a mystery. Some historians believe that the regime had never taken roots, although if this be true one wonders why it had not collapsed long before. Religious differences with the subject population are often cited, as well as the activities of a Jewish minority, hostility toward the regime by serfs and peasants, divisions amongst the aristocracy, and other factors. But if the causes are still obscure, the results of the unexpected occupation are clear enough. The Moslems came in unprepared for a total and permanent occupation and had no immediate plans for such. Some time elapsed before their schemes for Al-Andalus came to anything more than hasty improvisations. The history of the Moslem world seems to show ample evidence that political genius was not one of the gifts of the Arabs, Berbers, and other Islamic peoples; instead one finds a rather high degree of political instability. Certainly this was true of Spain, where periods of internal harmony during the Moslem occupation were very much the exception rather than the rule.

Futhermore, the relative ease of the occupation prevented anything like a strong front from being forged out of the diverse forces of the victors. By this time it should be clear that an Arab conquest of Spain never took place. The attacking forces were small—probably never over 30,000 men at the most—and mostly Berbers. Since this small force was trying to hold down an area running from the Marches of Septimania to the Strait of Gibraltar, it is clear that almost from the beginning its members must have tended to merge with the subject population. Doubtless there were later infiltrations from Syria and Palestine, but even so these additions were probably very small in comparison with the huge majority of Berbers and native Spanish that inhabited Al-Andalus. As time went on, the Mohammedan rulers of Spain depended more and more on contingents from north Africa, and from 1090 to 1212 Moslem Spain was mainly ruled from Morocco.[5]

Given these facts, it is not surprising that the "Islamization" of Spain proceeded slowly, the early invaders being much more interested in acquiring land than in promoting cultural exchanges. Futhermore, if it is remembered that the conquerors were diverse, often mutually hostile toward one another, and not far removed from nomadic barbarism, it is not difficult to believe that they absorbed a good deal of the pre-existing Hispano-Gothic culture. In such a situation, the early Moslems were forced to treat the native population with a certain degree of consideration. The old administration was left largely intact; consequently the Christians were still governed by their counts, judges, bishops, and lower clergy.

But culturally, and demographically, the situation described above was profoundly altered during the first three centuries of the Moslem occupation. Two powerful forces effected a change. One was the fact that the Mozarabs (Christians living in Moslem territory who retained their faith, but adopted a Moslem way of life) had become thoroughly Arab in language and culture; and second was—the words

5. Louis Bertrand and Charles Petrie, *The History of Spain*, 2nd ed. rev. (New York, 1952), pp. 30–31.

are Vicens Vives'—the "sensational triumph" of Islam in converting the peasants south of the Duero River basin in the west, and south of the Pyrenees in the east, to the new faith:

> There can be no doubt about this phenomenon; it is the axis around which will revolve the future problems of Hispania—beginning with the repopulation, the reconquest, and the successive failures to assimilate the Moriscos. By the middle of the tenth century, Hispania was a country with a Muslim majority.[6]

In regard to land distribution, some of it was given directly to the soldiers as booty. One-fifth of the conquered lands was considered state property, and was farmed by Christian peasants who paid one-third of the proceeds to the government. Territory not conquered but merely surrendered during the process of the occupation was frequently left in the hands of the native Christians, the original proprietors. They retained occupancy, use, and the right of re-sale. These conditions tended to prevail north of the center; in the south a kind of Arab feudalism existed.

Given then a conquest undertaken by a small minority already subdivided internally, and carried out so rapidly that it could not interfere with religious and historical feuds, some already centuries old, one must admit it is not surprising that bloody fighting broke out among the invaders even before the conquest was actually over. The Arabs of the north turned against their more barbarous kin of the south. Yemenites turned against Kaishites, Syrians against Medinites, and the Berbers, the eternal auxiliaries of every regime, against the field. Such confusion in the south and center gave the remnants of the Visigothic monarchy, the Christians of the Pyrenean strongholds, their opportunity. This helps to explain the early victories, whether Pelayo and the battle of Covadonga are historical realities or not.[7] Certainly by the time of Alfonso I the Catholic (739–757), the Christians were beginning to reoccupy some of the vacant lands north of the Duero. Forty years after the conquest, the complete absence of any common policy among the Moslems and their murderous civil wars were placing the occupation in considerable danger. Unless some stabilization could be achieved, a Christian rally behind some able leader might drive them all into the Straits of Gibraltar. However, Fate decreed that the leader was to be found by the Mohammedans, not the Christians, and in 751 he was already moving westward heading toward Spain.

6. Vicens Vives, *Approaches to the History of Spain*, p. 31.
7. According to an early legend, a band of Visigoths under a chief named Pelayo took shelter in the caves of Covadonga in 718. When pursued by the Moslems, they sallied forth and inflicted the first defeat of the Reconquest upon them.

4

Abd-ar-Rahman (730–788) was the grandson of the caliph Hisham, and thus a member of the ruling Ommayyad family. After the death of the great caliph, the family declined rapidly and in 750 was overthrown in a violent upheaval which led to a massacre, exceptionally bloody by even the generous standards of the Arabs. All the members of the family but one were murdered. That one was Abd-ar-Rahman.

He, his younger brother, and his mother, a Berber slave, managed to escape the assassins of the new Abbasid caliphate and started on a wild and dangerous flight through Palestine, Egypt, and north Africa. Both the mother and the brother were killed and, after a series of adventures worthy of the Arabian Nights, Abd-ar-Rahman passed through Egypt and eventually reached Kairouan. The hostility of the local governor, who was neither Ommayyad nor Abbasid, forced him farther west and he finally ended up seeking the hospitality and protection of his maternal uncles in the Berber tribe of Nafza, near the modern Ceuta. The confusion of Spanish affairs, and the presence in Spain of many partisans of his family, must have quickly suggested his next moves. He sent an agent to the Mohammedans living near Elvira and soon received promises of support from the Yemenite Arabs. In 755 he crossed the strait and soon town after town opened its gates to him. Although the nominal governor, Yusuf, was at first friendly, he and another chief, named Somail, later combined against Abd-ar-Rahman. The issue was settled on May 14, 756, on the banks of the Guadalquivir River between Seville and Córdoba. Abdar-Rahman defeated his rivals, who thereupon recognized him as emir of Al-Andalus.

The Ommayyad dynasty, although in utter ruins everywhere else in the Moslem world, thus established in Spain an independent emirate which was destined to be the most glorious in the history of the Mohammedan occupation, reaching its climax in the famous caliphate of Córdoba (929–1030). Although the history of this caliphate really begins with Abd-ar-Rahman I and his victory over Yusuf and Somail, he was careful not to challenge the Abbasid caliph in Baghdad by assuming a rival title; he and his immediate descendants remained emirs to the end of their days. Abd-ar-Rahman was now able to begin his life's work of stabilizing the central authority and putting down revolts wherever they occurred. To do so required constant fighting that continued throughout almost the entire reign. First Toledo revolted on behalf of Yusuf and, although the former governor was soon slain, the city was not reduced to obedience until 764. Then the southern Arabs of Yemen, who had first welcomed Abd-ar-Rahman, became dissatisfied and revolted. After being defeated in their turn, a remnant of the Yemenites combined with the Berbers in a long and bloody uprising.

When peace at last seemed restored to southern and central Spain, a new danger arose in the north. A confederation of Arab chiefs led by the governor of Barcelona, the son-in-law of the late Yusuf, now rebelled and appealed to Charlemagne for aid. When the Frankish king held an assembly of his warriors at Paderborn in the spring of 777, he was approached by Al-Arabi, a Yemenite sheik who appealed to him for troops against the "usurper" Abd-ar-Rahman. The result was the famous Frankish invasion, more distinguished, perhaps, for its effects on poetry rather than politics, but a real danger, nonetheless, to the Ommayyad power. The Franks came in through the eastern Pyrenees and laid siege to Saragossa which had refused to open its gates to Al-Arabi. However, a revolt of the Saxons in far off Germany forced Charlemagne to raise the siege and return to France. As the rear guard of his army was defiling through the pass of Roncesvalles, it was attacked by the Basques, and Rhotland, unknown to history until this moment but henceforth immortal, was killed. Centuries later this episode, enormously expanded, formed the basis for the great medieval epic, the *Chanson de Roland*. Frankish influence in northeast Spain did not disappear, however, with the vanquished rear guard. A small corner of the northeast, approximately the same size as the modern Catalonia, remained to constitute the Spanish March of the Frankish empire. Here French influence and language, working on Roman and Visigothic survivals, began the creation of that Catalan culture, not strictly Spanish nor precisely French, but uniquely itself.

Although Spain was never entirely free of fighting during his lifetime, Abd-ar-Rahman I was able to establish a unified realm to an extent hitherto unknown in Spanish Islam. War was necessarily his great preoccupation, but in moments of peace he found time to be something of a builder. In his capital of Córdoba, he began the construction of the great Mosque which was eventually to become, after those in Mecca and Jerusalem, the third great mosque of medieval Islam. Ferdinand III turned it into a Christian church in 1236, but, still called *La Mezquita,* its size and decorations continue to astonish modern visitors to Córdoba.

In his capital, the emir lived in the old Roman and Visigothic *castellum,* and this may be somewhat symbolic of the regime as a whole. It was still something very definitely foreign trying to adapt itself to an unfamiliar situation. Even Abd-ar-Rahman himself seems to have suffered from the very modern disease of homesickness. Being, like many of his race, of a poetic bent, he expressed this longing in the following touching verse attributed to him:

*Traveller, you who go to my country*
*Take with you there*

*The salutation of half myself to my other half.*
*My body, as you know, is in one place,*
*But my heart and its affections*
*Are in another.*
*Marked out as it was by destiny,*
*The separation has had to be accomplished,*
*But it has chased sleep from my lids.*
*The Divine will that ordained this divorce*
*Will, perhaps, decree some day our reunion.*[8]

His descendants continued his work with varying degrees of success. Hisham (788–796) had increasing difficulties with the Christian kinglets of the north and was troubled with hostile Arab and Berber princes as in the time of his father. Hakam (796–822) had to face an outbreak of Christian fanaticism in Toledo which led to many new martyrs, and the famous "Day of the ditch."[9] During the reign of Abd-ar-Rahman II (822–822) an attempt was made to imitate the luxurious court of the Abbasid ruler at Baghdad, which the famous Caliph Haroun-al-Rashid had made the model of the Islamic world. There was continued opposition from Christians anxious to win a martyr's crown, and Toledo was frequently in revolt. In 844 occurred the first attack of the Northmen, who briefly occupied Seville. The reign of Mohammed I (852–886) clearly shows that a decline had begun to set in. He was not able to subdue Toledo, which appealed to Ordoño I, king of Leon. In fact, from the middle of the ninth century to the early years of the tenth, it appeared that Ommayyad Spain was in the process of dissolution. Districts and cities were now breaking away from the rule of Córdoba and asserting their independence. In the northeast the Benikazi, an old Visigothic family converted to Islam, succeeded in holding Saragossa and other nearby towns in virtual autonomy. Successful revolts even occurred in southern Spain in a manner which was prophetic of the *taifa* period to come. Seville was, for a time, outside the control of Córdoba, but the most famous center of revolt was located at Bobastro in the mountains around Elvira. Here Omar ibn Hafsun, descendant of a Visigothic count, organized a band of brigands about 800, and eventually openly revolted against the Ommayyad rule. In 899 he became a Christian, taking the baptismal name of Samuel. Repeated attempts to suppress him failed, and he became a rallying point for all malcontents, of either religion, against the regime. Meanwhile Mohammed I was suc-

8. Quoted in Bertrand and Petrie, p. 47.
9. After a revolt of Toledo in 806, Hakam sent out a renegade Christian as governor. According to a story reported, doubtless with many exaggerations, by the Arab annalists, he invited some 700 notables of the city to a banquet; and when they came into the palace courtyard, they were murdered and their bodies thrown into a ditch.

ceeded by Mundhir (886–888), who was poisoned by his brother, Abdallah, after a two year reign. Abdallah (888–912) struggled vainly with the forces of dissolution, and was deeply involved in family intrigue. The parallel with the contemporary Carolingians is remarkably close. As in the Frankish empire, the Arab, Berber, and even Christian landowners were setting themselves up as petty rulers in defiance of the central authority. Fortunately, a strong hand was about to appear. Abdallah, in keeping with what might be called the family traditions, had managed to turn one of his sons against the other, and then eliminated the lone survivor himself. Thus, when he died in 912, the emirate went to his grandson, Abd-ar-Rahman III (912 –961), who turned out to be the ablest member of the family and was able to postpone the break-up of Moslem Spain for another century.

The new emir first turned his attention to putting down disorder and rebellion within his lands. Most of the nobles and great landowners were brought back to submission. A son of Omar ibn Hafsun held out for a time in Bobastro, but he was forced to submit in 928. By 930 only Toledo was still independent, and it surrendered two years later. By this time Abd-ar-Rahman III had already been active beyond the frontier. Between 920 and 924, Ordoño II of Leon had been forced to surrender the Moslem territory he had occupied, and in 924 the Christians suffered one of the great setbacks of the century when Pamplona, the capital of Navarre, was sacked. With Abd-ar-Rahman begins the custom of annual raiding of Christian lands north of the Ebro and Duero Rivers. Eventually, between the Moslem lands and the Christian kingdoms a zone of desolation was created, thanks to the constant destruction of crops and extensive slave-raiding.[10]

There were also dangers from north Africa. In 909 a new caliphate had been founded at Tunis by a family claiming descent from Mohammed's daughter, Fatima. The Fatimids soon became an expanding and aggressive power, and a definite threat to the Ommayyad dynasty in Spain. When they raided the Spanish coast, Abd-ar-Rahman started building a fleet to oppose them, and took Ceuta in Morocco as a means of extending his influence amongst the petty sovereigns of the coastal area. It is perhaps because of the Fatimids that in 929 Abd-ar-Rahman dropped the title of emir which had been borne by his family since 756 and took the more imposing title of caliph, thus creating a third caliphate within the Moslem world.

Like many despots in this and other periods of history, Abd-ar-Rahman III relied on a strong force of foreign bodyguards. These

10. Ibid., pp. 90–95; Brockelmann, Carl, *History of the Islamic Peoples*, translated by Joel Carmichael and Moshe Perlmann (New York, 1947), pp. 186–87.

were the celebrated Slavs, the name being given indiscriminately by the Arabs to all European prisoners of war. A large number of them came from the eastern Slavic marches of Germany and were brought into Spain by way of France. A considerable number also came from the Levant and Black Sea region, from which they were brought by Byzantine or Jewish slave traders and were resold to the agents of the caliph. Verdun is reputed to have specialized in the manufacture of eunuchs, who commanded an especially good price because of their utility in the administration of the harem. After special training, these Slavs were assigned to important posts in the civil administration, the army, and the harem.[11]

The first Spanish caliph also found time to be a builder. He made important additions to the great mosque in Córdoba, and near that city constructed a magnificent fortress-countryseat, Medina az-Zahara, named for a favorite concubine. Moslem chroniclers go into raptures over the power, wealth, and civilization of Spain under this ruler. Many of their statements are obviously exaggerations of the most extreme sort; but, while rejecting these, it seems fair to say that the country was wealthier and more prosperous than it had ever been before, and doubtless the court of the caliph was a center of magnificence.

Under his son and successor, Hakam II (961–976), the intellectual life of the court was emphasized by a ruler who was himself a scholar and a bibliophile. The caliph seems to have been chiefly interested in his famous library and the agents that searched the Mediterranean for rare editions for it. He also expanded the school established at the Great Mosque by his father; students were given funds to attend it, and famous scholars from all parts of the Near East were invited to teach there.

A curious situation followed the death of Hakam II in 976. The legitimate ruler, Hisham II (976–1009), was still a child; and, as was to be expected, power fell into other hands, mainly those of Mohammed ibn-abi-Amir, better known to history as Al-Mansur. He had risen rapidly during the reign of Hakam. After the caliph's death, thanks to the aid of the sultana Aurora, a Basque woman, he became the real ruler of Spain, leaving the empty title of caliph to Hisham, who was kept in complete seclusion. Al-Mansur, in the opinion of Menéndez Pidal, was the last great Moslem of Spain.[12] Undoubtedly he was a man of tremendous energy and warlike ability. Once again the Christians reeled under his heavy blows. Barcelona was sacked

11. Ibid.; Bertrand, pp. 53–55.
12. Ramón Menéndez Pidal, *The Cid and his Spain,* translated by Harold Sunderland. Foreword by the Duke of Berwick and Alba (London, 1934), pp. 27–28.

in 985, Coimbra in 987, Leon in 988, and Osma and the strong places north of the Duero in 989. But his greatest blow against the enemies of Islam was the sacking in 997 of the most famous western European Christian shrine at Santiago de Compostela. These many successful attacks in the north probably helped to stimulate widespread resentment, and may have contributed to the rapidly growing force of the Reconquest after his death. Al-Mansur maintained the influence of the caliphate over the Barbary Coast, and tried to replace the influence of the Slavs with Berber and Christian mercenaries. He died at Medinaceli in 1002 after returning from his fifty-second campaign.

His son, Abd-al-Malik, tried to continue his father's administration under the feeble Hisham II and for a while maintained the prestige of the caliphate, but unfortunately he was poisoned in 1008 by his brother. This opened the door to violent struggles for power among members of the family, further complicated by the usual Berber revolts. After much confusion and rapid shifts of rulers, the caliphate came to an end in 1031 with the death of Hisham III, the last to bear the title.

5

Politically, the work of Abd-ar-Rahman III and Al-Mansur did not last long. After 1031 Moslem Spain was broken up into a number of petty kingdoms called *taifa* states from the Arabic word for party or faction. Political weakness, however, does not necessarily imply an intellectual decline as the latter part of the famed *Siglo de Oro* was to show. Culturally, then, the *taifa* period was not a retrogression but continued to show an intellectual and economic advance. It was a time notable for the development of royal libraries and some of the kinglets, such as Al-Kadir of Valencia, became notable bibliophiles and scholars. Moktadir and Mutamin of Saragossa were mathematicians while Mudaffar ibn af-Aftas of Badajoz compiled an encyclopedia of fifty volumes. An important school of astronomy, which grew up in Toledo, produced the famous Toledan tables of astronomical observations, later used by Alfonso the Wise of Castile (1252–1284).[13] Motamid of Seville has a real place in Moslem literature as a poet. Concerning him, one of his modern translators observed that

...though his sun of power went down so long ago
that the West has forgotten the colors of his
glory, and though the kingdom for which he gave
his blood and his children and the years of his
life now bows to other rulers, another faith, yet

13. Ibid., pp. 33–38.

among a beauty-loving race he still preserves—
by reason of those lines which wars have not
scattered nor Time effaced—a gentle eminence.[14]

The following charming lines inscribed to a fountain suggest that this "gentle eminence" is not undeserved.

The sea hath tempered it; the mighty sun
Polished the blade;
And from the limpid sheath the sword leaps forth;
Man hath not made
A better in Damascus—though for slaughter
Hath steel somewhat advantage over water.[15]

Years later, when his kingdom was gone and he an exile, Mutamid could write as follows:

Woo not the world too rashly, for behold,
Beneath the painted silk and broidering
It is a faithless and inconstant thing.
(Listen to me, Mu'tamid, growing old.)

And we—that dreamed youth's blade would never rust,
Hoped wells from the mirage, roses from the sand—
The riddle of the world shall understand
And put on wisdom with the robe of dust.[16]

Thus Omar Khayyam had his echoes in Spain.

As the caliphate broke up, the new states tended to fall into one or another of three types: 1) those ruled by former "Slav" leaders; 2) those seized by Berber soldiers of fortune; and 3) those taken over by the descendants of noble Arab families who had come over with the conqueror. Generally speaking, the *taifas* in the northeast were apt to be Slav while the Berbers and Arabs dominated those in the south and southwest. The principal states were situated at Saragossa, Seville, Málaga, Granada, Almería, Badajoz, and Valencia. Of these, only Seville under the Beni Abbad, Saragossa under the Beni Hud, and Badajoz under the Al-Aftas showed any expansionist tendencies.[17] Córdoba remained a kind of republic until after 1068, when it was briefly absorbed by Seville.

This city was probably the most important *taifa*, and its history has more than passing interest. The founder of the family's political importance was a *cadi* (judge), descended from an ancient south Arab line, who had risen to power during the last days of the caliphate. His son, Mutadid (1042–1069), inherited his authority and greatly

14. Dulcie L. Smith in *The World's Best Poems*, edited by Mark Van Doren and Garibaldi M. Lapolla (New York, 1929), p. 28.
15. Ibid.
16. Ibid., p. 29.
17. Menéndez Pidal, pp. 29–31.

extended it. He was able to resist the advances of the Christians, and disposed of his Moslem rivals by the simple expedient of killing them. When his son, the famous Mutamid (1069–1091), took over his power, Seville controlled a good part of the southwest, even including Córdoba. It was his misfortune that the latter part of his reign coincided with one of the great figures of the Reconquest, Alfonso VI of Leon (1065–1109). Although Mutamid saved himself for a time by paying tribute to the king, the pressure on him was constantly increasing. Moslem territory began to suffer under Christian raids from Leon and also from Valencian territory where Ruy Diaz de Bivar, *el Cid Campeador,* was establishing his power. When Alfonso captured Toledo in 1085 with a truly international army, Mutamid and the other petty rulers of the south felt they must have outside aid themselves or perish.

In a fatal decision, Mutamid and some of the other *taifa* rulers decided to appeal to Yusuf the Almoravid, head of a newly risen power in Morocco. The Almoravids were a Moslem military brotherhood led by Sanhaja nomads from the Sahara Desert. Being late converts to Islam, they still retained all the fanaticism of the new believer. Hence their real enemy was not so much the infidel Christian, but rather the backsliding Moslem who had failed to maintain the purity of his faith. This is important in understanding the events that soon followed. They established themselves in Morocco about the middle of the eleventh century under Yusuf, their greatest leader, who ruled from 1061 to 1106 and founded a great, barbarous empire with its capital at Marrakesh.

Answering the appeal of Mutamid, Yusuf invaded Spain with a large army in 1086, and in the same year inflicted a major defeat on Alfonso VI, who had hastened south to check him. Yusuf then returned to north Africa, but came back to Spain in 1090, this time as a conqueror of the *taifas* as well as the foe of the Christians. Appropriately enough Mutamid, who was responsible for bringing in the Almoravids, was quickly deposed and sent to exile in Morocco for the rest of his life. A poet to the last, the old ruler produced these lines on seeing a group of Moslems going to a mosque to pray for rain:

> And forth they went imploring God for rain;
> "My tears," I said, "could serve you for a flood."
> "In truth," they cried, "your tears might well contain
> Sufficiency, but they are dyed with blood."[18]

The Almoravid empire, which included most of northwest Africa and one-half of Spain, was a burden to all concerned. Christians, Moslem intellectuals, and Mozarabs suffered from the ignorance and fanaticism of these Berber nomads. After Yusuf's death in 1106 there

18. Hitti, p. 541.

was a rapid decay. As Hitti well observes, the Almoravid empire "fulfilled the fated cycle of Asiatic and African monarchies with rapidity: a generation of efficient militarism followed by sloth and corruption leading to disintegration and fall."[19] The disappearance of the Almoravids left the field open to a new power, the Almohads.

Led by Masmuda tribesmen from the Atlas Mountains, the Almohads, like their predecessors, began as a military-religious movement whose leaders preached a reformist, purifying doctrine (the Spanish name is a corruption of the Arabic term for unitarians). Approximately between 1130 and 1146 they won control of Morocco and destroyed the Almoravid regime there. They then entered Spain as allies of groups opposed to the Almoravids. By 1157 they dominated Al-Andaluz with the exception of Saragossa which held out against them; soon Moslem Spain was merely a province of a vast though diluted empire which extended from the Atlantic to the mouth of the Nile.

By this time, however, the Christian states of the north had become too strong to be long held in check by such a power. Although the Almohads won one great victory over the Christians at Alarcos in 1195, they did not follow it up and consequently were later thoroughly defeated by the Christians at Las Navas de Tolosa in 1212. From this time on, they lost territory and by 1269 held only Gibraltar and Algeciras; shortly after this, their empire in Morocco came to an end.

Before continuing, it might be desirable to make certain comments on the Almoravid-Almohad period of Spanish history. It shows us that when the Moslems were united, they were still stronger than the Christians—at least up to this time. Thus, the Moslem unity imposed by Yusuf was able to defeat the formidable Alfonso VI at Zalaca in 1086, and a century later under similar circumstances Alfonso VIII was defeated at Alarcos.[20] But for the most part, Moslem unity after the caliphate was as hard to come by as Christian unity. Consequently, in the words of Castro, "neither side was sufficiently strong enough to resolve quickly such an unusual situation—a long struggle between two insecurities."[21]

Viewed in terms of the seven hundred years of conflict between the two groups for control and occupation of Iberia, the Moroccan invasions could be described as a Moslem counterattack in response to the successes of the Christian states in the eleventh century. But in another sense, they represent a sharp break with previous patterns.

19. Ibid., p. 545.

20. Americo Castro, *Los Españoles: Como Ilegaron a serlo* (Madrid, 1965) p. 121.

21. Ibid., p. 158

In spite of the centuries of almost constant conflict between natives and invaders, the two religions had developed a certain amount of tolerance for one another. Both claimed to be "peoples of the book"—i.e., the Bible and the Koran—both acknowledged certain prophets in common as divinely inspired—Moses, Elijah, Jesus, to name a few; and both accorded a certain status to subjects of the opposite faith.[22] Historians have come to recognize that a desire for additional territory was as much a factor in the earlier Reconquest as religion. The desert tribesmen of Morocco changed all that. Being religious fanatics, they took a very dim view, as has been pointed out, of the cultural and religious permissiveness of Spanish Islam. In regard to the Christians, Vicens Vives observes that "from 1086 on, they fought with an intolerance of such fundamental intransigence as had never before been associated with the flag of the Caliphate. . . . This spiritual harshness, exalted on the crest of military victories . . . caused their opponents in Leon and Castile to react in the same manner."[23] Thus an element of religious warfare came into the picture, and eventually in the Christian states of the north it flowered into the ideal of *total* expulsion of the Moslems from the lands of Iberia not because they were intruders, or violators of the ancient unity of the peninsula, but because they were the enemies of the only true faith—Catholicism. The crusading mentality had made its appearance. This aspect of the Reconquest will be discussed at length in the following chapter, but we must now return to the main narrative of this section.

The collapse of the Moroccan invasions was followed by the rapid Christian advance to the very waters of the Atlantic. This will shortly be described. Here, all that need be pointed out is that within a short time the kingdom of Granada under the Nasrid dynasty (1232–1492) was the only *taifa* left. The founder of this dynasty managed to save himself and his state by entering into an alliance with Castile and paying homage and tribute to Ferdinand III (San Fernando). Fortunately, because of the rugged terrain and natural defenses of the kingdom, plus the increasing feuds of the northern rulers, Granada was saved from further danger and managed to maintain an existence, at times flourishing and prosperous, until 1492. It is to this happy chance that we owe that gem of late Mohammedan art and architecture, the Alhambra.

22. In addition to the important position of the Mozarabs in Moslem and Christian society, titles sometimes used by the kings of Castile or León, such as Emperor of the Two Religions or Emperor of All Spain, come to mind.
23. Vicens Vives, *Approaches to the History of Spain*, pp. 45–46.

6

By now we have discovered that there never was an "Arab" occupation of the Iberian Peninsula. It is equally true that the terms "Arab civilization" and "Arab culture" are misnomers. As has been pointed out before, about the only truly Arab contributions to the civilization of the Moslems were religion and language. Gradually, and their behavior during the early emirate in Spain shows how long this took, they began to absorb a good deal of the much higher cultures with which they had made contact—Byzantine, Persian, and Syrian in particular.

In Spain, the conquerors took over the remains of a once high civilization, the Graeco-Roman, and its Visigothic veneer. Obviously they did not bring much with them, but eventually they did open Spain once again, as it had been during the Roman Empire, to the influences coming from the ancient centers of civilization in the Near East. Again through trade and commerce, Spain was in contact with Damascus, Byzantium, Baghdad, Tunis, Kairouan, Cairo, and Alexandria. Little by little, the independent emirs and especially the caliphs began to collect in their libraries the ancient learning of the Graeco-Roman culture in Arab translation, along with much that came from farther east such as the mathematics of Persia or the numerals of India. The building operations of the Moslems in Córdoba, Seville, Toledo, and above all Granada were influenced by Persian and Byzantine styles. It is known that, in various building projects connected with the Great Mosque in Córdoba, Byzantine workmen were imported in large numbers to work on the structure.

Eventually these various elements and styles were fused together into a culture that was remarkably homogeneous. When we look at its greatest artistic masterpieces, the Great Mosque, or the Alhambra, we do not say that here it is Persian, or here clearly is a Byzantine influence; we instinctively feel we are in the presence of a work of art that is balanced and harmonious, in short, an artistic unity.

It is not necessary to accept the extreme statements of the contemporary Moslem writers with their "sands of the sea" type of statistics; and yet, Bertrand perhaps goes much too far in attributing so little original achievement to Moslem culture in Spain. During its some seven hundred years, Al-Andalus was filled with much violence and strife, but history shows that this, in itself, does not inhibit cultural development. In fact, Spain under the Mohammedans was provided with most of the factors that have proved highly stimulating to cultural advance: 1) trade and cultural contacts with centers of higher civilization; 2) the presence of a high civilization in the immediate historical past; and 3) the close proximity of two extremely different languages, religions, and *mores*, often in violent physical contact.

One evidence of the strength and vitality of Spanish Moslem civilization is the very respectable number of original geniuses it produced. For example, there was Ibn-Abd-Rabbihi (860–940) of Córdoba, who wrote a long work on religious sects, probably making him the earliest student of comparative religion. One thinks of the remarkable contributions of Spanish philosophers such as Avencebrol (ca. 1021–1058), Avempace (d. 1138), and above all, Ibn-Rushd of Córdoba (1126–1198) known throughout the West as Averroës. This great thinker was a physician and astronomer, but his greatest influence lay in his commentaries on Aristotle which profoundly influenced medieval Scholasticism and Renaissance philosophy. One also mentions the name of the great Jewish thinker Moses Maïmonides (1135–1204), likewise of Córdoba.

One of the great services of Mohammedan Spain to the entire West was as a transmitter of knowledge. By the close of the thirteenth century, most of the Arab learning based on Hellenistic, Persian, Byzantine, Syrian, and even Hindu foundations had been transmitted to the West, especially the University of Paris. This was largely accomplished by a group of Christian and Mohammedan translators who worked in Spain. Beginning with Constantine the African, attached to the medical school at Salerno (d. 1087), running through the next century to Gerard of Cremona (d. 1187), the great monuments of Near Eastern thought were made available in Latin. Toledo was the center of this activity, thanks to the efforts of Archbishop Raymond (1126–51), who established a school for translation. Some of the great names in Western intellectual history worked here. Among them were Michael Scot, Robert of Chester, and Adelard of Bath; but the most prolific translator was the aforementioned Gerard, who died at Toledo after having rendered some seventy-one Arabic works into Latin. These included parts of Ptolemy, Galen, Euclid, Aristotle, and Hippocrates.[24] Seldom, to borrow Mr. Churchill's happy phrase, "have so many owed so much to so few."

The Christian states of the north, which we shall examine shortly, were strongly affected by these intellectual currents. And obviously there were exchanges in both directions across the frontier. In general, a large number of Christians (Mozarabs) living in the important Mohammedan centers, while still retaining their Christianity, took up Moslem ways of life, used the Arabic tongue, and even developed their own art and literature. On the other hand, there were

24. For an excellent and detailed account of Moslem intellectual contributions, see Hitti, Chapter 40. I am pleased to acknowledge my debt to it.

the *Mudéjares*, Moslems who lived among the Christians and adopted their way of life while still remaining true to Islam. Menéndez Pidal tells us that about 1050 there were devout Moslems in Toledo who could not speak Arabic and some four hundred years later one could find Christian villages within the kingdom of Granada where only Arabic was known. And apparently some of the early kings of Aragón wrote Spanish in an Arab script. Obviously, the business of finding a linguistic frontier would be exceedingly difficult. As a matter of fact, there were at least six major dialects or languages spoken in the peninsula: literary Arabic, vulgar Arabic, Berber, Hebrew, "Roman" (the early beginnings of Spanish). and Basque.

From all this it is clear that, whatever important contributions Islam and Christianity made to Spain in the early Middle Ages, unity was not one of them. A great diversity of tongues, three major religious faiths—Christianity, Judaism, Islam—various cultural strains, and different political organizations; all this, even during the best days of the caliphate, indicates that the old Roman and Visigothic unity had gone, seemingly forever. With the disappearance of the precarious unity provided by the Ommayyad dynasty, it is remarkable how conditions on both sides of the frontier tended to resemble each other: to the north, the beginnings of the Christian *taifas*, Leon, Castile, Navarre, Aragon; to the south the petty kingdoms of Seville, Granada, Toledo, Córdoba—it is the same story. Yet from these poorly organized, unstable kingdoms of the north, feebly trying to live up to vague legends of Roman or Visigothic glory, eventually came an empire that extended around the globe itself. How the first institutions of empire grew out of Moslem-Christian contacts along the frontier is the real significance of the *Reconquista*.

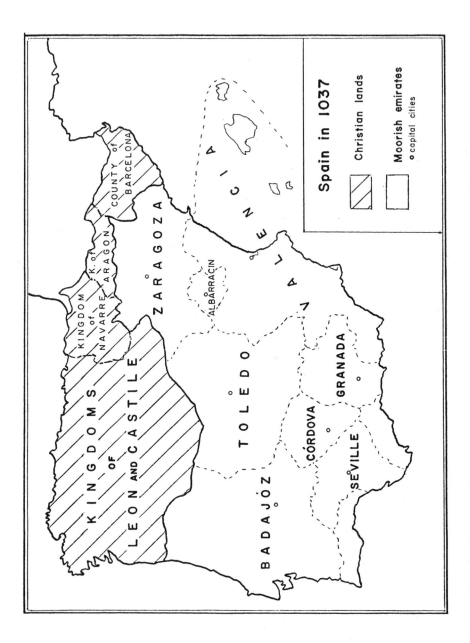

Spain in 1037

Christian lands

Moorish emirates
◦ capital cities

COUNTY of BARCELONA

K. of ARAGON
KINGDOM of NAVARRE

ZARAGOZA

KINGDOMS of LEON AND CASTILE

ALBARRACÍN

VALENCIA

TOLEDO

BADAJÓZ

CÓRDOVA

GRANADA

SEVILLE

# CHAPTER IV

# The Reconquest

MUCH OF THE CHARACTER OF IMPERIAL SPAIN OF THE *Siglo de Oro* was determined by the tremendous events of the *Reconquista*, which in one aspect or another occupied most of the Spanish Middle Ages. While all Spanish historians agree in emphasizing the transcendental importance of this vast resettlement, they often disagree strongly when they try to determine exactly *what it was*. Inevitably, the old problem of continuity versus discontinuity in history underlies these debates. In other words, do certain tremendous events sharply separate history into watertight compartments, or are certain aspects of the life of a people ineluctably carried across these traumatic divisions so that some things are never completely lost? Probably we shall never know, but this does not prevent Hispanicists from arguing the issue and evaluating the evidence. Without doing too much violence to individual theories, four basic interpretations of the Reconquest may be distinguished.

The simplest hypothesis might be described as the religious interpretation. This holds that the recovery of the Moslem lands was largely a religious movement, and that the warriors of the Reconquest were Christian crusaders. This theory is largely abandoned today, thanks to modern research which has shown that the crusading mentality simply did not exist in the eighth, ninth, and tenth centuries. Religion was certainly present in these early conflicts as the development of the Santiago cult shows, but in the cases of both Christian and Islamic territorial expansion, such a development was far too complex to be explained solely on the basis of religious fervor.

In 1925, the distinguished Spanish medievalist Ramón Menéndez

Pidal (1869–1969) published *La España del Cid*, which, while not ignoring the religious motive, added a Neo-Gothic twist to it. In his own words

> The states of the north nourished, in the midst of their rivalries, a concept of Hispanic unity which gave continuity and consistency to their efforts. This concept of unity was founded mainly on the cohesive power of Christianity then so vigorous [and] in the idea of the reconquest as a common enterprise for the restoration of the glory of the Visigothic state and nation, and in the recognition of the empire of Leon as the continuation of the dominion of Toledo.[1]

Critics of this theory later pointed out that it did not correspond to the historical realities of the time. In a primitive, rural economy there was no real idea of the state at all, much less an enduring tradition of it from Visigothic times.[2] Furthermore, the disunity of the north in the early Reconquest, Christian unity notwithstanding, has already been pointed out as a known historical fact.

Among critics of Menéndez Pidal, none have attacked him more sharply than Américo Castro (b. 1885). Approaching the problem somewhat obliquely, Castro holds that neither the Roman nor the Visigothic eras can be called Spanish at all. What was recovered during the Reconquest was simply not the same as what had been lost. The Seville conquered in 1248 was in no way like the Roman city of Hispalis lost in 711; and as for Toledo, "what resemblance could the conquering Christian find between the Visigothic city that they had lost in the eighth century, and the Toledo that they recovered in 1085 except the topography and a Roman monument here and there?"[3] To Castro, the beginnings of Spanish character—Hispanidad—are a product of the Reconquest, and do not exist before it. This character is formed by both Moslem and Christian elements in which the Christian contributed the heroic factor caused by the proximity and presence of the Moslems and the necessity of overcoming them. This led to the great emphasis placed on the importance of the person and his drive to overcome the insuperable, as evidenced in the literature of the Castilian epics, or in the reality of the conquest of the Indies.[4]

Without denying the stimulating nature of Castro's ideas, especially when considered as a catalyst in relation to the work of other historians, it must be admitted that the proof of his theories seems to lie more in the realm of the subjective rather than in objective histori-

1. Menéndez Pidal, *La España del Cid*, 5th edition (Madrid, 1956), Vol. I, p. 88 and Vol. II, p. 683.
2. Vicens Vives, *Approaches to the History of Spain*, pp. 124–125.
3. Castro, *The Structure of Spanish History, pp. 376–377.*
4. Castro, *Los Españoles: como llegaron a serlo*, pp. 123–125.

cal reality. However, a fourth interpretation of the Reconquest advanced by the late, distinguished historian of Catalonia, Jaime Vicens Vives (1910–1960) is perhaps more in keeping with the *Weltanschauung* of the late twentieth century. He maintains that the real motivating force of the early Reconquest was livelihood, the need for more land, for more adequate sources of food. "What the Christian cared about was to resettle, to conquer better lands and make them fertile for his children, creating a new spiritual climate which was impossible in the steep lands of the North."[5] Later, of course, religious and political factors enter in, but never completely cancel out the fact that the search for the basic necessities of life had much to do with determining the causes and aspects of the recovery of the Moslem lands.

This interpretation has led Vicens Vives to make an extremely interesting and significant distinction between the *military* Reconquest mentioned in all history books—very fast and vigorous after 1212; and what he called the *slow* Reconquest which was based on the resettlement of populations and internal colonization of southern Spain from about 1230 to 1609! The rhythm of the slow Reconquest began about the middle of the thirteenth century and continued until checked by the Black Death in 1348. After a lapse of almost a full century, it recovered its momentum and continued down to the era of Ferdinand and Isabella. However, the results of the discovery of America caused a drain of population overseas and weakened the capacity of Castile for internal colonization. This, thinks Vicens Vives, eventually led to the final stage of the slow Reconquest—namely, the expulsion of the Moriscos in the early seventeenth century since the population no longer had the capacity to absorb them.[6] Although future research in Spanish history may modify these concepts, at the present time Vicens Vives seems to offer us the most satisfactory explanation of the Reconquest that we now have.

To attempt to set up a chronological framework for such a complex movement as the Reconquest is probably necessary for the convenience of the reader although it is often a thankless and somewhat artificial task. The recovery of the Moslem lands is usually assumed to extend from sometime in the eighth century to the fall of Granada in 1492. Within these boundaries, four principal phases may be distinguished that are often characterized by quite different aspects.

The somewhat questionable legend of the battle of Covadonga in 718 will do as well as anything to inaugurate the initial phase of the recovery, which extends through the reign of Sancho the Great

5. Vicens Vives, *Economic History of Spain*, p. 125.
6. Ibid., pp. 157–58.

(1000–1035) of Navarre. During this phase, the Christians and their leaders brought off three major achievements: 1) through the development of the Santiago cult at Compostela they were able to open up contacts with France, and the northern European world; 2) the Duero valley was repopulated by settlers from the foothills of the Cantabrian range; and 3) the country of Castile emerged as a frontier community of great vigor. Their greatest failure during this phase was the inability of the kingdom of Leon to achieve the ideal of Roman and Visigothic unity, or to carry out the Reconquest single-handedly. By the end of the tenth century, the energy that had pushed the Leonese south-west to the Duero River had largely petered out. This initial phase of the Reconquest ended with the temporary supremacy of Navarre over all the Christian states of the north.

A second phase begins with the break-up of Sancho's realms on his death in 1035, and extends to the Almoravid invasion of the late eleventh century. This period is brief and essentially transitional, preparing the way for the great advances that marked the end of the eleventh, and the twelfth and thirteenth centuries. At this point (from 1085 on) the Reconquest passed from emigration into relatively vacant lands to large-scale attempts at territorial conquest. The break-up of the caliphate greatly facilitated such a trend, but the Christian states of the north were still too weak during the mid-eleventh century to carry out these enterprises by themselves. This transitional stage was characterized, therefore, by combinations of Christian states with each other, with the enemy, and also against each other. At the same time, they carried out various armed interventions in the feuds of the Mos-lem *taifas* in return for control of castles, land, and monetary tribute. Toward the close of the second period there was a steady trend toward large scale territorial conquest on the part of the Christians. However, until the opening of the third phase, and as long as the technique of mutual interventions prospered, it should be noted that the relations of Christian and Moslem were apt to be intimate and involved. This, of course, does not fit in with the concept of the Reconquest as a kind of eternal crusade. The crusading spirit was present, but only during certain times. Otherwise, the two faiths were not at each other's throats, and a considerable degree of cooperation took place. This was one of the characteristics of the second phase.

The third phase extends from the Almoravid invasion to the Cas-tilian conquest of Andalusia, or from 1086 to 1248. This was the traditional Reconquest of the history books. The appearance of Moroccan warriors fighting for their co-religionists intensified the feeling that the hated infidels were religious and cultural enemies. Consequently, many Christian military operations assumed the character of a crusade and were so proclaimed by the papacy. But here again it must be pointed out that the religious factor, while definitely present, did not rule out other motives. The conquest of Andalusia, for example, was marked by highly organized and very successful efforts on the part of the lay and clerical aristocracy to seize large tracts of land. The third phase, it should be remembered, was the phase of the military orders, and the great *latifundia* of the south, created by the crown to reward the northern nobles who had participated in the campaigns between Las Navas de Tolosa and the fall of Seville (1212–48). Unlike the other phases, it was also characterized by the expulsion of large numbers of Moslems from their lands to the great detriment of agriculture.

With the exception of Granada, the *taifas* were by now absorbed, and the Reconquest, definitely over for Aragon and Navarre, passed into a stalemate for Castile. The energies previously absorbed by the Reconquest were now turned into violent internal disorders in all the peninsular states.

The fourth phase was confined to the conclusion of the Reconquest in the reign of Ferdinand and Isabella and will be discussed in a later chapter.

2

If the battle of Covadonga is an actual historical occurrence, the Reconquest may be said to have begun before the Moslem conquest was completely terminated. The battle is probably more myth than reality, but there is little doubt that some kind of resistance was organized by the remnants of Visigothic refugees retiring to the shelter of the Pyrenean or Cantabrian foothills. But it was all on a very small scale. Doubtless the Mohammedans, engaged in the attempt to invade southern France, or occupied in furious feuds amongst themselves, paid little attention to what the Christians were doing. It seems probable that northwest Spain was relatively as unattractive to the Moslems as it had been to the Romans and Visigoths.[7] Certainly the earliest Christian expansion into the northwest from the mountains was into largely vacant territory, and consequently was almost unopposed.

A tiny kingdom, known as the kingdom of Asturias, gradually formed around Oviedo. According to legends that probably can never be precisely verified, Alfonso I (ca. 739–757) and his grandson, Alfonso II (ca. 789–842), pushed into what is now Galicia. By the

7. It should be remembered that the extreme northwest corner of Spain has always been hard to control. It was the last area to be occupied by the Romans in Spain, and for a long while it remained outside of Visigothic rule.

beginning of the reign of Alfonso III, "the Great" (866–914), the frontier had reached Tuy near the mouth of the Minho River, and straggled along to the northeast through the cities of Leon and Amaya. Alfonso III seems to have been a powerful personage, but again very little is accurately known of him. Taking advantage of a temporary weakness in Spanish Islam, he succeeded in moving the frontier southwest until he had acquired Burgos, Zamora, and Simancas. Still, it was relatively slow work because, when united, Moslem strength was far greater than any forces the small and poor Christian states could muster. Furthermore, the additional conquests of Asturias were mainly in the "no-man's land" of the Duero basin, a region largely depopulated through Moslem and Christian raids and counter-raids. As a matter of fact, both sides practiced a good bit of slave-raiding in an attempt to fill the vacant lands on each side of the shifting frontier.

Although intense religious fanaticism was still largely in the future, the Church and especially the monks played an important part in this early Christian expansion. Consequently, the establishment of the great shrine of Saint James (Santiago) at Compostela was a major development of this phase of the Reconquest. During the reign of Alfonso II it was believed that the tomb of the Apostle James was discovered near the town of Compostela in the far northwest. Amid great excitement, a church was built, there were the usual miracles, and eventually a bishopric was established. Possibly one of the reasons for the rapid growth of the cult was a curious confusion in the popular mind between the apostle James, and the James mentioned in the New Testament as the brother of Christ. Although the church carefully distinguished between them, public opinion often did not and local pride even went so far as to suggest that the shrine of Santiago de Compostela was actually superior to Rome because James, as Christ's brother, was obviously superior to Peter.[8]

Soon Compostela became one of the great religious centers of western Europe. *Santiago y cierra España* became the war-cry of the Christian forces in the peninsula, and great numbers of pilgrims from all parts of Europe began to take the "French road," as it was called, that led to Santiago's holy shrine.[9] This not only proved to be a great

8. Castro, *The Structure of Spanish History*, pp, 133–34.
9. Santiago was frequently portrayed as a young knight of commanding aspect, riding a white horse and carrying a banner. During the excitement of battle, many Christians believed they saw such a figure leading them on to victory. Castro has pointed out the interesting fact that the legend passed over to the Moslem side. Thus Aben Abizar, a Moslem chronicler who lived in Morocco, attributed their victory over the Christians at Alarcos to the intervention of a mysterious knight on a white horse who fought for them. Another

source of inspiration to the early Spaniards, but it also helped to bring them into much closer contact with the states of northern Europe, while at the same time it anticipated the later participation of the northern feudality in the Spanish crusades.[10]

One of the difficulties of the Christian states was the tendency of even some of the strongest kings to divide up their territory among their heirs, a fact which indicates how far we are, at this period, from any idea of political unity. Alfonso III is a good example. Apparently he abdicated a few years before his death and split up his lands among his sons Garcia, Ordoño, and Fruela; but after fourteen years and various deaths, all the territories were united again under Fruela. Sometime during these reigns, the capital was moved to Leon and the expanded kingdom took its name from this city. The king of Leon now ruled, more or less, in Asturias, Leon, and Galicia with some disputed claims to parts of Vasconia, Navarre, and the future kingdom of Castile. The institutions of this primitive state were mainly copied from the legends of Visigothic institutions—although after the rise of the Frankish empire, and particularly after Charlemagne's invasion of 778, there may have been some Frankish influences.

However primitive, the kingdom of Leon did achieve one great success during the first phase of the Reconquest: this was the repopulation of the Duero River basin by the emigration of mountaineers from the Cantabrian range to the plains southward. The result was an extensive displacement of peoples, involving Galicians, Asturians, and Leonese as well as Basques and even Mozarabs of the south. Leadership in the taking over of new land, or *presura*, often came from the king himself, who led expeditions to the south and west,

---

variation on the same theme related how the Moslem leader was promised the victory in a vision the night before the battle, the promise being made by a young warrior coming down from heaven on a white horse and carrying a green banner. Castro, *Los Españoles: como llegaron a serlo,* pp. 109–110, n. 2.

10. Vicens Vives points out that, while the religious theme has been emphasized by historians writing about Santiago de Compostela, very little has been written about its economic significance. He holds that the development of the Santiago cult wrought a veritable commercial revolution for northwest Spain. Since the greater number of pilgrims were French, Vicens Vives maintains that, by the end of the eleventh century, Compostela had become virtually a French town and all the more important towns along the route leading to the shrine contained French "quarters." The traffic along the road led to the preservation of roads, bridges, and the building of hospitals and inns for the use of the pilgrims. With the pilgrims there came an army of merchants, inn-keepers, artisans, and money-changers that constituted an incipient middle class. When fused together and assimilated at the end of the twelfth century, they constituted an important local force in the economy of the region. See Vicens Vives, *Economic History of Spain,* pp. 136–37.

building forts, refortifying cities, assigning lands, and fixing boundaries. Sometimes this was done in the name of the crown by a royal representative. At other times, the initiative was private, coming from great families, ambitious nobles, cities, and monasteries.

Whether the result of official or private enterprise, one thing seems clear: the society which resulted from the resettlement was relatively free. The work of the frontiersmen, for of course this is actually what the resettlers were, could only be undertaken by free men, whether brought in by the king or a noble. Serfs were not wanted and, according to Sánchez-Albornoz, were actually prohibited from entering some areas.[11] By and large, the nobility did not play a major role. Probably a good deal of the resettlement was carried on without permission from anyone, "neither the count nor the monastery nor whatever Ramiro or Ordoño was reigning at the moment, but by those who set out on their own initiative from the valleys of the North in search of freedom and settled in some corner of the Meseta plains."[12] *Presura* and resettlement effectively dictated the social structure of early Castile, which was to be free, non-feudal, vigorous, and aggressive.

The problems of the resettlement and the constant conflict with the Moslems placed great strains on the primitive institutions of government. Efforts on the part of the kings of Leon to increase their power to deal with these problems were frequently unsuccessful. The crown was usually represented throughout the kingdom by officials known as counts who often ruled directly over large areas. Nominally royal officials, these counts strove to become as independent as possible; the farther they were from the royal residence, the more likely they were to escape royal control, as the history of the county of Castile clearly shows. The monarchs tried to combat certain elective traditions in the Visigothic monarchy by making their realms hereditary, or occasionally by employing the title of emperor, but this seldom added much to their power.

The fact is that the national unity of Spain had been entirely lost, and the ideal of Saint Isidore's *mater Hispania* seems to have been entirely forgotten. Nothing illustrates how completely *particularismo* had become the order of the day than the story of the foundation of the independent county and later kingdom of Castile.

While Spanish historians disagree as to what was the germinal force that led to the appearance of an independent Castile, they do agree that this event was of great significance, and that Castile was strongly differentiated from the other Christian states of the northeast and the

11. Sánchez-Albornoz, "The Frontier and Castilian Liberties" in *The New World looks at Its History*, edited by Archibald R. Lewis and Thomas F. McGann (Austin: University of Texas Press, 1963), pp. 31–37.
12. Vicens Vives, *Economic History of Spain*, p. 129.

northwest. This difference seems to have been the result of three forces working in the new county. First, there was the freedom of a frontier society, stronger in Castile than elsewhere because it was more recent and more mobile. Secondly, because of the lack of natural protection along the eastern frontier (by contrast, the kingdom of Asturias was protected by mountains, by the semi-desert country from the mountains to the Duero watershed, and by the Duero valley itself) Castile was exposed to over a century (791–907) of constant pounding, first from the armies of Córdoba, and later from the Banu-Kasi renegades of the Ebro Valley.[13] From this pounding came a harsh will to fight and resist that produced a consciousness of strength which eventually led to secession. Finally, as Castile tended more and more to assume the lead in the Reconquest, there came under her aegis, for the first time in the history of the peninsula, sizable minorities of Moslems and Jews. But this aspect of the development of Castile is more properly treated in the discussion of the second phase of the Reconquest.

The pre-Castilian phase, if one may use such a term, of this frontier area goes back to the kingdom of Asturias-Leon. The eastern flank of this state, peopled mainly by Basques and Visigothic remnants, was remote from the political center of the kingdom and often as hard to control as to defend. Castles were frequently built at threatened points and hence the name *Castilla* was generally applied to this area. The first capital seems to have been at Amaya and, after 884, at Burgos. The kings of Leon were represented in Castile by the usual counts, but they were hard to manage; and, as the frontier of Leon moved south and west, Castile became more and more remote from royal authority. From 925 on, the counts of Castile were obviously aiming at complete autonomy, if not more.

It was the redoubtable Count Fernán González (930–970) who brought this about and made life utterly miserable for the contemporary kings of Leon. In 939, he allowed Abd-ar-Rahman III to use Castile as a base for an attack on Leon, and again and again he intervened in the affairs of his neighbors whenever he saw some advantage in it. As Merriman put it, "the intrigues of the count of Castile were shaking all the realms of Christian Spain to their foundations."[14] Later generations, finding it convenient to forget that Fernán González owed his rise to Moslem support, praised him as a noble knight and the terror of the infidel.

Hubo nombre Fernando el Conde de primero
Nunca fué en el mondo otro tan caballero

13. Sánchez-Albornoz, "The Frontier and Castilian Liberties", pp. 27–28.
14. Roger Bigelow Merriman, *The Rise of the Spanish Empire in the Old World and in the New* (New York, 1936), 4 vols., Vol. I, p. 66.

Este fué de los moros un mortal homicero
Decíanle por sus lides el buitre carnicero.[15]

Futhermore, his shocking behavior paid off handsomely. By the time of his death Castile was recognized as an independent county and Fernán had acquired all the appointive rights of the kings of Leon in his territory. In 1029, Castile was temporarily absorbed in the broad lands of Sancho the Great, but after his death it became independent under his son, Ferdinand, who assumed the title of king in 1032 or 1033. Shortly thereafter it became deeply bound up in the fortunes of the parent state. Ferdinand I of Castile conquered Leon in 1037, and ruled both until his death in 1065. They were apart between 1065 and 1072, from 1072 to 1157 they were united, and were separated for the last time between 1157 and 1230. They were finally brought together by St. Ferdinand III, and have never been separated since.

The establishment of Castile and its eventual absorption of Leon was an event of tremendous importance in Iberian history and has always been recognized as such by Spanish historians. Américo Castro expressed his view of the uniqueness of Castile by saying that Galicia-Leon was largely sustained by the Santiago cult, and Catalonia by Frankish imperialism, but Castile was the land of self-reliance and individualism.[16] Sánchez-Albornoz saw the union of Basques, Cantabrians, Goths, and Celtiberians in the original Castilian homeland as forming an "explosive mixture" that created the dynamic structure of Castilian society.[17] Perhaps the most eloquent testimony to the significance of Castile in Spanish history came from Vicens Vives. Speaking of the rise of this kingdom over both Leon and Navarre during the reign of Ferdinand I he wrote:

We have here a transcendental moment in Peninsular affairs in which Castile actually made her appearance in history. The Castilian people—of Cantabrian and Basque blood—were in agreement that their society was to be open, dynamic, and bold, as are all social structures on an advancing frontier. A people of shepherds and peasants, they led their flocks beyond the Duero River ... or they worked the fertile plains of the Arlanzon or Carrión rivers; and they would exchange their shepherd's crook or plowshare for sword and bow either to defend themselves against the invader, or to strike a blow for booty beyond the mountains of the central range. In the midst of these clashes (trivial perhaps,

15. "By name Fernando was the first count dight
    Never in the world was there such another Knight
    Ever to the Moslems a cause of mortal plight
    They called him Killer Vulture for his prowess in the fight."
Altamira, p. 119.
   16. Castro, *The Structure of Spanish History*, pp. 253–60, *passim*.
   17. Sánchez-Albornoz, "The Frontier and Castilian Liberties," p. 27.

but psychologically decisive) Castile forged her warrior temperament, her will to command, and her ambition to achieve a great destiny.[18]
Henceforth, Castile dominated the later phases of the Reconquest. Moreover, the traditional concept of the Spanish nation as dedicated to the Church, and to the destruction of heretics and infidels both in the old world and in the new, is mainly the achievement of Castile in the later Middle Ages. Here, Aragon was definitely the lesser partner.

Faced with disputes over the succession, and the emergence of Castile, the kingdom of Leon was clearly declining during the latter part of the tenth century. Not unconnected with this was the resurgent caliphate of Abd-ar-Rahman III and Al-Mansur. It is true that the kings of Leon could still win victories. In 914 Ordoño II got as far south as Mérida, and in 932 Ramiro II took the fortress of Madrid, but these advances were not permanent and the caliphate was clearly the stronger power. This was especially true during the rule of the energetic Al-Mansur when Leon not only had to cope with this formidable figure but also with the intrigues of Fernán González. Shortly thereafter a new danger came from the direction of Navarre, where the famous Sancho was rapidly emerging as the dominant figure in the north. By frequent appeals to the Moslems for assistance against its powerful neighbors in Castile and Navarre, Leon managed to maintain its independence until the year before Sancho's death. At that time, he occupied the city of Leon and proclaimed himself emperor. During these quarrels, little was done to acquire additional Moslem lands.

The failure of the kingdom of Leon to continue its earlier successes against the Moslems (which marks the end of the first phase of the Reconquest) was largely due to its failure to solve three problems: 1) it was not able to set up a competent military organization; 2) it was incapable of fusing together the interests of the mountaineers with those of the small agricultural proprietors of the Duero valley; and 3) it could not absorb the militant, rural masses of Castile. Henceforth, the leadership of the Reconquest would pass to other hands.

One strange development must be briefly touched upon before we turn to the second phase of the Reconquest, and that is the assumption of the imperial title by some of the early Leonese kings. According to legends, the title was used about 900 by Alfonso III and again in 917 by Ordoño II. Ramiro II (931–951) and Ordoño III (951–956) seem to have used emperor and *rex magnus* interchangeably in their titles, and Ramiro III occasionally employed the rather *outré* cognomen of *basileus*. Modern Spanish writers, such as Beneyto and del

18. Vicens Vives, *Approaches to the History of Spain,* pp. 41–42.

Arco, feel that the use of the imperial title by these kings of Leon indicates that the ideal of peninsular unity was not entirely forgotten. To them this title also suggests the idea of one sovereign with superior authority over the other rulers of the peninsula.[19] On the other hand, Menéndez Pidal believes this development was possible only because of the insignificance of the contemporary Carolingian rulers and because of the relative remoteness of Spain from the rest of Europe.[20] It is, however, doubtful that these vague and shadowy Ordoños and Ramiros had much of a concept of peninsular unity. The frequency with which they and others divided up their lands amongst their heirs seems to disprove this idea rather effectively. It is much more likely that immediate contemporary events influenced the choice of a title. What could be more natural, after an outstanding victory, or an important and successful siege, than for the victorious troops to salute their chief with a grandiose appellation. And indeed there is some evidence to suggest that this is exactly what happened. With the decline of Leon in the last part of the tenth century and the supremacy of the caliphate under Al-Mansur it is not surprising that this title lapsed. It is equally natural to find it in use again during the second phase of the Reconquest by the great, warlike kings of both Leon and Castile. It should hardly be necessary to point out that there is nothing in this usage of emperor intended by contemporaries to imply a rivalry with the Holy Roman Empire. Such an attempt, it is true, was undertaken by Alfonso X of Castile, but that was a very different affair, and will be dealt with in a later section.

3

As has been pointed out before, the second phase of the Reconquest has an essentially transitional character and is rather short, occurring mainly between the break-up of Sancho the Great's premature unification and the great wave of invasions from Morocco. Yet it is a phase of importance marked by new and interesting combinations of Moslem and Christian, by the appearance of new powers in the west and northwest, and, in its last decades, by dynamic warrior kings clearly foreshadowing the great conquests of the twelfth and thirteenth centuries.

During this age of adjustment, the Mozarabs had an especially important role to play as mediators and intermediaries between the two contending forces. In spite of the introduction of the Cluniac

19. Juan Beneyto Pérez, *España y el problema de Europa. Contribución a la historia de la idea de imperio* (Madrid, 1942), pp. 44–45; del Arco, p. 41.

20. Menéndez Pidal, *España y su Historia*, pp. 464–466.

order into Spain by Sancho of Navarre, the great age of crusading fanaticism was still almost a century away. A good deal of mutual toleration between the faiths made possible many cultural exchanges. As early as the ninth century a Mozarab saint, Alvaro of Córdoba, complained of the attraction of Arabic literature for the Christian intelligentsia. "All the young Christians illustrious for their talents are acquainted with the language and literature of the Arabs only; they read and study Arab books zealously; they expend huge sums collecting libraries of such works; and on every occasion they proclaim loudly how admirable this literature is."[21] As might be expected, a large number of Arabic words found their way into the Spanish language. While it is not so easy to tell if the reverse were true, the term *cristianos algaraviados* (Christians speaking Arabic) is matched by contemporary references to *moros latinados*, which speaks for itself. It was this relative tolerance and mutual interest of each culture that lay behind and made possible the great translation centers of the eleventh century.

The Mozarabs served in other ways. When the Mozarab Count Sisnando of Teutugal was captured by Motadid of Seville, he became the favorite of this king and later, when the same count served Ferdinand I of Leon (1033–1065), he often acted as mediator between his new master and the Moorish princes. Royal visits between Christians and Mohammedan rulers were common, and Christian fugitives, such as Sancho I, Queen Tota of Leon, and Alfonso VI of Castile, sought a temporary asylum in the *taifa* courts. There were many mixed marriages. Abd-ar-Rahman III had a Christian grandmother, and Al-Mansur a Christian wife. Alfonso VI of Leon (1065–1109) married, among others, a daughter of the Moslem king of Toledo; and a daughter of the royal house of Navarre married a Moslem prince. However, as the second phase gave way to the third, these cases became fewer and fewer.

After the middle of the century, there were clear signs that a new phase was approaching. The frontier began to move south and east, and certain consolidations of power such as the growing unity of Castile and Leon, the fusion of Aragon and Catalonia, and the appearance of Portugal, began to take place. The long and important reign of Ferdinand I, who inherited Leon and conquered Castile two years later, showed the beginning of these new trends. Taking advantage of his increased resources and the relative weakness of the Moslem states, he pushed the eastern frontier of Castile to the Ebro River while in the west he moved along the Tagus into the territory between that river and the Duero; between 1057 and 1064 he took Coimbra

21. Altamira, p. 98.

and other important centers in the future kingdom of Portugal. He also forced the petty Mohammedan rulers of Badajoz, Seville, and Toledo to become his tributaries. Unfortunately, the end of his reign was marked by the frustrating division of his hard-won territories among his three sons. However, the ablest, Alfonso VI, who inherited Leon immediately upon his father's death, succeeded in getting the other fragments in his own hands in a fairly short time. Although the latter part of his life was marked by tragic misfortunes, Alfonso VI must be accounted as one of the great rulers of the eleventh century and, in his sphere, almost as great a spoiler of other people's territory as his more famous contemporary, William of Normandy.

Everything about him made a powerful impression on his contemporaries. He appears in many legends, both Arab and Christian, and usually in a highly favorable light. Likewise in many a fragmentary *cantar de gesta* he appears as the typical hero-king; and in the great Castilian epic of *Mio Cid Campeador* he plays a role somewhat analogous to Charlemagne in the *Chanson de Roland*. Although he was a fierce opponent of the Moslems, his relations with them were touched with a kind of gallantry—one thinks of the love he had for his Moslem wife, Zaida, who bore him his only male heir and his chivalrous friendship with the Mohammedan king of Toledo—which was not unknown during this transitional age, and helped to make Alfonso the popular figure that he undoubtedly was. At the same time he had a good deal to do with the spread of French culture into Castile-Leon. His second wife was Constance of Burgundy, and apparently through her influence the French Cistercian order came into Spain. Two of his daughters married French princes, and many French knights found their way through the Pyrenees to fight in his armies. All in all, Alfonso managed to bring his lands into the general current of French culture, the most civilizing force in eleventh century Europe.

Although Toledo was almost ready to fall before the death of Ferdinand I, Alfonso, because of his friendship for its ruler, left it alone while he moved southward. By 1082 he had gone through the Guadalquivir Valley to Tarifa and seems to have already adopted the title of "Emperor of all Spain". By 1085 when his friend, the ruler of Toledo, was dead, he turned to that city and took it in the greatest single exploit of his long reign. Shortly after this, he appointed a French Cistercian as archbishop of the captured city, and barred the Mozarabic ritual from all but two of its churches, thus bringing Christian Spain closer to the papacy. He also called for new settlers to people his conquests and, typical of his relatively tolerant and international attitude, approved *fueros* or charters recognizing the special rights of the four classes of his subjects: *Mudéjares*, Jews, Franks (foreigners), and native Christians.

It has already been related how the very success of Alfonso VI brought about his undoing. The fall of Toledo united the *taifa* rulers against him and, under the lead of the king of Seville, they turned for aid to Yusuf the Almoravid from Morocco. This marked the beginning of Alfonso's difficulties. Yusuf beat him badly at Zalaca in 1086, and although the frontier held except in Murcia, and Toledo remained in Christian hands, this was more because of the divided interests of Yusuf rather than the efforts of Alfonso. Furthermore Valencia, briefly Christian thanks to the Cid, was abandoned by his widow on the advice of Alfonso, who was further shaken by the death of his only male heir in battle against the Mohammedans in 1108. He died the next year. Although his last years were darkened by these disasters, and after his death his realms were torn by a fierce dynastic struggle, the reign of Alfonso VI marks a great step forward in the history of the peninsula, and Castile-Leon in particular. The important things in his work survived, and, as it turned out, the victories of the Almoravids were ephemeral.

No account of the great warrior king can afford to omit the name of Ruy Díaz de Bivar, his sometime friend and enemy, immortalized as the Cid. Unlike the heroes of some of the medieval epics, the Cid is a historic personage, and his career throws additional light on this complex period.[22] A member of the lower nobility, the Cid seems to have become an important figure during the last part of the reign of Ferdinand I, and the brief reign of his son, Sancho II (1065–1972). When Alfonso VI acquired Castile in 1072, the Cid was at first welcomed at his court, but later an estrangement developed and in 1081 he was expelled from Castile. For a considerable period thereafter he served the Moslem king of Saragossa, sometimes even fighting against the Christians, and somewhat later he was apparently on his own. During this later period he achieved his most famous exploit—namely, the taking of Valencia in 1092. Although technically a vassal of the king of Castile, Ruy Díaz ruled the city as an uncrowned

22. Earlier writers have emphasized the fact that there is a solid historical base for the Spanish *cantares de gesta* which differentiates them from similar poems of heroic deeds in other European languages. Castro has spoken of what he calls "their disconcerting historicity," which he considers a unique phenomenon. Castro, *The Structure of Spanish History*, p. 256. More recent studies have suggested a considerably later date for the actual composition of *Mio Cid Campeador*, but I do not believe that this necessarily invalidates Castro's point. There is much less use of symbol, abstraction, and myth in this Spanish epic than in, for example, the *Chanson de Roland* or the *Nibelungenlied*.

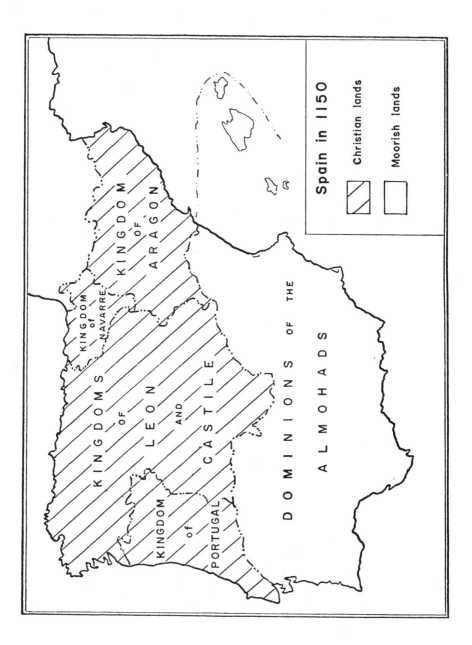

Spain in 1150

Christian lands

Moorish lands

KINGDOM of NAVARRE

KINGDOM OF ARAGON

KINGDOMS OF LEON AND CASTILE

KINGDOM of PORTUGAL

DOMINIONS OF THE ALMOHADS

king, greatly admired by both Moslem and Christian alike, until his death in 1099. His widow attempted to hold the city for a time but, on the advice of Alfonso, finally withdrew in 1102; whereupon the Mohammedans reoccupied the place. Although later ages considered the Cid a great fighter for the Cross, what strikes the student of his history is the fact that he lived intimately with the Moslems all his life, was fluent in Arabic, and often served them as willingly as he did his Christian masters. Thus his life was symbolic of conditions during the second phase of the Reconquest. A century later it would have been impossible.

4

The twelfth century was destined to be a great period in the third phase of the Reconquest and in the forward development of the Christian states in general, with the exception of Navarre. No one, however, could have predicted this, for its opening years were marked by violent internal conflicts in both Castile and Aragon, while the unexpected appearance of a new kingdom along the Atlantic coast seemed to presage an additional rival to the power of the Castilian-Leonese state.

In 1093 Alfonso VI had given his daughter, Urraca, to Raymond of Burgundy in marriage, and eventually a son, the future Alfonso VII, was born to the royal couple. Upon her father's death, Urraca, by this time a widow, succeeded to the throne of Castile and Leon, and she reluctantly agreed to marry Alfonso I (1104–1134), the Battler of Aragon. For a brief moment it appeared that the work of Ferdinand and Isabella might be consummated some three hundred and fifty years ahead of schedule. However, it was not to be. Alfonso was well-named the Battler, and Urraca soon took a violent dislike to him, probably well-mixed with fear. Faced, like his more famous successor Ferdinand II, with the delicate problem of his relationships within his wife's territory, Alfonso tried to solve matters with a heavy hand. The result was war between husband and wife for control of Leon and Castile, later complicated by the emergence of the young Alfonso, who was strongly backed in Galicia where he had been raised under the protection of the famous archbishop of Compostela, Diego Gélmirez. Urraca's marriage was conveniently dissolved in 1113 although Alfonso of Aragon refused to recognize that this terminated his rights in Leon or Castile, and the war continued as fiercely as before. A second or subsidiary conflict between mother and son added to the confusion. Doubtless there was a certain feeling of relief when Urraca expired in 1126 and Alfonso I was involved in a wide swing through Mohammedan Spain. This enabled the young Alfonso of Galicia to succeed in Leon and Castile as Alfonso VII (1126–1157). Perhaps determined to have the last word over his ex-stepfather after the latter's death in 1134, Alfonso VII staged a resplendent coronation at Leon in 1135 where he was saluted with the impressive title of *emperador de los dos cultos.* Since Alfonso the Battler's successor in Aragon had to be extracted from a monastery with the help of the pope, there was not likely to be further danger from that quarter, and so it proved. Nor did any one attempt to unite Castile and Aragon for centuries to come.

While the Mohammedans obtained a certain respite through these quarrels—although not Alfonso the Battler, who managed to wage war with everybody at the same time—the chief beneficiary was the emerging new state of Portugal. This state might be called a historical accident. Neither race, geography, nor religion affords any excuse for Portugal's existence; it was a product of the conditions of the Reconquest, and its origin throws considerable light on the nature of the Reconquest during the third phase.

During the heavy fighting that accompanied the Toledo campaign and later campaigns against the Almoravids, Alfonso VI was assisted by various foreign knights. Two of the most prominent were Henry and the above-mentioned Raymond of Burgundy. Both were rewarded by generous grants of territory in the northwest, and Count Raymond received the dubious reward of Alfonso's unruly daughter, Urraca. By this time the number of legitimate offspring was about exhausted; but from his always generous supply of natural children Alfonso selected a daughter, Teresa, and she was bestowed on Count Henry. Perhaps because of the slight stain on her lineage she was generously dowered with lands between the Minho and Tagus Rivers, later called Portucalia or Portugal. Instead of winning two devoted friends by his generosity, Alfonso's sons-in-law became intensely jealous of him and tried to weaken his position in every way.

The golden opportunity came during the dynastic difficulties after 1109, and it was Count Henry who was able to take advantage of it. Repeatedly intervening in the civil wars of Urraca, her husband, and her son, Henry was able to achieve considerable additions of territory. Indeed, at one time he seemed to be considering the possibility of getting Castile and Leon for himself. Had he done so, Portugal would doubtless have disappeared in an enlarged Castilian state and the history of the Iberian peninusla and the New World might have been quite different. But Count Henry died in 1114, and his widow, in spite of being the daughter of Alfonso VI, became the instrument of the forces of separation and independence. In 1128, she was forced to relinquish her power by her son, Afonso Henríques

(1128–1185), and the nobility. Afonso I at once embarked on a twofold struggle to secure independence from his feudal lord, the king of Castile and Leon, and to win additional territory from the Moslems. In both he secured notable successes. Although he made some kind of acknowledgment of feudal obligation to Alfonso VII in 1137, he was virtually independent after 1143, and in 1179 Pope Alexander III formally recognized the independence of the kingdom of Portugal. During his younger days Alfonso was frequently victorious over the Mohammedans. He defeated them at Ourique in 1139, and in 1147 he took the important fortress of Santarem. His crowning victory was the capture of Lisbon in the same year, thanks to the support of a band of crusading English, German, and Flemish knights who were persuaded to interrupt their journey to Palestine to take part in a crusade much nearer home. When Afonso Henríques died, his kingdom was established on foundations too strong to be overthrown. The struggle against the Moslems continued; there was a Portuguese contingent at Las Navas de Tolosa, and the Portuguese Reconquest roughly kept pace with the great Castilian advance down the Guadalquivir valley until the middle of the thirteenth century. These events firmly developed a national sentiment in the new kingdom, enabling it to resist all the efforts which the Castilians made from time to time to reconquer it.

Meanwhile Castile and Leon under Alfonso VII, the emperor, were still bearing the major share of the Christian advance in south central Spain. Both Almería and Córdoba were taken by Alfonso, but were later lost. The last ten years of his reign were darkened by the second invasion from Morocco in less than a century, that of the Almohads.[23] On his death the Christian forces were weakened by another division of territories, Castile being awarded to his olderst son Sancho III (1157–1158), and Leon going to the younger Ferdinand II (1157–1188). However, Sancho died within a year and was succeeded by his son, Alfonso VIII (1158–1214), who had a long minority. During this period, the Almohads strengthened their hold on Molsem Spain, and Alfonso VIII was not able to take the field against them until after 1170. At first he was successful, but in 1195 his allies failed him, and he was heavily defeated by the Almohads at the battle of Alarcos. This disaster was all the more unexpected since the Almohads had been in Spain for some time and had not, as yet, constituted an acute danger. However, Portugal and Navarre remained aloof as the campaign began and Leon, for the last time separate from Castile, was actively hostile under the ambitious Alfonso IX (1188–1230). The result was a defeat which shook the Christian states

23. See page 43.

of Spain. Preparations were made almost immediately for a second trial of strength. An attempt was made to improve relations with Leon by the marriage of a daughter of the king of Castile with Alfonso IX. The marriage actually took place and from it came the future Ferdinand III, the saint and great warrior who finally united the two states, but it cannot be said that the marriage improved the troublesome character of the king of Leon, who continued to intrigue against his father-in-law, and later against his own son.

In spite of these difficulties with Leon, Alfonso VIII maintained good relations with the other Christian states and in 1212 he notified them that he intended another major campaign against the Moslems. Although Alfonso IX of Leon ignored the invitation, the court of Portugal sent troops and Pedro II of Aragon, a heroic figure, came to the campaign in person. Navarre also sent troops. The pope was appealed to, and Alfonso dispatched Don Rodrigo Ximénez de Rada, member of a long line of distinguished archbishops of Toledo, to Rome to obtain the sanctions and special privileges of a crusade. Pope Innocent III agreed to all the requests made of him, and even threatened to excommunicate any Iberian sovereign who refused to assist the enterprise. Eventually a great host of Spaniards and many distinguished foreign knights assembled at Toledo in the spring of 1212. Although some of the strangers dropped out during the long, hot march southward through the Sierra Morena, battle was eventually joined with the enemy on the broad plain known as Las Navas de Tolosa on July 16. The active participation of Alfonso VIII and Pedro II, in addition to the archbishop of Toledo, lent an epic quality to this greatest and most decisive of engagements between Moslem and Christian in Spain. Indeed, the exploits of Don Rodrigo, prelate, scholar, and warrior, remind one inescapably of Archbishop Turpin in the Pass of Roncesvalles.[24] The Christian victory ended forever any danger to the northern Iberian states from Spanish Islam, and in a short time most of the remaining *taifa* states were overrun. Unfortunately, this moment of glory in the lives of the two sovereigns present at the battle was soon followed by tragedy. Pedro returned to Aragon to die the next year on the field of Muret, and Alfonso spent

24. Archbishop Turpin is the great feudal prelate of the *Chanson de Roland* who shrives and blesses the Frankish host just before the battle in the Pass of Roncesvalles. After killing innumerable Moslems, Turpin is himself killed thus achieving a perfect feudal and Christian death. Henry Adams felt that Turpin was the prototype of such fighting bishops as Odo of Bayeux, half-brother of William the Conqueror. Henry Adams, *Mont-Saint-Michel and Chartres*. With an introduction by Ralph Adams Cram. (New York, 1933), p. 23.

the remaining two years of his life in a vain effort to check the quarrels between his allies which had broken out almost immediately after the victory.

For a short interval of two years, the now triumphant Reconquest was halted by family quarrels involving Castile and Leon. These occupied the brief and meaningless reign of Henry I of Castile (1215–1217). On his death the throne went to his nephew, Ferdinand, son of Alfonso VIII's daughter and Alfonso IX of Leon. In spite of his father's intrigues, Ferdinand III successfully claimed the throne of Leon in 1230, and the last separation of Castile and Leon ended in a permanent union.

Ferdinand III (1217–1252) was not only a very able king and competent warrior, but he showed to the full that remarkable piety which was almost a family trait. Thus it is pertinent to recall that the famous Blanche of Castile, regent of France for the young Louis IX, was his aunt, and Saint Louis (1226–1270) of France his first cousin. Ferdinand was himself canonized by Pope Clement X in 1671, probably as much for his persecution of the Albigensians as for his spectacular crusades against the Spanish Moslems. Nevertheless, it is for this latter activity that history chiefly remembers him. After the union of Castile and Leon, Ferdinand was able to resume the final drive southward to the sea which had been initiated by his grandfather, Alfonso VIII. While his great contemporary in Aragon, James the Conqueror, was occupying the Balearic Islands and pressing southward along the Mediterranean coast toward Valencia, Ferdinand was preparing to conquer Andalusia. Córdoba fell in 1236 and this victory opened up the Guadalquivir Valley. He was then able to turn against the Moslems in Murica, which submitted in 1241. This advance not only carried Castile to the Mediterranean for the first time, but also brought it close to territory recently acquired by James the Conqueror. A treaty between Castile and Aragon in 1244 settled boundary difficulties for the time, and Ferdinand was then able to proceed against the Nasrid emirate of Jaén. The emir surrendered in 1246 in return for permission to retain some of his lands to the south in vassalage to Ferdinand. Thereupon he moved his seat of authority from Jaén to Granada, where his descendants were able to maintain the last Islamic state in Spain for the next two hundred and fifty years. Two years later Ferdinand attacked Seville, the capital of Andalusia and by now the major Molsem city in Spain. The siege was notable for the activities of a Castilian fleet which sailed up the Guadalquivir to take part in the operations against the city and also to prevent supplies and troops being sent from Morocco. Seville was taken on November 23, 1248, and the Christian occupation of Andalusia was now virtually complete. Ferdinand III was deeply involved in many plans during the next few years; he seems to have given some thought to a revival of the imperial title, that *ignis fatuus* of the Leonine and Castilian rulers, and to a great expedition against the Almohads of Morocco.

> In the midst of his preparations, however, the king was overtaken by an untimely death (May 30, 1252)—one of the noblest figures in the history of the Spanish empire, and deservedly venerated by his successors and their subjects long before he was canonized by Pope Clement X in 1671. He had dedicated his life with singlehearted devotion to the work of the Reconquest: he was valiant in war, generous in victory, loyal in the observance of his word.[25]

If the rich and variegated tapestry that was the Middle Ages can be symbolized in certain human lives, it seems clear that three thirteenth century rulers were typical of its noblest and most colorful aspects: Louis IX, the saintly French king and devoted patron of justice; Ferdinand III, the heroic warrior saint; and lastly, James the Conqueror of Aragon, certainly no saint, but warrior, poet, lover, and, like Richard Coeur de Lion, an outstanding representative of the rich culture of the *langue d'oc*.

At this point, it is desirable briefly to survey the changing conditions affecting the resettlement of the newly acquired lands. The conquest of Toledo carried the frontier from the Duero region to the Tagus valley, well into the central Meseta. Although the Almoravids recovered a good part of these lands after 1086, this proved to be only a temporary setback; by 1212 the area was permanently in Christian hands. The next and more rapid advance, from the Tagus River to the Sierra Morena range, was mainly an achievement of the twelfth century. In dealing with their territorial and demographic problems, the kings seem to have followed two general policies: in the cities, Moslems and Jews were left relatively undisturbed as Alfonso VI had done in the case of Toledo; however, in the countryside there was a reshuffling of peoples, with the Christian resettlement turned over to the towns and their newly established municipal councils. Later, the aristocracy and the military orders were to take over the control of the resettlement policies.

However, during the early part of the third phase of the Reconquest, the appearance of significant municipalities at Ávila, Valladolid, Medina del Campo, Segovia, and elsewhere was one of the most important developments. In order to strengthen the new towns which were so important in the maintenance of the frontier, considerable freedom and local autonomy had to be guaranteed by the crown. The *fuero* or charter bestowed on Oreja, an important town for the defense

25. Merriman, I, 85.

of Toledo, by the Emperor Alfonso VII in 1139 is a good example of the inducements offered to settlers. All those who wished to settle in Oreja were given amnesty for past offenses; the emperor surrendered his tax rights over the town and also his right to the royal fifth of booty taken in campaigns against the Moslems. Likewise, he offered to provide certain sums of ransom money, and to reimburse settlers for the loss of livestock taken in border raids at double the value.[26]

After 1212, the rich grazing land of the south was mainly turned over to the military orders, who introduced *latifundia* and a grazing economy, developments quite different from the earlier resettlement. The two principal beneficiaries of this change were the owners of the great flocks of Merino sheep, who were predominant in the military orders, and the Jews who rapidly took over the financial and commerical management of the wealth of the great landowners.[27]

With the great conquests of the mid-thirteenth century, the third phase of the Reconquest begins to draw to a close. The rest of the century saw Castile torn by violent internal conflicts involving the succession. However fascinating the reign of Alfonso X, *el Sabio* (1252–1284), may be from the standpoint of literature, astronomy, and law, it is not important for the continuation of the Reconquest, by now largely completed. From this time until the era of Ferdinand and Isabella, the increasing pretensions of the nobility will become a major problem to all the Iberian states, and it is more to this fact than to any other that Granada owed its long survival.

After a considerable lapse of military activities, the city of Tarifa fell in 1292 and early in the fourteenth century Gibraltar was taken. The first part of the reign of Alfonso XI (1312–1350) was a minority filled with the usual troubles, and even after the king came of age in 1325, the early years of his actual reign were not years of great accomplishment. When Granada was attacked by Castile and defeated, she appealed to the Merinites of Morocco for help. As a result of their aid, Gibraltar was retaken by the Moslems in 1333, and both the Moroccan emir and the king of Granada seem to have considered the idea of a holy war against Christian Spain. Moroccan troops invaded Spain, joined forces with Granada, and both besieged Tarifa. However, the Castilian fleet helped the town hold out until Alfonso could come to its assistance. The decisive battle was fought on the Rio Salado on October 30, 1340, and was another Christian victory. Three years later, Christian success on the Palmones River enabled Alfonso to besiege Algeciras which fell to him in 1344. After

26. Sánchez-Albornoz, "The Frontier and Castilian Liberties," p. 41.
27. Vicens Vives, *Economic History of Spain*, p. 162.

a five year truce, the king renewed the war by investing Gibraltar in 1349, but unfortunately he was one of the victims of the Black Death the next year and the siege was immediately raised. With his death the third phase of the Reconquest finally came to an end. With the exception of Granada, it brought the Mohammedan occupation to a close, and stabilized the frontier. For over a century Castile, satiated with territory, would forget conquest in her involvement with internal struggles of ever increasing severity.

5

The beginnings of the northeastern states of the Iberian Peninsula—Navarre, Aragon, and Catalonia—go back to the first Frankish expansion south. In 759, Pepin the Short, father of Charlemagne, took Narbonne and drove the Moslems back to the Pyrenees. Nineteen years later his son led a large force south of the mountains and besieged Saragossa although he failed to take the city. A second invasion brought about the capture of Barcelona by the Franks in 801; and although the frontier fluctuated somewhat, they made good their claim to this northeast corner of Spain which was first added to the duchy of Aquitaine. Later on it achieved an autonomous status as the Marquisate de Gotha (Spanish March) and after 865 was cut off from the lands north of the Pyrenees. During the confusion and troubles of the later ninth century, the counts of Barcelona began to absorb many of the local lordships, and also to ally themselves with the great families of southern France, in particular the rulers of Auvergne, Toulouse, Carcassonne, and Gascony. Meanwhile, petty wars against the Moslems in the early eleventh century brought the borders of the county of Barcelona (or Catalonia) to the Ebro valley.

About the same time as the establishment of the Spanish March, a small county began to form along the Arago River, which eventually lent its name to the tiny principality. Some early expansion took place in the direction of Sobrarbe and Ribagorza, but it seemed likely that Aragon would be absorbed into one or the other of its larger neighbors. At first, it seemed about to fall under Frankish control, but eventually Navarre, by now completely out of the Frankish sphere of influence, assumed the dominant role in Aragon. This was especially true during the reign of Sancho the Great (1000–1035). Born about 970, this man, little known, it is true, outside of the Iberian peninsula, was the dominant figure in Spanish affairs during his lifetime. He was able to weather the danger which the caliphate represented under Al-Mansur, and then, after the latter's death, he was able to weld Navarre, Castile, Aragon, and a part of the Spanish March into one considerable state. This remarkable achievement did not survive his death, for on his deathbed Sancho divided his estates among his sons. García, the eldest, got Navarre; Castile went to Ferdinand, who conquered Leon two years later; Aragon went to Ramiro, and the small countships of Sobrarbe and Ribagorza went to Gonzalo. However, Gonzalo soon died childless and his lands were seized by Ramiro, who united them to his kingdom of Aragon. By the time of his death in 1063, Aragon was completely independent of foreign control and in a position to expand both against her Christian neighbors and against the Moslems.

It cannot be said, however, that Aragon played a distinguished role in the Reconquest until the reign of Alfonso the Battler (1104–1134), "a notable disturber of the peace of those kingdoms."[28] This, of course, was the Alfonso I who married Urraca, daughter of Alfonso VI of Leon, and caused so much trouble to both wife and son through his unsuccessful efforts to obtain control of the western kingdoms. In spite of these wars, Alfonso managed to fight the Moslems as well. In 1118 he was able to capture Saragossa, and carry out raids into Valencia and Murcia. Alfonso died without legitimate heirs and Navarre was able to recover her independence. In the thirteenth century she passed into the hands of a French family and played little part in Iberian history until the era of the Catholic Kings.[29]

The problem of finding a successor to Alfonso I in Aragon led to a great turning point in the history of that state. Alfonso had a brother, Ramiro, but unfortunately he was a monk. However, with the aid of the papacy, Ramiro was persuaded, or forced, to come back into the world as king of Aragon, and even to marry a daughter of the ducal house of Aquitaine. When a daughter, named Petronilla, was born to the ex-monk and his wife, Ramiro evidently felt he had done his duty and once again renounced a world that seemed to hold no attractions. The infant Petronilla was betrothed to Ramón Berenguer IV, count of Barcelona and prince of Catalonia, with the understanding that she would be placed under the control of her future husband until they were of an age to wed. The union of Aragon and Catalonia which came from this marriage, for Ramón Berenguer also was given succession rights in the former state, was an event of the greatest importance. Since it had broken away from Frankish authority, the principality of Catalonia with its great port of Barcelona had become an important state, notable for its remarkable economic development. The beginnings of an urban market in Catalonia go back to the late tenth century, and the development of trade was greatly stimulated in the eleventh century after the fall of the caliphate. Barcelona's special importance in medieval Catalonia, according to Vicens Vives

28. Merriman, I, p. 275.
29. See below, Part II, Chapter I, *passim.*

and J. N. Oller, probably goes back to the beginnings of a trade in gold and slaves with the Sudan. This trade flowed toward the coast of north Africa and thence to the Spanish *taifas* of Denia, Valencia, and Tortosa. It was finally concentrated in Barcelona, which became the principal center for the export of African slaves and gold to the countries north of the Pyrenees.[30]

Concurrent with these developments in Barcelona and other Catalan cities was the expansion of feudalism in rural areas. As might be expected, Spanish feudalism, being affected by the special conditions of Iberian life, such as the destruction of Germanic elements and customs by the Moslems, did not take the forms of northern feudalism. Rather, it consisted of two types: one, in rural Catalonia, which did come closer to French feudalism; and a second type, which might be called seignorial feudalism and could be found in the Meseta. Seignorial feudalism was conditioned by the fact that the resettlement of the Moslem lands produced a society mainly of free peasants; and because of the absence of a land shortage, personal servitude was definitely limited. The first type was apt to be harsh and oppressive, but the second permitted much greater freedom in the terms of the feudal contract, the free towns of the Meseta, for example, being able to choose their own lords.[31]

Meanwhile, the counts of Barcelona contributed to the growing strength of the principality of Catalonia by carrying out raids against the Moslems and attempting, with considerable success, to acquire territory in southern France. In 1137, Catalonian territory north of the Pyrenees included a large part of Provence as well as such border regions as Cerdagne, Gevaudan, and Millau. During the remainder of the century this expansion continued, especially during the reign of Alfonso II (1162–1197), by now ruler in both Aragon and Catalonia. His northern acquisitions included Foix, Nîmes, Béziers, and Roussillon; Montpellier was added just after his death. Thus it might be said that Alfonso was on the verge of creating a Pyrenean kingdom which would have included both the Garonne and the Ebro valleys.

Obviously, in the marriage of the somewhat backward mountain kingdom of Aragon with the most advanced and least Hispanic state of the peninsula, it was the Catalan interests and outlook that now prevailed, and these interests were highly aggressive, mercantile, and intellectually exciting. The great port of Bacelona not only brought a large share of the wealth of the Mediterranean into the principality, but also the wealth of new ideas and cosmopolitan tastes and interests. Moreover, through their marriages into the families of the feudality of southern France, the princes of Catalonia and their subjects were

30. Vicens Vives, *Economic History of Spain*, pp. 147–148.
31. Ibid., p. 98–101.

able to tap the rich cultural sources of the *Midi*. Indeed, with the possibility of continued expansion against the Moslems to the south, eastward into the Mediterranean, and north into the trans-Pyrenean region of France, the future of the newly united Aragonese-Catalonian kingdom must have seemed bright.

The events of this dynamic century (the twelfth) transformed the Catalan mentality. This feudal, peasant Romanesque people of other times gave way to a brilliant and expansive society of colonizers and merchants. With the harsh parsimony that characterizes their history, the Catalans stored up enormous moral and material reserves that would, in the thirteenth century enable them to climb in one leap to the front ranks of Mediterranean politics.[32]

At first, it appeared that the Reconquest would claim the greatest attention of the rulers of Aragon. Alfonso II (1162–1196), son of Petronilla and Ramón Berenguer, continued the work of the Battler; he captured Teruel from the Moslems and, like the first Alfonso, continued to people his new lands with Mozarabs. As we have seen, he also added greatly to his possessions in southern France. His warlike son, Pedro II (1196–1213), played an important part in the Castilian Reconquest by being present at the Battle of Las Navas de Tolosa, where he played a valiant role. Unfortunately, his French possessions involved him in the complex fanaticisms of the Albigensian crusade and in 1213, answering an appeal from his vassals in southern France, he was killed at the battle of Muret by the troops of Simon de Montfort. Pedro's death was the first step toward the ultimate loss of all the Aragonese lands north of the Pyrenees. The de Montfort family eventually made over all their claims in this territory to the French crown, and Louis VIII in time took over many of them. When James I, the son of Pedro, and one of the great figures of the thirteenth century, came of age, he tried to retain the trans-Pyrenean lands, but found it impossible. Eventually, in a treaty signed with Louis IX at Corbeil on May 12, 1258, James renounced all Aragonese claims to these territories, with the exception of Cerdagne, Roussillion, and Montpellier.[33] Whatever James may have felt at the moment about these losses, in the long run it worked to the advantage of his kingdom. Aragon-Catalonia was now free of an expensive distraction. She was henceforth able to play a more significant role in the Reconquest, and in the building of that most remarkable medieval phenomenon—the Aragonese empire of *outremar*.

James I the Conqueror (1213–1276) was the outstanding figure of the Aragonese Reconquest, and also the founder of the overseas empire. In fact, during his tempestuous lifetime, he dominated every

32. Vicens Vives, *Approaches to the History of Spain*, p. 55.
33. Montpellier was later sold to France. Cerdagne and Roussillon were ceded to France by the Treaty of the Pyrenees in 1659.

aspect of his state. Merriman has brilliantly described his character as follows:

> Warmth and intensity of passion, both good and bad, formed its basis; restraint and self-control had no part in it at all. Waves of ferocious anger and tender pity succeeded one another like the showers and sunshine of an April day. In the heat of a terrible campaign against the Valencian Moors, when it was essential for him to be everywhere at once, he found that a swallow had made her nest by the roundel of his tent and 'so I ordered the man not to take it down till the swallow had taken flight with her young ones as she had come trusting in my protection.'[34]

James' greatest achievement was the conquest of Valencia. Pope Gregory IX was induced to proclaim a crusade there in 1229 and the war began in 1233. However, there were many delays and the city did not fall until 1238. Shortly afterwards, the occupation of territory between the Júcar River and the Moslem state of Murcia brought James into direct contact with Castile. A temporary agreement in 1244 adjusted the boundary line. In 1263 the Moslem king of Murcia revolted against Alfonso X of Castile, his feudal overlord. Alfonso appealed to James, who was by now his father-in-law, and the Aragonese king agreed to help. Murica was therefore occupied by his troops, but, in keeping with their agreement, James turned it over to King Alfonso. A permanent boundary between Castile and Aragon in the south was finally set up in 1304 and was more favorable to Aragon than had been the earlier agreement. The fall of Murcia marks the end of the Reconquest as far as Aragon was concerned. She was no longer in touch anywhere with Mohammedan territories and could henceforth devote her entire attention to expansion into the eastern Mediterranean.

As I have pointed out previously, the marriage of Petronilla with Ramón Berenguer of Barcelona in 1137 brought Aragon under the influence of the commercial and expansionist aims of Catalonia. However, it was not until the thirteenth century that these interests were able to achieve the beginnings of an overseas empire. In September, 1229, James the Conqueror of Aragon invaded the Balearics and was able to complete their conquest by 1235. The next eastward step brought the power of the eastern kingdom to Sicily. To understand how this happened, a short digression is necessary.

After the death of the Emperor Frederick II in 1250, the great struggle between the papacy and the House of Hohenstaufen was continued by his descendants. By 1268 the papacy seemed victorious, and its ally, the House of Anjou,[35] firmly established in Naples and

34. Merriman, Vol. I, p. 292.

35. Charles, Count of Anjou (1227–1285), was a younger brother of Louis IX of France. Brought into Italy by the papacy in the hope of destroying the Hohenstaufen power, he was crowned king of Naples and Sicily by the pope in 1266.

Sicily. However, the heir to the Aragonese crown, the Infante Pedro, had married a granddaughter of Frederick II in 1262 and was prepared to assert his wife's claims at the first opportunity. The cruelty of the French in Sicily had turned the natives strongly against them and local leaders begged Pedro III (1276–1285) to intervene. This he did after the famous uprising against the French, known as "the Sicilian Vespers," in 1282. Aragonese naval power enabled Pedro to retain the island despite all the efforts of Charles of Anjou, and of his nephew, Philip III of France, who attempted to assist him by an unsuccessful invasion of Aragon in 1285. The fact that Charles, Pedro, and Philip all died in 1285 led to a stalemate in regard to Sicily, but Pedro's intervention had made France and the papacy henceforth the bitter enemies of Aragon. For some time to come, the popes did everything they could to dislodge the eastern kingdom from its Italian holdings. James II (1291–1327) tried to hold on to both Aragon and Sicily, but, faced by the adamantine ferocity of Pope Boniface VIII, he abandoned Sicily by the Treaty of Anagni (1295). Although shocked by this catastrophe, the Sicilians were determined to maintain their independence and turned to Frederic, younger brother of King James, whom they crowned as king of Sicily on May 25, 1296. He proved too strong to evict and, with the rapid deterioration of papal relations with France, Boniface VIII eventually recognized Frederic as king of Sicily by the Treaty of Caltabelotta in August, 1302[36]. Thus was established the line of the independent Aragonese sovereigns of Sicily which was to endure for more than a century before the island was directly incorporated in the kingdom of Aragon.

The story of the Catalan duchy of Athens, although fascinating and romantic, is hardly directly concerned with the official expansion of Aragon into the eastern Mediterranean, nor did it represent a permanent acquisition. The next sizable addition was the island of Majorca. After its conquest by James the Conqueror, the island had passed into the hands of a branch of the royal family and a line of independent (save for a feudal allegiance to the crown of Aragon) sovereigns was set up. This line was ended by the skillful intrigues of Pedro IV (1336–1387) against the feeble James of Majorca, the last of the independent rulers. Taking advantage of a quarrel between James and the king of France over Montpellier, Pedro provoked James into open defiance. It was then a simple matter to declare his domains forfeited and annexed to the crown. A brief campaign of a month (June, 1343) enabled Pedro to occupy the island. Cerdagne and Roussillon, the mainland fiefs of the Majorcan kingdom, were taken the following year.

36. There appears to have been some reservation of papal feudal rights over Sicily, but this was nothing more than a formality. Actually the treaty represented the failure of some twenty years of papal policy.

Sardinia, the last major acquisition of Aragon in the Mediterranean, had been assigned to King James by Pope Boniface as a part of the arrangement whereby he abandoned his brother. Most of Sardinia was occupied by James between 1323 and 1324, but a complete conquest was not achieved until 1421.

The recovery of all of Spain except Granada by the various Christian states, in addition to the remarkable expansion of Aragon into the Mediterranean, was the major achievement of the Iberian peoples during the eleventh to the fourteenth centuries. No other European population had such an experience during the Middle Ages, and, throughout the process, the Hispanic character, customs, and governmental institutions were profoundly and permanently marked.

## CHAPTER V

# Spain between the Reconquest and

# the Era of the Catholic Kings*

THE PRESENCE OF THE MOSLEMS IN SPAIN AND THE DETERMINED though sporadic efforts to expel them dominated the history of the peninsula throughout the Middle Ages. Even after the great activity of the thirteenth century came to an end, and the energy developed by the Reconquest was diverted into innumerable petty feudal conflicts, the effects of this great struggle continued to influence all aspects of Iberian life.

The wars had helped to strengthen the monarchy in Castile, and made the king an important landowner; even the dissipation of royal resources by John II (1406–1454) and Henry IV (1454–1474) could not completely eliminate the crown as a power in the land. Furthermore, memories of the great warrior kings like Alfonso VI and Saint Ferdinand persisted and, in the long run, proved more lasting than the influence of the weak rulers of the fourteenth and early fifteenth centuries. In all the Iberian lands, the wars led to the development of a martial and religious spirit. The heroes of this frontier society were the warrior, the monk, and the missionary—not, be it noted, the trader or merchant.[1]

There is undoubtedly a connection between the Reconquest and the rise of that form of militant Catholicism which seems so typically Spanish, but great caution should be used in trying to evaluate the relationship. It is easy to assume that, whenever Moslem and Christian

*The title bestowed upon Ferdinand and Isabella by Pope Alexander VI after their successful war against Granada.

1. Richard Konetzke, *El Impero Español: orígenes y fundamentos*, translated from the German by Felipe Gonzalez Vicen (Madrid, 1946), pp. 11–12.

came together, fighting followed; but, as I have attempted to show in the previous chapter, there were long periods in Spanish history when this was not at all the result. The early wars were mainly for booty and territorial conquest and a good deal of religious toleration was still possible. Nonetheless a change did occur, and the religious fanaticism which appeared sporadically before the twelfth century became more common during and after the thirteenth. Probably several factors were responsible. Among them must be cited the presence of foreign knights in Spain, and the influence of the crusades to the Holy Land. The foreign knights, although they may have been, and probably were, motivated by human greed as well as religion, emphasized the international aspects of the struggle with Islam just as the succession of unsuccessful crusades in the twelfth and thirteenth centuries dramatized the conflict of the two faiths and added everywhere to the tension. In the fifteenth century, the new danger from the Ottoman Turks coincided with the renewal of the Reconquest under Ferdinand and Isabella and this added greatly to the increasing fanaticism of the Spanish Church. It is not surprising, then, that after the fall of Granada the forces behind Castilian expansion were too powerful to be contained and the Reconquest was continued, with many of the original motives still intact, under the name and form of colonization.

Although the Reconquest helped to develop an energetic, warlike society with strong religious tendencies, its influence on the Spanish economy was probably adverse. This is certainly true as regards agriculture. Here, the peculiar nature of the Christian-Moslem frontier with its frequent border raids placed a premium on the more mobile forms of wealth. Thus while the spoiliation of farms was often unavoidable, flocks and herds could be removed to places of safety, and this was probably one of the reasons for the growing importance of animal husbandry over agriculture. Eventually the great sheepowners pooled their common interests in the powerful organization known as the *Mesta* and repeatedly forced from the crown a multitude of concessions, often very harmful to agriculture. In this relationship lay one of the causes of the economic collapse of the seventeenth century.

Agriculture also suffered from the changes in the resettlement of Al-Andalus introduced by the vast acquisitions of the thirteenth century. In the span of a few years, Ferdinand III had acquired the richest part of medieval Spain. This area was too large and too populous for the resettlement methods adopted by Alfonso VI.[2] In Andalusia, the resettlement was henceforth closer to a military occupation. The

2. Vicens Vives, *Economic History of Spain*, p. 162.

Moslem urban masses were forced out of the cities although in the countryside the peasants were undisturbed for the time being. The new policies led to a Moslem revolt in 1263 in both Andalusia and Murcia. When the revolt was put down, the rural Moslems were uprooted and dispersed either to north Africa or Granada. The new lands so acquired by the Christians were redistributed mainly to the nobles, the Church, and the military orders.[3]

According to the researches of Pascual Carrión, approximately 3,750,000 acres of land passed into the hands of the nobility in these areas while the common people who formed the base of the conquering army received very little.[4] It has been estimated that at the fall of Seville in 1248 some 300,000 Moslems were driven from their holdings.[5] Since the nobility seldom attempted to cultivate all of their estates, this growth of *latifundia* led to an increase of uncultivated lands, thus further complicating the problems of agricultural production. Moreover, the land transfers led to a decline in the techniques of farming. The new proprietors had no great interest in studying Moslem methods, nor did the agricultural workers brought in by the resettlement have the necessary skills to maintain the high level set by the Moslems. According to Vicens Vives,

> As a general rule, the military orders paid no attention to the technical problems of agriculture, and this was why, at the time of the great Reconquest of Andalusia, the Castilian state found it did not possess the elements essential to take full advantage of an occupation so vast as that of the old Roman Baetica.[6]

It will not be difficult to imagine how much stronger the lay and clerical nobility became after the occupation of Andalusia. Their newly acquired wealth made it possible for them to challenge the state and crown as never before, and emerge in part victorious. The knight class also grew in power as the old *hidalgos* of the north were rewarded with parcels of land and often entered into vassalage relationships with the greater nobles. In the cities, the hidalgos gained control of the municipal councils and this was at the expense of the democratic tendencies that characterized many of the towns during the second phase of the Reconquest. The migration south also led to an intensification of serfdom in the north during the late thirteenth century. In order to protect their supplies of cheap labor now threatened by the movement south, the lords of the north multiplied the devices by which the free peasants could be held on the land.

3. Ibid., p. 163
4. Pascual Carrión, *Los latifundios en España: su importancia, origen, consecuencias y solución* (Madrid, 1932), pp. 291–96
5. Ibid.
6. Vicens Vives, *Economic History of Spain*, p. 165.

This led in Catalonia to the *remença* serf and his problems, and in Castile to the *solariego*. Also for the first time, there is the appearance of the *jornaleros*, or migrant, landless labor.

We have already seen that the initial effect of the frontier on the towns was highly stimulating, and that the crown deliberately favored this development through the granting of fueros on highly favorable terms. Out of this activity came regional leagues of towns, or *herman-dades* which were a common feature of Spanish municipal life in the later Middle Ages and, indeed, of medieval towns everywhere. And yet these important trends failed, in the long run, to produce in Spain the flourishing middle class municipalities and institutions that parallel developments in other states might lead one to expect. In the opinion of some scholars a culmination was reached in the late fourteenth century, and beyond that point the Spanish towns and the middle class ceased to progress.[7] While much more research must be done before a definite explanation of the weakness of the Spanish bourgeoisie can be formulated, still it would seem that a few general comments may be hazarded. It appears likely that the constant drain of the most energetic and ambitious, and possibly the most intelligent, elements of the population into the pursuit of arms, or into the Church, had a restrictive effect on the development of the middle class.[8] The border forays, the difficulties of communication in a land whose internal topography naturally made for separatism, the relative poverty of natural resources, the restrictions on agriculture written into law by the Mesta, all cast a blight on Spanish economic development and prevented it from following contemporary patterns in England and France.[9] This relative ineptitude in commercial matters led to efforts by the crown to improve the situation through government regulation and monopoly, frequently involving fixing of prices, salaries, and the prohibition of the export of goods under a foreign flag. All these policies, as Konetzke points out, "are phenomena that cannot be described as commonplace in the political economy of the middle ages."[10]

On the evidence of these facts, the distinguished French scholar Fernand Braudel concluded that the peninsula was never sufficiently urbanized, and the middle class never sufficiently numerous.[11] Thus

7. Rhea Marsh Smith, *The Day of the Liberals in Spain* (Philadelphia, 1938), p. 35 *et. seq.* Smith maintains that the Cortes of Madrid, 1391, was the last great meeting of municipal representatives, after which a decline set in.

8. Konetzke, p. 17.

9. See above p. 71.

10. Ibid., pp. 66–67.

11. Fernand Braudel, *La, Méditerranée et le monde méditerranéen à l'époque de Philippe II* (Paris, 1949), p. 617.

Spanish trade, commerce, and manufacturing always required the presence of foreign intermediaries. In the Middle Ages these were chiefly Jews and Moslems. After 1492 much was still being done by converted Jews *(conversos)*and Moriscos, but as the sixteenth century wore on Germans and Italians came to play the leading role in Spanish economic enterprise. This is not to say that the Spanish middle class did not play an important role during the great periods of Spanish history. The legal middle class, the *letrados*, had infiltrated the highest ranks of the administrative hierarchy. But it was always a shared role, never an exclusive one, and the economic weakness of the middle class effectively prevented it from doing more. Furthermore, the *trahison des bourgeois*, the desire to pass into the ranks of the lower nobility through the purchase of a title or by marriage, operated powerfully in Spain and doubtless further weakened a class already in decline by the sixteenth century.

2

The conditions resulting from the southward moving frontier, which were so deleterious to the national economy, had an entirely different effect on the origins of the Spanish colonial empire. As I have pointed out previously, the forces of religion and greed—the desire to bring souls to Christ, and gold into the pockets of men—which played so large a part in the Reconquest were equally effective in the overseas expansion of Castile. Seen from this point of view, the Spanish colonial movement under the Catholic Kings and Charles I appears as an extension of the Reconquest overseas. In the case of colonial institutions, the connection between the Reconquest and the colonization of the New World is close. The movement of the Iberian peoples against the Moslems, it must be remembered, was not only an affair of booty and conquest, but it was also a movement of peoples, an affair of internal colonization which constituted an admirable preparation for what was to come after 1492. According to Konetzke, "in the course of centuries [the Spanish] developed a certain technique of expropriation, and this system of colonization *within* Spain was then applied and adapted to the new situation during the conquest of the New World."[12] It is not surprising that Castile, the power that had had the greatest experience with internal colonization in the peninsula, was best able to take advantage of the opportunity that came at the end of the fifteenth century.

A brief examination of the origins of some of the more conspicuous colonial institutions will show how they were first utilized in internal colonization before being later transferred to the New World. The

12. Ibid., p. 17.

office of *adelantado*, often used in the early days of the overseas exploration in the defense of newly established settlements, was originally established by the kings of Castile to replace the local counts with an officer more amenable to the royal wishes. First mentioned in 1255, there seem to have been three different kinds of *adelantados*: the frontier *adelantado* assigned land along the border for which he had military responsibilities, mainly defensive; the provincial *adelantado*, a combination of judge and captain-general over large provincial areas in Castile, Leon, and Galicia and, although a soldier, was usually advised and assisted by *letrados;* the *adelantado mayor,* a lawyer whose work was confined to judicial functions and who frequently served as a circuit judge.[13] Other officials widely used in the colonies were the *alcalde mayor* (1371), a municipal judge appointed by the crown; the *corregidor,* a royal representative with certain administrative authority in the towns; the *pesquisidor,* similar to the *corregidor* but with higher authority, and the *oidor* who served as judge of an *audiencia* or court.[14] The *audiencia* originally referred to a high court personally presided over by the king. First established for Castile and Leon, it came to have jurisdiction in Andalusia; and, since the sovereign could devote only a limited amount of time to hearing cases, additional judges had to be created. King Henry II of Castile (1369–1379) increased its powers and provided seven alcaldes and seven letrados to serve on it. He also raised it to the position of a superior court of appeals holding sessions at Seville in the south and Segovia in the north. This institution was first established in the New World in 1524 at Santo Domingo. Other audiencias were later set up throughout the empire.

In short, it may be said that it is questionable if Spain could have achieved her great success as a colonial power without the experiences coming from the Moslem-Christian frontier. Her only serious rival in the sixteenth century, Portugal, had also shared this experience and learned from it. By comparison, one has only to think of the difficulties encountered by the English in their attempt to colonize medieval Ireland, or the failures that constituted English and French colonial efforts in the sixteenth century, to see what an education the Iberian powers derived from the Reconquest. If Spain were able to put into operation a more effective colonial government in a shorter time than any of her rivals, it was because she had had the experience of appropriating other people's lands, and governing

13. Charles H. Cunningham, "The Institutional Background of Spanish-American History," *Hispanic-American Review,* I, No. 1, February, 1918, pp. 24–39. See also, Clarence H. Haring, *The Spanish Empire in America* (New York, 1947), Chapts. 1–2, *passim.*

14. Ibid., pp. 13–32.

frontier provinces for almost seven hundred years of her history. In the words of a recent Spanish historian, "no other people experienced so long an apprenticeship for the mission of discovery and colonization as the Spanish."[15]

This brief survey of the Spanish medieval preparation for empire cannot be concluded without mentioning the pre-colonial activities of the Castilian navy. The earliest operations seem to be associated with the name of Diego Gelmírez, the famous archbishop of Santiago, in the first half of the twelfth century. To prevent Moslem interferences with Christian shipping, the archbishop sought help from Pisa and Genoa, already prominent in naval matters, and in 1120 seems to have ordered a small number of ships built. Portugal had some kind of a fleet in 1179 and Catalonia much earlier; in each case, trouble with the Mohammedans acted as a spur to additional naval activity.[16] As the Reconquest surged southward in the twelfth and thirteenth centuries, fleets could be used to blockade hostile coastal cities. This was especially true of the campaign against Seville in 1248 when Ferdinand III used the Castilian fleet to cut off this city from contact with the Moslems of Morocco. His son, Alfonso X, established the marine crusading order of Santa Maria de España as a means of imbuing seamen with the crusading spirit. Sancho IV (1284–1296) did much for the navy. He followed the policy of purchasing ships from the Genoese and eventually could boast of a fleet of approximately one hundred vessels. With this force, he won victories over the Moslems in 1284, 1292, and in 1293. Still later, during the reign of the energetic Alfonso XI (1312–1350) when the last victories were won before the night of anarchy descended upon Castile, the fleet played an important role at the siege of Algeciras in 1343–44. Since Alfonso was planning a descent on the African coast, naval power was obviously important to him, but his unfortunate death at thirty-eight during the Black Plague ended such projects for many years to come.

But it was during the Hundred Years' War between France and England that the medieval Castilian navy may be said to have reached its heroic age. The alliance of Castile with France assisted the House of Trastámara to the throne, and the grateful Henry II (1369–1379) became involved in active naval intervention against the English. In 1372, a Castilian squadron defeated the English at La Rochelle and two years later the English coast itself was successfully raided.

15. Juan de Contreras, *Los origenes del imperio: la España de Fernando e Isabel* (Madrid, 1939), p. 228.

16. In Catalonia, the Marca de Ampurias was founded by Charlemagne to protect the coast from Arab-Berber attacks. The count of the March won a victory in 813 over the Arabs and captured eight ships.

This operation led the way to additional assaults on English coastal towns. In 1377 the Castilians attacked Walsingham, Plymouth, Folkestone, and Dover. Perhaps the greatest achievement took place in 1380 when the fleet sailed up the Thames to Gravesend, not far from London, and burned it. The death of Charles V of France in this same year led to a long truce in the Anglo-French struggle; and internal troubles in Castile during the reigns of the weak successors of Henry II put a stop to these operations. Nonetheless, the conquest and colonization of the Canary Islands (1402–1483) shows that maritime activity in Castile was quite vigorous. Clearly, the days of Spanish maritime supremacy in the first three-quarters of the sixteenth century were by no means an accidental development but were, to the contrary, a continuation of the traditions and achievements of medieval Castilian sea power.

3

The institutions of medieval Iberia show a certain similarity to medieval institutions in the rest of Europe: although Aragon, with its Cortes of four houses and the unique institution of the *justicia*, shows certain special characteristics. In both states, the earliest records indicate an elective monarchy which gradually became hereditary. In Castile, hereditary succession was common after the reign of Ferdinand I (1037–1065) but even after that date some elections did take place. The famous law code of Alfonso X, the *Siete Partidas*, provided a scheme for hereditary succession which was almost immediately violated by his own son. Still, this was of the nature of the exception that proves the rule, and with the designation of the king's eldest son as Prince of the Asturias, first instituted in 1388, the trend toward hereditary succession may be said to have been completed. The history of Aragon shows a similar pattern, with such a respect for the royal blood that, as has already been mentioned, one of the royal princes was forced to renounce his monkhood and marry in order that the royal line might be continued.[17] Primogeniture was established in Aragon by the time of Pedro IV (1337–1386) when, except for Sicily, the lands of the various branches of the royal house were absorbed by the crown.

The rulers of the Iberian states were, in the beginning, surrounded by various officers who did little more than manage the simple needs of the royal household. Little by little, as in the other European nations, these officials evolved into great officers of state responsible for many phases of governmental administration. Sometimes their titles show a conscious imitation of the Arabic titles, such as the title

17. See above p. 73.

of *almojarife mayor* which was applied in early days to the treasurer of the Castilian crown.[18] Although in theory the crown in Castile was all powerful, in actual practice in king's authority was limited by customs, traditions, the Church, his own personality or lack of it, the rights of the Cortes, and the feudal nobility. As a part of the theory of absolutism, the ruler had the right of appointment to all important posts at his court, but here again this power was often restricted by the special privileges of certain noble families. Thus the Enríquez family monopolized the office of admiral of Castile, the Velascos kept the position of constable of Castile (commanding general) in their house, and in Aragon the post of *justicia* was controlled by the Lanuza family.

Every medieval monarch was advised by some sort of council, at first made up entirely of nobles and prelates, but soon invaded by members of the middle class who gradually took over most of the work. In Castile, such a council seems to have existed from early times as a nameless, amorphous group of friends and allies of the monarch, men who were closely associated with him but without permanent appointments or clearly prescribed duties. During the reigns of Ferdinand III and Alfonso X, the tendency toward a permanent organization became much greater and frequently nobles, clergy, and merchants were called to advise the crown. The reference to *hombres buenos* on the royal council can only refer to men of the middle class.[19] During the minorities and civil wars of the fourteenth century, the royal council (*consejo real*), as it was now called, increased greatly in importance. John I (1379–1390), on the eve of his unsuccessful invasion of Portugal in 1385, made formal, legal recognition of the council in a document setting its membership at four prelates, four nobles, and four citizens; he divided it into two *salas*, one dealing with administrative problems and the second hearing appeals from the *audiencias*. Henry III (1390–1406) increased the membership to sixteen, composed of *prelados, condes, caballeros y doctores*, which was essentially the earlier arrangement. Unfortunately, during the confusion of the reigns of John II and Henry IV, the Castilian council sank into a state of corruption and inefficiency that affected all institutions until after the advent of Isabella. How Isabella rescued the Council of Castile and made it the principal organ of her government will be told in a later chapter, but in this as in much else, the great queen was a renovator, not an innovator. There was ample precedent for what she made of the council.

By the beginning of the fourteenth century, most of the royal

18. Later the title of the officer was changed to *contador* and still later to *tesorero*.

19. Merriman, I, 211–12.

administrations in Europe had developed some sort of body representative of the major social classes or "estates" of the kingdom. Such bodies were termed Parliament in England, Estates-General in France, Reichstag in Germany, and Cortes in the Iberian peninsula. These institutions of the late Middle Ages should not be confused with modern representative legislative bodies, from which they differ in many ways. For one thing, they were not entirely representative since the majority of the population (serfs and agricultural laborers of varying status) were not represented. In addition, they were not exclusively concerned with legislation since the sovereign himself possessed this power. Actually most of their time was occupied in presenting petitions for redress of grievances, making special grants of money (here the middle class was very important) when they could not get out of it, and sometimes advising on problems of succession. While the Cortes of Castile was typical of these bodies, it was especially distinguished by its early origin—perhaps the first of its kind in Europe—and by the energy it usually showed in defense of its rights against encroachment by the crown. Already noted has been the remarkable development of those early Visigothic assemblies of clergy known as the Councils of Toledo. Carried to the north after the Moslem invasion, they became exclusively concerned with church affairs. Apparently the medieval Cortes attained its permanent form in 1189 when representatives of the towns were included in a gathering of nobles and clergy held that year in the city of Leon. Eventually the term "Cortes" was used only when all three estates of the monarchy—clergy, nobles, and townspeople—were summoned and present. Each meeting was usually named from the town where it took place; a permanent meeting place was never established, the Cortes being called to whatever city suited the convenience of the sovereign.

At first two Cortes met, one for Castile and another for Leon, but these were later combined into one after the unification of the two states. It might be noted that such an amalgamation never took place in Aragon, where three Cortes continued to meet separately even after all the realms were ruled by one monarch. In Castile, all three estates were represented in the early meetings, but eventually the members of the Cortes consisted mainly of town representatives who were not elected by popular vote, but usually selected by the town council. The towns themselves had no permanent right of representation, but came only when invited to send *procuradores* by the king. Apparently fifty-eight towns were represented at the 1189 Cortes of Leon, but by the era of the Catholic Kings the number had been drastically reduced since Hernando del Pulgar, confidential secretary and chronicler of Isabella, states that only fifteen cities and two villages sent delegates to the very important Cortes of Toledo in 1480.[20] While in the north of Spain many important municipalities usually had representation in the Cortes, a different situation prevailed in the south, where each kingdom added by the Reconquest was represented by *procuradores* from its capital. Therefore, the essential decentralization of Spain was reflected in the Cortes representation, for New Castile at least.

There were no regular meetings, the Cortes coming together only when convoked by the crown. There were no meetings at all in Castile between 1482 and 1498. When convoked, the delegates first presented their credentials and then listened to a speech from the throne, to which a formal reply was usually made. They then retired for deliberation. As has been pointed out, their powers and duties were varied: they were consulted on marriages, alliances, annexations, taxation, and the like. The plans for the *Santa Hermandad* and the expansion of the Council of Castile were first submitted to a Cortes by Isabella. They were always summoned to swear the traditional oath of allegiance to the heir to the throne, or on the accession of a new monarch. But from the sovereign's point of view, undoubtedly their most important duty was to vote the *servicio* or special grant of money for extraordinary expenses. Although their power in this regard was firmly established, it is clear that they never realized what they could do with it, and consequently never used this right to grant the *servicio* as a basis for constitutional opposition to the throne, or as a means of expanding their own authority. Within the limits indicated, members of the Cortes enjoyed considerable prestige and were treated by the crown with respect. They had judicial immunity, in theory at least, and the rights of free speech while in session; these conditions prevailed until the middle of the sixteenth century, when the institution began to decline rapidly—a decline, be it noted, that was affecting, as a whole, the middle class in Spain. As a summation of the whole institution, Livermore's evaluation seems just and appropriate:

> The system thus evolved was eminently suited to a conservative people, most of whom dwelt in rural towns maintained by a stable agricultural and stock-raising economy, and felt no enthusiasm for the vicissitudes of mercantile life. Its whole interest lay in the preservation of ancient privileges, rather than in the acquisition of new rights or opportunities.[21]

Still, in its great days, the Cortes of Castile compares favorably with the medieval Parliament of England, and is clearly superior to the Estates-General of France under the Valois, or the Reichstag of the

20. Jean Hippolyte Mariéjol, *L'Espagne sous Ferdinand et Isabella. Le gouvernement, les institutions, et les moeurs* (Paris, 1892), pp. 137–42.
21. Harold Livermore, A *History of Spain*, New York, 1959, p. 187.

medieval Holy Roman Empire. Probably its only rival was the sister Cortes of Aragon which shall be discussed later.

One of the chief characteristics of the Middle Ages was the wide gap in almost every field between theory and practice. Certainly, this was true in the organization of justice and the judiciary in medieval Castile. Until the thirteenth century matters were chaotic, with royal justice and royal courts in confused competition with feudal justice, church courts, and petty seignorial courts. During the reign of Alfonso X, known to the Spanish as *El Sabio* (the Wise), matters began to improve. Some twenty-three royal judges were engaged in the administration of royal justice, and the king himself appeared in court on Fridays to sit as supreme judge. This was the royal court later known as the *audiencia*. Evidently justice in the lower courts was still flouted with ease by the higher nobles, and this situation prevailed until the times of Ferdinand and Isabella. The law of Castile was a mixture of Roman and Visigothic practices somewhat unequally fused together in a code known throughout the Middle Ages as the *Fuero Juzgo* which was in fairly general use down to the middle of the thirteenth century, and in some areas a good deal later. Again it was the wise Alfonso who brought about a change. In 1255 the *Fuero Real*, consisting of a recodification and reconciliation of all existing *fueros* used in the royal courts and in a number of municipalities, was promulgated under his seal. This code shows a strong Visigothic influence. Much more Roman was the famous code issued between 1256 and 1265, known as the *Siete Partidas* from its seven sections. This system was mainly derived from (1) the old laws and customs of Castile and Leon, (2) canon law, and (3) the Pandects of Justinian and the commentaries thereon. Just what Alfonso himself expected from this new compilation is not clear. In any event, it was violated in the next generation when his rebellious son, Sancho the Brave, refused to obey the regulations regarding the succession to the throne.[22] The *Siete Partidas* do not seem to have been formally accepted until 1348, but doubtless before this date they strongly influenced a good many jurists in the direction of Roman law.

One special institution very important in Castile during the Middle Ages is almost without a counterpart elsewhere. These are the three military orders of the kingdom. While there is some superficial resemblance to such crusading orders as the Knights of Saint John or the

22. According to the *Siete Partidas*, when Alfonso's eldest son, the Infante Ferdinand, died, the inheritance should have passed to his children, the Infantes de la Cerda; however, Sancho, Ferdinand's younger brother, managed to seize the crown for himself, initiating a conflict with his nephews that lasted most of his reign.

Templars, these military orders of Castile were really quite different. For one thing, they were not based on operations in the distant Holy Land, but in Spain itself. Consequently, instead of growing weaker as the international crusading movement decayed, they drew nourishment from the continuance of the crusading spirit in Spain (which, in turn, they greatly stimulated) and the constant wars with the Spanish Moslems. They dominated the resettlement of Andalusia, and through the introduction of latifundia and a grazing economy helped to bring about those changes which were equally hostile to the earlier resettlement as well as to the Moslem agrarian tradition. But perhaps the greatest change they were connected with was in the development of "the harsh spirit of religious intransigence that characterized the Reconquest in Spain from that time forward. . .in this zone dominated by the military orders."[23]

Calatrava, the oldest, was founded in 1158 and took its name from a fortress bravely defended by a garrison of soldier monks. Santiago was organized about a decade later and, as its name implies, was especially concerned with providing protection for pilgrims en route to the famous shrine. Alcántara appeared in connection with an attempt by Ferdinand II of Leon (1157–1188) to introduce the Order of Calatrava into his kingdom. When there was some objection to the intrusion of a foreign order, Ferdinand in 1183 got Pope Lucius III to recognize these warriors as a new and independent organization; henceforth they were known by the name of the town where they had first been established. All three orders at first fought bravely against the Moslems and as a result received many privileges and lands from the generosity of the crown. However, as the Reconquest was practically suspended for a century after the death of Alfonso XI, they ceased to perform any essential functions. Still, their power, great wealth, and prestige made them a danger to the crown; and it was not until the reign of Isabella that they were forced to submit fully to the royal authority.

It is hardly proper to speak of a national army before the times of Ferdinand and Isabella. The sovereign, of course, had the same right as any feudal lord to call upon his vassals for a limited amount of military service. These vassals included both laymen and clerics, and undoubtedly some of the towns sent soldiers when great expeditions were afoot. Most feudal armies, and the Castilian was no exception, were usually noted for their complete lack of discipline and high rate of desertion. Some feeble attempts to improve matters were made in the fourteenth and fifteenth centuries. A royal guard was established, and the office of Constable of Castile was created in order

23. Vicens Vives, *Approaches to the History of Spain*, p. 49.

to provide a permanent commanding general. The basic arm was cavalry, whose fleetness was useful in the zone of raids and counter-raids along the frontier. By general European standards, these forces were considered to be light-armed troops. Cannon were not really important until the Granadine War, but may have been introduced into the army during the reign of Alfonso X.

4

While the institutions of the triple kingdom loosely called Aragon show some similarities to those of the neighboring state of Castile-Leon, there are also marked differences. Administrative decentralization had gone a good deal further than in Castile. Under the general name of Aragon there were actually three separate states, old Aragon, Catalonia, and Valencia, each with its own Cortes and distinctive administrative system; the person of the sovereign constituted the only bond of union among them. Although an Act of Union in 1319 provided that the three realms should never be separated, they were often held together with considerable difficulty derived in part from differences of social structure, language, and customs. Aragon, especially in the mountain districts, was essentially feudal, aristocratic, and hostile to royal pretensions. Socially it was extremely backward. The principality of Catalonia, on the other hand, contained very important bourgeois elements concentrated in the great city of Barcelona, proud of its wealth, its economic power, and its important connections throughout the entire Mediterranean world. Here in this city was the complete antithesis of feudalism, while in the Catalan countryside, feudalism persisted. Valencia, on the other hand, still retained much of its Islamic civilization and served as a kind of colonial area where a minority of Aragonese nobles and wealthy Catalan bourgeois exploited the unfortunate Moslem majority. The differences between the realms of the crown of Aragon were reflected in the everyday language of these areas since the regional speeches of Aragon and Valencia were quite distinct and Catalan was, and is, an entirely independent language. When, somewhat later, the Balearics, Sardinia, Sicily, and Naples were added, each with its own customs and institutions carefully preserved, it can clearly be seen that the task of holding together such a diverse assemblage of states, continental and insular, was immense, and, one would normally suppose, a task requiring a strong hand backed by almost unlimited royal power.

And yet it was exactly this power that was denied a king of Aragon. In many areas—old Aragon has already been noted above—feudal customs remained in full force. In Castile, in theory at least, grants made by the crown were to be limited and temporary; in Aragon, however, many feudal lords obtained a great deal of authority over their holdings and over their own vassals to the great detriment of the royal power. Consequently, the nobility of old Aragon frequently showed a degree of boldness and independence in dealing with their ruler that was hard to equal elsewhere. It is possible that the famous coronation oath, supposedly sworn by the Aragonese aristocracy before their king at his coronation—"We, who are as good as you, take you as king and lord, as long as you keep our laws and privileges, and if not, not"—was never actually used in that form, but it correctly represented the spirit that animated the nobility and which repeatedly flared out in violent reaction against extensions of royal power.[24] According to the *Fuero* of Sobrarbe, the king was "elected" by the nobility on condition that he should maintain their territory, rights, and privileges as well as promise not to make war, peace, or conclude a treaty with any foreign power without the knowledge and consent of the *ricoshombres*, or higher nobility.[25]

The Cortes in the eastern kingdom likewise displayed greater independence and more authority than its counterpart in Castile. Although there was a general Cortes for the entire kingdom, the separate Cortes for Aragon, Catalonia, and Valencia met more frequently and were probably more important. Since the *corts* of Catalonia was apt to be most sympathetic with the expansion of royal power, especially overseas, and since the Cortes of Valencia was the least important, it was in the Cortes of the kingdom of Aragon that opposition to the royal policies was most likely to be expressed. This famous body was divided into four branches, or *brazos*; one for the *ricoshombres*, one for the *infanzones* or lower nobility; one for the clergy, and one for the towns. While eight or nine great families claimed the right of permanent representation in the first *brazo*, the king could summon additional representatives of *ricoshombres* as he pleased. The *infanzones* came solely on the basis of the royal invitation. The cities, three confederations of towns, and eighteen villages claimed the right to sit in the fourth *brazo* as representatives of the towns.[26] Theoretically, they were supposed to meet every two years and attempts were sometimes made to obtain annual meetings, but it is clear from the evidence that they did not even meet every other year. Between 1481 and 1515 the Aragonese Cortes met ten times while, in the same period, the general Cortes met only three times.

24. The actual form usually cited for this oath seems to have come from Antonio Pérez or from Francis Hotman, who mentioned it in his *Franco-Gallia* of 1573. Neither were accurate historians.

25. This *fuero*, once believed to date from the earliest years of Aragon, is now thought to be no later than from the fourteenth century.

26. Mariéjol, pp. 146–48.

Sessions of the Aragonese cortes were opened according to an elaborate and traditional ritual with the king always present. Debates were often long and stormy and, in theory at least, unanimity was required to reach an accord. Actually this requirement seems often to have been waived upon general consent. Between sessions, a permanent deputation consisting of eight members—two from each *brazo*—remained at Saragossa to keep watch over governmental matters. As in the case of Castile, the Aragonese Cortes met to advise the sovereign, to make special grants, to present requests and petitions for redress of grievances, and to sanction foreign wars and the accession of new rulers. Unlike the procedure in Castile, in Aragon redress of grievances always had to precede the granting of special *servicios*.

Perhaps the most remarkable institution of the kingdom of Aragon was the office of *justicia* or chief justice, called the greatest lay office in the world by one of its holders.[27] The *justicia*, during the period of his greatest authority, was the chief interpreter of the law, and the final referee in legal disputes involving the liberties of subjects and the power of the crown. In addition he was the first of all the royal advisors and was supposed at all times to be close to the person of the sovereign. It was his special responsibility to see that the citizens of Aragon were not deprived of the special privileges and liberties accorded them by their precious *fueros*. Where such seemed to be the case, a very important power, *manifestación*, permitted him to withdraw the litigant to his own prison and transfer the case to his own personal court. The *justicia* is first mentioned during the reign of James I, but may be even older. In 1283 it was decided that he was to judge all cases involving violation of *fueros* by the crown. The high water mark of the office occurred during the days of the famous organization of the nobles known as the Union (1283–1301) to be discussed below. It was then decided that the crown could not proceed against a member of the Union without the prior approval of the Cortes and the *justicia*. After the defeat of the nobles at Épila in 1348 by Pedro IV, the importance of the *justicia* continued, although after this date the chief justice utilized the influence of the office in favor of the crown by which he had been appointed. The *justicia* sat at Saragossa with two lieutenants to assist him, along with a large staff. After Épila the Cortes attempted to get the crown to agree to a life-tenure for the office. At first the crown resisted, but in 1431 it was decided that a *justicia* could not be removed without the Cortes' consent. This appeared to be a victory for the antimonarchical forces, but actually it came much too late, since the office was by now almost hereditary in the Lanuza family, which was

27. Merriman, I, 471.

noted for its royalist sentiments. It was not until the end of the sixteenth century, in connection with the celebrated case of Antonio
Pérez, that the *justicia* again became involved against the crown.

From the above, it will be readily seen that the constitutional history of the kingdom of Aragon was quite different from that of Castile,
and this was especially true of the late Middle Ages. This is partly
due to the composite nature of the triple kingdom as previously
described. But it is also due to the fact that in Aragon especially,
and to a lesser degree in Catalonia and Valencia, a spirit of independence was preserved that strongly resisted the expansion of any arbitrary authority. On the local level, this often meant the resistance
to anything that might threaten the special privileges of towns and
villages, carefully preserved in the dearly cherished *fueros*. On the
national level, it meant the determination of the nobility, often
assisted by the middle class, to force the crown to respect not only
the local *fueros*, but all the special concessions it had been induced
to grant across the centuries to nobility, clergy, and townsfolk,
summed up by the somewhat vague, but undoubtedly inspiring slogan
"the liberties of Aragon." Thus, while the internal history of Castile
in the fourteenth and fifteenth centuries seems too often a dreary
chronicle of petty feudal civil wars, the realms of Aragon witnessed
"the crises of the great struggle against monarchical absolutism which
raged intermittently from the reign of James the Conqueror to that
of Pedro IV."[28] In this conflict, which must now be briefly mentioned,
we find ourselves on a much higher level than the feudal wrangling
of Castile-Leon. Here real constitutional principles were at stake and
both sides were represented by dedicated and determined men.

The struggle opened with a somewhat feeble prelude in the reign
of James the Conqueror (1213–1276). When James tried to levy an
unfamiliar tax in Aragon, and attempted other acts which were considered an infringement of their rights, the nobles struck back at him.
A league of nobles was formed, a formal statement of illegal acts
drafted, and James was forced to promise to respect the *fueros*. At
this time (Cortes of Exea, 1265) special powers were conferred on
the *justicia* as mediator between the crown and the nobility. But the
storm, vaguely hinted at here, did not break until near the end of
the next reign, that of James' son, Pedro III the Great (1276–1285).
It will be recalled that Pedro had been invited to assist the inhabitants
of Sicily in the expulsion of the French and their Angevin ruler
Charles, brother of Louis IX of France. On his return from this successful expedition in 1283, Pedro found himself formally deposed
by the pope, and his nobility up in arms over his failure to consult

28. Merriman, I, 430.

with them properly before his intervention in Sicily. Eventually a powerful league known as the Union was formed in 1283, and the king was forced to accede to major concessions to the aristocracy, in a document known as the General Privileges. Other concessions had to be made in Catalonia and Valencia. In the next reign, that of Alfonso III (1285–1291), the Union went a good deal further in its demands, which the king only partly resisted. In 1287, Alfonso was forced to sign the Privileges of Union, which involved, among other things, the right of the Union to depose him if he violated the Privileges.[29] However, he deliberately failed to carry out some of his promises, such as that of providing for an annual Cortes. The first ten years of the next reign were peaceful, but in 1301 it appeared that the nobles were ready once more to attack the royal power. However, a very different outcome awaited them. The Cortes supported the king and, when the *justicia* was invited to render a decision, he supported the crown. The result was that the Union was formally dissolved and its acts revoked; however, James II showed a wise moderation and the rest of his reign was untroubled internally.

The final struggle occurred in the reign of Pedro IV, who, although sickly and undersized, was one of the most formidable figures to occupy the throne of Aragon. A dispute within the royal family involving the succession led to an attempt by Pedro to get his daughter recognized as heiress to the crown, an action involving a major violation of the *fueros*. The old Union was revived in 1347 involving both the nobles and the middle class; shortly afterwards, it spread to Valencia. In fact, it was only in Catalonia that the harassed Pedro could find any support. It is not necessary for the purposes of this study to go into the complicated struggle that occupied the next two years. Suffice it to say that the Union undoubtedly went too far, and its excesses, in addition to Pedro's uncanny combination of audacity, duplicity, and courage, permitted the formation of a royal party to defend the prerogatives of the crown. The climax was the battle of Épila, fought between the king and the nobles of the Union on July 21, 1348. With most of the rebel chiefs either dead on the field or Pedro's prisoners, his victory was complete. On the whole, he used it with commendable moderation except in a few cases where he carried out a ferocious personal vengeance. All the acts of the Union, as well as the Privileges of 1287, were annulled, the king himself hacking its official seal to pieces with his dagger and cutting himself

29. The members of the Cortes were to have the right to assign certain advisors to the king who were to sit in the royal council. Alfonso could now proceed against members of the Union only with the consent of the *justicia* and the Cortes. Sixteen castles were given to the Union by the monarch as security for his word.

slightly in the process. But on the whole the liberties of Aragon remained as before. The nobles had gone too far and had been properly punished, but the crown's authority did not become overweening.

5

Although this study does not attempt to present an evaluation of medieval Spanish culture, a brief comment will not be out of place at this point. This culture, it might be said, had the advantages of an intense cross-fertilization. From the south came the Moslem influences, already discussed in the previous two chapters. From the north, ever since the famous "French Crusade" and the attempt of Aragon to rule a part of the *Midi*, came the potent influences of medieval France, of both the *langue d'oc* and the *langue d'ouil*. The marriages of Alfonso VIII with Leonora of Aquitaine (a daughter of the famous Eleanor) and Blanche of Castile with Louis VIII of France (thus making her the mother of Saint Louis) strengthened these influences as the French Gothic style of Burgos and of some of the other Spanish cathedrals shows. A kind of climax was reached during the reign of Alfonso X. Although particularly unfortunate in his political activities, the wise king was an important figure in the culture of his time, and achieved a kind of international reputation as a patron in general, and more especially as a poet. Under his direction an extensive work in the field of translation and compilation was carried out which contributed to brilliant original work in the next century. His legal achievements have already been mentioned. In addition, he started the *Crónica general,* the beginnings of Spanish historiography, and, with extensive borrowings from Arabic sources, his mathematicians and astronomers compiled the famous "Alfonsine tables" *(Libro de Saber de Astronomía).* His intense interest in music led to another famous compilation, the *Cantigas de Santa María.*

The first effort to establish an institution of higher learning in Spain was attempted by Alfonso VIII, who set up a *studium generale* at Palencia, but the school was apparently premature as it did not survive the monarch. A little later, Alfonso IX of Leon founded a university at Salamanca (1230) thus establishing the first Spanish university, later to become one of the most famous in Europe. As might be expected, it did especially well under Ferdinand III and Alfonso X, when its schools of canon and civil law attracted students from Paris and Bologna.

Secondary influences on medieval Spanish culture came from Italy and Byzantium. Naturally Catalonia, with its extensive commercial contacts in the Mediterranean basin, felt these influences first. Such episcopal and monastic centers in Catalonia as Seo de Urgel, Ripoll,

Gerona, Roda, and Tahull display a remarkable development of Romanesque painting, in which both Byzantine and Lombard traits are strongly present. Especially outstanding is the imposing Pantocrator from the main apse of Saint Clement's Church (1123) at Tahull. Although its form is strongly suggestive of similar figures in Byzantine churches at Ravenna and Constantinople, its intense bluegray and ochre tints as well as its delicate line work show the Lombard influence. A particularly vivid cherry-red which often appears in Spanish Romanesque painting also seems to have originated in certain Lombard paintings.[30]

That both Moslem and Jew participated in the culture of medieval Spain is without question. And as has been pointed out earlier, the idea of constant hostility and warfare between the different faiths of the Iberian peninsula is not true for all times and places. As late as the reign of Alfonso X, both minority religious groups of Castile shared in the general advance although each maintained its own language and customs. The Spanish Jews had, on the whole, fared much better than their brethren elsewhere in Europe. Not only were they important in finance and in the administration of both Castile and Aragon—Alfonso VIII's chief economic advisor was Jewish—but they entered many of the different crafts and professions as well. Jews were important as tailors, leatherworkers, metallurgists, weavers, embroiderers, as well as doctors and lawyers.[31] In view of their wealth, it is not surprising that the great Jewish families often formed connections with the nobility through marriage, for, as Mariéjol remarks, it only took a baptism to do it. As the Inquisition was to discover later, many noble families had Jewish blood, and there were rumors that the royal family of Castile itself was not exempt. Converted Jews frequently rose high in the Church. At the opening of the fifteenth century, the archbishop of Burgos was an ex-rabbi originally named Solomon Levi. Juan Arias, archbishop of Segovia, as well as Isabella's confessor, Fernando de Talavera, both came from families with a partly Jewish background.[32]

In spite of this relatively favorable position, the situation of the Jews began to deteriorate in the fourteenth century. There were several reasons for this. The Church, of course, had always been opposed to them and even the presence of distinguished Jewish converts in the priesthood did not change this attitude. Furthermore, the weakness of the Castilian crown in the fourteenth and fifteenth centuries made the government less able to resist Church propaganda against the Jews. Naturally, their general prosperity and the great

30. *Spain, Romanesque Paintings* (UNESCO World Art Series), p. 18.
31. Mariéjol, pp. 40–46.
32. Ibid.

wealth of some Jewish families excited jealousy, and, in addition, their connection with the always unpopular profession of tax-collecting made them an object of popular hatred. And lastly there was a tradition of anti-Semitism handed down from the early days of the Visigothic Church and never entirely forgotten.

The growth of anti-Semitism in Spain must also be viewed as a local phase of a general European crisis. By the middle of the fourteenth century, a great wave of social unrest was sweeping western Europe, leading to serious disturbances in England, France, Italy, and Flanders. The basic causes of this unrest were probably twofold: 1) a general economic depression caused by an agricultural decline, itself the result of wars and the Black Death; and 2) depopulation and inflation. The resultant social turmoil took the form of violent "confrontations" between lords and peasants, urban workers versus the urban patriciate, and nobles versus the crown. In Spain, this social unrest eventually focused on the religious minorities, sometimes Moslems, but much more often Jews because of their conspicuous prominence in the financial administration of the state, the church, and the military orders. The result was an increasing schism between the Christian and Jewish communities which heretofore had worked out considerable toleration in the intercourse of daily life. Some of this toleration was still maintained in urban areas, but in the rural areas where the crusading ideals were increasingly powerful it was being lost very quickly. Ironically, the drive for religious uniformity now began to produce a new and extremely important religious minority—that of the *conversos*, or newly baptized Jews. As a result of the persecutions and other forms of pressure, thousands of Jews came into the Church between 1391 and 1415. As their numbers increased, they were regarded with suspicion and eventually hatred. The very word, *converso*, came to carry a heavy load of scorn in Castile. In Catalonia, where Jews did not have a monopoly of the money-lending business, there was not so much hostility toward them.

The governments of the Christian states were more tolerant than the masses because of the indispensable financial aid rendered by the new Christians, although the new dynasty of the Trastámaras in Castile seems to have been less friendly than the earlier reigning house. Nonetheless, the rulers of Castile continued the traditional tolerance and did not decide to go over entirely to the side of the Old Christians until the last decade of the fifteenth century. It is a matter of some surprise that, given the increasingly hostile public attitude, the crown waited as long as it did.

The first signs of trouble came from the Castilian Cortes, always something of a barometer of public opinion. The Cortes of Burgos in 1315 imposed many new restrictions, and the rest of the century was marred by outbreaks of anti-Semitic violence. The worst occurred in 1391 and affected large areas throughout the whole peninsula, even reaching the Balearics. After each outburst, a certain number of Jews converted to Catholicism, and the orthodoxy of these New Christians continued to be highly suspect. In 1473 there was an outbreak in Castile, with particularly shocking atrocities at Jaén, Andujar, and Córdoba. The government was still officially tolerant, but it was beginning to be obvious that it could not remain so much longer.

6

The thirteenth century shows an important change in the international relations of the Iberian states. The relative isolation of these kingdoms behind the mountain barrier of the Pyrenees was coming to an end. The Spanish rulers began to seek their queens in France, Germany, and Italy. The international reputation of Alfonso X has already been pointed out. Through his mother, Beatrice of Swabia, he could claim kinship with the Hohenstaufens, one of the leading ruling families of northern Europe; and, because of this tie, he vainly sought to win the crown of the Empire. Although unsuccessful, through him Castile might be said to have begun to play a role in international affairs for the first time. In the next century, the Hundred Years War between France and England proved the difficulty of maintaining Iberian neutrality in a major struggle. Castile's valuable naval assistance to France has already been discussed.

And yet the growing importance of Castile, and to a lesser extent Aragon, in the affairs of northern Europe contrasted strangely with the growing anarchy in the western kingdom. With the Reconquest at a virtual standstill after the victories of Alfonso VIII and Ferdinand III, the fact is that the nobility was no longer occupied in the expansion of the frontier; its energy was no longer absorbed in wars against the Moslems. The aristocracy, therefore, turned its attention inward, so to speak, and became a major threat to the securtity of the state and throne in Castile. In increasing numbers the nobles infiltrated the Church, and were able to dominate the military orders. The royal army was now too small to stand against them, and Henry IV was reduced to relying for his personal safety on a Moorish bodyguard. The aristocracy acquired large parts of the crown lands, repeatedly obtained favorable tax exemptions for itself, intrigued in disputed successions, frequently defied the royal power, and, in general, provided an excellent example of feudal irresponsibility at its worst. We have seen that Aragon did not entirely escape these internal dissensions, but they were usually fought on a higher level and never were carried to such extremes as in Castile.

One purely fortuitous factor that greatly contributed to the anarchy in Castile was the frequent appearance of royal minorities. "Unhappy the land where the king is a child" states a medieval proverb, and this was especially true of Castile. Thus Ferdinand IV (1295–1312) succeeded at the age of nine, his son and heir Alfonso XI (1312–1350) succeeded at the age of one, Henry III (1390–1406) at eleven, and John II (1406–1454), Isabella's father, at the age of two. During these regencies, the wealth of the crown was frequently plundered with impunity by the aristocracy, usually beginning with the council of regency itself.

The land also suffered from two major disputes over the succession, one in the thirteenth century and an even more serious one in the mid-fourteenth century. In 1275, the heir to the throne, Fernando de la Cerda, died. According to the law code which Alfonso X himself had promulgated, the succession should have passed to the eldest son of the dead prince, the king's grandson; but this arrangement was challenged by Alfonso's second son, the Infante Sancho. A violent civil war ensued as the nobility rushed to take sides, while both the king and the prince distributed wealth and favors to win supporters. Generally speaking, Alfonso was unsuccessful in protecting the rights of his grandson, and was himself deposed in 1282 by the Cortes of Valladolid in a shameful spectacle. Upon his death two years later, the Infante Sancho succeeded as King Sancho IV (1284–1295) but the struggle with his nephews, known as the Infantes de la Cerda, continued throughout most of his reign and eventually involved the neighboring kingdom of Aragon. In such struggles, the members of the aristocracy were invariably the sole beneficiaries.

A second and more serious dispute broke out after the tragically early death of King Alfonso XI. This ruler possessed great qualities, but he did not hand them on to his successor who, because he frequently murdered his enemies, is generally known to Spanish historians as Pedro I the Cruel (1350–1369). Pedro's atrocities eventually united large numbers of the nobility against him under the leadership of Henry of Trastámara, an illegitimate son of Alfonso XI. Henry thus became the representative of Castilian conservatism since the nobles opposed Pedro's use of the middle class lawyers (legists) in the government of Castile. This internal conflict merged with the international diplomacy of the Hundred Years' War as Pedro was the friend and admirer of the Black Prince, while Henry of Trastámara could count on French support. The Black Prince briefly visited Pedro I in 1367, won the battle of Najera against Henry, and received as a personal gift from Pedro the famous red stone which now adorns the front of the English crown.[33] His health ruined by the rigors of the Spanish climate, the Black Prince returned to England an invalid,

33. This large and impressive stone was for a long time known as the "Black Prince's Ruby," until an investigation in modern times revealed that it was not a ruby but a spinel of much less value.

dying in 1376. Meanwhile, Henry continued the struggle with his half-brother after the withdrawal of the English and, with the help of France, finally succeeded in defeating Pedro and taking him prisoner in 1369. A personal interview between the two rivals in Henry's tent ended in an explosion with Pedro attacking Henry, who finally succeeded in killing him after a violent hand-to-hand combat. However, Pedro's sons and their followers continued the war and Henry II (1369–1379) was forced to make so many grants to the nobility that he is known in Spanish history as *el de las mercedes*—he of the gifts. Once again it was only the aristocracy that profited.

Still another factor which contributed to the Castilian disorders was the relatively low character of some of the rulers, and the weakness of others. It is clear that both Alfonso X and Henry II made far too many grants to the nobility, but they were exceeded in this by John II and Henry IV in the fifteenth century. Pedro was a thoroughly vicious character, and Henry IV, although lacking the strain of cruelty, was not much better. The ablest rulers of the later Middle Ages in Castile were probably Alfonso XI and Henry III, and both died prematurely.

Castile and Aragon were frequently involved in disagreements during the period between the reigns of Alfonso X and Isabella. Aragon became a party in the disputed succession during the reign of Sancho IV by supporting, for a time, the Infantes de la Cerda. The eastern kingdom also supported Pedro I against the Trastámara-Valois combination. A double reconciliation was effected during the reign of John I (1379–1390) by the arrangement of a marriage between John's son Henry and the granddaughter of the unlamented Pedro; and a second marriage of John himself and Eleanor of Aragon. Thus the Trastámaras were reconciled with the old legitimate line, and the potential hostility of the eastern kingdom was appeased by the marriage of an Aragonese infanta with the king of Castile. Although not quite in the category of the more famous match of 1469, this marriage was an important one in Iberian history since it eventually brought the House of Trastámara to the throne of Aragon. When the line of the counts of Barcelona died out in 1409, the Infante Ferdinand, a son of John and Eleanor, was chosen to succeed as King Ferdinand I of Aragon (1412–1416), thus becoming the grandfather of the more famous Ferdinand II, the future husband of Isabella. Although this change of dynasty in Aragon eventually facilitated the union of the two greatest states of the peninsula, its immediate result was confusion twice compounded since the Aragonese Trastámaras still retained their standing and possessions in the western kingdom as members of the royal house. From this fact sprang the constant quarrels between Aragon and Castile during the first half of the fifteenth century.

Relations between Castile and Portugal during these last two hundred years were frequently marked by Castilian interference in Portuguese affairs, and by several major efforts to conquer the seaboard kingdom. Alfonso XI was at war with Portugal between 1328 and 1330. Relations grew worse after the death of Pedro the Cruel. Ferdinand of Portugal claimed the Castilian throne, but was induced by papal intervention to agree to marry a daughter of Henry II. When Ferdinand married his mistress instead, Henry was not impressed by this example of domestic fidelity and invaded Portugal up to the walls of Lisbon. However, peace was made in 1374, thanks to English intervention. But trouble broke out again during the reign of John I of Castile when Ferdinand renewed his claim to the neighboring crown. There was a brief peace in 1383 only to be terminated the following year when John invaded Portugal and invested Lisbon. Since King Ferdinand had died only a short time before without male heirs, the danger to Portugal was critical. However, it was successfully met. An outbreak of plague forced John of Castile to raise the siege of Lisbon, and the famous constable of Portugal, Nuno Alveres Pereira, twice defeated the invaders as they withdrew. A Portuguese Cortes met at Coimbra in April, 1385, and elected John of Aviz king, thus marking the end of the dynasty of Count Henry of Burgundy.

The final blow to Castilian ambitions toward Portugal took place on August 14, 1385, when the new king of Portugal, aided by five hundred English archers, utterly defeated John I of Castile at the battle of Aljubarrota. This engagement had important consequences besides proving that the Portuguese-English alliance of 1386 was too strong for Castile. With the crown disgraced by this defeat, and a large part of the nobility killed in the engagement, the chief beneficiaries were the towns and the Church; and later meetings of the Castilian Cortes showed their increasing influence. An indirect and unexpected result of Aljubarrota was the growing hostility to the Jews and Moslems which came from the increased influence of the clergy. The culmination of this hostility was the great outbreak of anti-Semitic and anti-Moslem atrocities known as the Fury of 1391, in which the old tri-communal system of Jews, Moslems, and Christians broke down in many areas.[34]

Following the disaster of Aljubarrota, a truce was signed in 1387 and repeatedly extended until 1411, when a formal peace treaty was signed between the two states. For almost two hundred years to come, Castile ceased to be a threat to Portuguese independence. It is rather remarkable that a unification of the two states was not achieved

34. See below p. 185.

through marriage during the Middle Ages. Four times, prior to the era of the Catholic Kings, Castilian kings married into the Portuguese royal house, and three times Portuguese sovereigns married Castilian infantas. However, it was not until the latter part of the reign of Philip II (1556–1598) that such policies bore fruit. On the whole, Portugal emerged unscathed in her intermittent medieval struggles with Castile.

7

The rulers of the fifteenth century in Castile, down to the accession of Isabella, are among the worst in the history of that kingdom. Admittedly, this is hardly fair to Henry III (1390–1406), sometimes known as Henry the Sickly or the Pallid. During the long and turbulent minority that preceded the beginning of his actual rule (1399), the crown lands were again pillaged by the importunate nobility. However, during the seven years of his personal rule, Henry showed himself a man of remarkable force despite his physical weakness and, had he lived longer, might have succeeded in reversing the trend toward decentralization. Unfortunately, he died in 1406, leaving an infant son one year old and his kingdom to the troubles of another royal minority. One unusual event that occurred toward the close of this brief reign deserves mention. This was the famous mission of Ruy Gonzalez de Clavijo to the court of Tamerlane. The rise of Tamerlane, and his hostility to the Turks, was of great interest to the princes of the west. As a result, Henry III sent Clavijo with a small party to the court of the aged ruler. The Castilians were present at the battle of Angora in 1402 when Tamerlane defeated the Turks and later were received by him in a friendly fashion. Although nothing permanent came of this embassy, it does indicate a certain interest in foreign travel and exploration on the part of Castile, especially when it is remembered that Clavijo's embassy was contemporaneous with the voyage of Bethencourt to the Canaries.[35] As Merriman has pointed out, "the embassy of Clavijo will always be remembered as an early proof of the Spaniard's passion for adventure in distant lands—of the quality which furnishes the key to his later conquests in the New World. It showed that he had the stuff in him of which empire builders are made."[36]

The early minority of John II (1406–1454) was not as disastrous as might have been expected owing to the wise rule of his uncle Ferdinand of Antequera, who served as regent. However, the regent was forced to leave Castile in 1412 to assume the crown of Aragon

35. See Part II, Ch. V.
36. Merriman, I, 164.

and there was no one competent to replace him, least of all John II. The king showed little interest in affairs of state and, after attaining his majority, preferred literary and artistic pursuits in the pleasant society of his friends. He was fond of poetry and showed a slight talent in this. A few of his charming little poems occasionally appear in a modern anthology, but aside from these modest literary achievements, his reign must be called a disaster. Actually, it should hardly be called "his reign" since most of the important decisions were made by his favorite, Alvaro de Luna, constable of Castile. Between 1420 and 1453 de Luna, a bold and magnificent noble, ruled the state. Unfortunately, most of his time was devoted to enriching himself and his family, or putting down the constant plots against him. Thus waste, corruption, misrule, and weakness were the watchwords of the reign.

John II married twice. By his first wife, a princess of Aragon, he had one son, the Infante Henry, Prince of the Asturias. In his old age, after the death of his first wife, he married Isabella of Portugal. It was through this second wife that Alvaro de Luna was finally brought down, being executed in 1453. Queen Isabella also presented her lord with two children; a son, Alfonso, and a daughter, the Infanta Isabella, born in 1451.

When John II died in 1454, he was succeeded by his son of the first marriage. Henry IV had been born in 1425 and as he grew up seemed to justify great hopes. For some reason, they were never fulfilled. A true son of King John, he soon lost interest in governmental matters, signed documents without reading them, and was prepared to make almost any concessions to the nobles to keep them quiet. He cannot even be said to have made any contributions to Castilian literature. In short, he was a weak ruler and a contemporary sums him up in lapidary style: "all his face was disagreeable . . . his manner, and course of life were wholly addicted to debauchery and lewdness."[37] The court soon acquired a reputation for immorality which shocked that relatively tolerant time, and led the queen-mother to keep her daughter Isabella as far from courtly society as possible.

In 1453, after several years of a childless marriage, Henry divorced his first wife, Blanche of Navarre, a daughter of the troublesome Infante John of Aragon, on the interesting grounds that sorcery had prevented the consummation of the marriage. From this time on he was known to his subjects as *el Impotente*. Perhaps doubting his marital prowess, he was in no hurry to marry again, and during the interim his half-brother, the young Infante Alfonso, was heir apparent of Castile. However, in 1455, shortly after ascending the throne, Henry mar-

---

37. Juan de Mariana, *Historiae de rebus Hispaniae* as cited by Merriman, II, 8.

ried Joanna of Portugal, perhaps to establish a counterpoise to the constant interference of the Aragonese infantes in Castilian affairs. The long delay in the appearance of children again reminded Henry's subjects of his embarrassing nickname, but at last the long awaited child appeared in 1462. Unfortunately, it was a daughter, also named Joanna. Henry at once acknowledged the child, but his enemies professed to believe that Beltran de la Cueva, one of the king's closest friends, was the father. Henceforth, the unfortunate princess was known to contemporaries and posterity alike as "la Beltraneja." The real facts in the case will never be known, but it should be pointed out that from the beginning it was greatly to the advantage of certain highly placed persons that Joanna's illegitimacy should be accepted as an established fact and doubtless many persons were convinced of this for one reason or another. Obviously, another succession crisis was in the making, but a further discussion of these events must be reserved for the next chapter.

8

The internal history of Aragon, after the tumults of Pedro IV and his violent struggles with the nobility, was relatively calm. Pedro had conquered the aristocratic opposition with the firm support of Catalonia, and henceforth, until the arrival of the Trastámaras, the principality dominated affairs in the triple kingdom. Within the principality itself, the main development was the remarkable growth and prosperity of Barcelona during the fourteenth and the early part of the fifteenth centuries. This was a part of a larger phase, namely, the growth of the industrial and commercial city-state in the Mediterranean world, and what happened in Barcelona was being repeated in Marseilles, Milan, Florence, Naples, and Venice, to mention a few examples. In fact, the fifteenth century, which may be called the golden age of the Mediterranean city-state, was, at least up to about 1450, the golden age of the Catalan capital. Intensely proud of their city and its commanding position in Mediterranean trade, the citizens felt that to be awarded the title of *ciudadano honrado* (honored citizen) of Barcelona was the highest privilege urban life afforded. In addition, its enormous wealth, greater than all the other realms of the crown of Aragon put together, made it the principal support of royal policies, and established its hegemony in the eastern kingdom. Supported by this great economic power, the successors of Pedro IV, themselves descended from the ancient line of the counts of Barcelona, were not troubled by the nobility. Moreover, the anarchy that was blighting Castile in the fifteenth century does not turn up in the triple kingdom. Nor was Aragon cursed with such rulers as a John II or a Henry IV of Castile. The successors of Pedro IV were average men and reasonably competent. The last of his line, however, died with Martin I (1396–1410) and thus early in the new century a succession crisis was precipitated.

After a considerable delay, nine judges met in the little town of Caspe to consider the rights of those with a claim to the throne. Although six candidates presented claims, only two were serious contenders, James, count of Urgel, was a great-grandson of Alfonso IV and had married a daughter of Pedro IV. His principal support came from Catalonia and Barcelona in particular. Ferdinand of Antequera, infante of Castile, although a foreigner, was the son of Eleanor of Aragon who had married John I of Castile and he was, therefore, a grandson of Pedro IV. He found considerable support in Aragon and might be considered the candidate of the aristocracy as opposed to the commercial interests supporting the count of Urgel. The judges finally awarded the crown to Ferdinand, and this decision was proclaimed on June 28, 1412. Although accepted in Catalonia, he was not popular there, and occasional clashes occurred between the royal authority and the cherished *fueros*. Herein lay the germs of the contest between Barcelona and the Trastámaras which was to flare up into civil war during the latter part of the century.

The advent of the House of Trastámara to the throne of Aragon was an event of great importance in Iberian history, and even more significant in its implications. Henceforth, much more intimate relations prevailed between Castile and Aragon than ever before, and a major step in the direction of ultimate unity had been taken. Furthermore, John, Pedro, and Henry, the younger sons of Ferdinand I, retained their holdings in Castile and were considered infantes in that state as well as in their new patrimony of Aragon. Taking advantage of the weak character of John II of Castile, and the confusion in his government, they intrigued in Castilian affairs constantly. And although they must have been a constant source of provocation to the officials of the western kingdom, undoubtedly they accustomed Castile to the presence of Aragonese royalty. The step from this situation to the marriage of Ferdinand and Isabella was, relatively speaking, a small one.

Although there was the Catalan opposition to King Ferdinand, his moderation, wisdom, and personal charm seemed about to overcome all hostility. Unfortunately, his reign ended almost as soon as it had well begun. He fell ill in April of 1416 and died in the same month, at the age of thirty-seven. He had reigned only four years, and his death was widely regarded as a great misfortune.[38] His contemporaries bestowed on him the titles of "el Justo" and "el Honesto."

38. H. J. Chaytor, *A History of Aragon and Catalonia* (London, 1933), p. 211.

His oldest son succeeded immediately as Alfonso V (1416–1458). His reign properly belongs to the history of Italy, a land he loved and where he spent most of his time in a vigorous contest for the throne of Naples. Although his victory was long delayed, he was ultimately successful and after 1443 took possession of Naples without opposition. The importance of his reign for Aragon lies mainly in the fact that he left local matters almost entirely in the hands of his brother, the Infante John, who served as regent. Alfonso left Aragon in 1420 in company with his brother Pedro and spent the next three years fighting for the crown of Naples. However, the tangled interrelations of Castile and Aragon finally forced him to drop his Italian projects temporarily and return to the peninsula. During his absence, his younger brothers John and Henry had become involved in an attempt to control the young king of Castile, John II. During the course of intrigues much too complex to be narrated here, Prince Henry was made a prisoner by some Castilian nobles and was taken to Madrid, at the time a small village which had once been a Moslem fortress. It was about this time that Alvaro de Luna began to exercise his remarkable ascendancy over·King John and soon became virtual ruler of the country and head of the anti-Aragonese party in Castile.

Twice Alfonso V invaded Castile to force his cousin to adopt a more cooperative attitude toward Aragon, but on both occasions a pitched battle was avoided and a compromise arranged. In 1430 both parties signed an armistice for five years and, on the strength of this commitment, Alfonso again departed for Italy never to return to Spain. It is pertinent to point out here that fortune again indicated her preference for the eventual union of the two crowns. If John II and Alfonso V had been forced into a long and bloody war, the resultant tensions might have effectively prevented or long delayed the future unification of the two powers. As a step in the direction of unity, the armistic of 1430 must rank as second only to the succession of the Trastámaras to the crown of Aragon.

The troublesome Infante John and his brother Henry continued to intrigue in Castilian affairs, and did their best to involve their royal brother; but although at times it looked as if he might intervene, Italy's fascination for him always won out in the long run and he never returned to Spain. Toward the close of his long reign, he became interested in his nephew, Charles of Viana, and when that young prince flew to Naples to escape his father, Alfonso welcomed him warmly. If time had been left to him, it seems likely that the king would have involved himself in the struggle between father and son to protect Charles' rights to Navarre and eventually his succession to Aragon. However, death intervened on June 27, 1458, before he could do anything for Charles. The realms of Aragon then passed to his brother John, except that Naples went to his only surviving son, the illegitimate Ferrante. The quarrel between John of Aragon and his presumptive heir Charles of Viana therefore continued unabated with momentous consequences for the future of Spain and Europe.

Alfonso was undoubtedly a man of ability equal to his great ambitions. His court at Naples was a brilliant one, and he was a great patron of the art and learning of his time. Personally, he was an attractive man, and even his enemies found it hard to resist his personal charm. A certain generosity and chivalry in his nature led contemporaries to give him the nickname of "the magnanimous." He carried to a conclusion the Mediterranean ambitions of the kings of Aragon, and the acquisition of Naples was, in a sense, the logical culmination to the Aragonese domination of Sicily, already one hundred and fifty years old. From his reign on, Aragon was more deeply involved in Italian affairs than ever before, and the stage was being set for the future expansionist policies of Ferdinand II and Charles I. Whether his immediate successor would follow him in his imperialism in Italy or return to a more peninsular policy was, in 1458, completely unknown. In spite of his unquestioned prestige in European affairs, Alfonso's reign was not popular at home. The costs of his foreign policy, his lengthy absences from his Iberian kingdoms, the greatly resented involvements of his brothers in the internal affairs of Castile, all contributed to the repeated demands made on Alfonso that he return and devote himself to home affairs. In 1452 the Cortes sent a special deputation to Naples to implore him to come back:

> Sire, the war which has continued for seven years without ceasing has depopulated your frontiers to such a degree that men have ceased to till the soil there; Aragon, during these seven years, has expended four hundred thousand florins in the ransom of prisoners alone; all industry, all commerce is at a standstill. . . . For such manifold evils, the country can find but one remedy—and that is the presence of its king.[39]

From this, one thing is clear: public opinion in Aragon was still isolationist, to use a modern term. Imperial policies were not popular except perhaps in Barcelona, where overseas trade was still the overwhelming consideration. In the rural and agricultural areas, little urbanized and still dominated by feudal considerations, overseas expansion was viewed as the private affair of the sovereign and resented when it interfered with his local obligations. This feeling was to come to a head during the early years of Charles I with the twin revolts of the *Comuneros* (1520) and the *Germanías* (brotherhoods) of Valencia (1519).

39. Eugène R. Saint-Hilaire, *Histoire d'Espagne* (Paris, 1844–79), 14 vols., V, 278, as cited by Merriman, I, 425.

9

By the mid-fifteenth century the Iberian states, with the possible exception of Portugal, do not present a very encouraging picture. In Castile, feudal anarchy seemed unchecked, in Navarre a violent conflict between the sovereign and his heir was about to break out, and in Aragon an absentee ruler with quarrelsome relatives was creating a situation soon to lead to civil war. Certainly no one could have foreseen the brilliance of the era about to be born after a brief and violent labor. This is not the place for a debate on determinism versus chance in history, although this eternal argument is never more intriguing than when it is concerned with the Iberian peninusla during its next great century and a half. Obviously, contemporaries did not expect it or consciously plan for it. Yet, it is fascinating to observe with all the advantages of hindsight how, out of the many lines of development possible during some six or seven hundred years of Iberian history, those that actually took place tended to favor large political units, aggressive policies, control of remote regions and different cultures, and fanatical devotion to ideals. Without the presence of these factors, the era of Ferdinand and Isabella could not have taken place. Thus one notes the influences stemming from the presence of a foreign and sometimes hostile culture and religion, in no other area of western Europe so closely associated with Christian and feudal institutions. As I have tried to suggest, from this came an acquisitive, vigorous, warlike society. Likewise, the moving frontier literally forced on Castilians the creation of special institutions dealing with the occupation and control of newly acquired territories already peopled with natives possessed of a high civilization. The experience of Aragon added the problem of controlling political units separated from the homeland by extensive bodies of water.

Moreover, these developments in the Spanish states reached their culmination at a time when the historical climate was highly favorable to the formation of large, multi-ethnic states. Along with this went the decline of what had been, up to that time, the highest form of economic and political development—the Mediterranean city-state. Its difficulties began early in the fifteenth century when some of the smaller cities fell under the control of the larger and more prosperous ones. Thus Verona was taken by the Venetians in 1404, Pisa fell to Florence in 1405, and Padua lost her independence to Venice in the following year. Genoa became a prey to conflicting French and Spanish influences, with the latter predominating early in the sixteenth century.

The larger cities were also not exempt from this fate; Constantinople fell to the Turks in 1453, Barcelona was reduced to obedience in 1472 by John II of Aragon, Marseilles came under the control of the French crown in 1480, while in 1492 Granada passed into the hands of Ferdinand and Isabella. Thus during the final decades of the fifteenth century many of the important Mediterranean cities were losing their independence, and many of them were still feeling, to some degree, the effects of the serious economic depression a century earlier.[40]

It is generally realized that the difficulties of the Mediterranean city states were not caused by the famous shift in trade routes from the land-locked sea to the Atlantic. As previously indicated, these troubles long antedated Columbus, and did not prevent Mediterranean trade from enjoying a considerable revival in the latter sixteenth century, although it was gradually being overshadowed by the increasing importance of the Atlantic commerce and the American trade. In spite of these facts, however, it seems clear that the Mediterranean city state was too small and too lacking in resources to take advantage of the profound changes in economic conditions between 1450 and 1550, and this incapacity helped to make it extremely unstable politically. The favored species in the struggle for existence in the late fifteenth century were large territorial units. Of these, the two outstandng examples were the emergent empires of Spain and the Ottoman Turks. The words of Fernand Braudel seem particularly appropriate in this case:

> Without denying the role of individuals and circumstances, I think that with the increasing economic development of the fifteenth and sixteenth centuries, you have a conjunction steadily favoring the very large states. . . . Actually, history at one time is favorable, at another unfavor-

40. J. H. Elliott, *The Revolt of the Catalans. A Study in the Decline of Spain* 1598–1640 (Cambridge, 1643), p. 4. This depression was the result of trade interruptions caused by a variety of factors, such as war, piracy, and the Black Death. Even a century later, as Braudel's great study has indicated, economic conditions in the Mediterranean were still unstable. Two relatively new powers, Spain and the Ottoman empire, were acquiring control of great grain producing regions, and were ousting some of the older states from the relatively favorable positions they had occupied in the past. Thus by the middle of the sixteenth century, competition from both the Spanish and the Turks had forced France out of its traditional position of providing food supplies for the Mediterranean basin. Fernand Braudel, *La Méditerranée et le monde méditerranéen à l'époque de Philippe II*, p. 283. According to Braudel, another factor which adversely affected the Mediterranean economy was a serious gold shortage (*faim grandissante de l'or*). This shortage, lasting roughly from 1470 to 1540 or 1550, coincided with and was partly caused by the decline of the German mines, the diversion of at least a part of the flow of African gold from the Mediterranean to the Atlantic, and the increasing demands made on states involved in the Turkish and Italian wars. It was terminated by the beginning of massive shipments of American treasure about the mid-century. Ibid., pp. 373–74.

able to these vast political structures. It works to bring about their growth, expansion, and then their decay and dislocation. Evolution is not politically oriented once and for all; there are no states inevitably condemned to die while others are predestined to expand no matter what, as if they had been charged by destiny with the power of consuming territory and devouring their neighbors.[41]

History is, after all, a form of evolution. And while no one can predict day-to-day events, any more than the biologist can predict which mutations will appear in an organism, the historical environment makes some events meaningful while others are irrelevant and recede into the past without forming any kind of historical structure. Thus a series of fortuitous events in the Iberian kingdoms—a permanent union of the two strongest states, the overseas discoveries, a successful religious war against Islam—happened to occur at exactly the most favorable time for the formation of a super-state, a world power. And now we must turn to a second factor in the growth of large states, a factor which has nothing to do with economic development. Economic forces are rarely sufficient in themselves alone to produce the drive, the spirit, the *élan vital* without which, even in our time, the great agglomerations of territories cannot be asembled or held together. In our own time we have seen what nationalism and communism can do to create a unifying *mystique*; in the fifteenth and sixteenth centuries this unifying *mystique* in the case of both the Spanish and Ottoman empires was provided by religion—Christianity or Islam, as the case might be. And in the case of Spain this unifying mysticism took the particular form of the crusading spirit.

We have already seen that generalizations about the degree of Christian fanaticism in the Iberian kingdoms are apt to be unreliable. Periods of religious strife were succeeded by periods of peace and cooperation among Christian, Jew, and Moslem. But it will be noted that this is more apt to be true of the early rather than of the later Middle Ages. It seems that from the third period of the Reconquest on,[42] racial and religious intolerance was on the increase in Spain, and the crusading spirit which so uniquely appeals to the best and the worst in human nature had been and still was stronger in Spain than anywhere else. Granted this, the sudden and unexpected appearance of the Turkish and Protestant threat to the Catholic world in the early sixteenth century had exactly the effect in Spain that one would expect. The Spaniards had always thought of themselves as dedicated to the defense of Christianity within the peninsula; now, slowly and with some hesitations especially during the early years

41. Fernand Braudel, *La Méditerranée et le monde méditerranéen à l'époque de Philippe II*, pp. 508–509.
42. See above pp. 50 *et seq.*

of Charles I, they began to see themselves as especially dedicated soldiers of Christ anywhere in the world against the two enemies, Islam and Protestantism. It was this, added to the European and overseas expansion, as well as the influx of American treasure, that made the Spanish empire possible. It was this spirit, recognizing no obstacles and brooking no restraints, that conquered time and space, the constant enemies of the empire. It was this spirit, ignoring differences in geography, language, and customs, that for a time fused a mixture of peoples and cultures into what we call the Spanish empire. It was a similar spirit that made possible the parallel developments of the Ottoman empire. And last, it was the prolongation of this will to unity and empire in a century less favorable to the superstate that destroyed both the Spanish and Ottoman creations.

# PART II

# The Organization of the Dual Monarchy

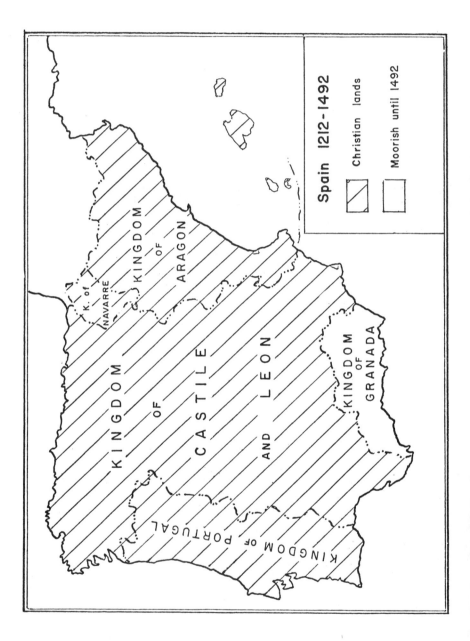

Spain 1212-1492

Christian lands

Moorish until 1492

KINGDOM OF NAVARRE

KINGDOM OF ARAGON

KINGDOM OF CASTILE AND LEON

KINGDOM OF GRANADA

KINGDOM OF PORTUGAL

# CHAPTER I

# The Famous Marriage

AS WE HAVE SEEN, THE MEDITERRANEAN CITY STATE HAD PROVED TO be too small to take full advantage of the commercial opportunities the age afforded, and too weak to sustain itself in competition with larger economic and political entities. The times then were favorable to the formation of large, associative states, provided two conditions were present: first, an extensive commercial development which would supply the economic resources necessary in the formation of such a structure; and second, a sense of dedication to a common ideal which would excite a loyalty and devotion capable of overcoming the obstacles of space and distance as well as diversity of tongues, institutions, and customs. When such conditions were present, as they were in the Iberian peninsula and the Ottoman lands, the result was a tremendous and rapid increase of power accompanied by an enormous expansion of territory.

This rapidity of historical change, this sense of rising tide in the affairs of men invariably follows a long, and often unnoticed, historical development. Thus when these subterranean forces of history, released by some fortuitous event, burst out into the open, we are given the illusion of something supernatural or superhuman in dramatic intervention; this we often personify under such edifying concepts as Divine Providence, the will of God, the *Übermensch*, the God-favored hero, and the like. Contemporaries, less informed than we concerning the historical background of events in Castile and Aragon, sought such explanations for the work of Ferdinand and Isabella. However, it is clear that the remarkable commercial development of Aragon in the Mediterranean in addition to the religious fervor of medieval Castile—repeatedly aroused during several centuries of local crusades—provided exactly the conditions required for empire-building in the late fifteenth century. Despite their undoubted ability, amounting almost to genius in political matters, Ferdinand and Isabella of themselves alone could not possibly have created the remarkable structure that bears their joint names, nor set the Spanish kingdoms on the path of empire without these favoring conditions.

The situation we are considering in the fifteenth century bears striking resemblances to certain conditions in the mid-twentieth century. In the case of the Communist bloc, we find a rapid expansion of territory based on a messianic ideology, and the technological development which in our time takes the place of the fifteenth century commercial expansion. On the other hand, it must be admitted that, in the rise of the Spanish world power, much that was medieval came to flower in the Iberian peninsula later than elsewhere. It is certainly not accidental that the Cid, the last of the great epic heroes of the Middle Ages, was actually an historical figure of the late eleventh century, and the Spain of the Catholic Kings is, in a definitely medieval sense, the last heroic age of the West. It is this fascinating mixture of medieval and modern that is typical of Iberia in these times, a fact which the great Spanish scholar Menéndez Pidal clearly recognized:

> All this output of our golden age, as has already been said, is not independent of the Renaissance, but it is a renaissance of a peculiar kind, profoundly medieval for all its modernity .... And yet highly modern for, if Spain cultivated medieval survivals, it was to fertilize them with the thought of modern times.[1]

2

The story of the famous marriage properly begins with John of Trastámara, also known as the duke of Peñafiel, John of Navarre, and finally John II of Aragon, plus many less flattering titles bestowed upon him by those who were frequently his dupes. Although none of the participants foresaw the historical significance of their activities—sometimes they do not really seem to know what they are doing—still, if any one person can be called the architect of the union of Castile and Aragon, John of Trastámara probably has a better right to the title than anyone else. Even without this, he may be called one of the most remarkable men in a century filled with *"singulares personalidades politicas,"* as a recent biographer has described him.[2] Constantly involved in turmoil, and constantly unsuccessful in his

1. Menéndez Pidal, *La España del Cid,* p. 473.
2. J. Vicens Vives, *Juan II de Aragón (1398–1479), monarquía y revolución en la España del siglo XV* (Barcelona, 1953), p. xiv.

early and middle life, success came late to him, at a time when many of his contemporaries were out of action, or in their graves. He excited intense hatreds and intense loyalties, and gave as good as he received. Perhaps his most striking characteristic, aside from his duplicity, was his tenacity, both in love and hate. Although devoted to his second wife and her son, his burning antipathy to his eldest son by an earlier marriage was to become famous and literally to tear his realm apart. Typical of his determination, and, one must also add, his courage, was his undergoing a double operation for cataracts at the age of seventy which, incredible to relate, was successful. During his long lifetime he united in his own career some of the most burning issues of the day: thus in Castile he was typical of the worst sort of feudal subversion; in Navarre he represented an absentee monarch struggling with feudal pretensions; and in Catalonia he was buffeted by the winds of social revolution.

He was born in Medina del Campo on June 29, 1398, the second son of the Infante Ferdinand of Antequera, himself the second son of King John I of Castile and Leon. This was a time when second and third sons of royalty received great *apanages* which they often built up into powerful holdings, as witness the state of the Valois dukes of Burgundy. The age was singularly blind to the dangers of this practice and King John I was no exception. In 1390, at the age of ten, the Infante Ferdinand was invested with many and rich estates. His marriage to Leonor de Alburquerque three years later also brought him extensive territories that created a solid block of lands from Portugal to Aragon, cutting Old Castile in two. The family lived at Medina del Campo in great splendor.

After the premature death of Henry III, Ferdinand became regent during a part of the minority of John II. In spite of his great power and opportunities for disloyalty, he showed himself both loyal and honorable. No serious complaints can be found with his conduct of Castilian affairs, except perhaps his efforts to increase the patrimony of his sons. Unfortunately, the means he followed in this involved the military orders more deeply within the mire of Castilian feudal politics. In 1409 his third son, Sancho, became grand master of Alcántara, and in the same year his fourth son, Henry, was accorded the same honor for the order of Santiago. His oldest son, the future Alfonso V of Aragon, was allowed to contract a marriage with a royal infanta and received 30,000 *doblas* of Castile and the marquessate of Villena within the western kingdom close to the Aragonese frontier. With this marriage, the grandmasterships, the extensive lands, the position of Ferdinand and his family was now firmly established in Castile. But more honors were to come.

As we have already seen, in 1412 Ferdinand of Antequera was

called to the throne of Aragon. At the coronation ceremonies, his oldest son Alfonso was recognized as heir apparent with John as next in line. John also received the title of duke of Peñafiel. Since the junior branch of the House of Trastámara now reigning in Aragon still kept its position and lands as a part of the ruling family of Castile, a delicate situation was created—one which was to bring trouble and discord on all parties. For years the energy and ability of the younger sons of Ferdinand were absorbed in Castilian intrigues; in this role the duke of Peñafiel was recognized as the chief of the Castilian interests of the family, especially after the death of Ferdinand of Aragon in 1416, when the bulk of the Castilian inheritance passed into his hands. He was now duke of Peñafiel in Castile, duke of Montblanc, and count of Mayorga in Catalonia. Moreover, he controlled the Castilian cities of Castrogeriz, Medina del Campo, Olmedo, Cuellar, and Villalón; in Rioja he held Haro, Belorado, Briones, and Cerezo. Some years later the duke stated that his holdings in the western kingdom were worth more than his total income from Navarre, Aragon, and Catalonia.[3]

Shortly before the death of his father, King Ferdinand, John had been sent to Sicily as lieutenant governor of the island. While here, he was briefly considered as a possible husband by Queen Joanna of Naples, and even went so far as to cancel a previous betrothal to Blanche of Navarre. However, nothing came of this possibility and, on the death of Ferdinand, he received permission from his new sovereign and brother, Alfonso V, to return to the mainland. Later he went to Castile with his younger brother Henry, grand master of Santiago. Important events in the western kingdom had opened up a new field of action for these restless spirits. King John II of Castile, already married to Duke John's sister, Mary of Aragon, had recently declared his majority on March 7, 1419; but he almost immediately began to display his complete incapacity as a ruler, a fact which was pointed out in the preceding chapter. As a result the court became a center of turbulent intrigues, and various factions began to form about the two infantes of the younger branch of the Trastámara family. Another powerful group of nobles began to cluster about the royal favorite, Alvaro de Luna, who was just on the threshold of his notorious career. Meanwhile it was necessary to find a wife for the duke of Peñafiel, and negotiations were once more revived for the hand of Blanche of Navarre.

Although less powerful than Castile, Aragon, or Portugal, Navarre was still considered an important state, especially because of its significant location straddling the Pyrenees. A French dynasty ruled it since the thirteenth century. Its present ruler, Charles the Noble,

3. Ibid., p. 20.

was considered a *preux chevalier* by his contemporaries and enjoyed considerable prestige. As he had no sons, on his death the crown would devolve on his daughter Blanche, already the widow of Martin of Aragon, last king of the old line of the counts of Barcelona. Duke John's suit was finally accepted by Charles and the pope issued the necessary dispensations; the marriage between John and Blanche took place on June 10, 1420. An elaborate marriage contract was signed by both parties which provided that, if Blanche died without heirs, John would withdraw from the kingdom; however, by a notable error, it failed to name the responsible ruler if Blanche, becoming queen, should die before her husband and leave no heir of age to rule. From this failure to allow for every eventuality there came a long development of the most tragic consequences. When Blanche should succeed her father, John would be allowed the courtesy title of king of Navarre, but final authority would rest firmly in the hands of the queen.

The next few years were filled with intrigues of a particularly barren sort. There is little point in outlining the various combinations that formed, broke up, and reformed again at the court of Castile. A son was born to John of Aragon on April 29, 1421, who was later given the name and rank of Charles, prince of Viana; however, this does not seem to have kept John in Navarre, where he was regarded by the native nobility as something of a foreigner and interloper. In Castile, violent intrigues continued around the weak person of the monarch and the powerful favorite Alvaro de Luna. The Infante Henry was imprisoned for a time and broke with Duke John; in the general confusion, war nearly broke out between Castile and Aragon. However, as we have seen before, a truce was arranged and eventually the disputes were settled. Henry was released in 1425 and, in the same year, Charles the Noble of Navarre died; Duke John could now use the style of King of Navarre, and by that name we shall know him for some years to come.

3

After the reconciliation between King John of Castile and his cousin, the Infante Henry, John of Navarre and Henry drew together in a cabal against Alvaro de Luna. After a brief success which forced Alvaro to retire from the court, he returned more powerful than ever. Henry was sent to the Granadine frontier, and John was invited to make an extensive visit to Navarre where he established himself in August of 1428. By this time a daughter, Blanche, had been born to him—she was later to marry Henry, Prince of Asturias. Alvaro de Luna now felt the time had come to eliminate the Aragonese infantes once and for all from the Castilian scene. To do this he planned nothing less than forcing a war between the two major states of the peninsula; in this way he hoped to rally the Castilian aristocracy around him; furthermore, he promised a general distribution of the rich estates held by John and Henry. Without waiting for the tiresome formality of a declaration of war, Alvaro began to attack the Aragonese holdings of the two princes in the spring of 1429; the formal outbreak of war was only officially announced in June. The temptation to the local aristocracy proved to be too great and de Luna was able to muster sufficient forces to defeat the Aragonese princes. Their lands were confiscated and distributed among the various nobles of the de Luna faction. However, a Castilian thrust into Aragon failed to penetrate the strong frontier defenses.

Alfonso V, making one of his brief appearances in his native land, wished to assist his brothers and attempted to stop the Castilian victories by an invasion of that kingdom. The efforts of the queen of Castile, herself a princess of Aragon, to prevent a fratricidal clash between the two armies, even to the extent of pitching her tent between them, succeeded, but the war continued in spite of her efforts. More effective in bringing matters to a close was the fundamental weakness of Alfonso V and his brother: that is, lack of any national support for their policies in Castile and the fact that Alfonso's real interests lay with his beloved Italy, from which he had been separated now for a number of years. Perhaps the most significant factor was the attitude of Catalonia. Without the financial support of the richest part of the Triple Kingdom, no really intensive war could be carried out. To the practical businessmen of Barcelona, the intrigues of the Aragonese princes in Castile must have seemed utterly pointless and wasteful. They made no secret of their opposition, and Alfonso V soon learned that he could not obtain funds from this source. The nobles of Aragon were equally hostile to the war, and in Navarre John found himself facing the same resistance. No one in the Pyrenean kingdom saw the slightest reason for risking life and limb to serve the foreign interests of a king-consort. A retreat was in order.

Negotiations were therefore once again begun between the two kingdoms in June of 1430. It was soon clear that Alvaro de Luna, finding himself in a strong position, was determined to concede practically nothing. From arrogant demands for the total restitution of the Castilian holdings of the two infantes, the Aragonese were forced to retreat to a simple claim on the rentals of the estates and even this was not allowed them. Eventually the Truce of Majano (from the village where the signatures were affixed) merely allowed the infantes of Aragon to retain what they *then possessed,* which is to say practically nothing, and made a vague promise of negotiations to settle other issues between them and King John of Castile. The truce was to be in force for five years, during which time the infantes were not to enter Castile.

Thus ten years of constant agitation and intrigue had resulted in a complete debacle. This was probably not too serious a blow to Alfonso the Magnanimous, whose interests, as we have seen, were elsewhere. But to John the check must have seemed well-nigh fatal; the great estates in Castile which his grandfather John I had bestowed on the family were now in the hands of his enemies. Doubtless seeing little hope of altering such an unfavorable settlement, John turned, for the time being, to the affairs of his own country and to Italy.

The next few years are mainly concerned with minor matters. King Alfonso returned to Italy in 1432, but John remained in the peninsula; he pursued his litigation in the Castilian courts but with little success, traveled widely in Aragon and Navarre, and occasionally yielded to the Cortes' urging to write his brother requesting his return home. All to no avail. Doubtless it would have greatly suited his purposes to have Alfonso return to take up again the issues with Castile and it may well be, as Vicens Vives thinks, that the reason for his journey to Italy during the summer of 1434 was to urge upon his brother exactly that course.[4] Certainly he could not have been of much military assistance as he brought with him neither fleet nor troops. Whatever Alfonso may have contemplated in regard to his Iberian interests was abruptly terminated by the deaths, early in 1435, of his principal Italian rivals, Louis of Anjou and Joanna of Naples. Once again Italy won over Castile as a field of activity, and he plunged ever deeper into the complexities of Italian politics.

But success continued to avoid him. All three brothers were present at the disastrous battle of Ponza on August 5, 1435, when Alfonso's fleet was utterly defeated by the Genoese and Alfonso, John, and Henry were taken prisoner along with many Italian and Spanish nobles. John shared his brothers' captivity in Milan for some months, but at the end of the year he was permitted to return to Barcelona, doubtless by this time thoroughly satiated with Italian politics. Early the next year Alfonso conferred upon him the rank of lieutenant governor of the realms of Aragon. He was now in a position to return to his interests in Castile.

It was a most propitious time since the Truce of Majano was shortly due to expire and a permanent treaty was desired. To this end, John sent an embassy to the court of his cousin asking for a prolongation of the truce with the kingdoms of Aragon and Navarre in order to allow for peace negotiations. The appeal came at a favorable time for Aragonese interests since the influence of Alvaro de Luna, unres-

4. Ibid., p. 75.

trained after the defeat of his rivals, was increasingly offensive to the aristocracy not directly of his party. The Castilian government agreed to the prolongation, and in the spring of 1436 formal negotiations were opened between the two crowns. The Peace of Toledo, signed on September 22, marked a partial recovery of John's position in Castile. His daughter Blanche was to be betrothed to the Castilian heir Henry and her dowry was to consist of a considerable portion of the lands taken from her father in 1430. Pending the consummation of the marriage (because of the extreme youth of both parties this was postponed to some time during the next four years), John was to recover possession of these lands. Castile also promised an annual grant of 10,000 florins to King John of Navarre, 21,500 to his son Charles of Viana, 15,000 to the Infante Henry and 5,000 to the Infante Pedro. Both sides agreed to return forts, castles, and towns taken from one another during the recent war, and the Aragonese infantes were not to enter Castile without the permission of the government. Later on, John is supposed to have remarked that he agreed to certain clauses unfavorable to his interests "for the sake of peace." No one need be deceived by this smug remark. Actually John had done very well in getting as much as he did, and, most important of all, he was once more reestablished in the western kingdom to watch over his own interests. This, rather than his sudden love of peace, led him to conclude the treaty.

Not long after the end of the war, Castile was torn again by her perennial internal disturbances. A new league of nobles was formed against Alvaro de Luna. In 1439, John of Navarre and his brother Henry came to Castile, perhaps at the request of the king, to mediate the strife between his favorite and the nobles. Such, at least, was the opinion of Zurita.[5] But efforts at a compromise failed and, as usual, the Infante Henry was the first to plunge into open opposition to de Luna by joining the faction forming against him. John, in keeping with his more subterranean tactics, appeared to remain apart for a few months at least, but he too finally came out openly against the favorite in 1440. He now became the chief of the insurgents, who included some of the greatest families in Castile. Moreover, the marriage of his daughter Blanche to Henry, Prince of Asturias, seemed to establish him firmly with the heir to the throne. The celebration of this marriage during September, 1440 at Valladolid was the occasion of a great gathering of the anti-de Luna faction and was ominous for the continuation of peace. As all expected, the long feared civil war broke out early the next year.

5. Jerónimo de Zurita (1512–80), archivist and historiographer of the Crown of Aragon.

At first the league of nobles carried all before it. By midsummer they had taken Medina del Campo, seized the person of John II of Castile, and forced Alvaro de Luna into open flight. For the next two years John of Navarre seemed to be the arbiter of Castilian politics. But nothing is more unstable than coalitions of feudal nobles, as history so frequently shows. The very completeness of the victory produced defections. Nobles dissatisfied with their gains began to drift into the opposite camp. Obviously, it was important for John to reach some sort of permanent agreement with the captured king of Castile, but this proved to be difficult. In the long run, John's difficult personality, his connections with the old feudality, and his status as a foreign sovereign prevented him from reaching any real agreement with the king. It soon became clear that powerful forces were gathering against him, including the heir to the throne, his erstwhile son-in-law, and the powerful Pacheco family, which was to play such an important role in the final union of the two crowns. The new combination demanded the "liberation" of the king, and—ominous note—the expulsion of foreigners; but with the king in his control, John apparently felt personally secure. Such was not to be the case.

Civil war again broke out at the end of March, 1444. Things went badly for John, the king succeeded in escaping, and he was forced back into Navarre. Appeals to his brother Alfonso V only produced letters of advice and formal embassies to Castile; Alfonso, recently in possession of the kingdom of Naples, his goal for so many years, had no intention of abandoning his great acquisition to assist in his brother's Castilian intrigues. In February of 1445, John issued forth from Navarre at the head of some troops and invaded Castile, making a junction with the forces of his brother, the Infante Henry. But these proved to be insufficient and, at the battle of Olmedo on May 19, the forces of Alvaro de Luna and the heir thoroughly defeated the brothers. Futhermore, Henry was critically wounded during the engagement and died on July 15.[6] Once again, the Castilian ambitions of John of Navarre seemed utterly frustrated.

### 4

After the great defeat of Olmedo, John withdrew from the struggle for the time being while the victors began the inevitable wrangling among themselves. Once again the aid of Alfonso was solicited and an understanding was finally reached whereby the king of Aragon agreed to support his brother in an attack on the Castilian province of Murcia. However, the first attempt failed, and John evidently decided to withdraw from the south and henceforth to use Navarre

6. The other brother, Don Pedro, had been killed at the siege of Naples in 1439.

as the base for activities in northern Castile. His status in that kingdom now became a matter of the first importance and marked the
beginning of the tragic struggle with his son, Charles of Viana.

Queen Blanche of Navarre had died in 1441. Since the marriage
contract between her and John had not specified what arrangements
should be made in case she died before her husband, her will
specified that their son, Charles of Viana, should inherit full rights
of sovereignty over Navarre but should not assume the royal title
or exercise his powers without the consent and blessing of his father.
Presumably this consent and blessing was not forthcoming, but a sort
of compromise was worked out which left Charles the *de facto* ruler
of Navarre (without the royal title) while John was left free to pursue
his ambitions in Castile. So long as these were paramount, John was
apparently willing to allow the ambiguities that surrounded both his
status and that of his son in Navarre to remain unresolved. But after
the misfortunes of Olmedo and other defeats, Navarre once again
assumed a major place in his schemes and it was clear that some
kind of reckoning between father and son could not be longer
delayed. Furthermore, after 1447, a new factor entered the situation:
John married again. His second wife was Joanna Enríquez, a daughter
of Don Fadrique Enríquez, hereditary admiral of Castile and distantly
related to the royal house. Younger than her husband, Joanna equalled
him in ambition, determination, and capacity for hatred. From the
first, she seems to have regarded Charles of Viana as a natural enemy
who would normally stand in the way of any children she might have.
Just how great a role she played in the first rupture between Charles
and his father is hard to say, but it seems obvious that she was
involved, especially after John sent her to Navarre with instructions
to take part in the administration of the country. Such a task was
not likely to win Joanna much popularity in a small provincial nation
traditionally jealous of foreigners. Therefore, it is not surprising that
the Beaumont family, long closely associated with Charles, urged him
to resist the pretensions of his step-mother while their traditional
enemies, the Agramonts, supported the new queen and her absent
husband. The family quarrel was going to become national.

The conflict became open when John came to Navarre early in
1450 and formally held court at Olite. Exercising the full powers of
sovereignty, he proceeded to reward his own supporters and confiscate the holdings of Charles' friends and allies; the Beaumonts were
among the principal victims of this policy. By summer the break
between father and son was complete; Charles fled to San Sebastian
with some of the Beaumonts and became involved in negotiations
with King John of Castile and Alvaro de Luna. To the indescribable
rage of John of Navarre, the prince of Viana signed a treaty with
his father's enemies while a Castilian army invaded Navarre. From

this moment on, the son was a traitor in the eyes of his father. After the signing of the treaty, the Castilian forces withdrew from Navarre and John was not able to take vengeance on the prince of Viana. In a battle with the Beaumont faction, royal troops led by Rodrigo de Rebolledo and Alfonso of Aragon, a bastard son of John of Navarre, completely defeated the insurgents and counted the prince of Viana himself among the spoils of victory. With Charles the prisoner of his father, the war should have ended, but the Beaumont faction still fought back fiercely and were by no means without allies. And the prince of Viana now began to command that general popular sympathy and affection which was to be his strongest support in adversity. While the war went on in Navarre, John was eventually forced to release his son, although on his own terms pending a final adjudication by the distant head of the family, Alfonso V, in 1453.

Meanwhile the entire political situation in the peninsula was affected by a momentous series of births and deaths. The queen of Castile, who had so many times attempted to prevent war between the land of her birth and the land of her husband, had died. In 1447, under pressure from the favorite, John of Castile had been induced to marry again, and the constable's choice had fallen on Joanna of Portugal, in spite of the fact that there was a taint of insanity in her family. By this second marriage John II had two children, a son Alfonso, and a daughter Isabella. Although the new queen owed her position to the favorite, she soon turned against him. Alvaro's power had been less secure in the years since Olmedo and the enmity of the queen and the heir, the Infante Henry, proved to be more than he could withstand. John was finally induced to order his arrest on a charge of witchcraft and three months later de Luna was executed at Valladolid on July 5, 1453, to the great satisfaction of his many enemies, especially John of Navarre. The position of the titular king of Navarre had also been changed by a birth; to his great delight Joanna Enríquez had given birth to a son at the little town of Sos in Aragon on March 10, 1452. Named Ferdinand for his grandfather, the first of the Aragonese Trastámaras, the child was henceforth the object of a consuming ambition on the part of both parents. In such a situation, Charles of Viana was more bitterly hated than ever by his father and his step-mother.

John of Castile did not long survive the loss of his remarkable favorite, who had ruled him for almost thirty years. He died on July 21, 1454, after one of the longest and most disgraceful reigns in the history of medieval Castile. As Prescott remarks, his reign "if reign it may be called . . . was more properly one protracted minority."[7]

---

7. William H. Prescott, *History of the Reign of Ferdinand and Isabella the Catholic*, 3 vols., tenth edition (New York, 1849), I, p. 28.

The advent of a new sovereign was greatly welcomed in Castile, and, indeed, Henry IV as prince had sometimes shown bursts of energy which gave hope for the future. But it soon became apparent that the new reign was going to repeat many of the worst features of the old one. Henry's energy was abated. He too turned to a favorite, Beltrán de la Cueva, and his dissipation of royal domains was even worse than his father's. His courtiers soon ceased to have much respect for him, and, as previously mentioned, his failure to produce an heir after several years of marriage had earned him the embarrassing epithet of "the impotent."

The war had been renewed in Navarre by Charles of Viana in the fall of 1453, but Henry was anxious to establish peace and one of his early acts as king of Castile was to negotiate with John. A treaty was signed between them on September 8, 1454, and ratified early the next year. This restored many of John's possessions in Castile to that crown in return for subsidies. However, Henry's efforts to mediate the quarrel between father and son were less successful, especially in view of the almost continuous fighting that went on between the rival clans of the Beaumonts and the Agramonts. Truces were made in the mountain kingdom only to be broken; and, after two violent battles between the factions in 1455, the last hope of reaching an accord between them, or between Charles and John, was destroyed. It was then that the king of Navarre decided on a drastic move which he had probably been considering for some time. This was nothing less than the disinheriting of Charles of Viana. This act, which in view of the marriage contract between John and his first wife, Queen Blanche, was probably illegal, could not succeed without powerful support, and this John now sought from the strong and ambitious Gaston IV, count of Foix, a most influential personage in border politics.[8]

After negotiations conducted in Barcelona, an agreement was reached on December 3, 1445. By its terms John disinherited his oldest son and bestowed full succession rights in Navarre to Doña Leonor,

8. The county of Foix was a significant principality, and its counts were among the most important of the feudal magnates of southern France during the fourteenth and fifteenth centuries. Although technically a French fief, Foix had close contacts also with Navarre and often took an active part in the petty wars of the border country. In the early fifteenth century, John of Foix married a daughter of Charles the Noble of Navarre and played an important role in the politics of the time. His son, Gaston IV, married Leonor, youngest child of John of Aragon and Queen Blanche. In 1447 he had purchased the viscounty of Narbonne from Charles VII of France, and later received the counties of Cerdagne and Rousillon from Louis XI. He was eventually made royal representative in Languedoc and Guienne. Obviously, he was a person to be reckoned with.

his youngest daughter and Gaston's wife. The next year, Charles VII of France ratified the agreement as Gaston's feudal lord and thus a door to French influence was opened into the peninsula. Fortified by this agreement as well as by the formidable artillery of the count of Foix, the Agramonts renewed the war successfully. The Beaumont forces were beaten and, to cap these disasters, Charles of Viana was now abandoned by Henry IV of Castile, formerly his help and support in time of trouble. Henry, giving up the cause of Charles as virtually lost, had decided to attempt to put relations between Castile, Aragon, and Navarre on a more solid basis. To this end he proposed a series of marriages between the two branches of the House of Trastámara, involving his half-brother, the Infante Alfonso, and Joanna of Aragon. More significantly, he also suggested a union between Isabella and the young Infante Ferdinand of Aragon. Thus, in the words of Vicens Vives, "for the first time, in the wake of the Navarrese civil wars there entered into the area of diplomatic possibilities the celebration of a betrothal destined to have such pregnant possibilities for the history of Spain."[9] The agreement was signed in May of 1457. The proclamation of Charles as king of Navarre by the Beaumonts a short time before was largely nullified. The prince of Viana was beaten and he knew it. He therefore decided to abandon the struggle temporarily and appeal to higher powers; this meant France, and , above all, the absent Alfonso V.

In fact, Alfonso seems to have felt something of the almost universal sympathy that Charles of Viana seemed to attract so easily. When the young prince arrived in Naples he was warmly received by his uncle. Both shared an appreciation of literature and the arts, and a friendship seems to have developed. The alarm that these developments caused John of Navarre can easily be imagined; especially when letters arriving from Naples indicated that King Alfonso intended to intervene in the quarrel between father and son on behalf of the prince of Viana. But before he could take concrete steps to protect his nephew, Alfonso V died on June 27, 1458, in his castle at Naples, and the situation was instantly altered in the most drastic fashion.

5

With the exception of Naples, which might be called Alfonso's personal acquisition and which had long been intended for his illegitimate son Ferrante, all of the realms of Aragon and the overseas territory went to the king of Navarre, who will now be known as John II of Aragon. This represented a great blow to the fortunes of Charles

9. Vicens Vives, *Juan II de Aragón*, p. 159.

of Viana. How could he possibly hope to stand up against his father, no longer a mere king by courtesy in Navarre, but lord of the realms of Aragon and undisputed head of the Aragonese Trastámaras. And to make matters worse, in his second son, Ferdinand, he now had an heir who could succeed him if Charles were again disinherited.

A realization of these facts may have been behind Charles' trip to Sicily. Once again something in his personality, or sympathy for his misfortunes, won the hearts of the Sicilians, and stimulated the tendencies toward independence which were never long absent from the island. Before long the usual delegation offered the crown of Sicily to Prince Charles. He refused, but his father was alarmed and took steps to avoid the possibility of a second Sicilian Vespers. He quickly recognized the government of his nephew Ferrante in Naples and opened negotiations to get Charles out of Sicily. Eventually the prince set sail for the peninsula, stopped briefly in Salou in Catalonia to send another embassy to his father, and finally landed in Mallorca on August 20, 1459, while the negotiations continued. After lengthy talks, a compromise agreement, known as the Concord of Barcelona, was reached in January of the next year. The lands and honors of Charles' supporters in Navarre were restored to them, but to obtain this concession he had to promise not to establish his residence in either Navarre or Sicily. Worst of all, from Charles' position, was the failure of the Concord to make any statement about his rights as first-born to the Aragonese realms—a much more important issue than his inheritance in Navarre and one which soon overshadowed everything else. Late in March Charles sailed to Barcelona and was received with enthusiasm by the population. In May there was a general family reunion in Barcelona when John and Joanna made their formal entry as king and queen. Although we are told an atmosphere of superficial cordiality prevailed, there were undoubtedly deep suspicions on both sides. Among other things, plans were discussed for a possible marriage between Charles and the Infanta Catherine of Portugal, and arrangements were made for a session of the Aragonese cortes, at which time Charles' supporters hoped he would be proclaimed officially *primogenit* of the Triple Kingdom.

Meanwhile, with these issues still unsettled, John sought to clear his hands of less vital matters. This explains his willingness to recognize Ferrante, and thus avoid Italian entanglements. He also hoped to improve relations with France, traditional enemy of the crown of Aragon. Therefore, he withdrew Aragonese interests from Genoa, which France was trying to control. In regard to Castile he was still hoping to recover his lost territories and this led him to resume his former role of disturber of the peace. By the Pact of Tudela (April 1460) he was now leagued with a group of dissident Castilian nobles, including such powerful forces as Alfonso Carrillo, the bellicose archbishop of Toledo, and the Mendoza, Enríquez, and Toledo clans. But these intrigues in Castile were soon forgotten by the explosion of the Catalan revolution.

Henry IV was naturally angered by the Pact of Tudela and his answer was to begin secret negotiations with Charles of Viana. Having failed to reach any understanding with his father on the matter of his succession rights, this prince was ready to seek help wherever he could find it. The result was another violent scene between father and son. The court learned of Charles' secret talks with Henry IV while John and his wife were at Lérida for the meeting of the Cortes. During a week of intense strain and suspicion, John was probably induced by his wife to assume the worst about his son. In a moment of anger he ordered the arrest of Prince Charles on December 2, 1460. This was a mistake, as he himself later realized. It was badly received throughout Europe, it contained the possibility of renewed war with Castile, it did revive the civil war in Navarre, and it led to a violent uprising in Catalonia.

6

During the early part of the fifteenth century, while economic conditions were generally improving in Catalonia, the lot of the peasant, especially the class known as *remeca*, was deteriorating. This class consisted of agrarian workers who could not leave the land without making a payment to the lord; however, this was not considered a personal condition like serfdom, but a legal category. It did not derive from ancient traditions, but was deliberately enacted in 1283 to check the movement of peasants to the cities. The most important element was not the person, but the *mas*—the unit of land which was to be cultivated. Rights of ownership were considered divided between the lord, who had the *dominio directo,* and the peasant, who had the *dominio útil.* The heavy losses caused by the Black Death worked both to the advantage and disadvantage of the *campesino* since the more energetic or ambitious *remençajeros* could now move into additional *masos* depopulated by the epidemic; on the other hand, to make up for their own losses, the lords were greatly increasing the feudal rents and redemptions which they now claimed the peasants owned them. The peasantry naturally attempted to resist the increased demands as a violation of their rights, and gradually a question of personal liberty was involved. In a region so ready to rise in defense of its ancient charters and privileges, and so addicted to litigation as Catalonia, the question of agrarian rights could easily become explosive,especially if connected with other burning issues.

Some of the peasants, especially in the mountain districts, wanted to obtain full rights and the abolition of the lords' *dominio directo*, but most did not wish to go so far. The majority who had acquired new *masos*, while insisting on the recognition of their personal freedom, were willing to accept obligations which tradition, custom, and law had sanctioned. To obtain these more moderate aims, the *campesinos* had formed peasant syndicates which had been legalized by Alfonso V in 1448. Later these organizations became a serious problem for the Infante John when he became lieutenant governor of the principality in 1454.[10]

The Catalan peasants were not the only class in difficulties. The famous merchant community which had for so long taken a leading part in exploiting the commercial opportunities of the Mediterranean was losing its prosperity and its leadership. Of the upper middle class, more than half now lived in Barcelona and were withdrawing from trade and commerce to invest their wealth in land. Those who did this naturally came into closer contact with the forces seeking to restrict peasant expansion into the *masos mortos*, or vacant lands. Thus they tended to lose touch with the mercantile interests which had created their wealth and political influence, and were undoubtedly drawing closer to the aristocratic point of view. The Catalan middle class, therefore, was divided in its sympathies and interests just at a time when a fierce political crisis was about to break. From a political point of view, the Triple Kingdom presented a combination of personal rights and economic progress that could be found in few places during the Middle Ages and which bears certain resemblances to nineteenth century England. To a great extent the Aragonese overseas empire was the creation of Barcelona—its ships, money, and the energy of its citizens. And it was here that this curious mixture of imperialism and safeguards for personal liberties was strongest. Yet, so long as these liberties were recognized by the governing power, there was no desire to interfere with the political institutions of the principality of Catalonia. This fact had never been lost sight of by the old line of the counts of Barcelona, who had ruled in Aragon until 1410, even in the midst of their most violent discords with the nobility. The new dynasty of the House of Trastámara had been accepted in the kingdom, yet with a certain reluctance, and in Barcelona there was an increasing sensitivity to the question of rights and privileges. This often took the form of stern resistance to the political activities of the younger princes of the dynasty. As has been pointed out, John of Aragon could get little support from Catalonia

10. For an illuminating discussion of this and other economic and social problems in Catalonia in the later Middle Ages, see Vicens Vives, *Juan II de Aragón*, especially Chapter VI.

for his projects in Castile and Navarre. During his administration of the principality for his brother, John was regarded by the aristocracy and the upper middle class with fear and suspicion, for it was recognized that he tended to support the peasantry and the lower middle class in their quarrels with the social levels above them. However, he really did not have sufficient power to settle these great questions and preferred to occupy himself with political intrigues on a fairly low level as we have already seen.

With the death of his brother, John's position was radically changed. As king of Aragon he could no longer ignore the potential social strife within Catalonia, especially since it might be expected to spill out into the other realms of the crown. His new position also meant a radical change in his relations with his oldest son. The succession to the crown of Navarre might be a minor matter to the magnates of the eastern kingdom, but when John became king of Aragon the rights of his son in Navarre became merged into the much greater problem of succession rights in the Triple Kingdom. Charles as a person was not too important—indeed he had been virtually unknown to the Catalans until 1460—but Charles as a symbol of the liberties of the land was a very different matter. It was this change in Charles' status which was dramatically brought about by John's blunder in ordering the arrest of his son. It was felt in Barcelona that this arrest had violated several of the principality's rights, and a delegation soon called on the king to demand Charles' release. Furthermore, the city council of Barcelona called the country to arms, summoned a fleet, and in general displayed a most bellicose attitude. When John went to Saragossa, he found the Aragonese aristocrats almost equally alarmed; and with Henry IV of Castile threatening an invasion, he was forced to yield. Charles of Viana was released on February 25, 1461, and turned over to the Catalans, who conducted him in triumph to Barcelona.

But John's humiliations were not yet over. With the queen as his personal representative, he was now forced to enter into negotiations with Charles and the principality as to the succession, the rights of the crown in Catalonia, and his future behavior. The complicated negotiations that led to the Capitulation of Villafranca were handled directly between the queen and the representatives of the principality. Joanna Enríquez showed great skill and evinced a real desire to reestablish the position and prestige of her husband in Barcelona. But she soon found that negotiating, not with a venal aristocracy as in Castile but with men supported by popular institutions guaranteed by well-known traditions, was a very difficult matter. During the first reading of the demands made by the principality, the queen was frequently moved to tears, but to no avail. The document finally signed on June 21, 1461, represented one of the most humiliating surrenders ever made by a king of Aragon to his subjects. John was forced to admit the injustice of his acts against Charles, and those who had assisted him in the arrest of the prince were to be dismissed. He promised a complete reform of the higher administration of the principality, henceforth to be completely Catalan in composition, once again agreed to swear to all its rights and privileges, and, in short, became little more than a figurehead in the administration of Catalonia. As for the succession, Charles of Viana was recognized as *primogenit* and lieutenant governor of the principality and in this official capacity possessed real executive powers. What no one seems to have foreseen was that in case anything happened to the prince of Viana, the capitulation would greatly strengthen the position of the Infante Ferdinand. Such was the extent of the royal surrender.

Doubtless even under relatively normal conditions the capitulation could not have been maintained. John had conceded too much, and if Charles of Viana had succeeded him as king it is doubtful if he would have accepted such limitations of royal authority. But the treaty was almost immediately thrown into jeopardy by the death of the prince of Viana on September 23. Coming at such an unbelievably opportune moment for the royal position, contemporaries could only believe that man had assisted the hand of God. It became almost an act of faith to believe that he had been poisoned by his stepmother. Popular hysteria broke out during the funeral in Barcelona and, as might have been expected for the time and place, miracles were soon reported at his tomb. While Joanna Enríquez was probably capable of poisoning Charles if she had had the opportunity, the work of Desdevizes du Desert and other scholars has pretty well cleared her name. Charles was never very strong and in recent years had followed a way of life that imposed too much on a weak constitution. He was a sick man throughout the negotiations of Villafranca, and the evidence clearly indicates that he died of natural causes, probably tuberculosis. Regardless of the cause, his death saved King John and enabled him to return to the policies temporarily checked by the Capitulation of Villafranca.

Such, however, was not immediately apparent. Joanna Enríquez and the Infante Ferdinand came to Barcelona and were received by the city authorities on November 21. A long period of intrigue and negotiations followed, in which the queen tried to calm the authorities and each side jockeyed for power. In the midst of the growing political tension, everyone feared the possibility of an agrarian uprising. Actually violence was constantly breaking out between the nobles and the *remençajeros,* especially in north Catalonia; in such cases the peasants appealed to the king for help. This added to the embarrassment of John and Joanna; for, while the crown could see political advantages in helping the peasants, it did not wish to go so far as to use them as allies in a social war. In such difficulties, Joanna finally decided to leave the city; on March 11, 1462, she and Ferdinand left for Gerona. She had failed to do anything to restore the position of the crown. Meanwhile in Barcelona it was decided to form a municipal army to be used against the peasants. The fact that it was to be commanded by a representative of the city and not by the crown made it clear that it was to be used against the crown, if necessary, as well as against the agrarian lower classes. Following so soon after the Capitulation of Villafranca, this decision of the city authorities represented another step in the rapidly worsening relations of the crown and the principality.

7

The great Catalan revolution thus initiated was to last a full ten years and do incalculable damage; among other things, it ruined the prosperity of Barcelona and the principality for a generation. It may be called the first violent effort of Catalan separatism to resist the growing power of the center of the peninsula, efforts repeated in 1640, 1704, and 1934. It is not the purpose of this study to trace the revolt of 1462 in detail; that has been thoroughly done in many monographs. Only enough needs to be given to enable the student of the period to see the general outlines and understand the connection between the Catalan revolution and the future marriage of Prince Ferdinand to the heiress of Castile.

In general, the movement in Catalonia went through three main phases. The first was mainly of aristocrats and the upper middle class with the intent of forcing the sovereign to observe the constitutional rights and privileges of the principality. The peasants and workers were not directly involved. The movement succeeded with the previously mentioned Capitulation of Villafranca. The unexpected death of the *primogenit* led directly to the second and more violent phase. In spite of contemporary opinion to the contrary, this phase was far more the result of the lack of generosity of the nobles and upper middle class than anything the intrigues of Joanna could have accomplished. At this time, the movement passed byond *pactismo*, or constitutionalism, into the area of political and social revolution. Supported actively for the first time by lower economic groups, the movement became definitely anti-royal and, as it developed, the ardor of the upper strata became much cooler and some of them turned definitely to the side of the crown. This phase ended when it became apparent by 1463 that the province could not resist the king indefinitely without outside help. With the third phase, the Catalan rebels passed beyond a rebellion against an unpopular king believed to have violated the laws; instead they were involved in a movement for complete independence under some foreign prince. Since the Catalans now offered the leadership of the movement to various foreign princes, the revolution, while retaining some of its aspects of a class struggle, also assumed the aspect of an international movement against Aragon by its potential enemies, chiefly Portugal, Castile, and France. These last two phases will now be briefly discussed.

John's first acts were to clear himself of foreign entanglements. Treaties were quickly negotiated with Louis XI of France and Henry IV of Castile, but nothing seemed able to quench the enthusiasm of the Catalans. They advanced boldly, taking several minor strongholds and finally besieging the queen and the Infante Ferdinand where they had taken refuge in the citadel of Gerona. When King John drew near with troops loaned by the count of Foix and the king of France, the Catalans were forced to raise the siege; and as the royal forces continued to advance, the rebels took the final step of proclaiming the king and queen enemies of the country. It was now clearly necessary to appeal to foreign powers.

The first approach was made to Castile. On the advice of his councilors, Henry IV decided to violate his previous commitments with Aragon and accept the appeal. Therefore, he sent 2,500 cavalry to the aid of Barcelona, which was already under attack. Strengthened by this help, the city resolutely rejected all proposals for peace. Meanwhile, Louis XI of France rewarded himself for his assistance to John II by the occupation of Cerdagne and Roussillon. Barcelona, now virtually an independent republic, acknowledged Henry IV as its sovereign.

The king of France offered his good offices to Castile and Aragon as mediator, and a preliminary conference was held at St. Jean de Luz. After failing to win Louis to a plan for the dismemberment of Aragon, Castile finally agreed to the mediation. At Bayonne on April 23, 1463, Louis announced his judgment: the Catalans were to recognize John as their rightful sovereign after full pardons for all and a three-month truce; Henry IV was to withdraw his troops and to cease supporting the rebels. Naturally these terms failed to satisfy anyone except Louis XI. A meeting on the French side of the Bidasoa River five days later between Louis and Henry did not help matters, as the French chronicler Commines, who was present, reported that both sides parted with intense mutual distrust. The formation of a hostile coalition of nobles in Castile the following year rather effectively kept Henry out of further intervention in Catalan affairs for some time to come.

With the defection of Henry IV, and the refusal of Louis XI to come to their aid, the rebels turned to Pedro of Portugal, constable of the kingdom, brother-in-law of the king, and a descendant of that count of Urgel who had vainly opposed the candidacy of Ferdinand of Antequera to the Aragonese throne. He had little ability except in literature, and his choice angered the French. Although he came to Barcelona and was officially installed as chief of state, he accomplished little. Meanwhile John's position was becoming stronger; he continued to advance in Catalonia and, on January 28, 1465, Pedro was badly beaten at Calaf, where the young Ferdinand served as titular commander of the royal forces at the age of thirteen. Don Pedro died the next year, and the important city of Tortosa surrendered to John. In these desperate circumstances, some of the leaders of the revolt considered surrendering, but a majority was still determined to continue the war. Since Pedro had died, it was necessary to appeal again for outside support, and this time the choice fell upon Duke Réné of Anjou, another claimant to the Aragonese crown. In possession, through marriage, of the powerful duchy of Lorraine, he was also the brother of Duke Louis of Calabria, who had contended with Alfonso V for the crown of Naples. Thus he might be called an ancient enemy of the crown of Aragon..Furthermore, he had a son, John, who was considered one of the best commanders of the age, and whom he now dispatched to Barcelona to represent him. The French maintained a benevolent neutrality, having allowed John of Calabria to pass through France on his way to Barcelona, and there was evidence that Louis XI intended to do more. The Angevin troops in Catalonia seemed able to change the balance of power, which had hitherto favored the royalists. The Infante Ferdinand was badly beaten in an attempt to save the city of Gerona, and once again his father's fortunes seemed at their lowest ebb.

By this time nearing seventy, nearly blind from cataracts in both eyes and facing a coalition of forces that seemed likely to dismember his kingdom, the position of John of Aragon was truly pitiable. Furthermore, at this critical moment in his career, he was deprived of his strongest support by the death of his wife. Yet the old man struggled on with his incredible tenacity and, as had happened before in his strange history, various unexpected developments altered the situation in his favor. Early in 1468 he recovered his sight, thanks to the famous operation performed on him by a Jewish doctor, in which the cataracts were successfully removed. He was now able to take the field in person and succeeded in recovering Gerona. His old enemy, Louis XI, found himself in serious difficulties with Charles the Bold, duke of Burgundy, which temporarily eliminated France as a factor in international affairs. John also reached agreements with as many enemies of the House of Valois as he could: Edward IV of England, Charles of Burgundy, and the disloyal Armagnac family in southern France. But even with these agreements, the power of the forces opposed to him, the firm grip of the Angevin forces on Barcelona, and his own lack of money and credit all combined to render his position precarious. As Zurita was to write about a century later, "It was clear that the king's policies were on the verge of failure without any possibility of improvement."[11]

Fortunately for John, his son Ferdinand was beginning to display those qualities of intelligence, calculation, and duplicity which were later to win the admiring praise of Machiavelli. Like his father in some ways, he was steadier, less given to explosions of the famous Trastámara temper, and more careful with his finances (later his stinginess would become famous). Ferdinand had been recognized as heir by the Aragonese Cortes as early as September 1464, and by a clever stoke John had induced the Sicilian authorities to give their official confirmation at the same time. Two years later Valencia had followed suit. But the dangers of 1468 forced John to go further; on June 10, he issued a pragmatic from Saragossa in which he bestowed on Ferdinand the title of king of Sicily and co-regent with himself for the island. Thus Ferdinand's position would be protected if John died suddenly—which, considering his advanced age, was not at all unlikely.

We have already seen the fascination that Castilian affairs had exercised over John, amounting almost to an obsession. It was the one consistent factor in his long and confusing career. There are two aspects of his Castilian policy: one, to hold on to his share of the grants of King John I to his father; and, second, to use his position and influence in the western kingdom as a means of support when he found himself embattled, first in Navarre and later in Aragon. In the first instance he had failed, as the inheritance had escaped from him, but the second still represented a promising field of action. This was especially so in 1468 since his desperate circumstances forced him to explore any possibility, and the prospects of a new civil war in Castile suggested that his intervention might be particularly effective at this juncture. What could not be recovered in Catalonia by himself might be secured with the help of Castile. It was in this sense that the famous marriage proposals he was shortly to make to the Infanta Isabella were an aspect of John's immediate necessities, but in a deeper sense they represented the culmination of almost forty years of intrigue and intervention in the affairs of the western kingdom.

## 8

We have already seen that the hopes generated by the accession of Henry IV did not materialize. His vacillations, weakness, and per-

11. As quoted by Vicens Vives, *Juan II de Aragón*, p. 310.

sonality defects made it impossible for him to dominate the quarrelsome and venal nobility while his gifts to them merely made them
more demanding.[12] He had returned to the older policy of raids
against the Moorish state of Granada. These, if successful, might have
won him some popularity; but in this as in all else he accomplished
nothing, and the Moslem rulers were able to defy him with impunity.
After twelve years of marriage to Blanche of Aragon,[13] he obtained
a dissolution on the grounds that a spell cast upon him by witchcraft
had prevented a successful consummation. Some years later, in 1455,
he had married Joanna of Portugal; but again, as in the case of his
former wife, no children resulted. In such a situation, the heir apparent to the throne was Henry's half-brother Alfonso, son of John II
of Castile by his second marriage. The existence of this prince, and
the somewhat unlikely possibility of children being fathered by
Henry, seemed to bar effectively the chances of Isabella's succession.
It is interesting to note that, exactly as in the case of Ferdinand, a
half-brother stood in the way.

Much to the surprise of the court, the queen became pregnant and
gave birth to a daughter in 1462. She was named Joanna after her
mother. The question of paternity, however, eventually became a
major issue for some of the courtiers refused to believe the child
was the king's and, as we have seen, attributed it instead to the
monarch's closest friend, Beltrán de la Cueva. Henceforth the young
infanta received the humiliating nickname of "la Beltraneja."[14] The
rise of Don Beltrán, so reminiscent of the late unlamented Alvaro
de Luna, naturally excited jealousy and resentment, especially in two
men who had previously enjoyed great influence over the feeble spirit
of Henry IV. These were the Archbishop of Toledo, Alfonso Carrillo,

12. An interesting attempt has been made to reinterpret the reign of Henry
IV in a sense much more favorable to that monarch. Orestes Ferrara believes
that Henry has been maligned by contemporary writers who were partisans
of Isabella and who were not above altering the texts, or suppressing entire
documents. Contrary to the usual secondary accounts, he holds that Henry
was a popular ruler, not impotent, and completely normal in his sexual life.
The allegations to the contrary came from chroniclers who had political
reasons (and no scruples) for wishing to discredit him. Such revisionism is
probably valuable, and Ferrara does help us to form a more balanced portrait
of Henry IV. However, I do not believe that he offers much evidence to
make us change our policial accounts of this reign. Henry simply cannot
be transformed into a strong king—a normal man, yes, but a strong ruler,
no. See Orestes Ferrara, *L'Avenement d'Isabelle la Catholique*, translated
from the Spanish by Francis de Miomandre (Paris, 1958).

13. This Blanche was the second child of Blanche of Navarre and John
of Aragon. See pp. 121, 124 of this study.

14. Ferrara, of course, strongly denies the charges concerning Joanna's supposed illegitimacy and Henry's supposed sexual inadequacy or outright per-

and his nephew Juan Pacheco, marquis of Villena. The archbishop ruled the largest and richest diocese in Spain with a stern hand; being of an ambitious and violent disposition, he was a force to be reckoned with. It goes without saying that he was a completely political prelate without a trace of religiosity in his makeup. His nephew was probably a more pleasant person, but equally ambitious and a better courtier. He had risen to prominence during the post-Alvaro de Luna period of the reign of John II and, the recipient of many royal estates in Toledo, Murcia, and Valencia, had become the most powerful vassal of the kingdom. Both men had taken a major part in forming Henry's policies and it is likely that the king's lack of success in dealing with Louis XI, especially at the time of the arbitration of Bayonne, may have contributed to the break. Whatever the cause, about the time of the birth of the Infanta Joanna, both men were in disgrace and very angry with their former benefactor.

The formal recognition of Joanna as heiress to the crown gave them an opportunity to make trouble. Using the supposed illegitimacy of Joanna as a potent argument in favor of Prince Alfonso, they formed a coalition of dissident nobles, never a very difficult thing to do in Castile, and demanded that the king should satisfy their complaints and surrender his half-brother Alfonso to them as the future ruler. In spite of an abject surrender to most of their demands, the hostile nobles eventually broke off negotiations with Henry IV and took part in the outrageous farce of his deposition at the city of Ávila in 1465. On this occasion, everything possible was done to humiliate the royal

---

version. His arguments are circumstantial, but must be given serious consideration. They can be summarized as follows: 1) the absence of any rumors or gossip concerning the paternity of the Infanta Joanna for two and one half years after her birth, and the fact that some of the nobles who later questioned her paternity assisted in the elaborate ceremonies of her baptism; 2) the failure of Henry's divorced first wife to support any of these charges, and the fact that she made him her heir in her last testament; 3) the strong probability that the Burgos Document (September, 1464) in which the question of Joanna's paternity was first raised by Villena and the rebellious nobles, has been altered by the later insertion of these charges, and that they did not appear in the original document; 4) Henry's willingness to marry Joanna first to his half-brother, the Infante Alfonso, and later to the King of Portugal, which would have hardly been possible if he knew that he was not her father; 5) the fact that the illegitimacy of Joanna provided the *only possible* legal justification for the claim, first of Alfonso and later of Isabella, to the throne of Castile. It therefore became almost an act of faith on the part of Isabella's partisans, especially after her enthronement, to insist on the dishonor of Henry as the cuckolded husband. Failing this, Isabella's reign was a usurpation and without any legal or constitutional justification. These are weighty arguments and offer strong, though indirect, support for the legitimacy of the Infanta Joanna. See Ferrara, chapter VIII, *passim.*

power. On a scaffold outside the city walls, a dummy dressed in the royal insignia was despoiled of its crown and scepter by the archbishop of Toledo and finally rolled in the dust to the accompanying jeers of the spectators. The young Infante Alfonso was then solemnly proclaimed with drums and trumpets as King Alfonso XII. But the insurgents had gone too far. There is evidence that the nation was disgusted by the shameful drama of Avila, and the more responsible of the aristocracy rallied around the king. Whatever they may have thought of the monarch, there was a great deal of latent respect for the institution itself in the fifteenth century, and this feeling was affronted by such a gross humiliation. Thus when Henry issued a call to arms to support the crown, there was a considerable response. Unfortunately, the king virtually threw away his advantage when he reopened negotiations with the rebels and, to win the support of Marquis Villena, offered the hand of the Infanta Isabella to the marquis' brother, Don Pedro Girón, grand master of Calatrava. To the disgust of his supporters, Henry obtained a dispensation from Rome, and arrangements for the marriage were set up in considerable haste. Meanwhile he dropped his military preparations. All these plans were ruined, however, by the sudden death of Girón before the marriage could take place. This was the first of a series of unexpected deaths that were to smoothe Isabella's path to the throne.

Since Girón's death ended any immediate prospect of a reconciliation between his family and the crown, the rebels once again became active. Eventually both sides mustered sufficient strength to force a battle, which was fought near Olmedo on August 20,1467, close to the site of a battle between John II of Castile and his rebellious nobles some twenty years before. Carrillo led the hostile forces, assisted by the young Infante Alfonso, while the chief figure among the royalists was Beltrán de la Cueva. The battle was indecisive, although Segovia fell to the insurgents not long afterward; however, the really decisive event was the death of the Infante Alfonso on July 5, 1468. This at once deprived the insurgents of their candidate for the throne and also the chance of legitimizing their conspiracy. Furthermore, it forced them to reach an understanding with the Infanta Isabella who, until this point, had been considered loyal to her royal half-brother.

It will be recalled that this princess was still a baby when her father died in 1454. At that time her mother retired from court to Arévalo and took her daughter with her. Here, remote from the confusion and corruption of court life, she passed a part of her childhood in a calm and religious atmosphere. Although King Henry required her to return to court in 1462, the impression of these early years was to be basic in the development of her fundamentally deeply religious character. With this went a profound reverence for the royal authority, which made the role of insurgency extremely repulsive to her. In spite of the fact that she may not have thought very much of Henry as a person, when approached by Villena, Carrillo, and the rest of the faction with an offer to the crown, she insisted first of all on an understanding with her brother. This was accomplished at a famous meeting between them at Toros de Guisando on September 19. By the terms of this understanding, Isabella was to be recognized as heiress to the crown with Joanna la Beltraneja next in line. A formula for Isabella's marriage was worked out by stating that it could only take place with the king's consent, the wishes of the infanta herself, and the advice of the marquis of Villena, the archbishop of Toledo, and the count of Plasencia.[15]

By this time the king of Aragon had already determined to act. Since the previous year, the Villena faction had been negotiating with John for a marriage between Ferdinand and a daughter of Villena. In May the Aragonese monarch had sent Pierres de Peralta and other agents to Castile with full powers to negotiate a marriage treaty. Peralta seems to have managed to avoid committing himself to either party in the Castilian civil war, although he was with the royal troops at the battle of Olmedo. However, the death of young Alfonso brought about such a change in the status of Isabella that John decided to make a proposal of marriage on behalf of Ferdinand directly to her. This, of course, was a shrewd move. Since there was a strong possibility that Isabella would now succeed her half-brother on the throne of Castile, this would mean a powerful ally for Aragon, now so deeply involved in the Catalan revolution. Furthermore, this was the only way John could counter the machinations of Louis, potentially hostile and a traditional ally of Castile. Such a marriage would probably break up the Franco-Castilian alliance and, with King Louis conveniently if temporarily involved in difficulties with Charles the Bold of Burgundy, there was likely to be no interference for the moment. Therefore, on July 17, 1468, Ferdinand made his formal proposal of marriage.

15. In describing the conference at Toros de Guisando, the *resumés* given by the contemporary chroniclers Palencia, Pulgar, and Valera are quite positive and consistent that Henry IV admitted that the queen was an adulteress and that the Infanta Joanna was not his daughter. In rebuttal, Ferrara states that the surviving document that describes the terms of the agreement is not nearly so clear as to the question of adultery. The illegitimacy of Joanna is vaguely *implied* only by a phrase in Article I of the agreement and nowhere referred to again. But Ferrara makes the point that even here we are not dealing with the original document, which has been destroyed. Our evidence comes from two later copies of the original, and Ferrara believes that the phrase referred to was inserted in the copies and did not exist in the original. Ferrara, pp. 238–44.

It was not a moment too soon. As soon as the reconciliation of Toros de Guisando had taken place, Henry began to consider the possibility of marrying his troublesome sister to the king of Portugal, and in this he was strongly seconded by the marquis of Villena, who, since Toros de Guisando, had been received at court and had once more resumed his previous influence. One has the feeling that both Villena and the king felt that the best place for Isabella was as far from Castile as possible. This must have been true for Henry if he ever expected la Beltraneja to succeed him. Meanwhile, Villena's return to the royal party had not endeared him to his uncle the archbishop. That energetic prelate now began to work with Peralta and the Aragonese mission as a strong proponent of the Aragonese match.

Since Isabella's recognition as heiress presumptive, she had not lacked for suitors. In addition to the king of Portugal, there was talk of an English prince, one of the brothers of Edward IV (although never specified, possibly Richard of Gloucester was the one referred to), and a really serious bid was put forward by Louis XI, who could deal with all sides. at the same time, for his brother the duke of Guienne, heir presumptive to the crown of France. But at this juncture Isabella seems to have favored Ferdinand—after all, they were of the same family, being first cousins, and he could hardly be called a foreigner, not at least as foreign as an English or a French prince. Furthermore, reports had it that he was comely, brave, supposedly the best horseman in his kingdom, and about the same age as herself. It is not difficult to see why she favored him above the others even though they had never met.

The negotiations proceeded more rapidly, therefore, and at the end of 1468 Peralta could write his master that everything was in order. In spite of the exorbitant demands of the princess' emissaries, the marriage documents were signed in their final form on March 5, 1469. They carefully maintained the separation of the two states; while both were to share in the administration of Castilian justice, Ferdinand was carefully excluded from any real power in the western kingdom, not even having the right to leave it to go to Aragon without "permission" from his wife. At the same time, Isabella was excluded from any share in the government of Aragon when Ferdinand should succeed there. It may be wondered why John of Aragon was willing to concede so much. But as I have tried to show, he needed help badly and he had no choice. He apparently thought that the price was not too high for what he was getting. As a matter of fact, there were no high or noble motives on either side, no brilliant historical insights, not even any references to what the future of the match might be. Both sides were engaged in violent struggles on a fairly low level. Each was seeking aid and each tended to see the other as a pawn in his schemes. Thus Ferdinand was doubtlesss seen by

Carrillo as little more than a piece in the complicated game he was playing in Castile, and Isabella was probably viewed by John of Aragon only in the light of his problems in Catalonia and the danger from France. Furthermore, in the summer of 1469 Isabella was in considerable personal danger from her brother and Villena and expected Ferdinand to get her out of it, as she so wrote him.

Aside from local dangers in Castile, the only possible obstacle to the marriage lay in the close family relations of the principal parties; papal dispensation usually took care of matters but in this case, owing to the Angevin sympathies of the pope, it proved hard to obtain and was not issued until several years after the marriage. To take care of the more legalistic minds in the clergy, and to remove the scruples of Isabella, a bull was forged purporting to have been issued by Pope Pius II in 1464. Although probably fooling no one, except perhaps Isabella, this spurious document did very well and took care of all matters until the papacy proved more pliant.

The Angevin victories of John of Calabria ceased by the end of 1469. Louis was still deeply involved with the duke of Burgundy and needed to use his money and soldiers nearer home. Therefore, he decided to resort to a more peaceful diplomacy directed toward reestablishing the traditional amity between France and Castile. To accomplish this purpose, he sent John Jouffroy, cardinal of Albi, as his personal ambassador to Henry IV. As a means of bringing about the renewal of the old alliance, he proposed a marriage between his brother Charles and the Infanta Isabella. Through some rather mysterious intrigues of Villena, the Cortes of Castile was induced to support this proposition, and Henry IV finally decided to agree to it. He therefore broke his previous treaty with Edward IV of England, and reached an understanding with Réné of Anjou. This created such a dangerous situation for Isabella that it may be termed one of the most critical moments of her life.

A few weeks previous to these events, she had transferred her residence from Ocaña to Madrigal. Here she found herself under such careful surveillance that practically everything she planned or did was reported to the marquis of Villena. Finding it impossible to prevent her marriage to Ferdinand by legal means, he decided on recourse to force, and had actually instructed Cardinal Mendoza to march to Madrigal with sufficient forces to effect the capture of the princess. Having no forces of her own to depend upon, the infanta now turned to Archbishop Carrillo, who had become a strong supporter of the Aragonese match. She was able to get word to him in time and it was his troops, not Mendoza's, that carried her off in triumph to Valladolid where she was received warmly by the citizens on August 30, 1469. From her new position of security she wrote two letters:

one to her brother justifying her actions, and a second to Ferdinand indicating the critical nature of the situation and appealing to him to claim his bride as quickly as possible. With the second letter was a formal embassy from the infanta led by Alfonso de Cárdenas, and the well-known chronicler Alonso de Palencia.

The ambassadors added their pressure to the urgent appeals in Isabella's letter, yet John II found his hands almost tied; the revolution in Catalonia had used up his treasury and his troops were involved there. The matter was laid before Ferdinand and the council and, in view of the dangerous position of Isabella, whose haven might be attacked by her enemies, it was decided to let Prince Ferdinand make the bridal journey *incognito*. He was to travel with very few followers so as to avoid capture while passing through hostile territory, mainly belonging to the Mendoza family, whose activities we have already encountered. The party left early in October, disguised as merchants, with Ferdinand acting as a servant who looked after horses, waited on table, and performed other menial tasks. On the second night, approaching the friendly city of Osma, they were mistaken for bandits and Ferdinand was nearly hit by a stone thrown from the walls. Fortunately, they were recognized in time and, from this point of the journey, they were able to travel with a considerable escort, which increased as they drew nearer to Valladolid. On the evening of October 15 Ferdinand was received at Isabella's quarters by Archbishop Carrillo, who formally presented him to his future wife. We are told that they had a private interview lasting more than two hours. The nuptials were celebrated three days later in the presence of Carrillo, Ferdinand's grandfather, the admiral of Castile (himself often a rebel), and a large number of their following. Preceding the ceremony, the archbishop solemnly read the forged papal bull granting these cousins the right to contract marriage. After a brief honeymoon spent in the city, the newlyweds dispatched an official announcement of their marriage to Henry IV in which they requested his formal approval and promised him their submission and loyalty. Henry's reply was curt and noncommital.

It is clear that of itself there was nothing new or remarkable in a marriage between the royal houses of Castile and Aragon. What made the nuptials of Valladolid so significant an event in the history of Spain and, indeed, of Europe and the future New World, lay in the special conditions in the Iberian peninsula and the general trends of the time. Unique in the annals of Iberian marriages was the fact that both parties might expect eventually to become reigning sovereigns in their own states. This meant, of course, that although the administrations of the two nations were to be kept strictly separate, they would follow parallel courses. The advantages coming from this situation were obvious and considerable. As will be shown, Ferdinand's role in the succession war with Portugal and the last war against the Moslems was exceedingly important; indeed, it seems doubtful if Castile could have succeeded in either war without his remarkable leadership. Isabella's influence in the affairs of Aragon is much less obvious, and it is clear that Ferdinand kept Aragonese matters firmly in his own hands; but he often copied her policies in internal affairs—the establishment of the famous rural police, the *Hermandad*, is a good example. The times, as has been observed several times, favored the creation of large political units; and, however separate the two administrations were to be during the era of the Catholic Kings, their successor reigning in both states might expect to rule over a powerful, unified collection of kingdoms—all of which did take place during the reign of Charles I. No one, in 1469, could have reasonably anticipated the formation of the great Spanish colonial empire but it is clear that, without the unified resources of the peninsula behind it, the government of Castile could hardly have taken advantage of the discoveries of Columbus, still less developed them so fully and so rapidly. Again we may cite the very important part Ferdinand played in the origin of the Age of Discovery, although much less publicized by later historians. In this, as in other matters, the two states complemented each other neatly: Castile providing the crusading spirit, the size and resources, and Aragon having the commercial experience and political know-how in dealing with overseas territories which she had developed in her long history of Mediterranean expansion.

The two sovereigns also complemented each other. Isabella, with her intense, fanatical faith, her stern sense of justice, and above all with her concern for the souls of her subjects, often seems to step directly out of the thirteenth century. On the other hand, Ferdinand seems very much the man of the Renaissance, and his concern for other peoples' territory, his deceit and duplicity, his egoism, strongly suggest the tyrants of northern Italy. Whatever quarrels and tensions these qualities produced, however incompatible they may have been in the boudoir, they worked beautifully together in the field of high policy. Thus Isabella was to provide the moral sanction to policies Ferdinand had often decided on for entirely different—and less worthy—reasons.

The marriage represented a great triumph for John of Aragon, although for the moment he got little out of it since Ferdinand and Isabella soon became so involved in Castile that they were able to offer little direct assistance to the old king of Aragon. Yet the years of constant intriguing in Castilian affairs carried on by the old man since his early youth had, in a way, borne fruit. For himself, these policies had accomplished little, but his son would continue them and expand them as king consort of Castile. Furthermore, John's policies had so accustomed the Castilians to the presence of Aragonese royalty that Ferdinand's position was made easier. The marriage was, therefore, an extension of John's earlier policies in Castile in different hands, and with slightly different methods.

Much of this, of course, is written with the advantage of historical hindsight. The situation could not have seemed anything like this to contemporaries. In fact, the immediate future of the famous couple was dark indeed. It was by no means clear that Isabella could overcome the opposition of her brother and some of the nobility to her rights of succession. The presence of la Beltraneja was a constant reminder that, if need be, there was another solution to the succession problem. Neither of them had any funds and thus were completely dependent on such uncertain forces as the archbishop of Toledo and his party. Furthermore, there was no guarantee in 1469 that John of Aragon would win his war in Catalonia. Had Ferdinand succeeded to a fragment of the realms of Aragon, or only in Sicily, it is possible that the history of the sixteenth century might have been quite different. Clearly then, much would depend on the courage and ability of Ferdinand and Isabella in the days to come if both were to obtain control in their own kingdoms. Only if, and when, this could be achieved were greater opportunities to await them.

# CHAPTER II

# The Administration of
# Ferdinand and Isabella

FERDINAND AND HIS WIFE HAD HOPED THAT HENRY IV MIGHT STILL be induced to accept their marriage and recognize Isabella as his successor, but such was not to be the case. Both the king of Castile and the king of France resented a marriage which they felt threatened them: Henry, perhaps because of jealousy of Ferdinand, dislike of Isabella, or affection for his daughter Joanna, whose chances for the throne had not been advanced by the marriage; Louis XI, because of his ambitions to acquire Cerdagne and Roussillon, which could only be done through cooperation with Castile, and a Castile in the hands of a son of John of Aragon was obviously going to be hostile. Once again the traditional Franco-Castilian alliance seemed about to reassert itself. Joanna la Beltraneja was again proclaimed by Henry to be the legitimate successor to the crown, and negotiations were opened for a marriage with the duke of Guienne, once considered a suitor for the hand of Isabella. The marriage was actually carried out by proxy, and recognized by some of the disloyal nobles, but death intervened. The duke broke with his brother, asked the pope to be relieved both of his oath of allegiance and his child bride, and turned for support to Louis' long-time enemy, Charles the Bold. However, before anything came of these developments, Guienne died on May 25, 1472. King Henry therefore was forced to look elsewhere for a son-in-law.

In rapid succession various candidates were considered, including Frederick of Naples (Ferrante's son) and Henry of Aragon (John's nephew), but the choice finally fell on Alfonso the African, king of Portugal, a strange and quixotic figure with a talent for knight-errantry. Meanwhile, the realm was in an uproar; public authority was virtually ignored, and the members of the nobility were able to carry out devastating raids upon each other with impunity. Andalusia, in particular, suffered from a violent feud between the Ponce de Leon and Guzman families, causing a considerable loss of life and damage to property. Both Ferdinand and Isabella continued their negotiations, however, hoping to achieve a reconciliation with Henry. He received Isabella in 1473 with apparent cordiality, and gave audience to the Infante Ferdinand at Epiphany the next year, but still held back from making any commitments. Shortly after this the marquis of Villena, long considered Isabella's chief opponent, died; but her enemies continued to intrigue against her. The end was not far off for Henry IV himself. He fell ill early in December and died in Madrid on December 11, 1474. Even in his last moments, he did not finally commit himself on the question of the succession. There was, apparently, no will, or if one existed it was destroyed; but some witnesses present later testified that he made a verbal statement asking that Joanna be considered the heiress of Castile. One need waste no great sympathy on Henry. He continued the worst policies of his father and left his kingdom in anarchy. Such might be his epitaph.

Who was the rightful successor? According to Merriman,

> There can be little doubt that she [Joanna] was the legal successor. She was unquestionably the daughter of the queen of Castile, born in the royal palace; and the allegations of her foes in regard to her paternity were never definitely proved. Finally, she had been formally acknowledged and sworn to by the Castilian Cortes as the heiress of the realm, and had been recognized as such by King Henry.[1]

On the other hand, Prescott felt that the early recognition of Joanna by the Cortes was due to pressure from Henry and placed great emphasis on the refusal of the later Cortes to take similar action. Comtemporaries were equally confused and, in the absence of any obvious answer to the question, were usually influenced by bribery, self-interest, or family loyalty. Of her own supreme rights, Isabella had no doubt. As soon as she had informed Ferdinand, who was in Aragon at the time, of her brother's death, she made arrangements for her immediate recognition as queen of Castile. This was done at Segovia on December 13. It should be noted that, while Ferdinand was proclaimed with her as king of Castile, it was only after Isabella's name that the title "queen proprietress" (*reina proprietaria*) was used. According to the marriage contract of 1469, Ferdinand's position was little more than king-consort.

Isabella's position was greatly strengthened by this formal act of accession. It was clear that she was acting for herself, and her energy and courage inspired admiration. Furthermore, she represented the

---

1. Merriman, II, 49.

cause of national unity and resistance to foreign intervention. By contrast, the Infanta Joanna, her rival, was still a child and her supporters were obviously dissident nobles in league with foreign interests. In a short time, Isabella was able to win over important adherents: by summer, many of the populous and important cities had followed the lead of Segovia and recognized her as sovereign. Beltrán de la Cueva, supposed father of Joanna, and the very important Mendoza family made their submission. According to the seventeenth century historian Mariana, a Cortes convoked at Segovia in February, 1475, recognized Isabella and swore allegiance to her.[2]

Perhaps only one person among the queen's immediate supporters was seriously disturbed by her elevation to the throne, but that person happened to be her husband. The sources for the period are not detailed enough to tell us whether Ferdinand had willingly accepted the marriage contract, or if he had signed it with reservations. However, in view of what happened, it might be inferred that he never liked it nor intended to abide by it. It is also possible that, on his return from Aragon, he was influenced by his Castilian relatives, particularly his grandfather, Don Fadrique. Whatever the motivation, Ferdinand now claimed the throne for himself as the nearest male Trastámara. One can only guess how the queen felt about this; the sources are silent. What is abundantly clear is that neither the queen herself, in spite of the deep affection she had for Ferdinand, nor the nation itself could accept this demand. Eventually a conference was held on the marriage contract with the advice and counsel of Cardinal Mendoza and Archbishop Carrillo. Although Isabella's sole right to the sovereignty was upheld, certain aspects of the contract were modified to give Ferdinand slightly more authority. Municipal and ecclesiastical appointments were to be made in the name of both sovereigns; justice was to be administered by them jointly when together, or separately by each one when apart. Royal proclamations were to bear both signatures, and both profiles were to appear on their coinage; and, last, their official seal was to display the united arms of Castile and Aragon with the motto *"Tanto monta, monta tanto, Isabel como Fernando,"* which certainly implied a complete

2. The great Spanish scholar and historian of the Counter-Reformation, Juan de Mariana (1535–1624), is the first to mention this meeting of the Cortes and there is some question as to what it was intended to do. Prescott has suggested that perhaps it was called to swear allegiance to the Infanta Isabella, oldest child of the sovereigns, who was born in 1470. Prescott, *History of the Reign of Ferdinand and Isabella the Catholic,* I, 143, note 7. Ballesteros holds that a Cortes did meet in Segovia to sanction Isabella's accession to the throne of Castile, Antonio Ballesteros y Beretta, *Historia de España y su influencia en la historia universal,* 12 vols., (Barcelona, 1922), Vol. III, 652.

equality. Whether this satisfied Ferdinand or not, it was the best he could get and he did not raise the issue again.

But the greatest danger came from Alfonso the African, who had been promised la Beltraneja by Henry IV some time before his death. Filled with excitement at the prospect of a new crown, and a war to be made notable by his knightly deeds and heroic actions, Alfonso made haste to claim his betrothed. Having previously been promised support by Louis XI, who enjoyed interfering in the involved politics south of the Pyrenees, the king of Portugal invaded western Castile in May of 1475 with a small army. While Ferdinand and Isabella seemed virtually helpless, he was able to join forces with the Villena faction (now led by the son of the dead marquis) and took possession of the Infanta Joanna to whom he was now formally engaged, notwithstanding the fact that his future bride had barely reached thirteen. He was also strongly supported by Isabella's good friend, the archbishop of Toledo. That touchy prelate had been angered by a real or imagined slight from Ferdinand; and in spite of everything mutual friends could do, even including letters from John II of Aragon and appeals from the queen, he now seceded to the Portuguese, boasting that he would soon reduce the queen to her former status of infanta.

The campaign opened disastrously for the Castilian cause. Although Alfonso failed to push his opening advantages, he occupied some of the frontier provinces and his opponents found the greatest difficulty in gettting sufficient funds or soldiers. However, after the Cortes of Medina del Campo in August, Isabella received a promise of financial assistance from the Church, and with these funds it was possible to raise and train additional troops. So passed the autumn and winter. Alarmed at the growing strength of his enemies, Alfonso also summoned help from his kingdom; his son, the Infante John, eventually arrived with reinforcements. Ferdinand was anxious to settle the campaign by a decisive engagement, but "the African" showed a certain reluctance; however, when Ferdinand moved to cut off his communications from Portugal by a march in the direction of Zamora on the Duero, Alfonso had to fight, and the result was the battle of Toro on March 1, 1476—"a noble combat of the ancient sort" by which the writer meant that swords and axes decided the day rather than such new-fangled unchivalric equipment as guns and arquebuses.[3] The archbishop of Toledo, it might be pointed out, commanded the Portuguese right wing. Both kings were heavily involved in the fighting, which was of the fiercest sort. The Portuguese had the worst of

3. Ferdinand had been in such haste to close with the enemy that he had left his own cannon behind as well as a part of the soldiery. The whole battle probably did not involve much more than six thousand men on both sides.

it; although, when night and a cloudburst had put an end to the fighting, a part of the Portuguese troops led by Prince John retreated to a small hill and remained there throughout the night. The following day Alfonso the African started back for his own country, accompanied by his thirteen-year-old fiancée. Thus all the strategic honors remained with Castile, and throughout the kingdom the battle of Toro was celebrated as a great victory.

But the king of Portugal was not yet ready to give up so easily. In spite of strong opposition in his councils and in his own family, he now determined to travel personally to France for an interview with Louis XI. Although he was received with all honor and many celebrations, he found it impossible to get very much out of the Valois, who very probably had recognized, by now, the crackpot nature of Alfonso's schemes. Disappointed in France, therefore, he resolved to visit his cousin and Louis' great enemy, Charles the Bold. After spending the winter with the duke, he was back in Paris early in 1477, and hoped to mediate the final differences between Charles and Louis; however, he was appalled to receive news of the duke's death at the hands of the Swiss at the battle of Nancy.

After waiting some months more in Paris, and sending word home that he intended to abdicate, Alfonso was finally persuaded to leave France and resume his crown, and this he did. Once more tempted by the prospects of a fame which had so far eluded him, he raised another army and invaded Castile again in 1479. But his time Ferdinand and Isabella were much stronger, and had already commenced their great work of reconstruction in the two realms. All that Alfonso could manage was to fight one inconclusive battle at Albuera on February 28, 1479.

Negotiations for a permanent peace had already begun, and were concluded by the treaties of Alcaçovas, signed in September of the same year. One treaty dealt with dynastic issues: Alfonso agreed to withdraw his claims to the Castilian crown although the Spaniards who had assisted him were to receive full pardon from the queen. The eldest daughter of Ferdinand and Isabella, the Infanta Isabella, was to marrry the Infante Alfonso, grandson of Alfonso the African. As for Joanna la Beltraneja, still the youthful fiancée of the Portuguese king, she was to be given the choice of marrying the Infante John (only son of Ferdinand and Isabella) or becoming a nun. Poor Joanna, the casualty of history, does not seem to have spent too much time coming to a decision. She promptly took the veil and entered the monastery of Santa Clara at Coimbra. Although she never again exercised political influence, she lived for many years in semi-royal state at the convent and died in 1530 at the age of sixty-nine when all the figures of her turbulent childhood had long gone and Spain was ruled by a foreign dynasty.

The second agreement involved, among other things, a kind of "demarcation" of colonial activities. Portugal recognized Castile's rights to the Canary Islands, while Castile recognized the rights of Portugal to other islands in the Atlantic and also to the coast of Africa—a kind of anticipation of the later treaties of Tordesillas. Thus with the ending of the Portuguese war, a ten-year period came to a close, during which Isabella finally and firmly established her full rights to the crown. Luck, of course, had played a certain part in it; death conveniently removed several obstacles from her path. Her own determination and courage were also major factors. But without the support of her husband, his determination equal to her own, and his leadership on the field of battle, it seems doubtful she could have done it.

2

The same year that saw the final recognition of Isabella's rights to her own crown brought Ferdinand into possession of his. At the time of the marriage, it will be recalled that the old king of Aragon had been too deeply involved to do much more than send Ferdinand his blessing. However, the sudden death of John of Calabria, leader of the foreign troops in Catalonia, had given King John's affairs a sudden turn for the better. With his usual diplomatic skill, the old man had negotiated treaties of alliance with Naples and Burgundy in hopes of keeping Louis XI too busy at home to promise additional aid to the Catalan rebels. Throughout 1471 he steadily advanced and during the first part of 1472 the area controlled by the rebels steadily decreased. In Barcelona, morale was worsening. Although an illegitimate son of John of Calabria remained in the city as the representative of his late father's interests, he quarrelled constantly with the city administration. Appeals to Louis XI first elicited a favorable response, but that sovereign was soon forced to defend himself from another attack by the duke of Burgundy, who invaded Vermandois and laid siege to Beauvais. At the same time the new pope, Sixtus IV, was much under the influence of Cardinal Rodrigo Borgia who, as a native of Valencia, was favorable to the royal cause in Catalonia.

Gold played a considerable part in John's offensive in 1472; through its persuasions, some of the previous leaders of the revolt were induced to rejoin the forces of the crown. Moreover, John offered mild and generous terms to the towns that now began to surrender rapidly to the royal forces. Barcelona was soon under direct siege and it did not prove difficult to bring about the final terms of the surrender. John II made his formal entry into the captured city on October 17, 1472, and the Catalan revolt was at last over after a decade of the most violent strife.

There now remained the problem of the French in Cerdagne and Roussillon. Soon after the fall of Barcelona, the royal forces pressed into the provinces and brought about a temporary recovery. Louis was able to involve Charles the Bold in a war with the Swiss and could again turn his attention to affairs in the south. France recovered the two provinces in 1475 and their incorporation into Spain was reserved for the future. Hostility to the Aragonese Trastámaras was one reason why Louis allied with Alfonso the African in the Portuguese war. However, when the shrewd French monarch realized the fantastic nature of Alfonso's policies, and his life-long struggle with Burgundy reached its climax, common sense dictated reaching some kind of permanent settlement with the Trastámaras. An agreement on many outstanding issues was finally signed between Louis XI and Isabella at Saint Jean de Luz on October 9, 1478. Both sides agreed to renounce earlier agreements against each other; of particular interest was the specific prohibition of treaties or "confederations" between the Trastámaras and the Archduke Maximilian of Austria, future grandfather, as it were, of the Spanish Habsburg dynasty. As Merriman aptly remarked, " ... thus the Franco-Aragonese quarrel of the past began to be transformed into the Franco-Spanish struggle of the future."[4]

It would be pleasant to write that, with the end of the Catalan revolution, peace descended on the realms of the crown of Aragon; unfortunately, this was not the case. The strong hand needed to bring order out of the chaos of ten years of civil war was wanting. John II was either too old, or too involved in the conflict over Cerdagne and Roussillon, to give the necessary attention to the complex problems of his states. In Catalonia, the *remença* problem still remained and there still continued the quarrels between the landowners and the peasants that had been one of the factors in the revolution. The royal government insisted that the peasants must meet their dues and rents owing to the landlords; to silence further protests Verntallat, one of the *remeçsa* leaders, was simply bought off by making him a feudal lord. Thus after 1472 nothing was done to solve the problems of the principality. In Aragon and Valencia there were violent feuds between hostile members of the aristocracy which the government was able to contain only with the greatest difficulty. And in Aragon proper there was almost a breakdown between John and his last Cortes. All in all, it was felt by many that only a change of ruler

4. Merriman, II, 59.

could bring about a turn for the better. This was not long delayed. Even into his eightieth year, John showed remarkable energy and still pursued his favorite sport of hunting, but his time was running out. His last boar hunt had to be broken off in mid-December 1478, and he returned to Barcelona a sick man. His last public appearance was on Christmas day in the cathedral for the services, and immediately afterwards he became much worse. On January 18, 1479, realizing that his end was near, he dictated a pious letter to Ferdinand urging him to disregard the world and its kingdoms and keep always in his mind the fear of God—a noble thought, but somewhat inconsistent with a life constantly in disregard of such sentiments. He died the next morning between seven and eight o'clock.

For those who believed that the duty of a prince was to increase his power as much as he could and by any means, John II of Aragon was a successful prince. Few in the complex fifteenth century would have recognized any other criteria for judging a ruler, as Machiavelli was later to point out. By such standards John was no worse that Louis XI, Charles the Bold, Edward IV, and most of the contemporary popes; in the long run he probably had more than his share of success, and his achievements influenced the era of the Catholic Kings about to begin.

At the end of the first Portuguese campaign, Ferdinand and Isabella now felt strong enough to begin the work of reform and restoration that was to be their greatest achievement. It will not surprise the reader to learn that this was chiefly done in Castile. Not only because the western kingdom was the larger and more powerful, but also because the chances of restoring the royal authority were better here. The Castilian crown based its claims on Roman law and divine right; Ferdinand himself favored this preponderance, and probably never forgot his early unpleasant experience with popular liberties in Gerona and Barcelona. It was not a case of Isabella's getting the upper hand over Ferdinand in some family *coup de main;* they seemed in complete agreement on this point and it should be noted that, while Valladolid or sometimes Madrid served the Catholic Kings as a joint capital, it was never Saragossa or Barcelona. Thus as the Spanish imperium expanded throughout the world during the sixteenth century, it was founded principally on the institutions of Castile and what Ferdinand and Isabella made of them.[5]

On the other hand, in regard to the personal position of the rulers in the union, Ferdinand was a more significant figure than Isabella. As the revised  marriage contract had provided, he had a share in

5. There are, of course, exceptions. The institution of the viceroy in the colonial system seems to have been borrowed directly from Aragon.

the government of Castile, although according to strict interpretation of the contract, a small one. In actual practice, his share was much greater. In addition to the influence that a man like Ferdinand might be expected to have over a wife who loved him, there were certain functions, such as those in the military sphere, that a king could perform much better than a queen. Furthermore, after Ferdinand took over the Castilian military orders, his influence was greatly enhanced. Isabella, however, seems to have had no corresponding authority in Aragon. Therefore, in a sense, both realms were united through their common sovereign who was Ferdinand, not Isabella.[6]

The most important work was done during a period marked, roughly, by the end of the first Portuguese campaign and the opening of the Granadine War. It was indeed time, for the very structure of the state seemed to be dissolving into total anarchy. According to a contemporary account cited by Merriman,

> So corrupt and abominable were the customs of these realms that every one was left free to follow his own devices without fear of reprehension or punishment: and so loosely were the conventions of civilized society observed that men practically relapsed into savagery, in such fashion that the wise and prudent deemed it next to impossible to bring order out of such chaos, or regulation out of such confusion; for no justice was left in the land. The common people were exterminated, the crown property alienated, the royal revenues reduced to such slight value that it causes me shame to speak of it.[7]

To make the crown as strong as possible was, therefore, the prime requisite, but this could be done in various ways. The policies chosen by the queen and her husband were generally conservative in that they were based on whatever traditions, history, institutions, and customs would serve the purpose of increasing the crown's power; this procedure was always preferred over the creation of something completely new. They were renovators, not revolutionists. More specifically, they attempted to increase their revenues, to govern more effectively, to establish an efficient and strong administration of justice (which had virtually collapsed), to curb the irresponsiblity of the aristocracy, and to increase the general prosperity of the country. These points will now be covered briefly while larger topics such as religion and colonization will be reserved for separate chapters.

In every fifteenth century monarchy, a large part of the royal revenues came from the crown lands. The conflict between the

6. Konetzke, p. 70.

7. Diego de Valera, *Forma en que estos reynos quedaron al tiempo que los serenísimos prínciples comenzaron a reynar* quoted in Merriman, II, 98–99. See also Note 1 in ibid, p. 99. Valera (1412–1487) was a contemporary chronicler who was a strong supporter of Isabella and a severe critic of Henry IV. His *Memorial de diversas hazañas* was published in *Biblioteca de Autores Españoles* (Madrid, 1846–80).

monarchs and the aristocracy for control of these lands is a special aspect of that social and economic revolution which swept through western and central Europe in the fifteenth century. However, in the countries of northern Europe the middle class was strong enough to act as a buffer (although inclining somewhat toward the crown) between the two contending forces and thus acted to moderate the confrontation. Unfortunately, in Spain, and especially in Castile, the relatively "low density" of the bourgeoisie made it difficult to play this role, and consequently, the clash between crown and aristocracy was more direct and catastrophic.[8]

In Castile, a process of alienation of crown lands had gone on, with varying results, ever since the civil wars over the infantes de la Cerda in the thirteenth century. However, the losses in land and revenue (the latter in the form of pensions granted to nobles) during the reigns of John II and Henry IV far exceeded all other reigns. By the accession of Isabella practically all of Andalusia was controlled by a few noble houses and the archbishopric of Toledo. During most of the fifteenth century, the key to the sordid internal history of Castile is the desire of the nobility to keep or extend their enormous fortunes in land, flocks, and economic privileges. To do this, they plunged the country into repeated civil wars of increasing violence.[9]

The Catholic Kings were determined to recover a portion of these lands and revenues; indeed, without the additional revenue it is difficult to see how their other projects could have been carried out. On the other hand, it would be highly anachronistic to read into their legislation a fundamental social reform such as that carried out against the French nobility by the Estates General of 1789. No one in the fifteenth century could contemplate a social structure without an aristocracy, least of all Ferdinand and Isabella.

The question of the recovery of crown property was discussed by the Cortes of Madrigal in 1476, but definite action was postponed. At the Cortes of Toledo in 1480, famous for the extensive reforms enacted, the municipal delegates begged the rulers, perhaps with some advance coaching, to recover the lost lands and pensions. As a result, a special summons was issued to the nobles most involved to appear at the Cortes and justify their acquistions. After negotiations of considerable complexity, a formula was worked out in consultation with Cardinal Mendoza and Hernando de Talavera, the queen's very influential and highly respected confessor. This formula required the surrender of lands seized illegally after 1464, meaning that the nobles gave up about half their income acquired after that date.[10] However,

---

8. Vicens Vives, *Approaches to the History of Spain*, p. 68.
9. Ibid., pp. 76–78.
10. Vicens Vives, *Economic History of Spain*, p. 295.

the Act of Resumption specifically confirmed the aristocracy in the possession of land acquired before 1464, which meant that very generous profits made by the Castilian nobility were left untouched.[11] In the case of pensions and annuities, those who had received them without performing any services in return lost them without compensation; those who had purchased annuities were to surrender them in return for reimbursement; others might retain a portion of their pensions based on the value of the actual services performed. The fact that the final arrangements were placed in the hands of Talavera shows how anxious the queen was to deal fairly with those who had just claims to land or income. In spite of this, the queen remained sensitive to those questions throughout the rest of her life, and it is worth noticing that she left a sum in her last will and testament to satisfy those who had a claim against the crown in this matter.

There is no doubt that these measures helped to end the civil war, pacified the country, and brought the nobles, *politically* at least, under the authority of the crown. But there is another side to these policies that recent historians have not been slow to point out. Economically and socially, the crown virtually surrendered all power to the nobility. With their principal economic activity enjoying the special privileges granted by the state to the Mesta, and their virtual monopoly of land not seriously threatened by the reforms of 1480, the final step was taken by the Laws of Toro of 1505, which permitted the founding of *mayorazgos* or entailed estates that could never be alienated. By this time, the privileged classes, either lay or clerical, had a death grip on the economy of Castile.[12] This eventually led to an informal alliance between the crown and the nobility at a time when the reverse was taking shape in the most progressive European states. All in all, it does not seem an overstatement to say, as does Vicens Vives, that the reforms of 1480

> served only to ratify the absolute social and economic control of the noble class over the state and the rest of the country. The known figures could not be more conclusive: about 1500 the nobles owned 97 per cent of the territory of the Peninsula either directly or by jurisdiction. This is the same as saying that 1.5 per cent of the population owned almost the entire Spanish territory. This fact is of capital importance.[13]

Although the long-range effects were deleterious, the immediate results of the reforms of 1480 were felt at once and were financially

---

11. Henry Kamen, *The Spanish Inquisition* (London, 1965), pp. 14–15.

12. Vicens Vives, *Economic History of Spain*, p. 295. The situation was not so critical in Aragon where Ferdinand's reforms (Sentence of Guadalupe, 1486) effectively gave the peasant control over his land. According to Vicens Vives, some 50,000 got access to a "fair-sized property". Ibid., p. 294.

13. Ibid.

beneficial to the state. In 1479 the national revenues of Castile were estimated at 885,000 reals. In 1482, two years after the resumption, the same author puts them at 12,711,591 reals; and for 1504, the year of Isabella's death, the figure given is 26,287,324.[14] Some of the greatest families were forced to return sizable amounts, and it is a measure of the integrity of the queen's advisors that the family of Cardinal Mendoza (the Toledos), who had helped to conclude the final arrangements, made one of the largest restitutions. One modern authority estimates the value in *maravedís*[15] of the surrendered properties of the four greatest nobles as follows:

| | |
|---|---|
| Admiral Enríquez | 240,000 |
| Duke of Alba (Toledo) | 575,000 |
| Marqués of Cádiz | 573,000 |
| Duke of Albuquerque (Beltrán de la Cueva) | 1,400,000[16] |

It is interesting to note, as an example of the essential conservatism of the rulers, that in spite of the constant and increasing demands for money as required by the expanding policies of the sovereigns, only two new sources of revenue were developed during the entire thirty years' reign of Isabella. The first of these was the income from the Indies, and the second was the well-known *cruzada*. This last was originally established by the Church as a system of indulgences whereby those who contributed to the costs of the Granadine War could obtain immunity from purgatory; it was continued long after the end of the war and became a regular source of revenue, even collected from places as remote from Granada as the New World. A meeting of the Cortes in 1512 complained bitterly against this form of taxation.

An old tax greatly expanded was the famous *alcabala*, long established as a sales tax. In 1491 its imposition and collection became the subject of elaborate regulations. Previously it was levied against all classes. As the result of Isabella's insistence, the members of the clergy were, for the first time, exempted. It remained at ten per cent throughout the reign.

14. Joseph Calmette, *La Formation de l'unité espagnole* (Paris, 1946), p. 207.

15. The value of certain Spanish coins is a technical and intricate subject. The *maravedí* was the most important Castilian money of account, and most royal revenues are expressed in it; later in the seventeenth century, the ducat was used for reckoning. There were approximately 375 *maravedís* to the ducat during the time of Ferdinand and Isabella. R. Trevor Davies, *The Golden Century of Spain*, 1501–1621 (London, 1937), pp. 297–98. See also Elliott, *The Revolt of the Catalans*, Appendix I, A note on coinage, pp. 553–55, and Vicens Vives, *An Economic History of Spain*, pp. 281–82.

16. Mariéjol, p. 31.

The administrative center of Isabella's government was the Council of Castile, and what she did with it affected Spanish administration for the next three hundred years. This council was an outgrowth or extension of the old *curia regis* of the earlier kings. We have already noticed the importance it assumed during the reigns of John I and Henry III. Isabella revised its membership to reduce the aristocratic influence and added greatly to its functions. Some changes were made at the Cortes of Madrigal in 1476, but in 1480 the council achieved its final form at the Cortes of Toledo, so important for its support of the royal reform program. The membership was now fixed at one prelate, three nobles, and eight or nine *letrados,* meaning middle class legists. This majority of non-noble persons pretty well established its royalist, anti-feudal character. Originally called the royal council, it later became known as the Council of Castile (*consejo de Castilla),* or often more simply "our council" (*nuestro consejo).* Rooms were assigned to it in the various royal residences on the assumption that its proper place was to be as close to the sovereign as possible; and, when the court was on tour, it usually traveled along. It met daily except Sundays and special religious holidays; usually its meetings were in the morning from six to ten, Easter to mid-October, and for the rest of the year from nine to twelve. Its competence was of the broadest sort. It had the authority to summon anyone and its regulations applied to all. Generally concerned with all matters of administration, it was particularly interested in questions of finance, royal marriages, succession problems, legal matters, and relations of Church and state. In short, there was virtually no issue that might not come before the powerful Council of Castile. Since most of its opinions were given in writing, and since it corresponded independently with officers and institutions throughout the kingdom, it began that extensive documentation that was to be one of the chief characteristics of Spanish administration under the Habsburgs. Other councils were set up as the reign progressed, but there was no question about the pre-eminence of the Council of Castile. As Merriman has stated:

> The Consejo de Castilla continued to vindicate its position at the head of the great conciliar system whose ramification is the salient feature of Spanish constitutional development during the next three centuries; under the king it was the supreme power in the Spanish Empire of which, as time went by, Castile became more and more unquestionably the centre.[17]

A discussion of the other councils used by the Catholic Kings in Castile involves difficulties. While some were clearly new and set up for specific purposes, the establishment of others was not nearly

17. Merriman, II, 118.

so definite. It is not always clear at this distance whether we are dealing with a really separate organ or merely a commission or branch of the Council of Castile.[18] Of the new ones set up for special purposes, we can be sure of the council of the military orders, the council for the *Santa Hermandad,* and one established to supervise the Inquisition known as the *Suprema.* The first was the logical outcome of the crown's control of the three military orders; united under the sovereign (in this case Ferdinand), they needed some sort of coordinating organ, and a council was the way Ferdinand and Isabella preferred to deal with such extensions of executive authority. From their point of view, a council had obvious advantages over a minister. It provided a wider sweep of opinion, and prevented any one man from monopolizing power, doubtless a major consideration with rulers as jealous of their authority as the Catholic Kings. The council of the military orders is often listed as a creation of Charles I, but there are references to it in 1515 and 1516 which puts it definitely, though barely, in the previous reign. The council of the *Suprema* was set up in 1483 ostensibly to supervise and to hear appeals from inquisitorial courts. It was made up of the grand inquisitor, three other ecclesiastics, and two doctors of law.

With others, matters are much less clear. Talavera, writing to the queen in 1493, distinguished three councils: those of state, justice, and finance. Here it seems justice refers to the Council of Castile. The council of state, or the "secret council" as it was sometimes called, seems to have been a highly informal body without any regularly established membership. It met, when called, with King Ferdinand, and its field was chiefly foreign affairs. As might be expected, this informal body retained a considerable aristocratic tinge inasmuch as diplomats were usually of noble extraction. Whether we should speak of a council of finance *(hacienda)* in this period or not is again difficult to decide. There was undoubtedly a group of specialists from the treasury functioning to advise the crown in the use of public monies. During the reign of Charles I it undoubtedly was a separate body, but in this period it may have been regarded as a branch or commission of the Council of Castile.

The same situation applies to the famous Council of the Indies. Clearly, it was established in its final form in 1524, but did it exist as a separate council in the previous reign? After Columbus' first voyage, their majesties turned problems connected with him and the mysterious lands of the Indies to an old and faithful servant, Bishop Fonseca, and various agents and commissioners. As details multiplied in volume and complexity, they established the House of Trade (*Casa*

18. Mariéjol, pp. 149–55.

*de Contratación)* in 1503. According to Mariéjol, a major authority on this epoch, Fonseca was allowed to have an assisting council in 1511.[19] Thus it would seem that 1524 was merely the final date in a long process of organization that began with the Catholic Kings.

These were the most significant of the administrative organs directly dependent on the crown of Castile. One other might be briefly mentioned: the Council of the *Hermandad,* or rural police force. However, this body hardly deserves inclusion among the previous ones since it was of so brief a life, being established for twenty-two years only. It should also be noted in this connection that Ferdinand established his own council in Aragon in which each state of the kingdom was represented by two lawyers, in addition to a few other officials. This marked the beginning of another phase of the Spanish conciliar movement—namely, regionalism. Under both Charles and Philip, a certain number of councils were added whose duties were not so much functional as geographical. Of these the Council of Aragon must be considered a prototype.

In addition to these councils, there were certain high officers of state who played a major or lesser role according to their positions, personalities, and the policy of the sovereigns. Chief of these was the chancellor, who had charge of all major documents and the royal seals. Both Mendoza and later Cardinal Cisneros made this office an important one, largely because of their own overwhelming personalities; later in the sixteenth century it declined, especially under a ruler like Philip II, who did not like strong personalities about him. The Constable of Castile had been set up in 1382 in imitation of a similar French office; this officer was a kind of generalissimo. In 1473 it became permanently established in the Velasco family and declined in importance. The Grand Admiral of Castile had charge of naval matters, war, trade, and commerce. He set up admiralty courts, could issue letters of marque, and in general functioned like a naval secretary. At this time it was considered an important and lucrative post. During a considerable part of the reign, it was held by Fadrique Enríquez, Ferdinand's grandfather, and later by his uncle. After the Age of Discovery, it was pretty well overshadowed by newer colonial offices and declined in importance.

Among the confidential and influential advisors of the crown during this period was Juan de Coloma, an Aragonese, who advised Ferdinand on matters of foreign policy, but who was also useful in other ways—for instance, it was he who drew up the contract with Columbus. Another figure in Ferdinand's entourage was Miguel Pérez de Almazan. He was a specialist in Italian affairs; and as foreign affairs

19. Mariéjol, pp. 149–55.

came to predominate more and more in the king's thoughts, he had more influence with him than anyone else. Cardinal Mendoza of the great Toledo family was a major figure at the Castilian court, in spite of the fact that initially he had been hostile to the queen. However, he eventually became one of her strongest supporters.

Mendoza is a good example of a type of warlike prelate, more soldier and statesman than priest, who is frequently met with in the eleventh and twelfth centuries, but who had largely disappeared from regions north of the Iberian peninsula. Born in 1428, the fourth son of the marquis of Santillana, Pedro González de Mendoza began his ecclesiastical career in 1452 when he was appointed bishop of Calahorra. In the wars of Henry IV, in which he took an active part, he commanded the troops of Calahorra, and was wounded at Olmedo fighting on the side of the queen. As the result of a love affair with a Portuguese lady-in-waiting of the queen, he had two sons who achieved a certain notoriety, one as a prospective husband of Lucretia Borgia, and the second as the grandfather of the famous princess of Eboli. In 1468 he was made bishop of Sigüenza and later, because of his services to Henry IV, he was made chancellor of Castile and cardinal archbishop of Seville in 1473. We have seen how Mendoza nearly captured Isabella at Madrigal in 1469. In spite of this inauspicious beginning, he made his peace with her after Henry's death and, at the battle of Toro, he fought on her side. His influence then grew steadily because of his powerful personality, ability, and acute intelligence. In 1482 he became archbishop of Toledo and primate of Spain. For the rest of his life his influence at court was so great that he was sometimes popularly known as the "third king." It is typical of his martial background that he took an active part in the conquest of Granada, although he was in his late sixties. Among other establishments, he founded the college of Santa Cruz at Valladolid. When he was stricken at Guadalajara by his last illness in 1494–5, Isabella moved her court to the neighborhood of the city so as to be near her faithful servant. Although from one of the greatest families of Spain, on his death bed he advised the queen not to bestow the archbishopric of Toledo on a powerful noble. He was not immune from the vices of the age, yet there is a certain grandeur about Cardinal Mendoza which makes him, along with other figures of the age of Ferdinand and Isabella, loom larger than life across the vistas of history. After his death, Mendoza was succeeded at Toledo by the famous Jiménes de Cisneros, who will be discussed later.

The last of the great ecclesiastics who helped mold official policy was Hernando de Talavera, a man of humble background and for some twenty years a monk of the monastery of Santa Maria del Prado. His proximity to Valladolid, often a residence of Isabella, and his reputation for sanctity led the queen to make him her confessor, always an important post, and especially so with a devout soul such as Isabella. Here his mild and gentle spirit was used to good advantage to moderate the sometimes stern religiosity of the queen. His most effective work was done at Granada, where he became archbishop after the conquest, but unfortunately he was not allowed to continue long enough to achieve the success his policies most certainly foreshadowed. Later, under the fanatical Cisneros, his work was entirely destroyed.

In addition to these important figures that surrounded the throne, no description of the administration of Castile under the Catholic Kings would be complete without a brief reference to certain secondary, but important, offices. Chief of these was that of *corregidor*, basically a representative of the crown in cities and towns. In spite of complaints at the Cortes of Madrigal, it was decided four years later at the meeting of Toledo to send them out to all the municipalities of Castile. In 1500 the institution was regularized with an elaborate description of duties and functions. These were mainly concerned with watching over financial affairs, enforcing the laws, and keeping an eye on the municipal lands. In this way it was hoped that the powerful tendencies to separatism might be checked and the various kingdoms with their divergent laws and customs brought under one supreme central authority. Spain never did develop a unity comparable to France, but without the *corregidores* the situation might have been a good deal worse. They were as important in the absolutism of the Catholic Kings as the *intendants* were in the government of Richelieu in the seventeenth century. Less important roles were played by the *pesquisidores* who were sent out to watch over municipal courts, and the *veedores* who served as inspectors reporting directly to the crown; both officials were also expected to watch secretly over the *corregidores* and report any irregularities.

The administration of justice was of great concern to Isabella and she did everything to improve its services. Doubtless after the internal anarchy of the two previous reigns there was much to be done. An *audiencia,* or high court, had been set up at Valladolid in 1480, but was soon so clogged with business that more were needed. A subsidiary court was established in Galicia in 1486, and a second *audiencia* was appointed for Ciudad Real in 1494. After the fall of Granada, a third *audiencia* was set up for that city in 1505. After 1494 the courts in Valladolid and Ciudad Real were known as *chancillerías.* There was also a steady increase in the number of royal judges, and an expansion of the duties of the *procurador fiscal,* or royal prosecutor. The Cortes of Toledo also took up the question of a general recodification of laws. It was decided to entrust this work to Doctor

Alfonso Diaz de Montalvo, a well-known jurist. After four years of work he succeeded in making some headway against the chaos and confusion of Castilian legal practices, and his *Royal Ordinances* were published in 1485. It is interesting to note that they were printed—one of the early examples of this technique in Spain. Although Dr. Montalvo's work was incomplete, it was in extensive use down to the era of Philip II.

In regard to economic policies, the major aim was to create an adequate supply of gold and silver for the needs of the state. Since the wars of unification and expansion had created a great need for bullion, the sovereigns tried hard to keep it from leaving the country. Thus the Cortes of Toledo forbade its export. In a manner strongly suggestive of twentieth century legislation on the same subject, an emigrating Spaniard had to make two declarations of the amount of gold and silver he was taking with him; one, to the *corregidor* of his home town, and a second to officials at the frontier. In this way a double check was secured against falsification. Foreigners were forbidden after 1491 to take more money out of the kingdom than they had brought in.

The attitude of the government toward trade and commerce was protectionist enough to delight the heart of any modern practitioner of autarchy. Export was strongly encouraged, especially the products of the native woolen industry, while imports were discouraged. To stimulate the textile industry, the sovereigns decreed that no more than two-thirds of the fine native raw wool could be exported, while at the same time they prohibited the importation of foreign cloth. For a time these measures showed results. Enjoying a brisk trade with the Low Countries, the Castilian woolen industry flourished, the period between 1480 to 1500 being its high point. Unfortunately, this prosperity was short-lived, falling a victim to the unwise fiscal policies and enormous needs of the Habsburg sovereigns of the sixteenth century. Shipping received a good deal of attention from Ferdinand and Isabella. In 1495 shipping interests were offered a large bonus for building ships of six hundred tons or over. Five years later, loading of foreign ships was forbidden if Spanish vessels were available, and a *pragmática* of the next year prohibited the sale of a Spanish ship in a foreign port. Once again there were temporary advantages to the Spanish merchant marine in these policies, but, as in the case of the woolen industry, favorable conditions did not outlast the sixteenth century or even half of it.

Coinage was always a serious problem for medieval states and Castile was no exception. Both rulers inherited a fearful monetary confusion when they took over their respective governments. There was a wide variety of coins in circulation, many private persons had the right to issue coins, and there was much counterfeiting. As early as 1471, attempts were made to end some of these evils but were generally unsuccessful because of inadequate enforcement procedures. The Cortes of Madrigal made a considerable reform when it reduced the number of persons having the right to coin money from one hundred and fifty to five. In 1493 in Aragon, and in 1497 in Castile, the sovereigns carried through to a successful conclusion their previous, tentative efforts at monetary reform. For the western kingdom, they now issued a new gold ducat, copied after the famous Venetian coin of the same name. The silver real was increased in value in terms of maravedís, and the amount of silver in the vellon coinage (basically copper) was reduced from ten to seven grains. This reform was important for it established a tradition of sound money in Castile that was followed, on the whole, throughout the sixteenth century.[20] All this was helpful to industry and for a time it prospered, but, in the words of Konetzke, "It did not achieve anywhere near sufficient strength to meet the necessities of the country and, at the same time, satisfy the increasing production requirements of the colonies."[21]

In the fourteenth century gold came into the peninsula from the Sudan via the ports of Málaga and Almería and thence to Granada. In the early fifteenth century after the Majorcans had reached the coast of Senegal, Castilian traders began to voyage along the African coast in search for gold, slaves, and ivory. In this new development the most important way station was the Canary Islands and the route thus developed went from Senegal to the Canaries to Cádiz. The larger share of this gold went into the pockets of the Genoese, who had established an important financial colony in Seville.[22] A lesser part went to Medina del Campo, where it served to pay for the luxury goods brought into the famous fairs of that city. What was finally left

20. Earl J. Hamilton, *American Treasure and the Price Revolution in Spain, 1501–1650* (Cambridge, 1934), pp. 51–53.

21. Konetzke, p. 101.

22. This colony began in a small way in the fourteenth century. In the second half of the fifteenth century, civil strife in Genoa, territorial losses by the republic to the Turks, and the opening of Africa by the Portuguese led to a considerable Genoese emigration to Seville. Between 1450 and 1500 the Genoese population of the city doubled, and in the sixteenth century, the colony was the largest of its kind in Spain. Typical is the remarkable career of Francisco Pinelo, head of one of the most important Genoese families in Seville. He worked with Luis de Santangel to find money for the first voyage of Columbus, and loaned the government 1,400,000 maravedís. Later he helped provide money for the second voyage. In 1503 he became factor of the newly established *Casa de Contratación*. He married into a noble family, and his two sons went into the church. Ruth Pike, *Enterprise and Adventure: the Genoese in Seville and the Opening of the New World* (Ithaca, New York), 1966. pp. 1–7.

over went to Burgos, where it was taken by wealthy *conversos* as payment on loans made by them to the king, nobles, and the Mesta. Vicens Vives has pointed out the astonishing similarities between these activities and those of the rapidly approaching Age of Discovery. Clearly, a pattern in the handling of bullion, in which native Spaniards played little part, was being established that would provide a basis for the exploitation of the New World with the same unfortunate results.[23]

A smaller but perhaps significant amount of gold came from within the peninsula itself—namely, the tribute from Granada. After 1430, the emirs agreed to pay their feudal overlords, the kings of Castile, 20,000 gold *doblas* annually. This outside source of revenue is almost never mentioned when historians are discussing the baneful influence of the American gold on the Spanish economy and character. Yet one scholar has suggested that it would be very interesting to study the effect on the Castilian psychology of being able to count in the national budget on a share of revenue which did not come from the labor of its vassals or peasants. "Therefore, when it is stated that the treasures of America perverted the procedures of the exchequer and the royal officials, this important precedent is forgotten: that before the 16th century there was also a treasure which came to Castile from outside—the treasure of Granada."[24]

In agriculture, Isabella attempted to ameliorate the conditions of the peasants. Since 1480 a serf had had the right to move to another place, taking with him his own possessions or selling them as he wished. This was virtually the death blow to serfdom in the western kingdom. Earlier legislation, which had forbidden the seizure of cattle or agricultural implements for debt, was revived at the Cortes of Madrigal; and much later the agrarain worker and his property were especially commended to the protection of the *Hermandad*. In spite of these measures, agriculture and the agricultural worker suffered considerably; for this the Catholic Kings were responsible.

The fact is that, for reasons political as much as economic, they favored using the land for grazing rather than for agriculture. The

23. "This means that, long in advance of Columbus' discovery, we have an exact precedent for the gold route of the American treasure. Gold arrived in Castile only to be siphoned off by foreign powers, especially Genoa....So the gold followed a straight line without the country profiting from it. And if we compare this situation with that of the sixteenth century we find the situation exactly the same. So the constant inflow of gold in the Late Middle Ages was the necessary precedent to the great machinery of the 1500's which also swallowed up the treasure of America without the Castilian commoner's receiving any benefit from it." Vicens Vives, *Economic History of Spain*, pp. 282–283.

24. Ibid., p. 281.

Mesta, the powerful organization of sheepowners, was important both politically and economically, and made large monetary contributions to the Castilian crown. Consequently, its wishes were heeded. In 1501 agriculture suffered a great blow when it was decided that, once land had been used for grazing, it could never be turned back to anything else. Merriman has stated that in good years, which were fairly common before 1500, Castilian agriculture "could just manage to hold its own; but was in no condition to resist bad ones."[25] Moreover, the increasingly strong economic position of the nobility, which was the result of these policies of the crown, made it impossible for the peasants to improve their own condition. Consequently, Isabella's very real desire to improve the standard of living of the agrarian masses was repeatedly being frustrated by measures enacted for the benefit of vested interests whose appeals were too strong to be denied. It is a fact that the depopulation of rural areas which was to make such an impression on foreign visitors to Castile during the sixteenth century actually began during the era of the Catholic Kings. Since the free peasants were unable to make a living on the soil, they began to emigrate to the cities after selling their land to those who had the money to buy—once again, the aristocracy.[26]

In his own realms, Ferdinand did what he could for agrarian workers, but in Aragon and Valencia he accomplished little. However, in Catalonia he was able to save the peasants from the heaviest exactions of the landlords by the famous decision of Guadalupe in 1486 which abolished the *seis malos usos* (six evil practices). The principality, however, was in the midst of a severe economic decline at his accession, for which five factors were probably responsible: 1) the devastation of the area during a decade of civil war; 2) the declining strength of the mercantile and artisan classes; 3) the effects of the Jewish explusion of 1492, which hit the productive classes hard; 4) the advance of the Turks in the eastern Mediterranean, which deprived the Catalans of valuable markets in the Levant; and 5) the shunting of trade from the Mediterranean into the Atlantic as a result of the opening up of the African coast and the later overseas discoveries.

In spite of this gloomy picture, a considerable recovery took place during the reign of Ferdinand. The Catalan *Corts* of 1481 restored a great deal of confiscated property and adopted a protectionist policy to assist in the recovery of trade. A few years later the currency was stablized. In 1495 trade relations were reestablished with Alexandria and regular fleets were sent out. During Ferdinand's last years (1503 to 1516) economic conditions were quite favorable. The popula-

25. Merriman, II, 137.
26. Vicens Vives, *Economic History of Spain*, pp. 293, 296.

tion of the Catalan cities grew, and once again the ships of Barcelona appeared at wharves in North Africa, Flanders, and England.[27]

An impartial observer, studying the Iberian economy during the era of the Catholic Kings, might have found it impossible to foresee the overwhelming decline that was to overtake it during the last years of the sixteenth century. However, he might have perceived certain elements of weakness in the structure that would have to be corrected if the economy was to advance. First, he might have noted that the relative prosperity of Castile was not uniformly distributed but was concentrated mainly in the woolen industry. The unsatisfactory nature of the distribution pattern also applied to the regions of the peninsula, the most prosperous areas being confined to the extreme north and to Andalusia in the south. In regard to technical devices for carrying on trade and transacting business—such as the handling of monetary matters—the Castilian economy was primitive and largely in the hands of Jews and foreigners. And lastly, the social structure of Castile was backward in comparison with Catalonia or the countries of northern Europe. In the simple agrarian economy of the region, the urban and industrial elements were not sufficiently developed to count for much. It was the persistence of these traits in the sixteenth century, coupled with the enormous demands made upon it, that brought the Castilian economy down.

4

In their dealings with the arogant and rebellious nobility, especially in Castile, the Catholic Kings were confronted by a class which was at the peak of its power. This commanding position was largely the result of six factors which can only be summarized here: 1) the very large land grants made by the crown during the conquest of Andalusia; 2) the vast expansion of the wool trade, of which the great landowners controlled the migratory routes; 3) the growth of the *mayor azgos*; 4) the penetration of the public administration and the Church by second and third sons of the aristocracy; 5) the dynastic wars of the fourteenth century and the advent of the Trastámaras, in particular Henry II, *el de las mercedes*; and 6) the utter weakness of the crown during the times of John II and Henry IV. The great families of Pimental, Ponce de Leon, Guzman, Mendoza, Figuroa, Córdoba, Santillana, Toledo, and others famous during the eras of the Catholic Kings and the first Habsburgs established their power at this time.[28] As has already been pointed out, Ferdinand and Isabella did not seriously challenge the economic and social aspects of this

27. Vicens Vives, *Economic History of Spain*, pp. 300–301.
28. Ibid., pp. 244–247.

position. What they, and Isabella in particular, did do was to force the nobility to abandon private wars and vengeances and to acknowledge the supremacy of the crown's political power.

This was carried out by the queen through a combination of severity and flattery. Not only did the crown insist on the fullest recognition of its rights, but the queen regarded acts of violence as a personal affront and usually attempted to deal with them on the spot. After two weak reigns, the nobility in some regions was virtually uncontrollable. In Andalusia, the dukes of Medina Sidonia fought the marquesses of Cádiz. In the north, Leon was frequently devastated by Alonso de Monroy, grand master of Alcántara. Valladolid, Zamora, and Salamanca were sometimes terrorized by Pedro de Mendana, the *alcalde* of Castro Nuño. Galicia was torn by the feuds of the count of Carmiña and Pardo de Cela. To put an end to such vendettas Isabella spared neither herself nor her relatives. Typical is the story of the quarrel between Don Fadrique Enríquez (Ferdinand's cousin) and Ramiro Nuñez de Guzman in the spring of 1481. Isabella had given Guzman a safe conduct until the affair was settled, but notwithstanding this he was attacked one night in the streets of Valladolid by hired bullies and severely beaten. When the queen heard of this violation of her safe conduct, she was furious, and correctly supposed that the young Fadrique was the instigator. Without a moment's delay, she personally rode to the residence of Admiral Enríquez, notwithstanding a heavy rain, and immediately demanded the surrender of his son. The admiral temporized and a search of the castle failed to locate him. Isabella returned to Valladolid so overcome with anger and chagrin that she became ill, saying that her body was suffering from the blows that Don Fadrique had given it. By this time the Enríquez family was becoming alarmed at the importance of the affair and eventually the young man was surrendered to the queen. After a public humiliation, he was imprisoned and finally banished to Sicily. The same severity was shown when two officials of the powerful Toledo family struck a royal officer; one was promptly hanged on the spot, and the other had a hand cut off and was banished from the kingdom.[29] Naturally Isabella's officials modeled their conduct after the queen's. The *corregidor* Chinchilla, for example, pacified Galicia in three months by the simple expedient of destroying seventy-six castles and executing the castellans without regard for family or political connections.

The most effective work in restraining the nobility and keeping peace in the countryside was probably done by the establishment

29. Mariéjol, pp. 29–30.
30. Navarro, p. 249.

of the famous *Santa Hermandad*, or Holy Brotherhood, actually a rural police force with a sanctimonious name. Here again we have an excellent example of the way in which the Catholic Kings adapted old institutions to their purposes. Town leagues were common throughout the Middle Ages, and had frequently appeared in the Iberian peninusla, where they were often called brotherhoods *(hermandades)*. These organizations usually enforced peace in the countryside; however, they were always instigated by the cities themselves and did not have royal connections. Such an *hermandad* seems to have been set up briefly in 1465–1467 when feudal anarchy was reaching new extremes. This league comprised the major municipalities of Leon, Castile, Asturias, and Galicia, and enjoyed a more elaborate organization than any other municipal *hermandad* in the past.

After Isabella's succession to the throne, the idea of a royal *hermandad* was apparently suggested by the treasurer, Alonso de Quintanilla, and Juan de Ortega, vicar general of Villafranca de Montes de Oca. The Cortes of Madrigal in 1476 approved the arrangements and, naturally, the towns gave it their warm support. However, the nobility hesitated to join in, and it was not until the constable of Castile, Fernando de Velasco, ordered his vassals to participate that the other nobles gave it their support—an interesting example of the still uncertain position of the royal power early in the reign.

The new organization known as the *Santa Hermandad* differed from the earlier medieval *hermandades* in that it applied to the whole kingdom and was completely under the control of the crown. From contributions levied on householders, an armed force of two thousand men was recruited and, being mounted, could be moved swiftly wherever needed. These troops might be called the first standing army in Spain. The first organizational meeting of municipal representatives was held at Dueñas, and a regular *junta* under the presidency of the bishop of Cartagena was established to manage its affairs. Later on, this *junta* was transformed into a council. The courts of the *Santa Hermandad* had a wide jurisdiction over crimes committed in the countryside. They dealt with cases of murder, theft, rape, arson, and robbery; they also pursued fugitives from municipal justice and suppressed acts of rebellion. Punishments were savage; those condemned to death were shot with arrows, and mutilation was frequently inflicted for lesser offenses. A contemporary speaks with horror of the "bloody vivisections" of the *Hermandad*, but such squeamishness is rare in the fifteenth century. Obviously the organization served its purpose well. After three years, there was a general request for its abolition; but, because of the Portuguese war, the sovereigns wanted it to go on. Later its forces played an important role in the war against Granada.

In 1498, its mission accomplished, the principal offices were abolished and the troops were mainly assigned the task of guarding highways and carrying out minor police assignments. In Aragon, Ferdinand established his own *Hermandad* in 1488. Like its prototype in Castile, it functioned so successfully that it could be disbanded in 1510. All in all, the work of reducing the countryside to obedience and establishing a considerable degree of peace and security must be regarded as one of the happiest achievements of the Catholic Kings.

Bringing the grand masterships of the three military orders of the kingdom into the hands of the crown also constituted an important aspect of Isabella's general policy of forcing the nobility to submit to the crown's authority. Moreover, it was one of her most original accomplishments, being without precedent. These orders were extraordinarily powerful in the fifteenth century. Each had its own private army, and the peninsula was covered with their castles and convents; even some of the towns were under their control. The grand masterships were greatly sought after; and, in the case of disputed elections, papal intervention was likely. Thus they offered the papacy an opportunity to interfere in matters of church and state. Although they provided the crown with a source of revenue and occasionally furnished troops when called on, they were a potential danger constituting a kind of state within a state. Moreover, entrenched in their great privileges, they also provided the baronage a convenient shield behind which to plot trouble for the state.

While Isabella as a woman was completely ineligible to exercise any direct control over them, in Ferdinand she had an admirable means of bringing them under the crown. An opportunity presented itself in 1476 when the grand master of Santiago died. With her usual energy, the queen immediately took horse and, after a ride of three days, reached Ocaña where the heads of the order were considering a successor. To their amazement she broke into the meeting and informed them that she had requested a papal bull of investment for her husband Ferdinand and requested them to suspend any further action. Alfonso de Cárdenas, whose election had seemed assured, tactfully withdrew his candidacy and, eventually, although with considerable reluctance, Rome granted the necessary permission. However, Ferdinand decided not to press the issue at this time and graciously reinvested the diplomatic Don Alfonso, who held the office until his death in 1499. In 1487 Ferdinand practically seized Calatrava by a threat of force, and in 1494 he forced out the grand master of Alcántara by offering him instead the archbishopric of Seville. When Santiago became vacant through the death of Cárdenas, Ferdinand appeared as a candidate for the grand mastership and was, of course, elected. With the king now firmly in control of each order, the government proceeded to unify and organize them in the usual way; a council having legal powers extending to civil and criminal jurisdiction was set up to administer their affairs. Ferdinand's tenure was for life only, but obviously the rulers did not intend to allow such a source of strength to pass out of their hands. The logical and obvious step was taken in 1523 when Pope Adrian VI issued a bull incorporating the three grand masterships perpetually in the crown of Castile.

In this way, the sovereigns put an end to the lawlessness of the two previous reigns. Still, it was not their purpose to drive the nobles again into open revolt, and in less vital matters the crown flattered them in as many ways as it could afford. They were urged to come to court; indeed, "the court" in a modern sense may be said to have begun at this time. Isabella had a taste for regal magnificence and liked to be surrounded by attractive ladies and gentlemen. This not only added to her state, but it enabled her to keep an eye on the great families and teach them the habit of obedience. Where a question of political power was not involved, no one was more solicitous of aristocratic pretensions than the queen of Castile. Hence she did not interfere with their ancient exemptions from torture, from imprisonment for debt, and from the payment of the ordinary taxes. She also created a certain number of new nobles and advanced others; thus, the number of dukes during the reign increased from seven to fifteen.

5

It has often been noted that when a vigorous people succeed in terminating a long period of civil war and internal strife, there is a release of creative energy that affects many different fields; this is as true of learning and scholarship as it is of political and social developments. Thus no one will be surprised to learn that the era of the Catholic Kings was marked by advances in literature and the arts, while all the institutions reflected a vigorous intellectual activity. The late fifteenth and early sixteenth centuries witnessed the founding of important Spanish universities—always a significant barometer for intellectual progress. In addition to the famous thirteenth century schools at Salamanca and Valladolid, nine new ones were founded as follows: Sigüenza (1472), Saragossa (1474), Ávila (1482), Barcelona (1491), Valencia (1500), Santiago (1504), Alcalá (1508), Seville (1516), and Granada (1526).[30] The church, of course, played an important part in the higher learning of the time. Much of the work of educa-

30. Davies, p. 26.

tional reform came from the great Cardinal Jiménes de Cisneros, successor to Mendoza and a giant of piety and learning. Devoted to the cause of clerical and monastic reform, he felt a better educated clergy was essential for the prosecution of the work of the Church. To this end he founded the University of Alcalá, which soon became a great center of humanist studies as well as theology. The new Colegio de San Gregorio at Valladolid became a model for the teaching of theology and the training of priests. One of the great achievements of Castilian scholarship was Cisneros' *Complutensian Polyglot*, or multi-lingual Bible which contained, among other achievements, the first Greek Testament ever printed and an unusally fine text of the Hebrew Old Testament. This work influenced biblical scholars for the next three hundred years.

Another sign of the quickening intellectual life was the early introduction of the craft of printing into the Iberian peninsula. It is generally assumed that the date of 1468 on the title page of the *Barcelona Book* is a misprint, but it is definitely known that one Lambert Palmart was printing books in Valencia by 1474. In 1480 Isabella permitted the importation of foreign books duty free, and by the end of the century Häbler estimates that some 720 books had been printed in Spain in twenty-five different towns. It is estimated by one author that in England during a comparable period only 357 books had been printed.[31] We have already seen that Montalvo's *Royal Ordinances* of 1485 were issued in *letra de molde*—namely, type.

In addition to the influence of the Church, the court itself set a good example for learning. Although Ferdinand's education had been interrupted early in his career by the wars in Catalonia, Isabella had had something of an education during the days when she and her mother were living in retirement from the court. Apparently Latin had been slighted, for in later years she resumed her study of it in spite of the tremendous demands on her time; and, we are assured by a contemporary, such was her genius that "in less than a year . . . she could understand without much difficulty whatever was written or spoken in it.[32] After the ending of the Granadine War gave the queen more leisure, she turned to the education of the aristocracy and asked the learned Peter Martyr to undertake to establish a school for the education of young nobles. Associated with Martyr in this venture was the Sicilian Lucio Marineo, who had been brought to Spain in 1486 as a part of a recognized policy of bringing learned foreigners to teach and work in Spain. A similar case was that of Arias Barbosa, a Portuguese who had studied in Italy, and who was situ-

31. Davies, pp. 26–27.
32. del Arco, pp. 650–51.

ated at Salamanca in 1489, where he taught Greek and rhetoric for many years.

Spanish scholars themselves often went to Italy to study classical languages. Chief among these was Antonio de Nebrija. After a ten year sojourn in Bologna and other important centers, he returned home in 1473 and settled for a time at Seville, where he taught Latin. Later he taught at Salamanca and Alcalá. In 1492 he published the first Castilian grammar, dedicated to Isabella. In view of the significance of the date, the phrase in the dedicatory statement that *"siempre la lengua fué compañera del Imperio"* is remarkably appropriate.[33]

## 6

Any attempt to summarize the spirit and nature of the joint administration of the Catholic sovereigns should properly begin by emphasizing its medieval heritage, organization, and practices. It was medieval in its system of councils. Every ruler in the Middle Ages was assisted by some sort of council. In the thirteenth and fourteenth centuries these councils were often subdivided into subcommittees or boards exercising highly specialized .functions. The idea of entrusting an executive department, even a primitive one, to the supervision and control of one man, a minister or secretary, is a modern concept that would have been highly repugnant to the fifteenth century. Although the Spanish system eventually prolifereated into a larger number of councils than other governments employed, it was still essentially a development of the old *curia regis* and in no fundamental way did it break with traditions.

In the same way, the close association of the crown with the system of estates was a method of government common to most states in the late Middle Ages and destined to survive well into the seventeenth century. While the Spanish estates showed unusual vigor and independence as we have seen, there was nothing unfamiliar or unconventional in the way that they supported Isabella in her reforms. In fact, much of the work of Ferdinand and Isabella might be called a legitimate exploitation of powers which medieval political theory assigned to the crown in a feudal society. Thus their religious policy, to be discussed separately, might be considered merely an outgrowth of every medieval ruler's obligation to prevent heresy and protect the faith; their internal policy, an extension of every sovereign's obligation to protect the weak and overawe the strong; their resumption of pensions and crown lands, merely the right of the crown to recover its own; their interference with the nobles' social irresponsibility, the right of a suzerain to enforce obedience and loyalty on

33. Prescott, I, 187.

his vassals; and their celebrated colonial policy, an extension of the crusading spirit to spread the faith by force of arms amongst the heathen. In short, the Catholic Kings were careful to avoid any violent breaks with tradition.

Their government was never more in keeping with past tradition than in the constant use it made of the church. Since the days of Charlemagne, every ruler had found in the church a potential reservoir of enormous strength. From it came most of the specialists trained in administration, and they had the added advantage of not usually establishing families and making their honors hereditary. The Spanish Church in the time of Ferdinand and Isabella was a tremendously wealthy corporation whose support in political matters would be invaluable. The forty bishoprics and seven archbishoprics of both crowns produced an annual revenue of 476,000 ducats, of which 385,000 came from Castile alone. The archbishopric of Toledo, considered one of the richest sees in Europe, produced an annual income of some 80,000 ducats. To use such an institution meant to control it and to gain control of it usually meant a fight with the papacy. Here again the policy of the two governments was strongly supported by a traditional dislike of foreign interference, and a certain xenophobic attitude toward Rome.

In Castile this tradition was of long standing. The ballads of the Cid frequently are cocky and irreverent where the pope is concerned, and there was a historic opposition in both Castile and Catalonia to the export of revenue, especially to foreign benefice holders. The jurisdiction of ecclesiastic courts was sharply limited in the peninsula, and here the layman received greater protection from church jurisdiction than anywhere else. It often turned out in practice that clerics who cited laymen before spiritual courts lost their case on appeal. Furthermore, Castile, unlike Aragon, had never accepted the papal inquisition of the Middle Ages.

The question of control of the Spanish Church came to a head during the pontificate of Sixtus IV, a pope long notorious for his unashamed nepotism. Although it was customary to accept royal nominees to sees, in 1482 Sixtus appointed his nephew to the bishopric of Cuenca without ascertaining if the appointment were agreeable to the sovereigns; unfortunately for Sixtus it was not, because the court had someone else in mind. A formal protest having no effect, the sovereigns prepared for drastic action. Their subjects residing in papal territories were recalled, and Rome was informed that their majesties were about to appeal to a general council to consider this issue and others. Sixtus, one of the most corrupt of the Renaissance popes, could hardly afford a careful scrutiny of papal policies, and doubtless Ferdinand and Isabella never really intended to go so far. However, the popes had always been extremely sensitive to the threat of a general council, and Sixtus yielded to the extent of sending a legate to Spain for further discussion. When the legate arrived and sent word to the court of his impending visit, he was sternly ordered to leave the kingdom at once since he had not been given royal permission to come. At this point a tactful letter from the legate, plus an appeal from Cardinal Mendoza, enabled both sides to meet without loss of face. Nevertheless, the papacy had to accept a complete defeat. Sixtus withdrew the offensive appointment and again recognized the royal right of "presentation"—i.e. nomination—to all episcopal appointments; Alfonso de Burgos, the royal candidate, was then formally invested with the see of Cuenca. Appeals to Rome were equally frowned upon except in cases of doctrine or theological questions, and no action of any kind was to be undertaken without advance notice. In 1508 when Julius II excommunicated a monastery near Naples, Ferdinand sternly reprimanded the viceroy for not having hanged the papal envoy on the spot because the government had not been previously informed of the excommunication. When the same pontiff wanted to send to Spain an envoy who was notoriously pro-French, Ferdinand in great anger wrote to his ambassador in Rome that "under no circumstances will we let him enter our kingdoms."[34] Henceforth it was clear that whatever the pope's legal position might be, the sovereigns were the *de facto* heads of the Spanish Church. A position, it might be added, almost identical with that of the Salian emperors of the eleventh century, who maintained the ruler to be *caput ecclesiae* as well as *rex et sacerdos*.

Perhaps the only original thing about the entire joint administration of the two rulers was the extent to which they were prepared to go to enforce their royal rights. Here of course there was much that was highly personal. Both of them had had their full experience with feudal anarchy and disregard of royal authority: Isabella during the reign of her half-brother, and Ferdinand in the Catalan revolution. Both of them were young when they came to power and full of energy which they expended without stint in the solution of their problems. Both of them had the highest concept of the royal estate, and were determined to make their concept prevail; and in this, as has repeatedly been pointed out, tradition and history were solidly behind them.

Furthermore, it was only through the establishment of a strong government that the basic *particularismo* of Spain could be overcome, and the great forces of the peninsula achieve their historic destiny. We have already seen that nature has not been favorable to the unifica-

34. Konetzke, p. 88.

tion of Spain. Beginning with the Romans, the geographic and climatic divisions of the peninsula have imposed major problems on the controlling power. The shattering of the old Visigothic state by the Moslem invasions was followed by a historical *particularismo* with the founding of the medieval states of Castile, Leon, Navarre, Aragon, and others. Add to these factors the introduction of religious disunity, the presence of Christian, Jew, and Moslem, and you have a diversity that could only be overcome by the most drastic methods and techniques. It is the great achievement of the Catholic Kings that they were able to devise these methods just at a time when historical forces were favorable to large political accumulations of diverse peoples and states. Out of this favorable conjunction came the Spanish and Ottoman empires.

Yet with all their skill and energy, the Spanish imperium would never have been created from the political or economic reforms alone of Ferdinand and Isabella. Its real source must be sought in their religious policy. By imposing a religious unity, even with the cruelest and most appalling methods, they succeeded in creating for more than a century and a half a spirit of dedication and fanaticism that made the Spanish world power possible. In the seventeenth century the empire was weakened by the unreasoning devotion of the country to its supposed religious mission, but at the opening of the sixteenth century the rapidly growing religious fanaticism of both the people and their government provided a convenient substitute in the absence of a scientific technology. In a word, religion took the place of modern skills in transportation and communication in holding the Spanish empire together.

# CHAPTER III

# The Religious Problem

IN NO OTHER COUNTRY OF EUROPE WAS RELIGION SUCH A COMPLEX problem. Three great faiths—Christianity, Islam, and Judaism—each long established in the peninsula, were closely and intimately involved. Because of the complexity of their relationships, almost any generalization about them can find some historical evidence to support it. We are confronted with examples of religious and racial strife, of massacres and destruction of property, but we can also find periods when the different faiths dwelt together with considerably less friction than one would find between various religions in such modern countries as northern Ireland, India, or Pakistan. If another generalization may be hazarded, it might be said that until the fourteenth century, outbreaks of religious violence were relatively isolated events; also, as we have seen, the more intelligent rulers protected the Moslem and Jewish minorities because of the valuable services that they rendered in various fields.

For example, the unconverted Moslems living in Christian territory, the *mudéjares*, performed many important functions. In Valencia, Aragon, and Catalonia, they served as valuable agricultural workers whose services were greatly in demand by the nobles who had land to be worked. In the professions, especially medicine, they did distinguished work, and the complaints emanating from various church councils about the undue number of Moslem physicians in the service of the crown testifies to their skill. They also contributed much to industry, especially in Valencia, where they were active in the production of sugar, oil, and wine. They were likewise noted for the high quality of their work in textiles, leather goods, porcelain, pottery, and metallurgy.

The church, of course, looked on this situation with little favor, and repeatedly attempted to establish a more effective segregation of religions in the peninsula. It urged the establishment of *morerías* or separate quarters in cities for Mohammedans, distinctive badges (for Jews also) and even total expulsion, but with conspicuous lack of success over a long period. Public opinion was not yet really aroused over the question of religious minorities except in certain areas along the frontier, and the historical evidence clearly shows that the different religious groups could live together with considerable mutual tolerance and intercourse. Moreover, the Christian rulers usually needed money, which the *mudéjares* could provide, or they had Moslem vassals whom they did not wish to provoke, or they were afraid of retaliatory measures against Christians living in Moslem states; consequently a variety of forces rendered nugatory the efforts of the church to stir up trouble. When Pope Honorius III ordered the decrees of the Fourth Lateran Council regarding distinctive badges enforced in Castile in 1217, he was forced to back down because of the protests from King Ferdinand III, who was supported by no less a personage than the archbishop of Toledo. Again in 1233 and 1250, when papal efforts were made to enforce the Lateran decrees, the same king, a future saint of the Catholic Church, simply disregarded the orders. When the church frowned upon commerical traffic between Moslem and Christian, the famous military order of Santiago confessed to Pope Innocent IV that it had Moslem vassals and requested permission to trade with them, which Innocent was forced to grant.[1] Thus a complex system of intimate relations, which for a long time resisted all efforts to destroy it, had been developed between the Christians and the *mudéjares*. Indeed, it was only through the rise of anti-Semitism in Spain, which in the long run was destructive of all religious toleration, that the favored position of the Moslem minority in the Christian states was ruined.

The history of Spanish Jewry presents a similar pattern of a mixture of persecution and remarkable prosperity. During the Roman period many Jews emigrated from Palestine to Spain, where they seem to have constituted an important minority in various commercial centers. At first tolerated during the early Visigothic state, their position began to deteriorate during its long disintegration and we have already noticed the increasing amount of anti-Semitic legislation enacted by the councils of Toledo during the seventh century. Doubtless the Mohammedan invasions brought about a considerable relief. Mohammed himself had considered Abraham and Moses as divinely inspired

1. Henry Charles Lea, *A History of the Inquisition of Spain*, 4 volumes, (New York, 1906), I, 68. In spite of its age, this work has not been superseded, and should be consulted by those interested in the Inquisition.

prophets, and much in his teaching was obviously borrowed from Jewish sources. As long as the Jews paid the tax levied on unbelievers and refrained from deliberate acts of provocation—not at all difficult for so unevangelical a faith as Judaism—the invaders were highly disposed to let them alone.

With the caliphate (912–1031) the golden age of Spanish Jewry began. Many Jews rose to high positions under the tolerant and civilized rule of the caliphs. Their schools flourished in Córdoba, Seville, Toledo, and other important centers. Even after the disintegration of the caliphate, this favored position continued in the *taifas* or Moslem succession states of central and southern Spain. With the Almohad invasion of the twelfth century, a change occurred. The Almohads were Moslem unitarians and armed with all the fanaticism of the newly converted. They closed the Jewish synagogues and schools at Córdoba, Seville, and Lucena, offering them the alternatives, so often repeated in Spanish history, of conversion or exile. As a result, many emigrated to the Christian states of the north where they were permitted to settle. Thus during the latter part of the twelfth century Toledo, now a Christian city, became also the major center of Jewish life in the peninsula.[2]

With that wonderful adaptiveness to new conditions which the Jews have always displayed throughout their long history, they soon became an important minority in the Christian states of the north. While they assumed a special importance in finance, to be discussed below, they were also important in the production of necessities. Thus they became tailors, leather workers, weavers, and buyers and sellers of high quality textiles in great demand by the upper classes. As closer ties with courts and administrations were assumed, they also began to establish connections with the nobility. To recover losses, many nobles married daughters of wealthy Jews, and, as Mariéjol has pointed out, it took only a baptism to accomplish it.[3] Eventually some of the noblest families in the peninsula had Jewish relatives[4], and this was also true of the church. In the time of Isabella, it was widely believed that there was Jewish blood in the families of Alonso de Burgos and Hernando de Talavera, both confessors of the queen, in Juan de Arias, archbishop of Segovia, and even in the first two grand inquisitors of the Inquisition, Torquemada and Deza.[5] Indeed, rumor had it that even the Trastámaras were not exempt.

But it was in the field of state finance that the Spanish Jews

2. Abram Leon Sachar, *A History of the Jews*, 2nd edition (New York, 1945), pp. 176–77.

3. Mariéjol, pp. 40–46

4. Kamen, pp. 19–20

5. Ibid.

achieved their greatest success and their greatest unpopularity. The weakness of the Spanish, particularly the Castilian, middle class provided them with their opportunity. Both Castro and Vicens Vives agree on this point.[6] Through their participation in the financial affairs of the state, the church, the military orders and the wool trade, the Jewish banker eventually came to control the money market in Iberia—a situation which did not exist north of the Pyrenees, where the Jew was excluded and control of the money market was absorbed by local merchants. This led to repercussions far beyond the merely economic aspects of life.

> The Christian lords shed their troubles by turning the care of their property over to the good Jewish bidders skilled in the handling of tangible things. This transfer signified the breakdown of the moral unity between vassals and lords, and ... the making of the Jew into a specialist in the heinous task of milking the poor for the benefit of the rich. Thus a permanent abyss was carved between the people and the government, and also between the state and the church, because in the Jew the kings had a convenient source of income and in the church a rival that was taking it away from them. What the King got from the *aljamas* in the way of tribute, and the technical services and public loans from the Jews, were the *facts* ... that kept them from participating in a common life with the Christians.[7]

Thus the Jews were able to move into the highest circles. Alfonso VIII of Castile had a Jewish mistress for whom he forsook his English queen for many years, and her father became his chief financial advisor. In the relative absence (up to that time) of a popular clamor against them, such an important minority could be and was protected against the fulminations of the church. After James I of Aragon had taken Minorca, he took all the Jews there under his special protection in 1247. Three years later the same ruler held that Jewish testimony was necessary to convict in any action, civil or criminal, brought by a Christian against a Jew. In Castile, we have already seen something of the tolerant attitude of Ferdinand III. After his capture of Seville he assigned the Jewish population a large quarter in the city and permitted the conversion of four mosques into synagogues. His son and successor, Alfonso X, used Jewish men of learning frequently in his government. Unfortunately, Alfonso's reign represents the high water mark of Jewish fortunes in Christian Spain; and, in the civil wars that took place after his death, their position began to deteriorate. This was especially true with the advent of the House of Trastámara. Pedro I had relied on Jewish financiers, and this was enough to make his rival and half-brother Henry officially anti-Semitic. After Henry

6. See Castro, *The Structure of Spanish History, passim,* and Vicens Vives, *Economic History of Spain,* pp. 248–49.

7. Castro, pp. 510–11.

wrested the throne from his brother in 1369, he continued this policy although he too was forced to rely on his Jewish subjects for frequent contributions[8]; still, it must be said that from this time on, there was a tradition of anti-Semitism in the House of Trastámara.

There is other evidence of the declining position of the Jews in the fourteenth century. The church returned to the attack with vigor. A council held at Vienne in France (1311–12) was unusually intolerant and hostile. The Spanish prelates who had attended it called their own council at Zamora in January of 1313 and indulged in the most violent denunciations of Jewish influence, while the council of Valladolid in 1322 fulminated against Jews being given authority over Christians. It also revived an old tale that Jews and Moslems went into medicine in order to murder Christians; and the council particularly forbade Christians to consult doctors of the proscribed faiths. Such accusations were not particularly new, but in the past they had not excited public opinion. The significance of the fourteenth century in regard to religious minorities in Spain is that public opinion now became aroused, culminating in the tragic "Fury of 1391."

2

What led to such a change in the public attitude toward the Jews? Never popular but accepted, for generations they had played an important role in almost all phases of Iberian life, except possibly agriculture. Powerful forces were at work in forming the new climate of anti-Semitism, but they do not yet seem to have been clearly identified. Certain factors seem obvious though superficial: the advent of a dynasty that regarded them with disfavor, their connection with taxation and tax-collectors—never very popular in any society—and increasing attacks by sincere but rabble-rousing monastics. But are these sufficient to explain such outbursts as the Fury of 1391 and the later violence of the fifteenth century? On the whole, perhaps not, although there is probably no easy answer. There is a need, however, for a more thorough investigation of the social history of western Europe in the fourteenth century, and from it we might be able to throw more light on the causes of its strains and tensions. One

8. At the Cortes of Burgos in 1367, Henry of Trastámara heard complaints over the use of Jews in tax farming and the collection of government debts. His reply is significant and tends to bear out the thesis of Castro and Vicens Vives: "To this [the complaints] we reply that it is true we farmed out the collection of said income to Jews because we found no others to bid for it. . . . But if any Christians should wish to collect said income, we shall command that the task be given to them for a much lower sum than the Jews are given for it." *Cortes de Leon y Castilla*, II, 15 as cited by Castro, p. 499, note 66.

has the feeling that it was a period of such rapid changes that people were unable to grasp what was happening and consequently were frightened and confused, as in all periods of transition. A century that contained the Babylonian Captivity, the beginnings of the Great Schism, the Hundred Years' War, and the Black Death was not likely to be stagnant. The old institutions were in the process of transformation. Chivalry was about to wear itself out on the battlefields in France, feudalism was decaying, serfdom was disintegrating west of the Rhine, and the great edifice of scholasticism was crumbling under the assaults of the later scholastics, such as Duns Scotus and William of Occam. Meanwhile, the economic and social structure was constantly being dislocated by production crises and popular revolts following the Black Death.

With everything taut and on edge, it is not surprising that tensions erupted into conflict. The fourteenth century was an age of great social upheavals, both in town and country. One thinks of the *Jacquerie* in France, Wat Tyler in England, Rienzo in Rome, and the urban revolutions in the Flemish cities. They were a part of the time, and in part a natural reaction to its rapid changes. The anti-Semitic riots in Spain seem another aspect of the same reaction. Popular protest can always fasten on a particular whipping boy to express its resentment over changing conditions; personification of abstract evils is always involved in deep-seated reactions. In England the source of trouble might be identified as the king's evil counsellors; in France, the wicked nobles; in Rome, the corrupt and absentee papacy; in Spain it was the Jews.

The Fury of 1391 was by no means an isolated event in fourteenth century Spain; it was merely the greatest of a series of riots and strife between Jews and Christians. These upheavals had become increasingly frequent in the Iberian cities after the mid-point of the century.[9] In so far as it had a personal cause, it might be attributed to the inflammatory preaching of the Archdeacon Ferran Martínez of Écija. Although a man of sincere piety and some learning, he was so blinded by his hatred and fear of all things Jewish that he completely accepted the wildest stories about ritual murders of Christian children and all the other old fantasies in the history of Jew-baiting. Ordered to cease

9. In explaining the catastrophic events of 1391, Américo Castro has written as follows: "This situation [the relatively tolerant relations between Jew and Christian] came to an end when the wild, demagogic reactions of the lower classes prevailed over the political empiricism of the kings as a result of a slow advance that lasted more than four centuries, *a kind of internal 'reconquest'*. [italics mine] The major episode in this movement was formed by the brutal massacres and pillaging of 1391 in precisely those cities whose life was most prosperous and luxurious: Seville, Valencia, and Barcelona." Castro, pp. 512–13.

his trouble-making by both ecclesiasticand state authorities, he defied all efforts to stop him and repeatedly flouted the orders of his superiors. His first attacks go back to 1378, but not until the death of John I and the establishment of a regency government for the young Henry III was he able to carry on without restraint. The regency was not stong enough to do anything about Martínez, and he utilized his opportunity to the full. As a result of his violent attacks on the Jews over a period of years, the rising anti-Semitism was fanned into a tempest whose storm center was Seville, where Martínez had been especially active.

The first signs of trouble came in March, when the *juderiá* (Jewish quarter) narrowly escaped being sacked by a mob and the authorities had great difficulty in bringing the situation under control. As the movement spread, violence erupted in Córdoba, Toledo, and Burgos. In spite of frantic efforts by the regency to preserve order, it was clear that the security of the Jewish communities was hanging by a thread. The thread was broken on June 9, 1391.

For some time Martínez had been demanding a general conversion of all Jews in Castile, and that seems to have been the inducement leading to the mob assault on the *juderiá* of Seville on that day. With the authorities helpless, or unwilling to risk their lives in defense of the Jews, the mob moved from house to house, sacking, burning, and murdering. Very few escaped, except those that saved their lives by instant baptism. The number of dead was estimated at approximately four thousand. With horrible rapidity, the uprisings spread across Spain in a tide of fire and blood. In Córdoba the Jewish quarter was entirely destroyed, with estimates of two thousand killed, and similar atrocities occurred in some seventy Castilian cities during the summer and autumn. The movement spread to Aragon, where the authorities were slightly more successful in coping with it, although there was a large death toll and much destruction of property. Even the Balearic Islands were not exempt.[10]

Spanish Judaism never fully recovered from the Fury of 1391. Many were killed, and many of the survivors fled the country. Much property had been destroyed and some of the *juderiás* were never reopened. These factors alone would have been sufficient to account for a large reduction in the Jewish population, but perhaps the greatest loss was sustained in another manner: conversion. Undoubtedly large numbers of Jews accepted a hasty baptism to save their lives at the time of the Fury. During the immediate aftermath, the relentless urgings of the monks, especially the Dominicans, must have

10. The Moslems were usually spared during the Fury, possibly because of the wholesome fear of reprisals on Christian captives or residents in the Moslem state of Granada.

accounted for an equally large number of converts among the survivors. Saint Vincent Ferrer, who was relentless in his preaching and teaching during the crisis, later boasted that he was personally responsible for the conversion of 35,000 souls—doubtless an exaggeration, but even so it does suggest that there was a steady movement of Jews into the Church for some time after the massacres. In this way, many Jews managed to survive and even recover a certain amount of wealth or power, but only as Christian converts, known as New Christians, *conversos* or, in a more uncomplimentary style, *marranos*. Thus an entirely new situation developed: Judaism revived, but from within the Church itself. The prospect was uncertain and fraught with danger.[11]

With great determination, many of the newly converted Jews embarked on fresh careers in both church and state. Some of them are known to us. Solomon Levi was an important rabbi of Burgos. Perhaps foreseeing the massacres, he accepted baptism in 1390 and took the new name of Paul of Santa Maria (Pablo de Santa María). Other members of his family entered the church, in which he acquired a remarkable influence. After studies at the University of Paris, he was ordained a priest and his advance continued. He was made bishop of Cartagena and eventually bishop of Burgos. Later he entered the government of Henry III and, after that king's death, he became an important member of the regency for the future John II. In his later years he was particularly admired for his violent writings against the Jews, having turned strongly against his former co-religionists, a thing not unknown to history. Other converts followed similar careers, and eventually there grew up in the Spanish Church a large community of *conversos* occupying important ecclesiastical positions and wielding a powerful influence. Because of their skill in matters of finance and taxation, the rulers of the peninsula were reluctant to part with their services, and after baptism a certain number returned again to government positions.

But their very success proved to be their undoing. If the Spanish Jews thought that their baptism would save them from future troubles, they erred greatly. As they grew more powerful, jealousy and resentment were excited, and antagonism sought an excuse to render hatred

11. For the losses sustained by the Jews during the Fury, Vicens Vives suggests the following figures: assuming the total Jewish community in Spain to have been approximately 200,000, 5000 to 10,000 perished. Perhaps one-half the survivors were converted to Christianity during and immediately following the massacres. Those still unconverted were about 75,000, which by the time of the Catholic Kings had doubled. Consequently Vicens Vives estimates that by 1474 some 150,000 Jews plus 100,000 conversos were the backbone of the financial, professional, and artisan classes in Castile. Vicens Vives, *Economic History of Spain*, p. 244.

pleasing to God. This could easily be found in the circumstances of their conversion. It was feared, and with perfectly good cause, that many had accepted baptism to save their lives; Christians had become Moslems for the same reason. Once in the church, it was suspected that they had not entirely lost an affection for the faith of earlier days, and perhaps even practiced Jewish religious ceremonies in secret. It would not have been at all remarkable that this should have happened, and it is precisely what did happen. Perhaps the only strange thing in view of the delicate religious situation is that, as time went on, many *conversos* made little secret of their apostasizing, and this added to the growing resentment. Furthermore, the considerable literature against the Jews contributed by distinguished *conversos* who had been earlier leaders of the Jewish community quite naturally added to the growing hostility toward the whole group. It was not surprising that a public with a tendency to believe the worst would find it apparently substantiated by the Jews themselves in the anti-Jewish literature written by the *conversos*. Heretofore, the anti-Jewish movement in Spain had been directed toward obtaining conversions; from about the mid-fifteenth century on it was directed toward elimination, either through death or expulsion. The very term "New Christian" had become a deadly insult in the opinion of the Old Christians.

Anti-Semitic violence therefore returned to the Spanish cities after the immediate effects of the Fury were over. Once again church councils denounced the use of Jews in government, medicine, and the like. There was an increasing pressure to increase urban segregation in *juderías*, and also *morerías*. In 1412 the Church ordered all Jews to move into these special quarters which had to be walled and could have only one gate. A time limit of eight days only was allowed, after which period Jews living outside the quarter would be severely punished. Any Christian women caught going in were to be especially castigated, which suggests the interesting possibility of sexual jealousy as a factor in anti-Semitism.[12] Probably these measures were not well enforced, as Ferdinand and Isabella intimated later on, but they do indicate the growing hostility of official opinion. And, unlike earlier periods, the public was now strongly behind measures

12. How these measures, especially sumptuary legislation, appeared to the victims is illuminated by the following striking contemporary comment: "They forced strange clothing upon us. They kept us from trade, farming and the crafts. They compelled us to grow our beards, and our hair long. Instead of silken apparel we were obliged to wear wretched clothes which drew contempt upon us. Unshaved, we appeared like mourners. Starvation stared us in the face." Abraham S. Neuman, *The Jews in Spain. Their Social, Political and Cultural Life during the Middle Ages*. 2 vols. (Philadelphia, 1944), II, 264.

directed against New Christian and Jew alike. When Alvaro de Luna attempted to collect a heavy tax in the city of Toledo using *conversos* as collectors, the citizens rose in rebellion and drove them out of the city. They then organized a court which considered the question as to whether or not a *converso* could legally hold a public office. Thus the issue was brought out in the open. The decision known as the *Sentencia Estatuto* was doubtless illegal, but significant nonetheless; it held that a *converso* was not eligible for public office, and denounced the entire body of *conversos* as false converts who had never really renounced their old faith, and practiced Judaism in secret. The riot in Toledo shortly spread to Ciudad Rodrigo where again there was mob violence and heavy destruction of property belonging to Jews and New Christians. The issue was significant since a new principle was actually being introduced. Previously throughout its entire history, the church had insisted that all new converts would have to be accepted on a basis of equality by the faithful. The *Sentencia Estatuto* attacked this doctrine by insisting in fact that the faithful were not a body of equals, but that Jewish converts would have to be treated as an order of second-class Christians. Obviously the church could not officially accept this theory and when appealed to judge the issue, Pope Nicholas V issued a bull dated September 24, 1449, in which he ruled that the faithful were one without division, regardless of whether born in the faith or brought into it. He authorized the archbishops of Toledo and Seville to excommunicate all those who denied it. Obviously the *Sentencia* could not be accepted or even enforced, but as in the case of other similar legislation it clearly shows that time was running out for the *conversos*.

During the middle of the century, the growing anarchy in Castile rendered the development of any consistent policy impossible. Alvaro de Luna had been friendly to the Jews on occasion, and many were afraid that his fall from power would lead to renewed difficulties. However, it was always possible to deal with Henry IV, as we have seen, and he proved willing to restore some of the privileges previously lost. But such was the weakness of the crown that it was almost impossible to enforce what privileges had been granted, and with the great nobles virtually petty sovereigns on their own lands, the treatment of both Jews and *conversos* alike depended as much on personal caprice as on any preconceived policy. The fact that many *conversos* had married into the noblest families undoubtedly offered some protection. We hear of Jewish blood in the Lunas, Mendozas, Villahermosas, and Enríquez; and, as we have seen, in the church; the first and second inquisitors-general, Torquemada and Deza, also had Jewish ancestry.

Meanwhile, public opinion was more and more enflamed by the

highly emotional preaching of fanatical monks. Chief among these successors to Martínez as a religious rabble-rouser was Fray Alonso de Espina, a Franciscan. Himself a New Christian according to some authorities, Espina was personally sincere and pious, with a high reputation for sanctity, and because of this became for a time confessor to Henry IV. Like Martínez, he was practically irrational in his anti-Semitism, and his *Fortalicium Fidei* or book against the Jews sums up every disgraceful myth and legend ever told against this unfortunate people. Espina frequently demanded the introduction of the papal inquisition as a means of rooting out infidelity among the New Christians.

Toledo was still a storm center of anti-Semitism. After a long argument, *conversos* and Old Christians turned to arms. On July 22, 1467, the cathedral was attacked. In the fighting that followed, a wealthy business quarter in the city was burned down. In 1470 Valladolid suffered from similar disturbances. Three years later there was a major tumult in Córdoba. The New Christians were supposed to be influential in the city government, and the Old Christians resented this; both sides had powerful backers among the local nobility and were ready for action. On March 14, 1473, a belief that a sacrilege had been committed during a religious procession led to a violent upheaval. The Jewish quarter was sacked and the disorders were put down by Gonsalvo de Córdoba, better known to history as the Great Captain. The mob rose again, however, and finally was suppressed after an orgy of murder and rapine. The result was that those *conversos* still left alive were banished forever from the city. As usual, these events excited similar atrocities in other Andalusian cities. The accession of Isabella in the next year produced no immediate changes, but it was becoming clear that the religious situation was producing almost as many disorders as the political anarchy; indeed both were closely linked and some policy would have to be devised to terminate an impossible situation.

## 3

To deal with conditions involving mass infidelity, the church had possessed since the thirteenth century the papal inquisition. This institution was devised after the Albigensian Crusade had indicated that a crusade was too uncontrollable to be the best way to deal with heresy. A letter of Gregory IX in April of 1233 is usually considered an important step in its founding, inasmuch as he states his decision to turn the inquisition over to the Dominicans. The organization thus established was something like a system of itinerant judges, with assistants in theology and canon law, who moved from place to place in the search for heresy. The chief inquisitor had a dual role that appears somewhat shocking to modern thought; he was chief judge, and also a prosecuting attorney. But the whole assumption behind the medieval inquisition was that any one who came up for investigation was very probably guilty. A system had to be devised to bring about conviction and make acquittals rare. This was easy to accomplish through the encouragement, use, and protection of delation, constant employment of torture, and the promise of a mild sentence to all who freely confessed. Furthermore, sources of evidence were kept from the accused as well as the names of those denouncing him, and the advantages of a defense counsel were denied him. Although bishops were theoretically responsible for the control of heresy in their dioceses, this had long since been proved insufficient, and the inquisition was to assist and often supersede episcopal functions. Thus, in addition to behaving like a series of special courts, the papal inquisition might also be described as a kind of police force, with the Dominicans serving as the policemen.

In spite of the efforts of the papacy, the medieval inquisition had a rather limited expansion. It was strongest in France, Italy, Aragon, and briefly in Germany; rather less so in Hungary, Poland, and Bohemia; it was in England only once, in 1309, and not at all in Scandinavia, nor, surprising to say, in medieval Castile. And almost everywhere in the fifteenth century, it was in decay. Obviously, this moribund institution did not offer much hope for bringing order out of the frightful confusion of Castilian religious affairs, but after the sermons of Fray Espina, there was some talk about establishing the papal inquisition in the western kingdom. Things even went so far that John II, in 1451, petitioned Pope Nicholas V for the delegation of papal inquisitorial power to be used against Judaizing Christians. The pope consented, but the extreme weakness of the secular power and the fact that John's reign was nearing its close prevented anything from being done. Henry IV did not attempt to reopen the matter.

In Aragon the situation was somewhat different, for here a branch of the papal inquisition had been established. At the end of the twelfth century, Pedro II had published a severe edict against heretics, and in 1226 James I had forbidden them entry into the kingdom. In 1233, a council at Tarragona ordered the confiscation of the property of anyone who should dare to protect a heretic, and ruled that any one suspected of heresy could not hold a state office. According to Lea, the papal inquisition was established in 1238, but was only spasmodically active. Its most famous inquisitor was Nicholas Eymeric, whose *Directorium Inquisitorum* was widely used as a manual for inquisitors during the later Middle Ages, and even had a considerable influence on the early inquisitors of the Spanish institution. From Eymeric's complaints over the shortage of money and lack of support from the crown, it may be assumed that the papal inquisition in Aragon was not overly active nor enjoyed much prestige.

Such was the situation at the opening of the reign of Ferdinand and Isabella. That there was a genuine religious crisis cannot be doubted. Relations between the faiths were worse than they had been in centuries, and were contributing to the general disorder which the sovereigns were trying to suppress. Since Isabella from the beginning of the reign had actually looked forward to a crusade against Granada (this was mentioned in the marriage contract), she would sooner or later have to face the problem of assimilating large numbers of Moslem subjects. This could hardly be accomplished until some degree of law and order had been established, and some general policy worked out for dealing with the touchy question of religious minorities. That this policy might be based on toleration and adequate protection for all faiths was, as we have seen, not totally foreign to the history and traditions of the Iberian peninsula, but to a mentality such as Isabella's it was completely out of the question. Moreover, the change in the public attitude toward Jews and Moslems during the last century and a half was such that the government could count on popular support for a stern policy. And yet, to Isabella and her clerical advisors, the task of dealing with the unconverted groups must have seemed by far the easier and less immediate than the pressing issue of the *conversos,* at this time more of a Jewish than a Moslem problem.

As the government was well aware, thousands had poured into the church since 1391 and often with the scantiest sort of preparation. It was an open secret that these New Christians were still sympathetic with the faith of their fathers, and many of them were still quietly celebrating the Jewish festivals in the privacy of their homes without any real attempt at concealment. Their servants, often as not Christian, were aware of this and doubtless talked freely of such goings on. However, they seemed protected by the fact that many of them had risen high in both church and state. As we have seen, important positions in the hierarchy were now controlled by *conversos,* and doubtless this gave them a false sense of security. These facts were well known to the queen, and must have occasioned considerable alarm in the inner circle of her advisors. The possibility that the Spanish Church might come under the control of those who were disloyal at heart, and "boring from within" to use a modern term, was not completely unlikely, and must have contributed to the desire for a drastic solution as soon as possible.

On the other hand, there were forces present that delayed a solution of the problem. As we have seen, nothing really constructive could be undertaken until after the first Portuguese invasion had been disposed of, and so the sovereigns were hardly free to turn their attention to internal matters until the meeting of the Cortes at Madrigal in 1476. There was also the fact that the queen was receiving good service from Jews and *conversos*, and probably hesitated to dispense with them, especially since both she and Ferdinand were in serious financial straits during the early years of the reign and needed all the help they could get. This, again, produced delays.

The problem could not be permanently by-passed, however, and was evidently considered at length in 1477 and 1478. The queen was in Seville from July of 1477 to October, 1478; and it seems likely, in spite of Lea's opinion to the contrary, that a decision was reached sometime between those two dates. It will be recalled that Seville in particular and Andalusia in general had been the scene of frequent outbreaks of religious strife. What seems to have happened was that the queen appointed a kind of preliminary commission to investigate the religious situation in Andalusia, and named to it Bishop Pedro Fernández de Solis of Cádiz, Diego de Merlo, Fray Alonso de Hojedo, and others in whom she had confidence. The commission seems to have reported that not only was Seville filled with heresy reaching into high places but also that the entire kingdom of Castile was infected. In this, the commissioners were supported by Cardinal Mendoza and the prior of the convent of Santa Cruz, Fray Tomás de Torquemada, sometime royal confessor. As a result, and doubtless with the concurrence of Ferdinand, Isabella made her fateful decision to introduce an inquisition in Castile, probably during the summer of 1478. As Lea observes:

> Wise forbearance, combined with vigorous maintenance of order, would, in time have brought about reconciliation, to the infinite benefit of Spain, but at a time when heresy was regarded as the greatest of crimes and unity of faith as the supreme object of statesmanship, wise forbearance and toleration were impossible. After suppressing turbulence the sovereigns therefore felt that there was still a duty before them to vindicate the faith.[13]

If, as seems probable, negotiations were opened with the papacy over the establishment of an inquisition during the summer of 1478, there was a considerable delay; for the final bull is dated November 1. Actually, what the sovereigns were asking was highly unusual in one sense: they were not asking for a branch of the papal inquisition, but for permission to set up a new institution which would be under, and supervised by, the crown. This was, of course, in keeping with their ideas of government and the fact of the absence of the papal inquisition in Castile; however, it was nonetheless something new as far as Rome was concerned. Sixtus IV eventually agreed and issued

13. Lea, I, 130.

the bull toward the end of the year. It merely provided that, because of the existence of false Christians in Castile, Ferdinand and Isabella might, as a remedy, appoint three bishops, or other suitable men, to act as inquisitors over hereitics and those who assisted and abetted them. The power of appointment and removal of these officials was lodged in the crown, and also the right to confiscate property of the condemned. These represented unusual concessions from the pope, especially a pontiff as grasping as Sixtus IV where power and money were concerned. Yet the papacy had long wished to introduce the papal inquisition into Castile, and Sixtus probably assumed he would have greater control over the new institution than he actually did. The subsequent history of the Inquisition in Aragon shows that Sixtus soon regretted the extent of his concessions and tried to force Ferdinand to relinquish some of the crown's authority.

On the other hand, the establishment of a royal Inquisition is remarkably consistent with the policy of the Catholic Kings in other matters. A situation of long standing develops to the point where it exceeds the power of traditional institutions to handle. The government intervenes, but rather than trying something revolutionary, or markedly new, it expands an old idea—in this case the moribund papal inquisition—strengthens it to do an efficient job, and makes sure it is entirely under royal control. Passing from generalities to specific examples, there is a surprising parallel in the working out of this technique between the *Santa Hermandad* and the Inquisition. In the case of the *Hermandad,* the problem of keeping the peace and putting down rural anarchy had become acute. Municipal brotherhoods had existed in the past and we have noted their efforts to achieve peace in the countryside, but the last private attempt in this direction in 1465–67 had not succeeded. The Catholic Kings had therefore revived the idea, the name, and much of the policy of the older institution in their own of similar form, the *Santa Hermandad.* However, it was now to operate on a national basis, with royal backing, an effective budget, and the usual governing council to represent the crown and coordinate the *Hermandad* with the other royal activities. It will be easily seen that the procedure in the case of the Spanish Inquisition follows a close parallel.

A delay of almost two years followed the issuing of the papal bull. It is not entirely clear why this was so, but a fair guess would be that the *conversos* realized that the new institution was primarily directed against them and used all their influence at court to block it. It should be pointed out that neither Jews nor Moslems *per se* came under the jurisdiction of the Inquisition. Since they were not Christians, they could not be accused of heresy, nor, unless previously baptized, could they be described as relapsed. Unless they committed acts of sacrilege or blasphemy against Christianity, they were entirely outside the power of the church and its organs. But once baptized, they were fair game, and religious laxity could bring the Inquisition upon them. Therefore, the *conversos* were the target at which the Inquisition was aimed and they knew it. Some writers have referred to Ferdinand's alleged lack of enthusiasm; but in view of his great activity in support of the Inquisition in his own kingdom, this seems most improbable. In any event, the necessary commissions were not issued by the queen until September 17, 1480, and the actual organization of inquisitorial courts was not set up until the end of the year.

There was, of course, much resistance to the new institution. It was resented because it was a new kind of royal interference in local affairs, and because it marked a sizable increase in the powers of the crown. Not all the bishops favored an organization that could disregard their authority at will, and the nobles were alarmed at their inability to protect friends and vassals from the inquisitorial authority. On the other hand, public opinion tended to approve the way in which the tribunals struck at the New Christians in their power and pride; and the lower classes, those who made up the mobs sacking the *juderías*, welcomed any humiliation brought on the upper classes. From this point of view, the Inquisition almost becomes an instrument of class warfare as there seems little doubt that, in its early years, its principal victims came from the upper classes.[14] However,

14. Kamen sees the Inquisition as a class weapon, but in a slightly different way. He feels strongly that it was a device utilized by the nobility to force their own ideology on the population as a whole. Since this concept, essentially feudalistic and economically backward, was mainly threatened by the middle classes and their incipient capitalism, the nobility used the Inquisition to attack the strongest elements of the bourgeoisie, namely the *conversos*, who were highly vulnerable to such an attack because of popular hostility to their supposed recusancy. "What emerges from this situation is that the Inquisition was neither more nor less than a class weapon, used to impose on all communities of the peninsula the ideology of one class—the lay and ecclesiastical aristocracy." Kamen, p. 8. This thesis can be accepted only with considerable reservations. That the Inquisition had a class aspect is undeniable. However, the class that mainly supported it was the class of non-noble Old Christians in the cities and countryside. Dr. Kamen goes too far in implying aristocratic control of the institution; as we shall see, the crown was extraordinarily sensitive to its authority over the Inquisition. Furthermore, many of its chief victims were from the nobility, the very class that was supposed to be using it for its own ends. Kamen's thesis is a special case of a more generalized theory he holds concerning the new monarchies in western Europe during the latter half of the fifteenth century. He writes: "This [the alliance between the Castilian crown and the feudal nobility] followed the general trend in western Europe where the rise of the new monarchies was based on alliances with the feudal nobility against the urban middle classes" Ibid., pp. 14–15. In the case of England and France the

the opposition played directly into the hands of the crown and the Inquisition by the utter stupidity of the policies it adopted to check the new organization. In Seville these policies soon involved a plot to murder the chief inquisitors and mobilize public opinion against the Inquisition by a show of arms. Betrayed to the government by one of the conspirators, the conspiracy was soon checked and the Inquisition struck back ruthlessly. Arrests were quickly made, the trials were prompt, and on February 6, 1481, Seville celebrated the first *auto de fé* (act of faith) in the history of the royal Inquisition. Six persons were burned at the stake—a curious sentence in view of the fact that the basic crime does not appear to have been heresy in this case, but resistance to the Inquisition.[15] It seems clear that the severity here employed was intended to strike terror into the hearts of the opposition and discourage others by suggesting that rejection of the new institution was the equivalent of heresy. Other arrests and condemnations followed in rapid order; by November 4 of the same year, the Seville tribunal had burned 298 persons and condemned seventy-nine to perpetual imprisonment.[16] As a part of the program to terrify and disorganize the opposition, additional tribunals were added as soon as legal machinery could be set up. A second court was established in 1483 at Ciudad Real; two years later it was transferred to Toledo. One was assigned to Valladolid in 1485, but its establishment was evidently delayed. In 1483 the famous *Consejo de la Suprema y General Inquisición* was formed which put the Inquisition in the conciliar system, and an inquisitor-general was appointed to serve as administrative head under the supervision of the *Suprema*. The famous, or infamous, Tomás de Torquemada was the first incumbent. The popes were obviously alarmed at the growth of the royal Inquisition and attempted to maintain some control as we shall see in the story of the Inquisition in Aragon, but they were not very successful. At one time Alexander VI dealt the organization a shrewd blow by appointing five inquisitors-general with equal authority, but the experiment was not repeated. The five were allowed to hold their offices until they died, but replacements were not appointed and by 1504 Deza had been recognized as the sole head.

4

At the time of the application for a papal bull to set up a royal Inquisition in Castile, Ferdinand had not yet succeeded to the throne

---

historical facts do not seem to support this interpretation. It is far more likely that the crown made alliances with the urban middle classes *against* the nobility rather than the reverse.

15. Lea, I, 160–65.
16. Ibid.

in Aragon, but after the death of his father in January of 1479, he was now in a position to take any action he wished. Apparently he decided to try first a revival of the older papal organization that had long been established in the eastern kingdom, provided he could fully control it. He therefore obtained a ruling from the general of the Dominican Order that the government might appoint and dismiss inquisitors at its pleasure. On the strength of this assurance, a court of the revived organization was set up at Valencia. The new tribunal showed great activity and began to excite the usual opposition among prominent *conversos*, when suddenly the whole business was checked by the papacy. Sixtus required the Dominicans to withdraw their permission to the crown to appoint and dismiss inquisitors. When Ferdinand wrote the general of the Dominicans a letter full of royal wrath, Sixtus issued the bull of April 18, 1482, which went much further in attempting to checkmate the crown's power. In this extraordinary document, the pope for the first time stated that heresy, like any other crime, required a fair and equitable trial and flatly stated that this was just what defendants were not getting at the hands of the papal inquisition in Aragon. Furthermore, he asserted that many of the inquisitors had been moved by cupidity rather than zeal for the faith, and that honest and sincere Christians had been tortured into confessing heresies which they had never committed in thought or deed. Henceforth, he ordered the episcopal vicars to take part in the inquisitorial process, he made changes in procedure to assist the rights of the accused, and ordered that those who wished to confess heresy should be permitted to do so secretly and with the promise of absolution. The bull—a direct challenge to Ferdinand's authority—was to be read in all churches.

It can be said at the outset that the bull should not be regarded as a tribute to Sixtus' humanity and toleration. Toleration was not accounted a virtue in the fifteenth century and certainly not in a pope. Furthermore, Sixtus, a coarse and vulgar *arriviste*, was the last person to show the slightest concern for anyone except himself and his family. He was really interested only in money and power; in the matter of the Inquisition in Valencia, he felt Ferdinand had done a little too well for himself and that he must be forced to pay up if he expected to continue. He was therefore executing a move in a game which he expected would yield him a pawn or two, or even a bishop at Ferdinand's expense, rather than acting in the name of mercy and justice. It should also be noted that the bull of April 18 applied solely to Aragon; nothing was said about the Castilian inquisition or its procedures. It may be supposed that important *conversos* in Aragon were not without influence in Rome, where bribery was the normal method of dealing with the papal court, as it was of most courts during the period. The bull of April 18 certainly gave them what they wanted.

Ferdinand replied angrily on May 13, rejecting all the insinuations and accusations of Sixtus.

> Things have been told me, Holy Father, which, if true, would seem to merit the greatest astonishment. It is said that your Holiness has granted the *conversos* a general pardon for all the errors and crimes they have committed... To these rumors, however, we have given no credence because they seem to be the things which would in no way have been conceded by your Holiness who have a duty to the Inquisition. But if by chance concessions have been made through the persistence and cunning persuasion of the said *conversos*, I intend never to let them take effect. Take care therefore not to let the matter go further, and to revoke any concessions and entrust us with the care of this question.[17]

Thus wrote Ferdinand to Pope Sixtus! He concluded by again requesting that the necessary powers of appointment and dismissal be restored to him as previously arranged with the Dominicans. It took Sixtus about five months to reply and meanwhile the inquisitorial courts continued to function. When the pope did reply as the next move in the little game he and Ferdinand were playing, he was conciliatory, indicating that he was open to agreement, and allowing the suspension of the bull until the cardinals, who had fled from Rome because of an epidemic, had returned. At this point, the negotiations went underground, but it seems likely that some division of the spoils was consummated; for on October 17 Sixtus issued a bull placing Aragon, Catalonia, and Valencia under Torquemada—in short, under the Castilain Inquisition. Henceforth, except for a short respite, 1507–1518, the various kingdoms of Spain were under one Inquisition "supreme and general" which thus served, among other things, the cause of Iberian unity.

However, the success in combatting the intrigues of the papacy was merely the first battle in the establishment of the Aragonese Inquisition as Ferdinand was soon to learn. The opposition now shifted from distant Rome to the Triple Kingdom itself, and from the game of power politics to the much more exciting issues of *fueros*, rights, and privileges, a field where the Aragonese were old and experienced antagonists. In Valencia, where Ferdinand had first set up a tribunal under the new arrangement with the pope, there were strong protests from the Valencian Cortes that the powers of the Inquisition violated the *fueros* of the kingdom. Ferdinand replied wrathfully in a series of letters during July, but the Cortes maintained

17. Kamen, p. 48.

its stand. A second royal explosion occurred on August 31. Ferdinand rebuked the Cortes, threatened severe punishment to all who attempted to impede the work of the Inquisition, and ordered his officials to proceed without any regard to what the people or the Cortes might say. However, in spite of the royal pressure, it was not until November 7 that the Valencian Inquisition was formally opened for business. It is clear from this episode that Ferdinand was prepared to violate local rights ruthlessly where the Inquisition was concerned, although in other matters he observed them, or at least made the pretense.

The next opposition came from Archdeacon Mateo Mercader, Borgia's representative; what happened is a good example of the role being played by Rome in the early days of the Spanish Inquisition. When Ferdinand had briefly revived the old papal inquisition, Rodrigo Cardinal Borgia was archbishop of Valencia and also papal vice-chancellor, an office in which he set a record for bribery remarkable even in those loose times. He had relinquished his episcopal functions over heresy to the local inquisitors, but apparently changed his mind when the tribunal in Valencia began to do a large business. He easily obtained a brief from Sixtus IV, dated December 4, 1481, which withdrew these powers from the inquisitors and put them under the supervision of Mercader, senior archdeacon of the see of Valencia. Borgia may have been involved, as Lea believes, in the bull of April 18, which was a means of regaining episcopal control over the activities of the Inquisition, which, obviously, were going to be profitable in confiscated property.[18] Whatever the underlying causes, Mercader soon quarreled with Fray Juan de Épila, one of the two inquisitors for Valencia. At this point Ferdinand decided to settle the question decisively, and he at once deprived Mercader of his episcopal functions, ordered him to surrender the bull appointing him to tribunal, and threatened him with banishment if he disobeyed. Although all this was in complete violation of church rights and the privileges of the kingdom of Valencia, he was able to get away with it, and we hear little more of Archdeacon Mercader. However, events were to show that there was still much opposition, both active and passive, and the king had to be constantly on the alert to crush all resistance. When the lieutenant-general of Valencia removed a prisoner from the control of the Inquisition in 1488, Ferdinand at once called on him to explain his action. In 1497, when lawyers objected that the notaries of the Holy Office lacked the authority to certify the sale of confiscated property, Ferdinand threatened them with prosecution by the Inquisition itself and stated

18. Lea, I, p. 233.

that the institution was not subject to any of the special privileges and rights of the kingdom. And in 1500, after a strong protest to the king over the activities of the Inquisition, all officials and members of the Cortes were forced to swear a special oath of obedience in the presence of the inquisitors. In this way, the opposition was eventually crushed by the unrelenting pressure of the crown.

In the old kingdom of Aragon proper, resistance to the new tribunals was more direct and more violent. The Inquisition had been formally set up here on May 4, 1484, with the appointment of Fray Gaspar Juglar and Maestre Pedro Arbués as inquisitors. A meeting of the Cortes at Tarragona had accepted Torquemada's jurisdiction over the work of the Inquisition in Aragon without apparent question, and the first *auto de fé* was held on May 10. Then a great clamor arose and the *converso* element, which was very strong in the kingdom, began to organize a protest. When some of the wealthier victims attempted to flee, the crown ordered that they be stopped at the frontiers. The four estates of the realm immediately protested this violation of their privileges and sent an embassy to the king, but to no avail. At Teruel the inquisitors were not permitted to enter the town and were forced to set up their quarters a short distance away. After severe warnings were unavailing, Ferdinand finally threatened to call in nobles from the nearby Castilian province of Cuenca and at this the town yielded. There were the usual ruinous fines and other heavy punishments for those who had resisted. But again, as in the case of Seville, the opposition destroyed its position by going to an extreme that outraged public opinion and played directly into the hands of the government. In the capital city, the *conversos* had become so alarmed at the progress of the new system that, in spite of all the evidence of the last few years that Ferdinand was not to be turned from his goal by a threat of force, they decided to have recourse to murder. A plot was formed to kill Pedro Arbués, who was struck down as he knelt before the altar of Saragossa cathedral during the morning service on September 15, 1485. Apparently he had expected something like this, for he was wearing armor under his robes; but it did not save him and he died two days later. It might be pointed out that efforts to obtain his beatification were strangely resisted by the Holy See in spite of efforts by Charles I, Philip III, and several attempts by Philip IV. This last finally succeeded during the last year of his life and beatification was accorded to Arbués in 1664. Canonization did not occur until 1867 during the pontificate of Pius IX, a pope who had also suffered from popular uprising.

Ferdinand was furious when the news of the crime reached him, but Arbués' murder held some advantages for the royal policies as it turned the scale of public opinion sharply in favor of the Inquisition.

Ferdinand was now in a strong position and he knew how to make use of it. As some of the murderers had already passed beyond the frontiers, the pope was asked to require all sovereigns, rulers, and magistrates throughout the Catholic world to deliver up anyone connected with the crime to the Inquisition, and this was done by Innocent VIII according to letters dated April 3, 1487. Had other rulers honored this request, which they did not, it would have made the Spanish Inquisition virtually an international organization. Some of the guilty were taken immediately, but the pursuit of others and their friends and associates went on for years. The prosecution struck far and wide, and some important *converso* families, such as the Sánchez and the Santangel (this last long active in the royal service), were practically wiped out. After this the resistance in Aragon was broken.

A similar story unfolded in Catalonia. The principality did not send representatives to the Cortes of Tarragona on the grounds that it was not required to attend meetings beyond its own boundaries and thus had not been party to the acceptance of Torquemada's jurisdiction. To avoid possible offense to popular feeling, Ferdinand had left the names blank in the orders sent to the principality establishing a tribunal of the Inquisition, but this had no effect. The Catalans stubbornly resisted, holding that Barcelona was directly under the Holy See and thus could not receive an inquisitor from the crown. Furthermore, they already had a papal inquisitor, with a formal commission, who apparently had been inactive for years. The king then turned to Rome and requested a withdrawal of the commission, but a long delay followed. It was not until February 6, 1486, that Innocent VIII issued a bull removing all papal inquisitors from Aragon, Valencia, and Catalonia. With exquisite irony the reason given for the removal was "excessive zeal"! Torquemada was then appointed a special inquisitor for Barcelona. A good deal of passive resistance must still have existed for the Inquisition proceeded more slowly here than elsewhere. Torquemada's representative was not received by the city until July 5, 1487, and it was not until the following year that the first *auto de fé* was held. The numbers involved are also considerably less, only seven reportedly being burned in 1488 and three in 1489.

As elsewhere, the Inquisition was sternly resolved not to accept the slightest resistance, and the events affecting the city of Tarragona in 1494 are significant although the incident was trifling in itself. When a plague broke out in Barcelona, Tarragona established a quarantine against anything coming from the stricken city. When the inquisitor and his court, presumably wishing to escape infection, arrived at Tarragona, the citizens objected to breaking the quarantine and refused to open their gates, asking him to establish his headquarters outside the city until the danger was over. Instead of heeding these reasonable requests, the inquisitor, Antonio de Contreras, demanded instant admittance, threatening those who had excluded him with excommunication. He was still excluded, however, and departed making wild threats. When he was finally admitted to the city on July 18, he took testimony, and the leading citizens and city officials were forced to present themselves before him and the lieutenant-general of Catalonia and humbly beg forgiveness. The following Sunday they were forced to undergo the additional humiliation of public penance after Mass. As one writer puts it, "men who wielded their awful and irresponsible power in this arbitrary fashion were not to be restrained by law or custom, and from their tyranny there was no appeal save to the king who was resolved that no one but himself should check them."[19]

By this time resistance on the local level was virtually over, but the cortes still occasionally attempted to intervene. At a general cortes of the three kingdoms meeting at Monzón in 1510, relations between the crown and the assembled estates were unusually good. Enthusiastic over the news of the taking of Oran and Algiers, the deputies made the crown a generous grant of 500,000 *libras* and in return Ferdinand graciously consented to abolish the Aragonese version of the *Santa Hermandad*. In spite of this general euphoria, the deputies managed to insert in their petitions serious complaints about the functioning of the inquisitorial courts, especially the extent of their jurisdictions and the burden of the special privileges bestowed upon them. The king evaded as much as he could and promised vaguely to correct abuses. Two years later, meeting again at Monzón, the deputies were in a less compliant mood and tried to force their wily sovereign to discuss specific abuses and provide specific remedies. The pressure proved to be too strong for Ferdinand to ignore; and, since it was no longer a question of the Inquisition and its right to prosecute heresy but merely of abuses in the functioning of an institution that most had come to accept, the crown evidently felt it could make concessions. The cortes proposed a series of reforms which the king agreed to accept. After receiving the royal assent, the inquisitors were required to swear an oath to obey each article separately. Ferdinand also solemnly swore that he would ask Rome to order all inquisitors to observe the Concordia of Monzón, as the document was now called. What Ferdinand actually got from the papacy was somewhat different; on April 30, 1513,Leo X issued a letter permitting Ferdinand to dispense with the vow he had previously sworn before the cortes. Thus

19. Lea, I, 265.

all efforts to curb the power of the Inquisition in the Triple Kingdom failed.

5

From the foregoing, the reader will see that the immediate *raison d'être* of the Inquisition was the problem created by the Jewish converts. In later years the tribunals would be much more concerned with the Moriscos, but it was originally the Jewish issue that brought the dreaded institution into being. With the establishment of the Inquisition, the government of Ferdinand and Isabella now possessed a weapon strong enough to deal with the *conversos*. There still remained, however, the problem of the unconverted Jews who, as non-Christians, were outside the jurisdiction of the ecclesiastic tribunals. There was nothing unusual about the idea of a mass expulsion—it had been frequently tried in other lands during the Middle Ages—but in Spain the Jews had been too valuable to the state for such a drastic solution of the religious problem. But, as we have seen, there had been a rising tide of popular resentment during the last century and a half against Jewish subjects, and this feeling was emphasized by Isabella's efforts to achieve religious unity in the peninsula. Perhaps as a result of her visit to Andalusia in 1477 and 1478, the queen had toyed with the idea of expulsion; for some kind of edict was drawn up against the Jews of Andalusia in 1480. But nothing seems to have been done. For one thing, the coming war with Granada was going to be very expensive and the aid of Jewish financiers was essential. Moreover, two important figures in Castilian finance were Jews, Abraham Senior and Isaac Abrabanel, and they doubtless used their influence to prevent anything so drastic as expulsion. There is also evidence that the sovereigns themselves hesitated for some time before agreeing to the expulsion, in view of the obvious economic liabilities involved. However, one can only agree with Lea that, although many profited temporarily from the elimination of the Jews, economic considerations were still probably not the main cause. The sincere though bigoted religious devotion of the rulers, the feeling that religious unity was the best way to establish political unity, the constant fear that Castile might slip back into the internal anarchy from which she had been so recently rescued, the belief that Jews of the old faith proselytized amongst the *conversos*, all these elements must be understood in order the explain the state of mind that finally led the Catholic Kings to decide upon total and permanent expulsion.

With the rapid deterioration of the kingdom of Granada in 1488 and 1489, it was clear that the acute financial needs of the Catholic Kings would soon be reduced, and hence the monetary support of the Jewish element would no longer be so essential. In May of 1486,

Ferdinand had ordered all unconverted Jews banished from the sees of Saragossa and Albarracın, as they had already been expelled from Seville, Córdoba, and Jaén. There were popular demonstrations against them in 1491, and by the end of that year the Granadine War was virtually over.

Early in 1492 it was clear that something was being prepared and apparently Senior and Abrabanel tried to bribe the court from taking any action by offering a large sum of money. Whether strictly true or not, contemporaries believed that the sovereigns were considering the offer until Torquemada dramatically appeared before them, cricifix on high, and compared them with Judas, who had also betrayed Christ for silver.[20] After that the offer was rejected. The Inquisition, obviously alerted in advance, played its part in the tragedy by inflaming popular opinion through trials and *autos de fé* that emphasized the recalcitrance of *conversos* and the proselytizing activities of their Jewish associates. An important case developed at La Guardia where, it was claimed, Jews had murdered a child and stolen her heart in order to use it in sorcery against Christians. Although, as Lea points out, the whole story was obviously a "creation of the torture chamber," several Jews and *conversos* were executed in connection with it, and the sentences were published throughout the country.[21] In a short time, as might have been expected, the Holy Child of La Guardia became the center of a cult. In the terminology of the twentieth century, the Inquisition was preparing a propaganda base for the new policy of the government.

The expulsion edict was signed on March 30, 1492.[22] All Jews had to leave Castile and Aragon by July 31 or accept baptism; those who returned were liable to the death penalty. They were permitted to sell their effects and property, but the time limit was so short that the greatest confusion arose and the unfortunate owners were terribly

20. This story is quoted by Juan Antonio Llorente (1756–1823) who was closely connected with the Inquisition after 1785 and wrote the first carefully documented history of the Inquisition; his work was published in French between 1817 and 1818. Since many of the documents he used have been destroyed, his work has the importance of a major source. Juan Antonio Llorente, *Histoire critique de l'inquisition d'Espagne, depuis l'époque de son établissement par Ferdinand V jusqu'au règne de Ferdinand VII, tirée des pièces originales des archives du Conseil de la Suprême et de celles des Tribuneux subalternes du Saint-Office.* 4 vols. (Paris, 1817–18), I, 260. See also Sachar, p. 214.

21. Lea, Vol. I, p. 134.

22. As Professor Kamen has pointed out, until 1492 Spain had a much better record than the other monarchies of western Europe in dealing with the Jews. England, for example, had expelled her Jews in 1290 and France followed suit in 1306. In Castile, the invaluable services in finance and adminis-

victimized. In Aragon the situation was even worse, since Ferdinand sequestered all Jewish property until claimants and creditors had been satisfied; the abuses possible under this procedure can easily be imagined. Worse yet was his decision to collect from all Jewish sales an amount finally equal to what they would have paid in taxes throughout the expulsion year. Thus everything was done to strip the last penny from these unfortunate people. Valuable pieces of property went for a pittance, for who could hold out long against the pressure of the embarkation date? Acts of personal violence could be carried out virtually with impunity since the victim or his family would be out of the country before the case could come up. It is true that, pending the embarkation, the two governments took the Jews under state protection; but in the inflamed condition of popular feeling, this meant little, and the sovereigns themselves led in the spoliation. We have already seen something of Ferdinand's chicaneries, but nothing could exceed in cruelty or cynicism the policy that forced the miserable exiles to pay out of their slender funds an embarkation tax of two ducats per head when they reached the nearest port. Anything left behind with friends or *converso* relatives was promptly seized, if detected, by the crown; correspondence and litigation concerning this was still going on several years later. To add to their troubles, Torquemada forbade any Christian from giving them food or shelter after August 9.

Everywhere they went in Christian Europe they were badly treated. Many fled to Portugal, where John II drove a hard bargain with those he permitted to enter; during the next reign there were many forcible conversions. Eventually, the Portuguese government, on the insistence of Ferdinand and Isabella, adopted the policy of baptism or exile. In Navarre, the exiles were decently treated at first; but in 1498 the government adopted the Spanish policy, and those who wished to keep their faith were forced to flee. Many went to

---

tration rendered by the Jewish minority protected them against the growing popular anti-Semitism, and greatly retarded its development into an official policy of the state. However, after 1391, when Jewish converts poured into the church and even achieved prominent positions in its administration, the official attitude began to change. The Inquisition was established to insure the sincerity of conversions, but even this formidable institution did not succeed in allaying the fears of the government—fears which were fanned by the Old Christians. More and more, expulsion must have seemed increasingly to be the only solution. Kamen, following the theory previously described, sees this expulsion mainly as a social and economic act: "The expulsion was, in its widest interpretation, an attempt by the feudalistic nobility to eliminate that section of the middle classes—the Jews—which was threatening its predominance in the state. It was a refusal of the old order to accept the new importance of those sections of the community that controlled the capital and commerce of the towns." Kamen, p. 7.

Italy, especially Naples, but here again trouble awaited them. In the year following the French invasion, the people blamed their troubles on the Jews and in 1495 there was repeated mob violence against them. Only in Turkey, where Christian virtues were not practiced, were they treated as members of the human race, and the Sultan Bajazet found them to be such admirable citizens that he ridiculed the folly of the Catholic King in driving off these valuable subjects.[23]

In the absence of reliable statistics, the actual number forced out will never be known. Andrés Bernáldez (1450–1513), chaplain to the archbishop of Seville, cites a figure of 35,000 Jewish households for Castile and some 6000 for Aragon, which might come to a rough total of 160,000 souls resident in the two kingdoms. Later, there was a tendency for expanding the figures enormously. Writing about a century after the event, Zurita offers an estimate of some 400,000 persons affected by the expulsion, and Mariana stated about 1592 that in his

---

This interpretation, although interesting, seems entirely too simple, ignoring as it does the powerful religious feelings that lay behind the expulsion. Regardless of what the twentieth century may think about it, the government of Queen Isabella was convinced that it was facing a major religious crisis caused by the masses of Jews of questionable orthodoxy now within the church supported by the powerful minority of the still unconverted Jews outside of it. It is perhaps correct to state that such a crisis was basically religious in nature, and only in a secondary sense socio-economic. It should also be remembered that the attempt to resolve the crisis first by setting up the Inquisition and second by total expulsion of the unconverted Jews was highly popular with the great majority of Castilians. In fact, when the policies of the two sovereigns in regard to the Moslems, the Jews, anarchy in the countryside, and financial reform be considered, it can be maintained that the joint rule of the Catholic monarchs was the first truly popular government to exist in the peninsula since the time of Ferdinand III, the saint.

23. The strange vicissitudes of Spanish Jewry are well illustrated in the moving story of the great Abrabanel family. Of ancient Jewish stock claiming descent from David, their Spanish phase begins in the fourteenth century with Judah of Seville, who became keeper of the wardrobe for the Castilian crown. His son Samuel became one of the wealthiest men of his time, and in spite of the prejudice felt by the Trastámaras against Jews, he was often used in responsible positions by King Henry II. Like many others, Samuel was caught by the Fury of 1391 and accepted baptism to save his life, taking the name of John of Seville. In the later calmer period, he recanted and fled to Portugal. Samuel's son Judah re-established the fortunes of the family in Portugal. He was prosperous and eventually became treasurer to a member of the royal family. The most famous member of the family, Isaac, was born in Lisbon and rose rapidly, becoming treasurer of King Alfonso the African, whose dizzy exploits have been previously mentioned. Unfortunately for Isaac, with a new king came new trouble. Isaac was implicated in a plot against the crown organized by the duke of Braganza; and while the duke was executed, Isaac fled to Spain. For the second time the family fortunes were prostrate.

But a third time they recovered, although briefly. Isaac Abrabanel, well-educated, intelligent, skillful in business, was too valuable a man to be

day the estimates varied from about 170,000 to 800,000 persons expelled.[24] Isadore Loeb, a modern scholar, after a careful sifting of all the available evidence, both Christian and Jewish, put the figures as follows: emigrants, 165,000; baptized, 50,000; died en route, 20,000.[25] And some consider these figures too high. Vicens Vives, taking the estimates of Fritz Baer, reduces the number of expelled to about 150,000.[26]

If the total population of the two kingdoms was approximately six million, which seems a conservative estimate, then it will be seen that a relatively small percentage of the population was affected, although this does not of course mitigate the outrageous injustice done to the Jewish subjects who had contributed so much to the welfare of the two kingdoms. It would seem that the *immediate* economic damage done was relatively slight, being quickly absorbed in the rapidly expanding economy of Castile during the first half century of the age of exploration and discovery. However, the long range results were much more harmful since, as Vicens Vives has pointed out, they tended to check the development of Castilian capitalism:

> ...[The explusion] eliminated from the social life of Castile the only groups that might have responded to the stimulus of an incipient capitalism; it undermined the prosperous economy of many municipalities; it mobilized an enormous quantity of wealth, a large part of which was used to finance the foreign policy of the Catholic monarchs, another part of which was dissipated in the hands of the aristocrats and functionaries....The wave of terror aroused by these measures would affect the Castilian mentality within a short time—that time necessary for Judaizers and crypto-Judaists to dig catacombs underground, and for

ignored. He became an important figure in the councils of Ferdinand and Isabella where his business ability was useful in obtaining supplies for the army during the Granadine War. Although he was unable to prevent the expulsion order, he was excluded from it; however, he decided to remain with his own people and during 1492 fled to Naples, where he was well received by Ferdinand I and for the third time became an important figure in the finances of a state. When the French invasion took place he fled to Sicily, where he remained until Ferdinand of Naples expired. He then sought refuge in Venice, where he died, leaving distinguished sons and grandsons. The last male descendant of the family died in Prussia in 1863. Sachar, pp. 218–20.

24. Lea, I, 142.
25. Ibid.
26. Vicens Vives, *Economic History of Spain*, p. 291. See also Fritz Baer, *Die Juden in christlichen Spanien*, 2 vols., 1929–1936. Other recent scholars who have considered this question usually accept figures close to those of Baer except Harold Livermore, who opts for a slightly higher estimate for the explusions. See J. H. Elliott, *Imperial Spain, 1469–1716* (New York, 1963); John Lynch, *Spain under the Habsburgs*, vol. I, *Empire and Absolutism, 1516–1598* (Oxford, 1964); Harold Livermore, *A History of Spain.*

there to appear upon the public scene (characterized by its sense of honor) a need to prove the legitimacy of one's blood.[27]

Of course, nineteenth century liberals in general attributed many of the economic evils of the seventeenth century in Spain to the earlier expulsion of Jews and Moslems, but the real cause of Spain's economic ills was the importation of gold and silver from the New World, and the terrific financial burdens that the Spanish imperium imposed on the backward economy of Castile. In this decline, the expulsion of the Jews, tragic though it was, was only one factor among many, and not necessarily the most important.

6

Having now related the origins of the Inquisition, it is necessary to comment more generally on certain of its aspects and functions, as well as its impact on Spanish life. We have already seen that considerable opposition to it developed in Castile, and a good deal more in the realms of Aragon. It should be noted that for the most part this opposition was not based on any ideals of religious toleration, human rights, or religious freedom—doctrines which meant a great deal in the eighteenth and nineteenth centuries, but not the sixteenth. Nor was there much feeling that death was too severe a penalty for the acknowledged heretic or relapsed convert. Instead, the critics emphasized the violation of local charters and royal concessions—violations that undoubtedly did occur and with the full concurrence of the court. Utilizing devotion to the faith as a pretext, Ferdinand and Isabella soon discovered in the Inquisition a weapon that could be used as effectively against local *fueros* as against local heretics. It soon became their avowed policy to recognize no local rights in restraint of the Holy Office.

Contemporaries also complained bitterly against corruption in the new organization. While some of these diatribes were based on fear and hatred rather than sober evidence, the case of Inquisitor Lucero and others indicates that some corruption did exist.[28] Moreover with both rulers determined to defend the inquisitors to the uttermost, it is clear that corruption would be and was extremely hard to discover, and even when uncovered equally difficult to root

27. Vicens Vives, *Approaches to the History of Spain*, pp. 92–93.

28. Diego Rodríguez Lucero was appointed inquisitor of Córdoba in September, 1499. His arrests of leading citizens, often on trivial or trumped up charges, created a virtual reign of terror in the city. In spite of widespread protests and complaints, he was able to pursue this course until 1507 when Diego de Deza, the inquisitor-general who had protected him, was forced out of office. In 1508, the *Suprema* arrested Lucero, who was imprisoned but eventually was allowed to retire to Seville without any further punishment. Kamen, pp. 63–65. See also Lea, I, 206–08.

out. Another cause for complaint was, curiously enough, that some of the lesser penalties, such as fines and public humiliations, were too severe.

The inquisitorial processes were commonplace enough in the sixteenth century (and also in the twentieth) to excite little comment. The fact that individuals were often arrested in secret, not allowed to communicate with the outside world, nor to know the exact nature of the charges against them, and that evidence was supplemented by the use of torture did not greatly disturb public opinion in the early days of the Inquisition. A frequent complaint stated that individuals sometimes remained in inquisitorial prisons for very long periods, even years, before their cases were settled, but judicial processes were not fast in the sixteenth century, and in the absence of any clearly defined principle of *habeas corpus*, this sort of misfortune might befall a subject in almost any European state. The fact that the defendant was allowed counsel at a certain stage of the process was considered, and properly so, a remarkable concession to the rights of the accused. The papal inquisition of the Middle Ages would never permit it. Torture was employed when the accused had made conflicting statements that could not be resolved by ordinary methods, when he refused to give information as to his accomplices, or when the evidence from other sources was defective. By the standards of the time it was used conservatively and, in theory, could not be repeated but various subterfuges were employed to get around this prohibition.

The greatest of the public acts of the Inquisition was undoubtedly the *auto de fé*, or act of faith. Voltaire, writing in the eighteenth century and admittedly not an impartial observer, is supposed to have remarked that if a stranger visited one of these ceremonies he would not know whether he was witnessing a festival, religious ceremony, a sacrifice, or a massacre; indeed, it borrowed a little from all four. Basically it was a public sentencing of individuals condemned by the Holy Office, with punishments ranging from fines for minor infractions to death at the stake itself. Celebrated with great pomp and ceremony, it attracted large numbers of people who often spent several days in the locality, frequenting taverns and brothels, which helped give the grim proceedings the air of a festival, as noted by Voltaire. An *auto de fé* was often held to celebrate an event of national importance such as a royal marriage or birth. Those condemned to death were "relaxed," to use the technical term, to the secular arm for punishment since the Holy Office claimed that it could not shed blood. Upon being relaxed to the state, they were promptly conducted to the *quemadero* or burning place and executed. A few who recanted at the last minute obtained the grace of being strangled just before the executioner applied the torch and thus escaped the horrors of being cremated alive. In addition to capital punishment, individuals were sentenced to various forms of imprisonment, and heavy fines sometimes amounting to total confiscation of property. The proceeds of these penalties were always turned over to the crown for disposal.

However they may have first reacted to these ceremonies, the people of Spain soon became highly addicted to them, and there are stories of outbursts of popular wrath when a victim received a less severe sentence than the crowd anticipated. Sometimes the officers of the Inquisition had to intervene to protect an accused from the vengeance of the mob if he had escaped the stake. One of the most severe sentences of the Inquisition was the wearing of the *san benito* for a period of months or even years. This was a coarse garment of yellow (black in the case of relapsed heretics) marked with Saint Andrew crosses on front and back. Wearing it subjected the individual to derision and gross insult, if not worse; and, when the period was over, the garment had to be publicly displayed with the owner's name in the local church, thus perpetuating the family's shame and disgrace. It must be borne in mind that even a mild sentence from the Inquisition brought utter social disgrace on the individual and his family, and often made it impossible for them and their descendants to hold any sort of public office. Thus the imposition of the *san benito* was a major calamity little less to be dreaded than life imprisonment or confiscation of property.

The critical period in the history of the Inquisition appears to have occurred during the brief reign of Philip I (1504–06) and the inconclusive period (1507–17) when his son Charles was still residing outside of the peninsula. In the case of Philip, the enemies of the institution were able to take advantage of a major scandal which involved the behavior of Lucero, the inquisitor at Córdoba. When Philip and his wife Joanna, Isabella's daughter, arrived to take over the government of Castile after the great queen's death, they received many complaints against the behavior of the Inquisition in general, and of Lucero in particular. To the scandal of the Church, Philip appointed two laymen (!) to look into the matter; and although the Holy Office took hasty and belated steps to disassociate itself from Lucero, it seemed on the verge of a major setback when it was saved by the unexpected death of Philip on September 25, 1506. Since Joanna was shortly afterwards incapacitated by her insanity, there was no immediate danger for the Inquisition, although Lucero was never reestablished, and eventually Inquisitor-General Deza, who had supported Lucero, was forced to resign. During Ferdinand's last years there were actually two separate inquisitions, one for Castile and another for Aragon. After his death in 1516, the young Charles I was strongly urged to abolish the Holy Office, but the influence of Cardinal Cisneros, who in Charles' absence was the real ruler of Castile, was thrown completely behind the Inquisition and doubtless helped to save it. Charles soon nominated his old tutor, Adrian of Utrecht, to the vacant post of inquisitor-general of Aragon and this further strengthened its chances of survival. When Charles finally arrived in Castile, the Cortes complained strongly of the injustices of the Holy Office and the king promised redress; but nothing was done, and the two parts of the organization were soon returned to their original unity. When the pressures of the imperial election forced the king to leave Spain with virtually nothing accomplished, the last chance to correct abuses in the Inquisition was lost. With the subsequent development of the Lutheran and Turkish perils, the Inquisition was considered more necessary than ever, and the government did not dream of lessening its powers. Thus the crisis which was partly induced by the advent of a new, non-Iberian dynasty passed, and the Inquisition emerged with none of its prerogatives curbed or abolished. While the crown was not unwilling on occasions to intervene in the functioning of the Holy Office, it was absolutely determined that no one else should have this privilege.[29]

It has sometimes been asked if the Inquisition should be regarded as a political or a religious institution. The question would have seemed meaningless to the Catholic Kings because neither they nor their contemporaries distinguished between the two categories. Actually, the Inquisition was both religious and political and the two aspects were completely complementary. On the religious side, it provided a spiritual power greater than the church itself which could be used to maintain ecclesiastical discipline, purity of dogma, and religious unity. At the same time, being completely under the crown, it represented a new instrument which the state could wield to achieve ends which were often as much political as religious. Furthermore, it is doubtful if the unity of the two states could have been secured by any other means. We have already noticed that the geography as well as the historical development of Iberia have emphasized disunity rather than unity. Against these trends the Inquisition provided a solid obstacle by establishing a jurisdiction that covered the whole of the peninsula except Portugal, and ignored all local rights and privileges. It also helped strengthen the religious fanaticism of the people, especially during the sixteenth century when the Catholic Church was gravely threatened by the Protestant and Moslem dangers. In the words of Turberville:

29. Surprisingly enough, Ferdinand's correspondence with the Inquisition shows an unexpectedly favorable aspect of his character. He constantly urged the inquisitors to be strictly fair and just, and in cases of property confiscation, he sometimes intervened to prevent undue hardship. Lea, I, 22.

No part of the country had met with any tribunal so efficient or so power-ful as this new institution to which the Catholic monarchs imparted not a little of their own characteristics.... The inauguration of the new Inquisition... must be regarded as an integral part of their policy of political organization and unification.[30]

Many writers have blamed the Holy Office for the intellectual decline of Spain in the latter part of the seventeenth century, and some have gone even further by attributing the decline of Spain in almost every field to the existence of the Inquisition itself. This is much too sweeping a verdict. Indirectly, the Inquisition may have been a factor in the collapse of the Spanish world power in so far as it helped to mobilize Spanish support for international Catholicism in the Counter-Reformation, in which Spanish strength was dissipated and the country ruined. But in certain fields of intellectual endeavor, a high degree of achievement and the Inquisition flourished side by side. One thinks immediately of the artistic and literary achievements of the famous *siglo de oro*. Evidently, certain aspects of intellectual activity are perfectly compatible with an authoritarian state and society. But in considering less direct relationships, a formidable case can be made against the Inquisition.

In early sixteenth century Spain, considerable intellectual freedom persisted. Erasmus was known, read, and admired. Copernicus could still be studied in the Spanish universities at a time when he was anathema to most of the Protestant theologians. Yet these freedoms were eroding as the century came to a close. In the passing from a relatively open society to a closed society, the Inquisition did make a considerable contribution. And in this closed Spanish society of the seventeenth century, speculations concerning the nature of the universe and new ways of elucidating its secrets were largely ruled out. Thus the scientific revolution of the seventeenth century, which opened up a new world to the middle classes of England, France, and the Netherlands, was excluded from Iberia, and in this exclusion the Inquisition played a role. This was the price Spain had to pay for its achievement of unity based on a militant and intolerant Catholicism.

30. A. A. Turberville, *The Spanish Inquisition* (New York, 1932), p. 29.

CHAPTER IV

# The War Against Islam

THE CONQUEST OF GRANADA IS RIGHTLY VIEWED AS ONE OF THE
major events in the reign of Ferdinand and Isabella, but it would
be entirely wrong to see it as an end in itself. Actually, it was an
initial step in a larger campaign against Mohammedanism in which
Spain eventually came to see itself as responsible for the defense
of a Christian Europe increasingly threatened by the resurgent power
of the Crescent. All the Mediterranean states had been alarmed over
the advances made by Islam in the fifteenth century. The growing
activity of the Mameluke rulers of Egypt made itself felt in the Egyptian capture of Cyprus in 1426, and three naval attacks on Rhodes
during 1440–44. Moreover the period was also marked by the rapidly
expanding power of the Ottoman Empire. After the fall of Constantinople in 1453, which sent a tremor of fear throughout the Christian world, there were Turkish threats to Otranto in Italy, and the
islands of Sicily and Malta. Hernando del Pulgar speaks of widespread
alarm in Spain over Ottoman conquests in 1480.

In all this Spain was deeply involved. There was always the fear
that the Moslems of Granada might call in the Turks, or the hardy
fighters of the Mahgreb. In 1489 the sultan Bayazid had threatened
Ferdinand and Isabella with persecutions of the Christians within
his domains if they did not desist from the Granadine War. They
countered by offering him help against the Mamelukes of Egypt. As
we shall see somewhat later, even the schemes of Columbus were
undoubtedly weighed for their possible advantages in a Holy War
against Islam in which not only the known but the unknown and
as yet undiscovered New World should all contribute to the success

of Christian arms. For these various reasons, the eventual conquest of Granada was not intended to be the end of the Reconquest but rather the springboard into a new area—the beaches of north Africa. These had to be secured to protect the Spanish coasts, prevent possible invasions, which had happened so many times before, and provide the bases for a farther advance into the interior. That this was no idle dream of Isabella's is proved by the famous clause in her will: "I beg my daughter and her husband [Joanna the Mad and Philip the Handsome] that they will devote themselves unremittingly to the conquest of Africa and to the war for the faith against the Moors."[1] But the war against Granada was the first and most obvious step.

2

Since the decline of the *Reconquista* in the latter part of the thirteenth century, Granada had maintained a precarious but prosperous existence along the southern coast of Spain. It owed its long survival to the disintegration of its enemies as well as to its own natural strength. Following Alfonso XI's great victory on the Salado River, the Reconquest had degenerated mainly into border skirmishes, raids, and counter-raids. In the fifteenth century the Castilians could point to only three engagements which could be dignified with the name of battles: the Infante Ferdinand's victory at Antequera in 1410, and lesser triumphs at Sierra Elvira in 1431 and at Gibraltar in 1462. The growing anarchy in Castile, and Alfonso V's preoccupation with Italian affairs, effectively prevented the large scale operations that would have been necessary if anything so ambitious as the actual conquest of Granada had been contemplated.

Furthermore, the natural strength of the little kingdom was great. Travel and transportation across it was difficult by reason of the rugged terrain—a countryside of steep mountains, narrow and deep valleys alternating with occasional *vegas,* or small level plains of great fertility. Roads were few and apt to be so precipitous that the inhabitants often preferred to use the Mediterranean instead since the kingdom possessed two excellent harbors, that of Almería in the eastern zone and Málaga in the west. Thus no operation against Granada could expect to accomplish much without the close cooperation of a blockading fleet. Almería and Málaga were not only important for trade and commerce in a locality not generously endowed with good ports, but they also facilitated close contacts between the citizens of Granada and their co-religionists across the narrow strait in Morocco. As long as Granada existed, the possibility of a repetition of Tarik's famous expedition in 711 was never completely ruled out.

1. Merriman, II, 242.

In addition to the natural defensive strength of the landscape, the emirs of Granada had fortified towns and strong points, and constructed castles at every strategic locality. There were probably more such places in Granada than in all Castile, and the capital city was surrounded by a belt of protective towns such as Illora, Loja, Alhama, and Guadix which constituted an advance defensive system far more difficult to crack than the massive walls of the capital itself. Moreover, a numerous and concentrated population, stimulated to warlike activities by a lifetime of border warfare, provided the military support necessary to maintain such a defensive system. The Moslems were famous for their light cavalry, an arm capable of extremely rapid maneuver on the field of battle. They were deficient in artillery, and their infantry was not especially strong although their crossbowmen were considered equal to the best in Europe. As the Granadine War was to show, they were certainly not deficient in courage, and it required the greatest efforts over a ten-year period by the two strongest states of the peninsula to overcome their determined resistance. Had their leadership at the top been better, and had not civil conflict broken out within the state, the Granadine War might have had an entirely different outcome.

Economically the kingdom, or, more properly, the emirate, was prosperous.[2] Its agricultural production was adequate for its needs, and its flourishing silk trade was a major source of wealth. Intellectually, it was probably in decay as compared with the earlier achievements of Spanish Islam, yet a certain creative spirit lingered in the arts as the delicate traceries and *arabesques* of the famed Alhambra testify. Able leadership seems to have been lacking. The rulers of Granada during its last century of existence were barely adequate; none of them were outstanding, and it is difficult today to find even a listing of their names, except, of course, the miserable Boabdil (Abu Abdaliah). For the most part, the history of Granada might be written as a series of minor struggles along the frontier, internal revolts and dynastic contests in addition to the steady decline of the central authority. Political instability is the dominant note. Furthermore, the important cities of Almería and Málaga pursued a policy of such independence that they might almost be said to be city-states themselves. This situation naturally invited intervention. While it was the Catholic Kings who eventually profited from it, the princes of Morocco had never completely given up the idea of staging a conquest of Granada on their own. This possibility of an invasion from the south may have been one of the factors that determined the sovereigns to undertake the Granadine War.

2. Nineteenth century writers used the words "king" or "sultan" frequently in referring to the rulers of Granada. Actually the title they usually bore was that of emir and they will be so referred to here.

The governments of John II and Henry IV were, of course, far too weak and disordered to undertake anything like conquest. On the whole, relations between Granada and Castile were reasonably friendly, and Henry IV's partiality for the Moors—witness his famous Moorish Guard—is well-known. In fact, it was one of the charges frequently brought against him. In the early 1460s,[3] the emir Ismail died and was succeeded by the hot-tempered Mulay Abdul Hassan. He refused to pay the tribute which had been paid by his predecessor to Castile, but in spite of this act of defiance, Ferdinand and Isabella found it expedient to agree to a three year truce in 1478 pending the final settlement of the succession war with Portugal. When the truce expired, the emir permitted an operation against the town of Zahara, a small fortified town on the frontier of Andalusia not far from Cádiz. On December 26, 1481, the place was surprised and successfully assaulted, the entire population being sold into slavery. It was this relatively minor event that led directly to the Granadine War.

It is clear that Isabella, at least, had long cherished the idea of the final expulsion of Islam from the peninsula. A statement in the marriage contract obligating Ferdinand to assist in operations against Granada proves this. But early difficulties prevented anything from being done. We have already seen that the war with Portugal occupied most of the rulers' attention until 1479, and from 1476 to 1480 they were also deeply involved with internal reforms. It was the misfortune of Emir Hassan that his successful attack on Zahara took place at a time when the Catholic Kings were at last in a position to do something about it. Previous wars had been mainly border raids; this one was going to be different in that the raids and destruction were going to be much more systematic and on a much greater scale. Furthermore, two campaigns were to be waged annually: one in the spring and a second in autumn after the heat of summer had abated. The earlier conflicts had frequently exhibited a local aspect, but this one was to be truly national in character with troops coming from all parts of Spain, even from the remote Basque provinces.

Because of the rocky terrain in which the armies had to operate, cavalry could not do much. It was therefore necessary to depend greatly on infantry and artillery since many of the operations were sieges. This was probably fortunate since, by emphasizing infantry, Ferdinand and Isabella were able to get away from a strictly feudal army and come much closer to the concept of a truly national force. Of course, they sought soldiers wherever they could get them; troops of the *Santa Hermandad* were frequently employed, and there was

3. So many different dates are given for the accession of Mulay Abdul Hassan that it can only be referred to in this rather general way.

even a corps of Swiss mercenaries, the most redoubtable infantry in Europe. Isabella, who acted more or less as the head of the services of supply, worked hard to develop an adequate artillery which would be needed in the numerous sieges of fortified places. Here she was aided by technicians brought in from France, Germany, and Italy. Eventually a considerable number of large-bore siege guns were accumulated. Although frightfully clumsy to handle and dangerous to friend and foe alike, they were usually able, in time, to batter a breach in the walls through which the besiegers could enter. Powder, always a scarce item, was imported from Sicily, Flanders, and Portugal. In addition to infantry and artillery, a significant role was played as the war developed by the Castilian fleet, which patrolled the coast and prevented any outside assistance from reaching the Moslems. Eventually Córdoba became a kind of field headquarters for the military and supply operations. Isabella was usually there or nearby and from this city streamed a steady supply of equipment and personnel to the combat areas where they were most needed. From here came the engineers, to use a modern term, the sappers, roadbuilders, bridge builders and the like who constructed new roads or repaired old ones so that the heavy ordnance could be brought to towns and forts under attack. One of the most modern of Isabella's activities concerned the well-being and recovery of the wounded. Contemporaries were greatly struck by her "hospital" tents where the sick and injured received special attention, thus giving the queen the distinction of founding the first field hospitals in modern military history.[4]

3

The response to the disaster at Zahara was not long in coming. A report had reached the marquis of Cádiz that the Moslem town of Alhama was so negligently guarded that a small band of determined men might be able to surprise and capture it. Although small, Alhama had great strategic importance. It was only a short distance from the city of Granada itself and lay across the regular road from the capital to its major port of Málaga. It was built on a rocky hill with a river at its base and was famous for its springs, which had led the rulers of Granada to make it almost a royal residence. It was also the administrative center for the public land taxes. Rodrigo Ponce de León, marquis of Cádiz, was exactly the man to be attracted to any wild scheme that seemed nearly impossible. He was at this time in his late thirties and for many years had conducted a famous feud against his hereditary enemy, the duke of Medina Sidonia. For the next decade he

4. Merriman, II, 68–69.

was one of the great animating spirits of the war—his own private war having completely lapsed—an excellent example of the value of the Granadine War in putting the turbulent feudality to better use than private carnage.

The marquis, his friends, and vassals succeeded in assembling a force of some twenty-five-hundred foot and three thousand horse and set out across the wild highlands of the southeast. Traveling mainly by night to avoid discovery, they reached the fortress without alerting the defenders and two hours before dawn on the morning of February 28, 1482, they began their assault. Thanks to the almost complete surprise they achieved, they were able to carry the fortress itself, but when they attempted to complete the reduction of the town of Alhama, the citizens rallied in the streets and a long and bloody battle followed. In spite of some critical moments when they were almost thrown out of the city, the attackers eventually carried all before them and thus the first conquest of the Granadine War was achieved.

But once taken, it became a serious problem to hold Alhama. It was almost immediately attacked by forces sent by Muley Abdul Hassan from Granada. As soon as the news of the capture of Alhama and the counter-attack from Granada reached King Ferdinand at Medina del Campo where he was holding court, he set out to relieve the garrison and succeeded in doing so. After he retired, a second attempt was made by the Moslems to retake the city and this time a close blockade was established in the hope of starving it out. At this point salvation came from the Guzman family, the aforementioned enemies of the Ponces de Leon. A third attack was planned but many of Ferdinand's advisors strongly recommended a permanent withdrawal on the grounds that a post so far advanced into Moslem territory could not be maintained. At this crucial moment, Isabella apparently intervened and convinced her husband that Alhama was too valuable to be surrendered. Marching from Córdoba, which now became the central headquarters for the Spaniards, Ferdinand again relieved the city and greatly strengthened the garrison. Then, after a lengthy foray into the *vega* of Granada itself, he returned to Córdoba and disbanded his forces. Henceforth, the Moslems were too deeply involved in internal difficulties to think of recovering the fortress which thus gave the Christians an advanced base not more than a dozen miles from the capital city itself, and partially blocked communications with Málaga.

With this victory, the Granadine War may be said to have commenced. If it had been decided to abandon Alhama, the conflict would have probably degenerated into the usual indecisive border raids and forays. But after the successful defense of the city, Ferdinand and Isabella were determined to continue the war, although even they were still not yet aware of the demands which the conflict would make on the organization and resources of their states. Isabella now called on the crown vassals and nobles for supplies, men, and artillery to assemble in the vicinity of Loja by July 1. At that time Ferdinand would take the field in person to attack the city, one of the outlying defenses of Granada itself.

Unfortunately, the operation was unsuccessful for lack of sufficient supplies and the retreat from Loja was conducted with considerable confusion, Ferdinand himself narrowly escaping capture by the Moorish troops. It was clear that the victories at Alhama had probably led to an underestimate of the enemy's strength and much greater preparations would be necessary. At this point a resolute show of resistance by Granada might have postponed its fall indefinitely. Instead, at this crucial moment, the outbreak of civil war in the emirate played directly into the hands of the Catholic Kings. The emir, Muley Abdul Hassan, had broken with his wife Zoraya because of her intrigues in behalf of her son, Boabdil. Using the failure to relieve Alhama as a means of fomenting dissatisfaction, Zoraya and Boabdil were finally able to force the emir out of the city, which they now took over. Hassan fled to his brother, El Zagal (the valiant), who held court at Málaga and enjoyed a reputation as the leading Moslem warrior, and the dread of the Christians. Thus to the dangers of a Christian war, Granada now was forced to endure an internal struggle amongst the ruling family—father, mother, son, and uncle. Obviously it was to the great advantage of the sovereigns of Castile and Aragon to keep their enemy disunited, and consequently they did all they could to keep the civil war going. Fate played into their hands by granting them an incredible piece of luck.

During March of 1483, the grand master of the Order of Santiago, Alonso de Cárdenas, led a disastrous raid into the Málaga area. Thanks to a successful ambush planned by El Zagal, the Christians were forced to flee in disorder leaving behind them some of the greatest names in Spain. This victory by his uncle and potential enemy more than ever underscored the feeble nature of Boabdil's rule in Granada, and forced him to undertake some daring exploit to recover his lost prestige. He decided to attack Lucena, a border Castilian fortress some forty or fifty miles south of Córdoba. He besieged the place on April 21, 1483, but in a battle fought outside the walls, the Moslems were defeated and Boabdil was captured as he hid along a river bank preparatory to flight. Nothing could have been of greater advantage to the Spanish sovereigns than this capture, and they used their advantage with consummate skill. Boabdil was granted a two-year truce for himself and those cities acknowledging his rule; he was to renew the annual tribute, surrender some four hundred captives without ransom, and grant the Spanish forces transit across his domains whenever they wished it. But the most astute Christian tactic was that, instead of keeping Boabdil captive, they proceeded to set him free and thus insured the continuance of those internal dissensions which had been of such great advantage to the Christians. Returning to Granada, virtually a vassal of Ferdinand, Boabdil found that his defeat had cost him all prestige and honor. Meanwhile, Hassan had gone blind, and his brother claimed the throne, proclaiming his nephew a traitor. Eventually, with Ferdinand's support, Boabdil was able to regain a part of Granada while his uncle held on to the famous Alhambra and other government buildings. Thus the unity of Spanish Islam was utterly destroyed.

While these events were taking place, the sovereigns appeared to have let the war lapse. Actually, this was more apparent than real, for during most of the next four years they were constantly engaged in preparations for massive operations against the last Moslem strongholds. The *Santa Hermandad* was of great help in convoying supplies to Alhama to keep that advanced post in Christian hands. Money, of course, was always a problem and consequently the help of the church, which made a grant of one hundred thousand ducats from ecclesiastical revenues, was highly opportune. It was also very useful in that religious age to have the papacy offer a generous indulgence to all those who bore arms in this "holy war" against the infidel. Nor did operations cease by any means, although major efforts were postponed to ,a later time. Since the next large-scale campaign was to be directed against Málaga, the border operations were designed to isolate that city and cut it off from the possibility of aid. In 1485, the western outpost of Ronda was taken, and the next year both Loja and Illora fell, thus driving wedges on the eastern side between Málaga and Granada. The capture of Marbella on the coast some thirty miles to the west of the threatened port gave the Castilian fleet a very good base very close to the theatre of operations.

In April of 1487 Ferdinand opened the last phase of the war by marching over the Sierra Nevadas and investing the town of Vélez, some miles east of the port and a part of its outer defenses. At this point, El Zagal left Granada in an unsuccessful attempt to succor Vélez. On his return, he found himself shut out of Granada by his nephew and finally forced to set himself up in Baza, Guadix, and Almería, so far to the east as to be virtually out of the immediate theatre of the campaign. Vélez fell on April 27 and Ferdinand proceeded immediately to the investment of Málaga, an event followed with great interest by other European leaders. The siege was long and difficult and fought with much animosity on both sides. The city was strongly fortified and a part of the garrison consisted of tough Moorish troops from Morocco and other parts of north Africa. Much hope was entertained in the city for help from Africa, but the work of the Castilian fleet, patrolling off the coast, put an end to these aspirations. When El Zagal attempted to relieve the city, his column was attacked by troops of Boabdil and cut to pieces. Later this loyal member of the family sent an embassy loaded with gifts to his liege lord, King Ferdinand. It is very difficult to feel much sympathy for the later fate of Boabdil, *el rey chico*, as the Spanish called him; on the other hand it is easy to feel that El Zagal, who at a different time might have been an outstanding Moslem ruler, deserved a better fate.

To instill a greater enthusiasm in the troops after the siege had lasted some time, Ferdinand invited Isabella to the camp. The queen arrived with great pomp; her presence seemed to have a significant effect in raising the morale and the religious dedication of the troops. An assassination attempt by a Moslem fanatic on the sovereigns also was an important factor in arousing further the martial spirit of the men. This helps to explain the terrible terms, in contrast to Ferdinand's usual policy, that were meted out to the unfortunate city. Eventually, to forestall a general assault which might have been followed by a massacre, the inhabitants surrendered on August 18, 1487. This did spare them their lives, but precious little more as they were sold into slavery, except certain handsome youths and maidens who were sent as gifts to the pope, the queen of Naples, the queen of Portugal, and various Spanish nobles. The captured city was repeopled by emigrants from the cities of Christian Spain.

Once again a relative calm fell upon the military operations. With the emirate in such desperate straits, the sovereigns doubtless felt that they could take time to carry out other policies delayed or postponed during the earlier years of the war. In the summer of 1487, both rulers went to Aragon for the important recognition of the Infante John's succession rights by the various cortes of the eastern kingdom. At the same time, it was necessary to take steps to restore public order in some areas where the long absence of Ferdinand had given feudal anarchy a brief chance to reassert itself. It was at this time, as mentioned previously, that Ferdinand decided to introduce into his state the counterpart of the hated and feared *Santa Hermandad* of Castile as a means of enforcing peace in the countryside.[5] He was in Saragossa during November, where he received a *servicio* from the cortes for the Moslem war. Moving southward, the court stopped at Valencia and then went on to the Castilian province of Murcia, where the king set up a field headquarters in June, 1488. It had been decided to move cautiously into the territory controlled by El Zagal,

5. See above, p. 171.

and here that tough fighter inflicted a brief but decisive defeat on Ferdinand's forces as they were edging along the eastern frontier in the direction of Baza. The king withdrew and El Zagal wound up the campaign by a series of raids into Christian territory. The old fighter was still quite dangerous even at the death.

The winter of 1488 found the sovereigns engaged mainly with internal matters. At the same time certain problems north of the Pyrenees demanded attention. An embassy was received from Maximillian of Habsburg, son of the Emperor Frederick III, who, as the husband of the late Mary of Burgundy, was endeavoring to protect his wife's inheritance from France by forming an anti-French league. The Catholic Kings agreed to permit a small force to be sent to the aid of the duke of Brittany in his wars with Anne of Beaujeu, the French regent, but there was definitely a feeling that problems of foreign policy, and many other issues, such as the schemes of the persistent Italian, Christopher Columbus, should be forced to wait on the successful conclusion of the conquest of Granada.

In the spring of 1489 the court moved to Jaén, almost directly north of Granada and where the queen was in residence. Plans called for the elimination of El Zagal and his holdings as a preliminary step to the final drive on Granada. Ferdinand took the field on May 27, and, after reducing several of the adjacent fortresses, finally invested Baza. The city presented tremendous difficulties for siege operations as it was surrounded by dense thickets and woods in addition to many irrigation canals. Preliminary operations led to an unsuccessful advance of the besiegers which put them into such difficulties that they were forced to withdraw. At this point some question arose whether to continue the siege at all. Here the opinion of the queen was solicited. In her reply, Isabella urged them not to abandon a cause so well begun and so nearly completed. Once again her influence, this time *in absentia,* carried the day and it was resolved to go on with the siege. In spite of the difficulties, the lines were gradually drawn tighter around the walls. When Isabella finally visited the camp on November 7, 1489, it appeared to the defenders that there was no hope. Negotiations were opened, therefore, and Ferdinand permitted the inhabitants to send a message to El Zagal; however, that chief informed them that he was unable to send a relieving force. When Ferdinand, in sharp contrast to his policy at Málaga, offered decent terms, it was decided to accept them. The city therefore surrendered on December 4, 1489.

El Zagal himself shortly followed suit. Convinced that there was no possibility of countering the massive forces of Christian Spain, or ending the treasonable hostility of his nephew, he decided to withdraw from the hopeless struggle. Again the victors were magnanimous, and gave him a small principality in the south, although they retained his cities. However, he soon found his new realm, like Napoleon at Elba, too small for his stature and voluntarily withdrew to north Africa where, according to a tradition, he died in poverty.

But time was also running out for the worthless Boabdil. The fall of Málaga and the elimination of El Zagal made the position of Granada hopeless. Apparently some time near the close of 1489, Ferdinand and Isabella summoned him, as their vassal, to surrender the city; but Boabdil alleged, doubtless with complete accuracy, that public opinion would not accept this and refused. On the verge of extinction as an independent state, Granada suddenly came to life. The city hummed with military activity. Boabdil renounced all his engagements with the Catholic Kings and even led raids into the Christian area. He also intrigued in Guadix, Baza, and Almería to stir up opposition against the new regime. But they were all straws in the wind. During the spring of 1490, Ferdinand retaliated by ravaging the *vega* up to the walls of Granada. He reestablished a firm control over the recently conquered cities, and their inhabitants were given the choice of submitting to an investigation of their loyalty, or evacuating their homes. Most of them feared to be put to the test, and in this way the cities of Guadix, Baza, and Almería were repopulated by Christians sent in by the crown.

The winter of 1490 was occupied with preparations for what the sovereigns believed would be the last campaign against Islam. In April of 1491, Ferdinand took the field and by the end of the month he had moved into the *vega* in front of the city itself. Granada was defended by massive walls and there was no shortage of manpower. According to Prescott, the population had been swelled to possibly 200,000 citizens by fugitives from the recently occupied areas. The besiegers probably did not exceed 50,000 foot and horse, although some writers have put the figure higher. Both the king and the queen, with some of their children, were present in the camp. The moment was historic and all realized it. After some seven hundred years, the sojourn of the Crescent on Spanish soil was about to end.

The siege itself was not nearly as dramatic and exciting, from a military point of view, as some of the romantic historians would like to make it. It was little more than a ravaging of the countryside by the Christians and occasional sallies leading to short, fierce skirmishes with the defenders. In July the besiegers sustained an unexpected blow. Apparently through the carelessness of an attendant, Isabella's tent, a grandiose affair belonging to the marquis of Cádiz, caught fire and ignited other pavilions near it. The blaze spread and did not cease until most of the camp had been destroyed. Once again the Moslems seemed unable to take advantage of the opportunity fate handed them, and the sovereigns had the camp rebuilt of wood, brick, and mortar, naming it the city of Santa Fé. Apparently this event dealt the last blow to the faint hopes of the defenders, especially the emir. In October Boabdil opened secret negotiations with Hernando de Zafra and Gonsalvo de Córdoba, the plenipotentiaries of Castile. By November the terms had been drawn up; the city was to be surrendered within sixty days and all military supplies and fortifications were to become crown property. However, the inhabitants were not to be molested in their property, laws, or religion—exceedingly generous terms for the time, and undoubtedly too generous to be kept. The formal surrender was originally intended for the end of January, but as rumors of the settlement leaked, the Granadine government feared a popular demonstration and so the date was moved up to January 2, 1492.

On that day the city was occupied by Cardinal Mendoza while the sovereigns waited for their formal entrance. For this great occasion, the utmost magnificence was assumed by the rulers and indeed the entire court shone out in a burst of gems, polished steel, cloth of gold and silver, and, above all, the bright banners of the units participating. Pending the occupation of the city, the king and queen received the unfortunate Boabdil with their usual stately courtesy and accepted from him the keys of the city. He then departed for the estates reserved for him, only to die in battle a few years afterward in north Africa. Eventually, the large silver cross, a gift of Pope Sixtus IV and which had been borne throughout the war wherever Ferdinand was present, was solemnly raised, along with the standards of Castile and Santiago, over the roof of the Alhambra. As the host burst into a *Te Deum*, Ferdinand and Isabella made their formal entrý, and the queen was saluted by all as the ruler of Granada. It was the great moment of their reigns.

4

The story of the conquest of Granada has an epilogue which begins heroically and ends tragically. It begins with the death of the marquis of Cádiz, and ends with the violation of the treaty provisions and the persecutions introduced by Cardinal Cisneros. The brave marquis had become the hero of the war, having been, in a sense, an immediate cause of it by reason of his successful raid on Alhama in 1482. Throughout the intervening ten years he had been present at all the major operations and had been universally admired by both friends and adversaries for his courage and ability. In this enterprise he literally wore himself out. Not long after the fall of Granada he retired to his estates and, on August 28, 1492, as Columbus was pushing into the reaches of the mid-Atlantic, the marquis died in his palace at Seville from what his contemporary Andrés Bernaldez calls fatigue and over-exposure.[6] He was forty-nine years old. The entire court at once went into mourning for him, and the sovereigns went out of their way to show their gratitude for his years of loyal service by bestowing honors on his descendants. Although married twice, Rodrigo had no issue by his wives. He did, however, have three illegitimate daughters and the court agreed to transmit his rank and titles to the son of the oldest daughter. Later when the crown reannexed Cádiz (it had passed out of royal control during the reign of Henry IV), the Ponce de Leon family received various estates in compensation, with the head of the family receiving the title of duke of Arcos.

As for the former kingdom of Granada, peace settled down wearily after ten long years of fighting. War fatigue, possibly, had something to do with the very moderate terms offered by the Catholic Kings, and for a few years there was a general tranquility. Unlike earlier arrangements made in the case of the kingdom of Valencia, or later in the cases of Spanish Navarre and Portugal, no attempt was made to preserve the administrative integrity of the kingdom. It was simply annexed outright to the crown of Castile and given seats in the Cortes of that kingdom. Probably the government feared that any attempt to preseve the Moslem state would delay the process of assimilation they hoped would soon take place. It is also of interest to note that there was no question of annexing any part of Granada to Aragon. It is true that there was no common frontier which might have given Ferdinand an excuse for making such a claim, but in view of the important contributions made by Aragon in the war it would not have been surprising if someone had raised the question; significantly, no one seems to have even thought of such a thing—proof of the extent to which a sense of *hispanidad* had developed since the joint reigns had begun. Granada was set up as an archbishopric with the incumbent being the gentle Talavera, former confessor of the queen, and presently bishop of Ávila. To represent the crown and command the military forces within the newly conquered kingdom, the queen appointed the count of Tendilla, a member of the famous Mendoza family, as captain-general. Both appointments were excellent. Tendilla had been a gallant soldier during the recent wars and had earned the respect of his new subjects. As for Talavera, the only criticism that can be made of him and his work is that it was too far in advance of the time to endure in an age of religious intolerance.

Personally, the archbishop carefully avoided unnecessary display and personal pomp and even insisted on an episcopal income con-

6. Andrés Bernáldez. *Historia de los Reyes Católicos* as quoted by Préscott, II, 106.

siderably less than he had received in Ávila. Although he, like everyone else, was anxious to see the conquered Moslems embrace Christianity, he wisely refrained from any form of pressure and preferred a smaller number of *sincere* converts to the masses of disloyal Christians that a policy of enforced baptisms might have brought into the Church. He required his clergy to learn Arabic and set about it himself. He also had an Arabic grammar and vocabulary compiled and even proposed translating parts of the Gospels into Arabic with the eventual goal of translating the entire body of Scriptures. If these wise measures had been carried to fruition, Spain might have been spared some painful chapters in her history, but unfortunately Talavera's slow and sure methods were much too dilatory for the time, and complaints were made that his conversions were too few. Signs that the very generous provisions for religious toleration established by the capitulation of Santa Fe could not be maintained were not wanting. In January of 1498 Ferdinand was forced to rebuke the too eager inquisitors of Valencia for attempting to suppress, on their own authority, the national Moorish dress worn by Moslems in that kingdom. At the court of Isabella there were those who urged the queen to order immediate baptism of all Moslems on the grounds that this would not really violate the treaty because they would thereby gain eternal salvation—a strange argument, but one that would eventually be effective although the queen refused to go so far at that time. However, in 1499 when the court had stopped at Granada, the question of religious policy toward the Moslems came up again and this time the sovereigns yielded to the extremists by appointing Cardinal Cisneros as an associate of Talavera to speed up the work of conversion.

It is now time to consider the career of this remarkable man who, from this point on to his death in 1517, plays a major role in the government of Castile. Born Francisco Jimenes de Cisneros at Tordelaguna in 1436, he came from a minor noble family that had seen better days. He was early intended for the church and studied first at Alcalá and later at Salamanca, where he received a double degree in both civil and canon law, a remarkable feat. Advised to seek preferment in the greater world of the Holy See itself, he went to Rome and spent six years in the Eternal City. The death of his father at the end of this period called him home, but not before he had obtained from the papacy promise for a benefice of a certain standing in the diocese of Toledo as soon as a vacancy should occur. In 1473 such a holding did fall vacant and, acting on the papal promise, Cisneros promptly took it over. Unfortunately for his ambitions, the fiery Carrillo was still archbishop and had already intended to bestow the benefice on one of his own party. When Cisneros refused to resign,

Carrillo had him thrown in prison to soften his resistance. We now can learn something of the unyielding temper of this man since he continued to defy the archbishop and remained in prison for six years, steadfastly refusing to surrender his holding. Eventually papal pressure forced Carrillo to release him and Cisneros withdrew from Toledo by accepting the chaplaincy of Sigüenza in 1480, where he first met Cardinal Mendoza, then that city's bishop.

While at Sigüenza he carried on his linguistic and theological studies which were eventually to lead to the *Complutensian Polyglot* and also found time to act as Mendoza's administrative vicar. But all through these (and later) years he was troubled by an urge to withdraw from the world and spend his life in meditation and prayer. About this time he joined the Franciscan Order in its strictest form— the Observantines—and soon won a reputation for sanctity by his violent self-mortification. At Castañar he built a small chapel where he lived for three years very much in the manner of an early medieval hermit. It is reported that Cardinal Mendoza, that very wordly prelate, objected to his withdrawal from the world and is supposed to have remarked that talents like his could not be long hidden in a cloister. Such proved to be the case. In 1492 Isabella lost her confessor when Talavera was advanced to the see of Granada, and Mendoza lost no time in suggesting the name of Cisneros. As might be expected, this intense, austere monk made a great impression on the queen, and all the more because here was no uncouth rustic but a highly trained and disciplined body and mind, a religious fanatic but also a learned man. In fact, it may be said that Cisneros embodied both the best and the worst aspects of Spanish civilization. There is no question of his sincerity, his piety, or his complete lack of self-interest; however, because of his blindness to the realities where religious problems were concerned, and because of his violent resistance to any opposition in the name of moderate policies, the judgment of Lea on him and his work must stand as true. "Much as Spain owes to this extraordinary man, his services were far overbalanced by the irreparable mischief which he wrought in a work for which he was particularly unfitted."[7]

It took no little urging to overcome a resistance undoubtedly sincere, but eventually Cisneros accepted the post of royal confessor and entered into public life, a career he constantly lamented, but which ceased only with his death some twenty-five years later. In 1494 he was chosen provincial of his order and in this position he began his monastic reforms, the most beneficial aspect of his work.

7. Henry Charles Lea, *The Moriscos of Spain, Their Conversion and Expulsion* (Philadelphis, 1901), pp. 29–30.

Finding the Franciscans well provided with material luxuries, he struck violently in an effort to restore the piety of the order's early days. In spite of intense opposition he carried out a remarkable change in morals and practices with the strong support and approval of the queen, who enlisted the support of that somewhat less than reforming pope, Alexander VI. Before Mendoza died in 1495, he had apparently recommended his protégé for the vacant see—next to the papacy perhaps the most powerful ecclesiastical post in Europe. According to a story which his biographers have all found most edifying, Cisneros literally fled from the appointment and had to be pursued in force and brought back to court, accepting only when ordered to do so by the pope. After his installation, he proceeded to the reform of his diocese and again his high-handed methods produced an equally high-handed resistance. Eventually the general of the Franciscan Order was brought into the picture by an appeal in 1496, and, this failing to produce a respite, the harried brothers succeeded in getting the pope to issue a bull prohibiting further action pending his own investigation. But the queen rushed to Cisneros' defense, he himself was resolute in his determination not to be stopped in the work of reform, and by 1497 most of the opposition had been overcome. In spite of the violence of his methods, and his ruthless crushing of opposition, his work in this instance was significant and all to the good. Monastic life in Spain was cleansed and purged of many of the evils later denounced by Luther, and while it is difficult to imagine Protestantism finding a permanent foothold south of the Pyrenees; it might have been a real threat in the sixteenth century had it not been for the work of Cisneros.

Such was the man who was associated with Talavera in the work of encouraging conversions amongst the Moslems of Granada. His worst characteristics came immediately to the fore. The pressure for conversion was soon increased. At first only argumentation and bribes, in the form of rich gifts to important converts, were used, but uglier methods followed. Forcible baptisms took place, especially among renegade Christians and their children. Although highly educated himself, Cisneros' religious prejudices allowed him no respect or understanding for Moslem culture. Particularly offensive was his burning of all the Arabic books and manuscripts, some of them works of art, that he could get his hands on. Only three hundred works on medicine, through some strange aberration, would he spare, and these were turned over to his new University of Alcalá. The Moslems deeply resented this sort of treatment, especially when it was in direct violation of the treaty, and even some Castilians urged a more moderate course, but nothing could stop his fanatical zeal. As might have been expected, a revolt was the final answer of the persecuted.

Taking advantage of an incident that inflamed public opinion, the Moslems of the Albaycin quarter of Granada rose, early in 1500, and besieged Cisneros in his residence. Although he was rescued by troops under Count Tendilla, the insurgents refused to lay down their arms and it required ten days of negotiations before order could be reestablished; this was achieved only through the personal intervention of Talavera and Tendilla. Ferdinand and Isabella were displeased and angered at the first reports reaching them, and Ferdinand is supposed to have reproached his wife bitterly for her support of Cisneros; however, when that unabashed prelate appeared at court to explain himself, he was able to win them over, or at least Isabella since Ferdinand never associated himself too whole-heartedly with the persecution of the Moslems after 1492. After the queen sent commissioners to render an official report on the Albaycin revolt, some citizens were executed, some imprisoned, and many sold their estates and emigrated to north Africa. But, in apparent justification of Cisneros' policy, there were many conversions since the government offered pardon for previous offenses to those who would accept baptism. Cisneros, it hardly need be added, was now firmly reestablished in Isabella's favor and his policy of persecution became official, the treaty notwithstanding.

But the fire lighted in Granada soon spread to other regions. A second revolt broke out in the wild, mountainous district of the Alpujarras which extended southeast from the capital toward the Mediterranean. This area was filled with tiny villages inhabited by primitive, backward Moslems barely touched by civilization. Alarmed at the reports of widespread apostasy in Granada, they decided to take up arms in defense of the faith and began seizing forts and passes and even carried out some raids in Christian territory. Tendilla, assisted by Gonsalvo de Córdoba, the future generalissimo of the Italian wars, took the field against them. In spite of the barbarity with which Huejar was taken and pillaged, the uprising continued, and at the end of February, 1500, Ferdinand himself took the field at the head of royal troops. One by one the little villages were taken, but the resistance was fierce and both sides showed little mercy. Eventually peace was restored on the basis of the surrender of all arms plus occupation of various strongholds by loyal forces. A fine of 50,000 ducats was levied on the entire region, but those who would accept baptism were excused from paying their share. Apparently a good many took advantage of this offer to enter the church, whereupon, as Christians, they were then subject to the tender mercies of the Inquisition.

An even more bloody conflict developed in the area of the Sierra Vermeja near Ronda. Alarmed at the report of widespread conversions in Granada, the mountaineers attacked Christian villages. In addition to widespread killings, a considerable number of Christians seem to have been kidnapped to be sold as slaves in the markets of north Africa. The government assembled a force at Ronda, under distinguished leadership, to deal with the situation. Present were the counts of Cifuentes and Ureña, Alonso de Aguilar who was a famous fighter, and the older brother of Gonsalvo de Córdoba. The expedition moved into the Sierra and encountered a Moslems force on March 18, 1501, which they defeated, but when the Christians dispersed to pillage, they were suddenly attacked again, this time with disastrous results. In the rout that followed, many distinguished figures were killed; among them were Alonso de Aguilar and the famous engineer and artillerist Francisco Ramírez of Madrid. This defeat caused a great shock in Spain, and much dismay. There was fear of a general uprising and the possibility that it might be reinforced from north Africa or the Near East. Ferdinand at once turned from the Italian situation which had been engrossing his attention and took the field at Ronda early in April. But the rebels were alarmed by their very success, and cooler heads opened negotiations to avoid having to face the full power of an aroused monarchy. Ferdinand's terms were stern: either baptism or exile. While some went to north Africa, undoubtedly the great majority became Christians, although exactly what they really thought about their new faith had best be left to the imagination. Some Moslems, of course, had existed for centuries in the old cities of Castile where they were protected by special privileges and grants made by the medieval kings, and some still persisted in the kingdom of Granada despite Cisneros, but most of them had accepted baptism under the circumstances described above and were known henceforth as *moriscos* and will be so termed in this book.

But the crusading zeal of Isabella and Cisneros could not allow even this remnant to remain in peace. There was always the fear that the majority of the converts, whose shaky Christianity was recognized even from the beginning, might be led into apostasy by a tiny minority. Furthermore, the convenient circumstance of the revolts, even though provoked by the initial Christian violation of the religious clauses of the capitulation of Santa Fe, gave Isabella the excuse she needed to escape from these restrictive clauses. Henceforth the elimination of all remaining Moslems, like the fate which befell the Jews in 1492, was not to be long deferred. As a step in this direction, the government of Castile in 1501 prohibited all intercourse between Moslems in any part of the kingdom and the new converts of Granada. The final step was taken by the *Pragmática* of Seville, issued on February 12, 1502. All unbaptized Mohammedans over fourteen years old if males, or twelve if females, were to be out of Castile by the end of April of the same year. They could sell their property and take all movable possessions, except gold and silver, with them. They could go where they wished except to the possessions of the Ottoman sultan, or the cities along the north African coast which were at war with the Christians. The short time limit set permitted virtual confiscation of property—a procedure which was doubtless suggested by the earlier edict against the Jews. No figures of the actual number of Moslems leaving the kingdom can be found that have any dependability whatever. Probably the number was small. By far the greater number seemed to have preferred to stay in the land of their fathers and accept baptism with all its risks. Significantly, Ferdinand took no such steps in the realms of Aragon where Moslems were permitted to remain until 1526. Such was the tragic outcome of this brief experiment in religious toleration, an experiment which, unfortunately, was not to be tried again in Spain until very recent times.

5

The fall of Granada marks a turning point in the history of the Catholic Kings. Henceforth, they had passed beyond the position of mere local success to become major actors on the European scene itself. This development was no accident. The Granadine War, by greatly increasing the prestige of both rulers and by consolidating the power of both states, now enabled them (in this case, chiefly Ferdinand) to engage in great power politics in a manner which would have been impossible before the war.

The news of Granada's capture was received with enthusiasm and excitement throughout Christian Europe, which had been very much on the defensive in the face of Islam's forward march prior to 1453. The foreign volunteers returning home from this and earlier campaigns spread the fame of the two rulers far and wide, and helped pave the way for the title of *"los Reyes Católicos"* formally bestowed on them in 1495 by the Spanish pope, Alexander VI, for their services to the faith. Within Spain itself their standing was supreme and long remained so. A century after the conquest, the Jesuit historian Mariana was so deeply moved by the thought of this achievement that he would write that

> ... as they were in the prime of life, and had now achieved the completion of this glorious conquest, they seemed to represent even more than their wonted majesty. Equal with each other, they were raised far above the rest of the world. They appeared, indeed, more than mortal, and as if sent by Heaven for the Salvation of Spain.[8]

In addition to the factor of personal prestige, the conquest brought in its train other advantages as well as additional problems. The crown

8. Prescott, II, 98.

of Castile had now acquired a rich territory blessed with an extensive, industrious population, and two major Mediterranean ports in addition to many smaller ones. But this acquisition brought with it an acute and burning issue: the problem of assimilation. Could the Spanish government and Spanish civilization, already so profoundly influenced by Islamic culture, assimilate and absorb these new subjects? Unfortunately, after well over a century of intensive efforts to deal with the problem, the government was forced to answer in the negative. While one can quarrel with the techniques used in trying to bring about assimilation, and call the final solution lamentable, it should be pointed out that the government and the people made a real effort over a long period of time to reach a solution other than expulsion—a fact for which justice has seldom been done them.

Another aspect of the conquest of Granada which has not always been sufficiently emphasized was its profound effect on the emergent unity of the crowns. Nothing had more to do with advancing the peculiar nature of Spanish nationalism—an inextricable mixture of political, racial, and religious filiaments—than this long-term military operation. We have already seen that from its inception it required much greater effort and organization than in previous wars with the Moslems during recent centuries. After a decade of almost continuous military activities involving men and material not only from Andalusia but from the distant provinces of the north along the Atlantic seaboard, a sense of common unity in a common cause had been powerfully advanced. Moreover, this sense of unity had been fired and hardened by the mystique of religious passions released in a burst of crusading ardor which was to make Spanish nationalism virtually irresistible for the next century and a half. As has been pointed out several times previously, none of the great fifteenth and sixteenth century agglomerations of territories could overcome the logistics of time and space without this passion, this mystique of empire which was inspired by both the noblest and basest motives of mankind. To this end the victory over the Mohammedans of Granada after ten long years of warfare was a powerful incentive.

More specifically, the functioning of governmental processes in the peninsula was made much more efficient by reason of the demands of the Granadine War. Practically every branch of government was affected; the earlier reforms were now matured, as it were, by extensive use. Money being constantly a problem, all the traditional devices were manipulated to yield larger and larger amounts—even the papacy was pressured into making its contributions.[9] Hitherto, even the most advanced states found any large-scale military effort over an extended period beyond their capabilities. The achievement of Fer-

9. See above, p. 219.

dinand and Isabella in organizing large numbers of men and the supplies necessary to support them for almost annual campaigns during the greater part of a decade is almost unique in the fifteenth century.

Naturally, the most direct influence was on the naval and military establishment itself. The Castilian fleet was extensively used in blockading the southern coast, and this inadvertently was preparing the way for the age of discovery and colonization. As for the land forces, it may be said that a national army was born during the war, a strange mixture of royal troops, nobles' armies, municipal levies, and mercenaries held together by religious fervor and the prestige of the sovereigns. The armies assembled were among the largest of the time and the government thus learned the techniques of holding such large masses of men together and supplying them with necessities. It was here also that the greatest captain of the age, Gonsalvo de Córdoba, learned the skills that were to bring him his laurels on the fields of Italy. As mentioned previously, the numerous sieges of the war helped develop the artillery under the direction of Francisco Ramírez, assisted by German, French, and Italian specialists. It is clear that the lessons of the war were not lost on the sovereigns. In 1493 they created the Old Guard of Castile, a permanent force of twenty-five-hundred men, and three years later they introduced the first step toward compulsory military service in European history. This was the requirement that one out of any twelve citizens between the ages of twenty and forty, in a given locality, might be liable for military service when called. Unfortunately, details on the enforcement of this regulation are lacking, but it is clear that Ferdinand and Isabella were in this way able to free themselves to a considerable degree from their dependence on the traditional and often highly undependable feudal levies.

With the war happily concluded, most of the internal problems of the peninsula were settled. The king and queen enjoyed good relations with Portugal and with Navarre. Any question of their rights to their thrones had long since passed and the internal pacification of Spain was proceeding apace. The first uproar over the Inquisition was over and the institution was gradually becoming a regular feature of Spanish life. Ten years of war had given the sovereigns new powers and new weapons. They were now ready to embark on bold new enterprises that would carry them far beyond the confines of the Iberian Peninsula.

6

With the conclusion of the Granadine War in 1492, Isabella was prepared to take the offensive against Islam across the Strait of Gibraltar and into the tiny Moslem states of the north African littoral. It does not seem likely that Ferdinand was much interested. To judge by his attitude ten years hence, the only value he attached to the Spanish conquests on the coast was as safeguards for his communications with Italy; certainly, he showed little interest in a "holy war" and was completely apathetic to the idea of a vast Spanish empire in north Africa. It was the queen and those near her who shared her medieval, crusading zeal that were the moving spirits behind these dreams.

Losing no time after the fall of Granada, the queen sent out a trusted advisor, Lorenzo de Padilla, to reconnoiter the coast near the Strait of Gibraltar in 1493. He went as far east as Tlemcen and returned to present his information. The old disputes with Portugal over her special areas were renewed when the sovereigns requested that Pope Alexander VI bestow on Castile the right to make conquests along the north African coast. The Portuguese promptly protested and urged their prior claims. After lengthy discussions, a compromise was reached whereby everything east of and including Melilla, a city less than two hundred miles southeast of Gibraltar, was assigned to Castile. In 1496–97, a force sponsored by the Andalusian duke of Medina Sidonia seized Melilla and turned it over to the Catholic Kings. And then followed a long delay. This was undoubtedly due to Ferdinand's steadily increasing ambitions in Naples—a family trait, it will be remembered—and the growing concern of both husband and wife over their future successor, especially after the lamentable death of the Infante John in 1497. With King Ferdinand openly at war with France and heavily dependent on the financial and military resources of Castile, there was no money or men readily available for pursuit of the infidel in Africa. Furthermore, with the death of the queen in 1504, there was only one person who still cherished her hopes for north African conquests, but Cardinal Cisneros' hands were tied as long as Ferdinand was prosecuting the war in Italy.

By 1505, however, the war ended and apparently the cardinal urged a renewal of the crusade against Islam by offering to pay the first two months' expenses of an African campaign from ecclesiastical funds. Ferdinand was never the man to reject military operations when they cost him little, and gave his consent.

It was decided to attack the fort of Mers-el-Kebir, a key work in the outer defenses of the important city and kingdom of Oran. The cardinal succeeded in asembling a force of some 10,000 men with about 140 warships and transports to carry them to the theater of operations. After raising anchor early in September of 1505, the armada made a landing near the fort on September 11, and shortly afterwards the place was taken. Here again a delay occurred. From the point of military strategy, the only way to be sure of holding on to coastal points would have been to occupy the back country and this, apparently, is what Cisneros wished to do. Unfortunately for his plans, Ferdinand had other and more pressing interests. He was about to be ousted from Castile by his daughter and her husband, Philip, duke of Burgundy, and already had made plans to go to Italy. Before the end of the year he was called back to Spain by the unexpected death of his son-in-law, and the increasing mental derangement of his daughter. Obviously in such crises north Africa was of small importance.

Meanwhile, the situation of the Spaniards in Mers-el-Kebir was increasingly precarious and Cisneros pressed the king for a second expeditionary force to make secure what had been acquired in the first campaign. Once again the cardinal offered to pay the costs from the revenues of the see of Toledo and again Ferdinand agreed. It was finally decided to make Cisneros commander-in-chief of the operation, but with the assistance of a capable military leader who should be in charge of the military operations. From the point of view of religious administration, all newly acquired territories would be placed under the administration of the diocese of Toledo, a promise Ferdinand had little trouble in breaking later. The obvious choice for military commander would have been Gonsalvo de Córdoba, the victor of Italy, but Ferdinand's intense jealousy of the man who won Naples for him precluded that appointment. It was finally given to Pedro de Navarro, a good enough commander, but a man of no scruples and not likely to get along with a superior who regarded the expedition from the point of view of a crusade. It turned out to be a poor choice, and has led some historians to believe that Ferdinand deliberately hoped to keep the formidable cardinal, whom he disliked, out of Spain by involving him in inconclusive military operations.

When the operation began, Cisneros' desire to move immediately on Oran was ignored and a preliminary expedition was mounted far to the west within the Portuguese sphere by an attack on the island of Vélez de la Gomera. After the island was taken, the Portuguese naturally protested and negotiations followed; eventually it was included in the Spanish sphere. The main operation got under way on May 16, 1509, when a relatively large force of perhaps twenty-thousand men was successfully landed in the vicinity of Mers-el-Kebir and three days later the city of Oran fell before a savage assault followed by a barbarous massacre of the defenders and inhabitants. Once again Cisneros wanted to move into the interior to form a large block of territory while Navarro, largely interested in personal plunder, wanted to attack other coastal cities. Ferdinand supported his general, and when the cardinal found evidence convincing him that the king was doing all he could to frustrate his plans, he retired in anger to Spain, where he went into retirement at his beloved University of Alcalá. Navarro was now left in full command in north Africa. It is possible that Ferdinand has been too harshly criticized for his policy. While he evidently did not share Isabella's dream of a great African empire, and was not interested in Cisneros' desire to open up routes into the interior, he may, as Braudel thinks, have been trying to create a new route from Spain to the grain fields of Sicily.[10] This route, which would have been largely overland along the African coast, would have been defended and maintained by the cities and forts taken in 1509, 1510, and 1511. From this point of view, a deep penetration south of the coast would have been relatively pointless and very costly.

In any event, the campaign of 1510 began promptly on January 1 when Navarro set sail for Bugia, about one hundred miles east of Algiers. The city was soon taken and held in spite of frequent efforts to recapture it. At this point in the story, the famous Barbarossa brothers make their appearance. The younger, Khaireddin, destined to be the most famous admiral of his epoch and a scourge of the Christians in the Mediterranean, attacked Bugia unsuccessfully in 1512 and 1515; however, his time had not quite arrived. Meanwhile, after the fall of Bugia, other cities hastened to recognize the authority of the conqueror. At the end of January, Algiers acknowledged the suzerainty of Castile. Tenes to the west, and Dellys to the east soon followed. Tunis had to be by-passed because of its strong fortifications, but in 1511 the important city of Tripoli was added to these acquisitions. Placed under the viceroy of Sicily (and therefore under the crown of Aragon, which lends support to Braudel's interpretation) it was destined to be the last conquest of the era of the Catholic Kings, and was shortly afterwards followed by a serious defeat. Under the joint command of Navarro and García de Toledo, father of the famous duke of Alba of Philip II's reign, an expedition was sent to capture the island of Gelves in the Gulf of Tunis. Inadequately prepared, the Spanish force was defeated with heavy loss. According to Konetzke, Ferdinand was shaken by this news and planned to retrieve the situation by taking the field in person, as he had so often done in the earlier battles of the war against Islam; he also hoped by additional conquests to create a solid block of Spanish holdings on the Barbary Coast that would be self-sustaining and capable of its own defense.[11] But once again Italian affairs intervened. The king

10. Braudel, p. 103, footnote 1.
11. Konetzke, pp. 269–70.

became involved with Pope Julius II in a new combination to expel the "barbarians" (and incidentally Ferdinand's rivals) from Italy. In the war of the Holy League that followed, Spanish armies played a leading role, and left few men to spare for an African campaign. And in the following year occurred Ferdinand's conquest of Navarre.[12] As a result, nothing more was done in Africa until the next reign.

Merriman, the able historian of the Spanish empire, feels that the abandonment of the north African campaign by Ferdinand was almost inevitable, given his more important interests elsewhere.[13] Later historians have not been so charitable. Konetzke believes that Ferdinand's failure to renew the attack in 1512 was a fatal mistake as he had a chance to get control of the entire coast, given the disorganized and demoralized state of the Moslem cities, and that such an opportunity never came again.[14] Braudel is even more unsparing in his criticism:

> It is truly a catastrophe in Spanish history that after these operations . . . this new war of Granada was not followed with determination, and that this *unrewarding but essential* task had to be sacrificed to the Italian mirage, and to the relative facility of American operations.[15]

This of course makes sense if it is assumed that Spain had an obligation to Europe after the fall of Granada to attempt the defense of Christianity whenever and wherever threatened by Islam—an obligation, it might be added, that the Habsburg rulers of Spain always kept before their eyes and tried, intermittently, to honor. Doubtless Ferdinand was little if any influenced by colonial considerations in the foreign policy of his late years, but his successors found the American gold and silver so essential, and the whole colonial operation so extensive and demanding, that it was only occasionally that a return to the ideals of Isabella and Cisneros could be indulged in. North Africa was sacrificed, not to the "mirages of Italy, but to the silver mines of San Luis Potosí." As a result, there was created in the eastern Mediterranean, in the phrase of Braudel, "a zone of least interest" and while the attention of Spain was focused on the New World, the renewal of the war against Islam, which Ferdinand and Isabella inaugurated with the attack on Alhama, was allowed to lapse, and eventually the Turk moved into the vacuum.[16] The occupation of Egypt by the Turks in 1517, which began a new phase in the history of the Mediterranean, was thus not unconnected with the rise of the

12. For these and other events in Ferdinand's foreign policy, see Chapter VI.

13. Merriman, Vol. II, p. 260.

14. Konetzke, p. 270.

15. Braudel, p. 86. Italics are mine.

16. Ibid., p. 513.

Spanish empire overseas. However, in view of the magnificence of that achievement, and viewing the history of Spain in broad perspective, it would be a rash historian who would say that Spain made the wrong decision in emphasizing America at the expense of north Africa.

*CHAPTER V*

# The Origins of the

# Spanish Overseas Empire

It is not the intention of this study to go into a detailed account of the Spanish colonies and their establishment. That has been done repeatedly by specialists in the field of Latin American history, and with great success. All that needs to be done, for the purpose of this work, is to show how the colonial movement arose from existing conditions within the peninsula, its historical background, how policies were evolved, and how existing institutions were transferred to the New World and there modified to suit conditions. In short, despite the fact that we must consider overseas expansion, the focus will be kept mainly on Spain.

That Castile should inaugurate the greatest imperial experiment since Rome was not so much of an accident as it may seem. All empires, when studied in detail, probably appear fortuitous, and indeed this element can never be ignored in history, but in the case of Castile both the historic past and the conditions of the present created a powerful impetus toward overseas expansion. Probably no other nation, except to a lesser degree Portugal and Aragon, had as much preparation for dealing with colonial conditions as Castile. The institutions connected with a moving frontier, the border raids and counter-raids, the presence of powerful cultural and religious aliens in close proximity to the Castilians, the early colonial laboratory of the Canaries, all provided experiences that were constantly utilized in the New World. After the initial phase of the *conquisitadores*, a much greater degree of organization was necessary; a model for this was found close at hand in Aragon's long experience in controlling its Mediterranean island empire.

But even with this unique training for empire which the blind forces of history were giving to medieval Castile, it is doubtful if much could have been done without what the twentieth century would call a "proper mental conditioning." There had to be a will to empire, a willingness to undertake tremendous exertions, a shouldering of huge responsibilities, the unremunerative as well as the remunerative. No empire can be created without these. Institutions alone will not do it; it is purely a state of mind, and it is essential. Braudel has pointed this out in a striking passage which also explains the peculiar mentality which led to the creation of the Spanish empire:

> Therefore, there are no empires without a mystique sense of mission and in western Europe no empires without that enormous prestige that comes from the *mystique* of a crusade, from its political implications of a mingling of heaven and earth.[1]

The centuries of war between Christian and Moslem had long acquainted Spaniards with the concept of a crusade; in fact, Spain may be said to be the original home of the crusading idea long before Godfrey of Bouillon and Peter the Hermit. Although, as we have seen, there were periods when the concept lay dormant, it was always capable of flaring up on occasions and it was Isabella's particular achievement through the Granadine War to have rewakened the crusading fervor in a particularly intense form. We have also seen how the creation of the Inquisition and the attacks on both Jews and Moslems had intensified the religious fanaticism of Spain. It was this situation that conditioned the Spanish mind to accept the burdens, as well as the profits, of empire; and since the burdens long preceded the profits, without this mental attitude there would have probably been no empire.

It is also no accident that the empire began in 1492—a date when all the favorable forces seemed to reach conjunction. The Granadine War had just ended with a victory and the queen was prepared to continue the holy war against Islam to the shores of north Africa. Anything that might assist in an operation obviously so pleasing to God was mandatory, from the conversion of the heathen to the pious appropriation of their wealth in the good cause. Moreover, for the first time in years, the sovereigns were free to consider the propositions of Christopher Columbus, the Genoese who had several times importuned them with his rather unsound ideas about a voyage to

---

1. Braudel, p. 507. Since I have translated this passage with some freedom, I cite here the original: "Or il n'y a pas d'empires sans mystique, et dans l'Europe occidentale, pas d'empires hors de cette mystique prestigieuse de la croisade, de sa politique entre terre et ciel."

the Indies.[2] And lastly, 1492 saw the election of the Spaniard Rodrigo Borgia (or Borja in its Spanish form) to the chair of Saint Peter as Pope Alexander VI. With a former subject of Ferdinand's from the kingdom of Valencia wearing the triple tiara it would now be much easier for Spain, or more correctly, Castile, to obtain recognition of new discoveries—especially in view of the almost certain challenge of Portugal—from the only authoritative international office which the times would respect.

There is also another favorable factor which has seldom been noticed. The ten years of war in Andalusia (1481–1492) had undoubtedly led to the usual conditions following a war: violence, a disregard for property and human life, insecurity, and generally unsettled conditions. In such a situation certain types seem to rise to the surface. They usually develop the qualities necessary for survival in a war-torn area: a certain desperate courage, boldness, mendacity, liking for violence and willingness to shed blood, cupidity, and the gambler's instinct to stake all on a last chance. Since the greatest number of settlers in the New World during the early period came from Andalusia[3], it seems reasonable to suppose that the characteristics of the *conquistador* period—a mixture of magnificent courage and the worst sort of villainy—were formed by conditions of the Granadine War whose greatest impact was on Andalusia.

Thus Castile and Aragon had unknowingly been preparing over the centuries for the great colonial expansion, and by 1492 the times were ripe. For these and other reasons cited later, Castile accepted the responsibilities of empire. It is astonishing how early these were understood, and goes far to explain why Castile in particular and Spain in general was one of the world's great colonizers. Another significant episode took place in the climactic year of 1492. In the preface to his *Gramática Castillana*, the first ever written, Antonio de Nebrija remarked that "always language was the companion of empire".[4] and dedicated the work to Isabella. The historic implications are even more marked in the scene that followed. When, sometime later, the author was presented to the queen at Salamanca, she inquired as to the utility of the work. Replying for Nebrija, Bishop Talavera stated that

> since Your Majesty has placed beneath your yoke many barbarous populations and nations with foreign tongues, and since with this conquest

2. Although Columbus' birthplace is claimed by many places, Genoa still seems the most likely, and the most generally accepted by historians.

3. For a detailed description of the sources of the early migration from Spain to the colonies, see an unpublished doctoral dissertation by Aubry Neasham in the Bancroft Library, University of California at Berkeley.

4. del Arco, pp. 650–51

these peoples must receive the laws which the conqueror imposes on the conquered, this grammatical art can therefore help bring to pass a better knowledge of our language.[5]

It was this early awareness of their "mission" that marks the Castilian people above all others in the history of European expansion until we come to the British of the nineteenth century.

The Spanish government, in the eloquent words of Professor Haring accepted the task of colonization with the most painstaking seriousness. With high ideals of order and justice, of religious and political unity, it extended to its ultramarine possessions its faith, its languages, its law and its administration; built churches and monasteries; founded schools and universities; in short endeavored to make its colonies an integral part of the Spanish monarchy.[6]

2

Undoubtedly an immediate stimulus to overseas expansion came from the rivalry with Portugal. We have already seen how this rivalry began with the Succession War, which had its naval and economic aspects. Alarmed at the Portuguese expansion in Africa, Ferdinand and Isabella attempted to get a foothold there through the encouragement of private expeditions to "Guinea" as west Africa was then known. They offered to license Castilian traders in return for one-fifth of the profits. They even went so far as to consider some kind of colony on the Guinea coast, for a decree of February 17, 1479, provided for the transportation of workers and miners to operate gold mines there. The peace with Portugal before the end of the year put an end to colonial projects within the Portuguese sphere, but voyages to west Africa from Spain were very frequent and there were numerous fights whenever Spanish and Portuguese ships met off the coast. Even after the signing of the peace treaty, various differences continued. The Spainsh rulers were anxious to obtain a modification of the clause prohibiting Spanish trade with Guinea, and this may have been involved in the famous plot of the duke of Braganza against John II of Portugal, an intrigue that was believed to have Spanish support. The plot was crushed with the execution of the duke, but in view of the disputes between the two governments over the Canaries, the Spanish sovereigns were doubtless anxious to improve relations. Consequently, a marriage proposal was made in 1490 between the Infanta Isabella, oldest child of the Catholic Kings, and the Infante Alfonso of Portugal. Unfortunately, the infante died the following year and Isabella returned to Spain. Meanwhile Hispano-

5 Ibid.
6. Henry Clarence Haring, *Trade and Navigation between Spain and the Indies in the Time of the Habsburgs* (Cambridge, 1918, p. xii.

Portuguese disputes had been focused on a new center—the Canary Islands.

At the stage then reached by overseas expansion, the Canaries were strategically important since they were located approximately sixty miles from the west African coast and thus were directly athwart the Portuguese routes southward. These islands had been long known to Europeans. The elder Pliny had given them their name (Canaria) because of the numbers of wild dogs supposed to be there. The original inhabitants were of primitive Cro-Magnon stock who had probably emigrated from north Africa in prehistoric times. By the time of the first European contacts they were divided into two groups: the *Guanches* who had settled in the western islands and the *Canaries* who were living in the eastern part of the archipelago. They were of brown complexion, with blue or gray eyes and light hair, and contemporary accounts enlarged upon their physical strength and vigorous activities. Their cultural level has been described as paleolithic with a slightly more advanced pottery. Apparently they were ruled by local chiefs who called them together in outdoor assemblies for ceremonies and sports. Although Christianity had not reached the islands before the fifteenth century, the native faith seems to have been monotheistic. In sum, it may be said that the islanders were only slightly more advanced than the inhabitants of the Caribbean who were still enjoying their last years in the happy state of the "undiscovered."

In the fourteenth century a grandson of Alfonso X had been crowned king of the Canaries by the Avignonese pope, Clement VI. Lack of funds, however, prevented anything from being done in this early period. In 1402, two Frenchmen, Gadifer de la Salle and Jean de Béthancourt, sailed together from La Rochelle and began the final explorations before the actual occupation of the archipelago by Spain. Béthancourt later went to Spain and obtained an investiture from Henry III of Castile, and both explorers sold and resold many times their supposed rights and claims over the islands. Eventually some of these claims were acquired by Prince Henry the Navigator while others had passed into the hands of the Herrara family of Castile.

After much negotiation, Ferdinand and Isabella on October 15, 1477, bought out a part of the claims of the Herraras, who were confirmed in their rights, but the crown henceforth acquired sovereignty over Teneriffe, Palma, and Grand Canary. Shortly thereafter an expedition was organized for the occupation of this last island. In many ways it was still a medieval enterprise. Members furnished their own arms, paid their expenses, and were promised land in return. Some who furnished part of the military contingent were allowed to count this as part of their feudal service to the queen. The church was also induced to pay some of the cost; and, because of this, certain commercial monopolies were given to the bishops involved, especially Juan de Frias, titular bishop of the Canaries. The expedition, under the command of an old soldier named Rejón, set out from Seville in the spring of 1478 and soon ran into trouble. There were violent quarrels between the soldiers and their ecclesiastical backers, the Portuguese protested, and the local inhabitants were anything but enthusiastic.

Eventually Portuguese claims were settled by what might be called the colonial compromise of the treaty of Alcaçovas in 1479. Castile recognized the exclusive rights of Portugal over the kingdoms of Fez, and Guinea in west Africa, as well as the archipelagos of Madeira, the Azores, and the Cape Verde Islands; foreign merchants could not trade in these places without the permission of the king of Portugal. On the other hand, the Canaries were now recognized as being under Castilian sovereignty. As for Rejón and his little expedition, although greatly outnumbered, superior weapons won the day, as was to be repeated for the next century throughout the New World. Meanwhile, the quarrels between Rejón and the churchmen present finally became so scandalous that the sovereigns decided to send out two special commissioners to settle matters, and for this purpose they selected Pedro Fernández de Algaba as *juez pesquisidor*, and Alfonso Fernández de Lugo, an old soldier of the Moorish wars, to go to the Grand Canary and learn the facts. Here again it will be recognized that this arrangement was to be repeated frequently when similar difficulties occurred in the colonization of the Americas. As a result of the investigation, Rejón was sent home in chains, but succeeded in recovering his standing and was allowed to return to the island with reinforcements. Here he promptly executed the man who had been sent out to replace him but did not harm Lugo, who was to have the final word on the whole business. But the queen was not yet satisfied and finally decided to send out Pedro de Vera, a well-to-do soldier whose capacities for quarreling and making trouble for his neighbors undoubtedly qualified him for colonial activities. Once again the pattern was repeated. Vera arrived, sent Rejón back in chains, Rejón's friends succeeded in rehabilitating him, and in June of 1481 he returned with two ships and some 320 men.

Meanwhile, Vera had greatly stimulated native resistance by his atrocious cruelty. On one occasion, when trying to entice some of them into boats so that they could be sold as slaves, he solemnly swore on the Host that they were to take part in the conquest of Teneriffe, having first carefully obtained an unconsecrated wafer so that he could break his oath with impunity.[7] Rejón was not able to

7. Merriman, II, 175–81; Konetzke, pp. 111–13.

land on Grand Canary and put in at one of the Herrara islands, where the family had him killed. His widow immediately sailed home to the court to obtain vengeance on her husband's murderers, and probably would have obtained it had not Ferdinand Peraza, head of the Herrara clan, saved himself by proposing marriage to a lady-in-waiting of the queen. Since Ferdinand had been showing undue interest in this lady, Isabella was happy over a solution which would settle several different matters at once. Peraza was pardoned, married, and returned to Grand Canary with his new wife as soon as possible. Resistance was ended and the island was pacified by 1483. But once again difficulties arose. Vera's terrible treatment of the natives became too scandalous to ignore and eventually, in 1485, the bishop of the Canaries made formal complaints. In 1489 another *juez pesquisidor* was sent out and in his turn Vera was sent home in disgrace—and probably in chains.

The government now turned to Lugo, the former companion of Algaba, and as he offered to mount an expedition largely at his own expense, he received a greater measure of authority than his predecessors. He was promised the office of *adelantado*, for the first time established beyond the confines of the peninsula, and given some rights over the nearby African coast.[8] As a result Palma was incorporated into the crown in 1492. In April of the next year, while Christopher Columbus was hastening to Barcelona to inform the sovereigns of *his* achievements, Lugo was beginning the conquest of Teneriffe. For this he had the largest force yet assembled for the Canaries, 1000 foot and 125 horse, but he ran into greatly increased native resistance and was forced to return to Grand Canary in 1494 for additional support. He returned in the same year and resumed his operations, completing the conquest of the island by September, 1496. He was now made governor of Palma and Teneriffe, and *adelantado* for all the islands. Since at about this time he married into the Herrara family he had, under the supervision of the crown, virtually the entire archipelago within his jurisdiction. Lugo remained in the Canaries for the rest of his life. He died in 1525, and must be considered, as Merriman describes him, "one of the most interesting of the Spanish conquistadores and one of the least known."[9]

As in the case of later colonial experiences in the Americas, the government, after early and generous concessions to private individuals to undertake the conquest and occupation, later did everything possible to reduce its concessions and increase the authority of the crown. The office of *adelantado* remained, as promised, hereditary

8. See above, p. 84.
9. Merriman, II, 84.

in the Lugo family, but in 1536–37 it lost practically all its political authority. Each of the islands was incorporated as a municipality of Castile and soon acquired the usual organs of local administration developed centuries past on the mainland—an *ayuntamiento, alguaciles,* and *alcaldes.* In 1526–27 an *audiencia* was set up for the entire archipelago.

In regard to the treatment of the natives, the government was chiefly concerned with their baptism—indeed, this had been one of the principal reasons for the occupation—and next that they be treated decently. While it was easy to baptize and keep the inhabitants Christian (the Inquisition was brought in during 1504), the good treatment of the natives at the hands of the *conquistadores* proved to be something else. Here, as in the case of the American Indians, distance and temptation effectively frustrated the good intentions and high ideals of the crown. The introduction of the *repartimiento,* in which natives were forced to contribute a certain amount of their labor to church and government officials under the supervision of the *adelantado,* probably did not help matters. From the earliest contacts with the Spaniards, the Dominicans and Franciscans had been active in the occupation and it is probably owing to their work that the natives did not fare worse than they did. Although slavery was sometimes used as a penalty for those guilty of rebellion, Ferdinand and Isabella were strongly opposed to the trade, especially where Christians were involved, and tried to stop it in the islands. Here also their good intentions were unable to prevent a considerable clandestine business in the selling of human beings.

In conclusion, it must be said that as a colonial experiment the Spanish experience in the Canaries was highly significant. In her government of the archipelago, the queen was careful not to permit any large scale transfer of feudal rights. After the troubles with the early conquistadors, so strongly suggestive of the crown's later difficulties with the Columbus family, the government hastened to send out its own officials with additional powers. And even these representatives were carefully watched by special commissioners, and *jueces pesquisidores;* furthermore, the constant bickering between the military and ecclesiastic authorities usually gave the crown frequent opportunities to increase its power. Since all these policies were extensively pursued in the Americas later on, it was in the Canaries that the government first began the "transplanting of the political institutions of the metropolis to the overseas and newly conquered territories, a typical phenomenon of Spanish colonization."[10]

10. Konetzke, pp. 117–18.

The Columbus story has been told and retold so many times that it seems unnecessary to do more than remind the reader of a few basic facts. For a man who has been so well-studied in all his later activities, the early part of his life is really little known. In spite of all the scholarly arguments about his birthplace, the safest assumption is still that he was born in Genoa in the late summer or fall of 1451, thus making him only a few months younger than Isabella. Until he reached his twenties, very little is known. He later said that he went to sea at an early age, and this seems likely. In 1476 he went to Lisbon and for the next eight or nine years sailed under the Portuguese flag, although the details of his activities are far from clear. Life in Lisbon in the early heroic age of Portuguese expansion was doubtless stimulating and here Columbus may well have picked up the seeds of his later projects. He married into a good family and his son, Diego, was born there in 1480.

Just when the *empresa de las Indias,* or the enterprise of the Indies as he called it, occurred to Columbus will never be known. It was not a very original idea since an intense interest in geography and exploration was in the air. Humanistic studies had led to a careful reappraisal of the ancient geographers and the Portuguese voyages down the coast of Africa added to the general interest. There was a widespread desire to reach the wealth of China and the Indies, so fascinatingly described by Marco Polo from his personal observations, and a hope amongst educated persons that this could be done. The belief that the earth was flat had never been more than a popular superstitution; well-read persons knew that it was round and humanists who had studied the ancient writers had a pretty good idea of its size. It was not held to be impossible to reach the east by sailing west; it was merely believed to be impracticable because of the distance between the coasts of Europe and Asia.

Columbus defied educated opinion, not in asserting the roundness of the earth, but in insisting that a voyage from Europe westward to Asia could be carried out. Here he was most original in his errors. Following Toscanelli, who got the idea from Marco Polo, Columbus assumed that the coast of Asia was some thirty degrees of longitude farther east than it actually was. To compound his mistake, he further assumed that Cipangu (Japan) was fifteen-hundred miles still farther out in the Pacific. Even with this most advantageous and highly erroneous reckoning, Toscanelli had postulated a journey of some five-thousand miles from Spain to China, but Columbus made additional corrections to cut this figure in half. By using the smallest estimate ever made for a degree, forty-five nautical miles instead of sixty, he reduced the size of the earth by twenty-five percent, and

by making other corrections in his favor, he finally reached the astonishing figure of twenty-four-hundred nautical miles for the voyage
from the Canaries to Japan. The correct figure as based on actual
air-line reckoning is 10,600 miles.[11] As his latest biographer puts it:
"Of course this calculation is not logical, but Columbus's mind was
not logical. He *knew* he could make it, and the figures had to fit."[12]
Unfortunately for him, there were many, both in Lisbon and
Salamanca, who knew the figures did not fit, and it was this, rather
than the usual fiction frequently printed in high school texts about
the flatness of the earth, that led to his repeated rebuffs. Samuel Eliot
Morison has constructed a delightful bit of fantasy in imagining the
kind of reply Columbus received from learned faculty members and
geographical experts when his propositions were referred to them:

> Unfortunately, Captain Colombo, we deny the validity of your calculation
> of the globe, we suspect the accuracy of your compatriot Marco Polo,
> we doubt the existence of his Cipangu; Ptolemy mentioned no such
> place. According to the close calculations of our mathematical experts,
> who were already studying the heavens when you were plying the shut-
> tle, it would be necessary to sail at least 10,000 nautical miles due west
> before reaching Catigara, the eastern verge of the known world. Master
> Paul (Toscanelli), on your own showing, makes it 5000 miles to Quinsay,
> if such a place there be. Even assuming that you find favorable winds
> over that vast expanse of ocean (which we strongly doubt), and that you
> can sail an average of four knots, which is what our best caravels can
> do on long voyages, your passage would require a hundred days. Over
> fourteen weeks beyond sight of land! We should not feel justified in
> risking the money of the king our lord (whom God preserve), or the
> lives of his subjects, on so dubious an enterprise.... You may go.[13]

Once convinced of the possibility of a voyage to the Indies via
the western route, Columbus offered his ideas to John II, the young
and energetic king of Portugal. After lengthy negotiations in 1484
and 1485, the offer was rejected. Columbus then went to Spain, but
with the Granadine War in progress, the Catholic Kings obviously
had no time for a penniless seaman with incorrect ideas about the
size of the earth. In 1488 he was writing the Portuguese court from
Seville asking for permission to return, and was in Lisbon in time
to see Bartholomew Dias enter the mouth of the Tagus on his return
from the discovery of the Cape of Good Hope. With all these expecta-
tions of opening up the eastern route to the Indies, John II again
lost interest in Columbus, who then returned to Spain.

During his first visit Columbus had at least made some connections
that might be valuable later on. He had stopped briefly at the monas-

11. Samuel Eliot Morison, *Admiral of the Ocean Sea, A Life of Christopher Columbus* (Boston, 1942), p. 68.
12. Ibid.
13. Ibid., p. 69.

tery of La Rábida, and perhaps met Fray Juan Pérez, later to be so helpful. He had also convinced Antonio de Marchena, head of the Franciscan sub-province of Seville, and a man of scholarly reputation. He appealed to the great duke of Medina Sidonia and almost succeeded. Then he turned to the count (later duke) of Medina Celi, who controlled a port and owned a fleet. It seems to have been the duke who first brought Columbus to the queen's attention. While he was awaiting the opinion of an advisory commission appointed by the queen, his illegitimate son Ferdinand was born, and then, as we have seen, Columbus returned to Portugal.

On his second arrival in Spain, about 1489, he was still waiting for the commission's report. Until Columbus arrived at La Rábida in the latter part of 1491, his activities are not well known. Apparently he visited the court during the siege of Baza and probably realized that until the Granadine War was ended he could hope for little from Ferdinand and Isabella. In 1490 a worse blow fell when the commission, speaking through Talavera, rendered an unfavorable report. After waiting some months more, Columbus decided to go elsewhere, apparently France, and stopped again at La Rábida to pick up his son Diego, whom he had left with the Franciscan friars. Here, as is well known, he became friendly with the prior Juan Pérez, who had had close associations at one time with Isabella. Pérez was urgent in his pleas that Columbus should not quit Spain without a second attempt to win over Isabella. To this end Pérez personally wrote the queen.

This is stated in all the accounts; what is less obvious, but equally interesting, is the important influence of the Franciscan Order in prelude to the age of discovery. Columbus had several times stopped at Franciscan monasteries such as La Rábida and others. The order had always been active in missionary work, especially in the Far East, as the achievements of William von Rubruck, Giovanni de Monte Corvino, and Giovanni de Plano Carpini attest. Plano Carpini, it should be noted, opened up Spain to Franciscan activities some fourteen years before he went to Cathay. Underlying the Franciscan interest in the conversion of the Far East, as Konetzke has pointed out, was a new attitude toward nature and the world,

> an immediate and intimate surrender of man to nature and all creation. Attention has already been called to the fact that in overseas missions among the infidels, there evolved—as the diaries and travel books show us—a new visual perspective which, through its naturalism, passed beyond the frontiers of the medieval world, and, like the love of St. Francis of Assisi which embraced all men and all created things, established a true mystique of geographical expansion.[14]

14. Konetzke, pp. 169–70.

Undoubtedly Columbus found the general atmosphere of Franciscan missions sympathetic toward his ideas and, as we have seen, Juan Pérez became an ardent supporter. As a result of his letter, the prior was invited to come to court for consultation. In view of the Franciscan background of interest in and trips to the Far East in the thirteenth century, it is hard to believe that Pérez did not emphasize the importance of Columbus' plans for the revival of Franciscan missionary activity in the Far East. Indeed, indirect evidence suggests that he did bring this to the queen's attention.[15] If true, given the intense piety of Isabella, a more powerful argument for getting Columbus a second hearing could have hardly been devised. At any rate, he received another invitation to come to the royal camp at Santa Fe, and, what was probably as important, the sum of twenty-thousand maravedís for new clothing and a mule.

Once again his ideas were presented to a commission of experts for consideration, and once again rejected, although Morison believes less for their errors than because of the great demands made by Columbus in terms of rewards, honors, and remuneration.[16]

However, in spite of this rejection, Columbus remained in camp until Granada surrendered and even marched in the procession that entered the city. When a final audience with the sovereigns indicated that all was lost, he packed his mule in great disgust and headed north. He had only covered a few miles on his journey when he was overtaken by a messenger from the queen calling him back immediately. The picture had suddenly changed for the better.

What was the cause of this strange reversal of royal policy? In the absence of documents that might answer the question definitively, one can only speculate. My guess is that the queen was mainly influenced by religious and economic factors, the first more than the second. We have seen that after the capture of Granada religious enthusiasm for continuing the war against Islam was high, and Isabella was thinking of extending operations to the Barbary Coast as Padilla's mission clearly shows. Furthermore, the Ottoman empire, the rising power in the Near East, had already shown a considerable interest in the fate of the Spanish Moslems and might become more dangerous if the war extended to north Africa. Columbus' plan offered interesting possibilities in this struggle. If an understanding could be reached with the powers of the Far East, who, according to Marco Polo, were not Mohammedan, Islam might be caught between two gigantic pincers. The concept, of course, went back to the thirteenth

15. Pérez' letter to Isabella about Columbus is now lost, but contemporary references to it suggest that the friar did mention the possibility of missionary work in connection with Columbus' voyage. Konetzke, pp. 170–71.

16. Morison, pp. 100–101.

century, when legends of Prester John suggested the same thing; yet it had never been completely forgotten. Castile had established one brief contact, as we have seen, with the Middle East during the brief reign of Isabella's grandfather, Henry the Palid (Henry III) when Ruy Gonsalez de Clavijo reached the headquarters of Tamerlane in 1404, just two years after the Mongols had inflicted a great defeat on the Turks and taken the sultan Bayazid captive. The implications of all this must have been inescapable and present in the minds of the Catholic Kings since on April 30, 1492, they gave Columbus credentials to present to the "Grand Khan of Cathay".

In addition, there was always the possibility of converting the Far Eastern people to Christianity, and we know that conversion and baptism were always present in Isabella's mind; the history of the Jews and Moslems during her reign proves that conclusively, to say nothing about the Inquisition. By implication this is always a little unfair to Ferdinand. Granted that the king seems worldly and sometimes cynical in comparison with his wife, it would be absurd to suggest that his Christianity was not sincere. His faith simply made more allowances for the realities of this world than did Isabella's. And it was Ferdinand, surprisingly enough, and not Isabella who made the classic statement of the religious causes of the discovery in the famous instructions to Diego Columbus of May 3, 1509:

> It [the reasons for the discoveries] has always been and still is in these matters of the Indies to convert the Indians to our Holy Catholic Faith so that their souls may not be lost, and therefore it is necessary for them to be taught the truths of our religion without any force whatsoever.[17]

Economically speaking, there had been a long-time desire to open up the rich countries of the Orient for trading purposes, and this had been especially marked in the later fifteenth century in connection with the trade in spices. As is well known, a combination of Arabs, Egyptians, and Venetians brought the spices from the Far East into the European market. By the time these condiments had reached the consumer's table, the price had reached astronomical proportions because of the taxes imposed upon them by the various states through whose territory they passed en route to the Venetians, who then added their own generous profit to the burden of costs. Moreover, as Donald F. Lach has pointed out, because of disturbed conditions in the Near East coming from the Turkish expansion, Venice imported very few spices in the last decade of the fifteenth century, which led to still further increases in price.[18] Obviously, the prospect of undercutting

17. As stated in del Arco, pp. 384–85.
18. For a full discussion of this subject, see Donald F. Lach, *Asia in the Making of Europe*, Vol. I: *The Century of Discovery* (Chicago: University of Chicago Press, 1965).

these various monopolies of the spice trade and dealing directly with the ultimate source in the Far East was very attractive and led to a revival of interest fostered in part by the accounts of medieval travelers such as Marco Polo. His account of his travels had been printed in 1485 and Columbus' copy is filled with marginal notations. China, however, had been generally unfriendly and virtually closed to foreign penetration since the establishment of the Ming Dynasty of 1368; and the hostile attitude of the Turks and Mamelukes made the overland journey especially hazardous. A new route to the Far East which would avoid all these obstacles would undoubtedly mean more trade for the two monarchies, especially desirable after such a long and expensive war with the Moslems of Granada. Furthermore, there was for various reasons a real shortage of precious metal throughout Europe, which was keenly felt because of the increased political activity of many states, all of which would be considerably relieved by the gold of Cathay and Cipangu so glowingly described by Marco.

More specifically, the immediate costs of Columbus' plans could be met. Apparently Luis de Santangel, financial advisor of Ferdinand and descended from a Jewish family of Catalonia or Valencia, had become convinced of the value of the scheme—"so great service to God and the exaltation of His Church, not to speak of very great increase and glory for her realms and crowns"—that he went to the queen and convinced her that money could be found. It was at this point that Columbus was recalled. Here it might be well to lay another old legend that shows surprising life at times: namely, the tale of Ferdinand's supposed hostility to the enterprise of the Indies. Quite the contrary is true. Ferdinand was apparently consulted from the beginning and some of his people took the lead in finding the money and making the contract. We have already noticed the role of Santangel. Gabriel Sánchez, Ferdinand's treasurer and Juan de Coloma, of the Aragonese chancellery, also worked for the plan, and the final text of the contract was not only registered in Castile, but in Aragon as well.

It was decided to get the money on a loan from Santangel and his Genoese friend Francisco Pinelo, backed by funds from the *Santa Hermandad* of which Santangel and Pinelo were both treasurers. Approximately a million and a half maravedís were so obtained.[19] Columbus himself contributed 250,000 maravedís which he borrowed

19. The exact amounts are not known. Morison gives 1,400,000 mds. and Konetzke 1,114,000. The latter raises the question as to whether or not the official funds ever came in, and suggests that possibly all the money was raised by Columbus and his Italian friends—a suggestion that this author has been unable to prove or disprove.

from various friends. All in all, according to Morison's estimates, the great enterprise cost some two million marvedís, not including the payroll, or, in our money about fourteen thousand dollars.[20]

Once the money could be found, the court agreed to Columbus' exorbitant demands and granted him the most generous terms ever awarded to a discoverer who, as yet, had discovered nothing. He was appointed admiral of the Ocean Sea and governor and viceroy of all islands and mainlands he might discover. He was to have the right to a tenth of all precious metals, stones, or other commodities produced or bartered in these lands tax-free, and, if he paid one-eighth of the costs of any vessel sailing to the new discoveries, he could collect an eighth of the profits. And these, and other privileges, were to be handed down to his descendants. The Spanish court was to be tied up in litigation for years to escape the results of such generosity. The various documents and orders concerned with the contract and the voyage were signed for the most part during the month of April, 1492; and on May 12 the admiral, to refer to him by his new title, set out for Palos where he would put to sea on the third of August at half an hour before sunrise. So began the most famous voyage in history.

4

Luck was with the great enterprise since the little fleet crossed the Atlantic in record time. At two o'clock on the morning of October 12, Rodrigo de Triana, look-out on the *Pinta* which was leading the fleet, made out a line of white sand in the brilliant moonlight, and cried out *"tierra"!* It was the end of one age and the beginning of another.

This same luck held with them until the first hour of Christmas Day, 1492 when the *Santa Maria* was hopelessly wrecked on a reef in Caracol Bay (Santo Domingo). Then things went from bad to worse. The first colong, Navidad, was planted near the site of the wreck. On January 4, apparently deserted by the *Pinta*, the admiral hoisted his flag on the *Niña* and started out on the return trip. The voyage was a horror since on February 12 the small over-crowded ship ran into dirty weather and until March 4 was constantly battered by the elements. On that date the *Niña* sailed peacefully over the bar and anchored in the Tagus estuary not far from Lisbon. Safe at last, but in Portuguese power.

Portuguese problems will be dealt with later on; suffice it to say that King John rose to the occasion and behaved gallantly. Columbus and his crew, including some Indians, were treated with honor and

20. Morison, p. 103.

allowed to proceed on to Castile. On March 15, the admiral sailed into the harbor of Palos exactly thirty-two weeks after his departure, and eventually he was able to start on the eight hundred mile journey (which must have seemed very short indeed to him who had been to Asia) to Barcelona where the sovereigns commanded his presence with "the best haste you can in your coming." Some time between April 15 and 20 he reached the city and the next day was received with great ceremony in the Alcázar, the king and queen actually rising from their thrones as he approached to make his obeisance. Later in the month there followed long conferences with Ferdinand and Isabella, Cardinal Mendoza, and other prominent persons as plans were made for the second voyage.

From the historian's point of view the second voyage is far more interesting than any other although it usually receives scant notice in general histories. In addition to being a marvel of rapid organization, it illustrates in a striking manner how quickly the Catholic Kings reacted to the implications of the first voyage, and also reveals the effectiveness of the organization which the sovereigns had perfected in the last nineteen years. The origins of the second voyage, which was a really imposing colonial expedition, can be found in the sovereigns' letter of April 7, 1493, after receiving the first news of the discovery from the admiral.

> Inasmuch as we will that that which you have commenced with the aid of God be continued and furthered, and we desire that you come hither forthwith ... so that you may be timely provided with everything that you need; and because as you see the summer has begun and you must not delay in going back there, see if something cannot be prepared in Seville or in other districts for your returning to the land which you have discovered.[21]

Doubtless one of the reasons for haste was the growing problem of what the Portuguese would do about the discovery. While they were having recourse to the weapons of diplomacy, the king and the queen probably felt that additional discoveries would strengthen their case. In any event, within the space of five months a great deal was done which probably could not have been equalled by any other contemporary state. In carrying out the royal instructions the principal figure was the famous Juan Rodriguez de Fonseca, sometimes called the first colonial minister in European history. Although often difficult to deal with, as we shall see, he seems to have worked with great industry and the sovereigns with him. Between the end of May and the beginning of September there were more than one hundred government orders dealing with all phases of the projected expedition. The ships had to be obtained, readied for sea duty, and supplied

21. Morison, p. 355.

with stores. It is interesting to note that the requisitioning of bread, a major staple of diet on shipboard, was turned over to an officer of the Inquisition. Doubtless his awesome connections facilitated his task. In addition to the usual supplies, there were numbers of plants, shrubs, domestic animals, and the like; for this was to be a real colonial project with a permanent settlement on the perimeter of Asia as the goal. There is nothing, in Portuguese history remotely like it before 1535.

Eventually a fleet of seventeen ships was assembled with a complement of somewhere between twelve-hundred and fifteen-hundred men. While most of the crew came from Andalusia (a few had sailed on the first voyage), there were also Basques and a few of the admiral's compatriots from Genoa. The father of Bartolomé de las Casas was present as were three Franciscans from northern France. The ecclesiastical work of the expedition was placed in charge of Fray Boyl, or Buil, a Benedictine from Montserrat. The special gift of Isabella to the second voyage was the equipment for an entire church which was to be set up at Navidad for the benefit of the colonists who had settled there. Curiously enough, in view of all the elaborate preparations, no one seems to have realized that the most important commodity in the establishment of a colony had been omitted: there were no women nor were any permitted in the New World until 1498, when bitter experience had taught the government that Indian husbands were strangely reluctant to part with their wives.

Special instructions were written for Columbus, dated May 29, 1493, giving him extended powers. He was to have a free hand in organizing the colony and in making what additional voyages of discovery he deemed necessary. The main object of the voyage was again given as the conversion of the natives. Second, it was a trading venture with the crown determined to set up a royal monopoly; no private business was to be permitted although the admiral was to get one-eighth of the profits. Everything else went to the crown of Castile. As Morison puts it,

> The first European colony in America was conceived as a means of converting infidels and acquiring gold; in practice the higher object became completely submerged by the lower. Apparently the sovereigns had lost all desire to exchange compliments with the Grand Khan. Perhaps they figured out that he would not be too well pleased with the mining and missionary game.[22]

The second voyage began at Cádiz on September 25. On October 8 the fleet arrived at Gomera in the still partly unconquered Canaries—a curious conjunction of the two oldest Castilian colonial operations. After a stop of two days to take on livestock and give

22. Morison, p. 392.

the admiral a chance to greet the proprietress of Gomara, Doña Beatriz de Peraza, later to become the wife of Alonso de Lugo, the fleet weighed anchor and moved southwesterly into the Atlantic. For the last time the admiral's amazing luck held and favorable winds pushed them across the middle Atlantic in the very fast time of twenty-nine days. Columbus landed on November 3 at Dominica (named by him) in the Lesser Antilles. Without knowing it, he had discovered the shortest and best route from Europe to the West Indies.

As for Navidad, no trace of the colony remained. Later the admiral learned that the settlers had been killed off, apparently after considerable provocation, by a native chief named Caonabó, or so the name sounded in Spanish ears. Columbus therefore planted a new colony on Hispaniola and appropriately named it Isabella. After rather lengthy explorations which took him along the northwest shores of Cuba, he returned to Isabella where trouble awaited him in the form of violent quarrels amongst the settlers. Here he gave proof of his really extraordinary ability to mishandle administrative matters, and, leaving much bitterness behind him, he sailed home, reaching Cádiz in June, 1496.

The last two voyages, however interesting to a biographer of Columbus, are not particularly important for a history of Spain. It was becoming clear to the crown that whatever his talents for long voyages and his amazing confidence that he would find Asia, the admiral could not be trusted with the organization of the small Spanish holdings in the New World. In that sense, his credit was diminished at court although the sovereigns, and especially Isabella, wished him treated with all honor and respect. The government also began to curtail some of the privileges bestowed upon him in the first contract thus initiating years of litigation with the Columbus family. There may have also been less confidence that he was where he was supposed to be, and the diminishing number of ships allowed him in the last two voyages—six for the third, and four for the fourth—reflects this growing lack of confidence on the part of the crown. It should also be remembered that the last years of the fifteenth century and the beginning of the sixteenth represented for Ferdinand a growing involvement in *weltpolitik*, while for Isabella they were overshadowed by the growing madness of her daughter, Joanna, and the great question of the succession. Very likely there was nothing Columbus could say or do that would distract the sovereigns from these great issues, but they did take the time to find the money for his last two journeys to the Caribbean. In 1498 he sailed his most southerly route yet and finally reached the coast of South America in the Orinoco region. It was on this voyage that he ran into difficulties on Hispaniola with the new governor, Bobadilla, and was sent home in chains to the great indignation of his old friend, the queen. In 1502 he made his last trip with four ships and cruised off the coast of Central America near the modern states of Honduras and Costa Rica. Still cherishing his illusions to the last, he believed he was only some nineteen days sail from the mouth of the Ganges.

On his return early in November, 1504, he received no invitation to court. Isabella was dying and affairs of much greater moment were afoot than the ideas of an old seaman who had not found the treasures described by Marco Polo, or a passage through the islands and land mass that seemed to bar the way. After the queen died on November 26, his last opportunity was gone. He was able to get to court in May, 1505, although he was suffering from various ailments, but Ferdinand, although courteous and friendly, was unwilling to restore to him his administrative powers. He was still hoping—he was always hopeful—that he might get justice from Ferdinand's daughter, Joanna, and her husband Philip of Habsburg, the new sovereigns of Castile, but death did not allow him to wait for them. He died at Valladolid May 20, 1506.

> One only wishes that the Admiral might have been afforded the sense of fulfillment that would have come from foreseeing all that flowed from his discoveries; that would have turned all the sorrows of his last years to joy. The whole history of the Americas stems from the Four Voyages of Columbus; and as the Greek city-states looked back to the deathless gods as their founders, so today a score of independent nations and dominions unite in homage to Christopher the stout-hearted son of Genoa, who carried Christian civilization across the Ocean Sea.[23]

### 5

The first European repercussions from the new discoveries precipitated a crisis with Portugal. From the moment of Columbus' appearance in the Lisbon roads, it was apparent that the Portuguese were very unhappy over what had been done, although King John II did not attempt to detain him as some urged him to do. After all, Portugal was the initiator of European overseas expansion, and had received papal confirmation of its claims from Cape Nun southward by Martin V, Eugenius IV, Nicholas V, and Calixtus III. While it might be argued that these bulls did not apply to the west Atlantic, the Portuguese felt that they did. Furthermore, as we have seen, they had tried to work out a division of spheres of exploration with Castile by the treaty of Alcaçovas which had settled the Succession War in 1479; this had been confirmed by the bull *Aeterni Regis* three years later. These documents created a line of demarcation running east and west just south of the Canary Islands, thus guaranteeing the

23. Morison, p. 671.

archipelago to Castile; however, everything south of the line was reserved for the king of Portugal. Nothing was said about voyages to the west, or to India. In view of the fact that no one, least of all the admiral, really knew where the new discoveries were, it was clearly expedient to obtain some sort of papal confirmation to strengthen Castile's position against Portugal in the diplomatic tussle which most certainly was coming.

Obviously no time was to be lost, and since the new pope was Spanish it was to be expected that Rome would be friendly. The sovereigns' request for a papal bull was not so much because they felt the need of validating what had been done, or because they accepted the Gregorian doctrine that the pope was *dominus orbis* —Spanish theologians did not, in any event, recognize this right; what they wanted was confirmation by the chief international authority of their sovereignty over what Columbus had and might discover in the future. Alexander VI responded graciously with the first of two bulls named *Inter Caetera*, dated May 3, 1493, which generously bestowed the Castilian sovereignty in conveniently vague terms on all lands discovered or to be discovered by "our dear son Christopher Columbus." However, before the bull could reach its destination, the Catholic Kings had talked to Columbus and he very probably suggested that they should have put their request in more specific terms, and with some sort of demarcation line between the respective Spanish and Portuguese areas. Such a line had already been used by the bull of 1481, but in the second *Inter Caetera* bull issued in June it runs from north to south one hundred leagues west of the Azores and Cape Verde Islands, with all unclaimed lands discovered to the west being assigned to the crown of Castile. This of course settled the fate of the line of 1481 and opened up the south Atlantic to any future voyages Columbus might wish to make, but something more was also involved. It appears that the admiral believed there was a physical distinction between the sea and climate east of the line and conditions westwards; thus to him the line corresponded to a distinction that actually existed, and was not a mere convenience.

When the Portuguese ambassadors finally arrived in Barcelona in August, 1493, they were dissatisfied with the placing of the line, wishing to move it farther to the west. About this time Pope Alexander VI issued his fourth and final bull[24] on the matter in which he outdid himself in trying to please the Catholic Kings. By the bull *Dudum*

24. Between the second *Inter Caetera* and *Dudum Siquidem*, Pope Alexander VI issued a third, *Eximiae Devotionis*, which, since it merely confirmed earlier concessions in stronger language, is not usually mentioned by historians. There is an excellent summary of The Castilian-Portuguese negotiations in Loch, *Asia in The Making of Europe*, I, 56–58.

*Siquidem* all previous papal recognitions, "whether to kings, princes, infantes, religious, or military orders", were cancelled. The Portuguese were outraged, and King John began to assemble a fleet in his ports while at the same time he urged his ambassadors to get Ferdinand and Isabella to agree to a modification of the line of demarcation which would give him some rights in the southwestern Atlantic. Fortunately, the sovereigns proved to be reasonable and they had doubtless achieved what they really intended from the beginning—namely, the elimination of the line of 1481. Furthermore, Portugal was well placed to cause much trouble to Spanish ships sailing out into the Atlantic, and the Portuguese navy was larger and stronger than Castile's; prudence, therefore, dictated that a peaceable solution be found. The result was the famous treaty of Tordesillas concluded between the two powers on June 7, 1494. The line of demarcation was now placed at 370 leagues west of the Cape Verde Islands. As now situated, the line cut through the easternmost tip of South America, eventually giving Portugal her colony of Brazil. Since it was believed that 740 leagues of water lay between the Azores and the new discoveries, the new placement of the line was a fair division of ocean. In the Western Hemisphere the line was honestly accepted, but in the East Spain violated it since the Philippines lay in the Portuguese sector.

In summary, it must be said that the pope really did not divide the world since he was not a mediator in the discussions as the king of Portugal had not asked for his intervention or judgment. The bulls had eliminated a possible Portuguese appeal to Rome based on former papal recognition of Portugal's earlier claims. After the four bulls, the pope ceased to be a factor in the crisis, which was solved by direct negotiation between the interested powers themselves. On the whole, it was an equitable solution.

6

In a sense, there was no colonial policy, nor colonial administrative organizations or personnel until Columbus returned from his first voyage. Almost immediately, however, it became necessary to improvise all of them as rapidly as possible, and it is amazing how many of these early decisions set the norm for the next two hundred years of colonial development. At the outset it was clear that the crown would tolerate no rivals to its supremacy in the colonies. When the first expedition was being organized, the duke of Medinaceli offered to help with the expenses on grounds that he had looked after the admiral for two years, which is doubtful, to say the least. The crown refused; and when the duke petitioned the government after the discovery to send a few of his ships annually to the New World, he was again refused.

Ferdinand and Isabella simply did not want the high nobility directly involved in colonial activities.

In their May to August correspondence with Columbus during the interim between the first and second trips to America, the Catholic Kings made certain basic policy decisions in their concern for the conversion and benevolent treatment of the Indians. This concern showed itself in the rigorous arrangements set up for the registration and listing of persons and commodities transported, and in the establishment of a judicial system based on the institutions of the metropolis. Thus the sovereigns were responsible for the genesis of the administrative apparatus later so widely expanded.[25] Also significant in terms of the later viceroys are the great powers given the admiral, who is actually termed viceroy and governor in the documents. He is given full authority to get the best ships and the needed supplies, and will be responsible for setting up the local administration in the colonies, naming the *alcaldes* and *alguaciles* responsible for handling criminal and civil cases at law. He will also establish a customs house in the Indies to match the one to be set up at Cádiz. While the sovereigns soon learned that Columbus was incapable of managing this administrative machinery, they never varied from the idea of giving some crown official broad discretionary powers under royal supervision. Later their successor was to expand this concept into the two great viceroyalties of New Spain and Peru into which the entire colonial empire was divided until the advent of the Bourbons.

As indicated earlier, it was decided in May of 1493 to make all trade with the Indies a crown monopoly regulated by a treasurer, a comptroller or business manager, and a factor who headed a kind of department of supply. This three-fold division of organization was to run through practically all the Spanish institutions controlling the colonies. Minute provisions were set up for the registration of every ship, every sailor, and each piece of merchandise so that the government could not be cheated of its profits. In 1495, however, there was an abrupt change. The pressure to participate in the American trade from Castilian merchants had become too great for the government to resist. Trade, therefore, was thrown open to all subjects of the crown (Aragonese were not formally admitted until 1591) and ships were to register, leave, and return to the port of Cádiz. One-tenth of the tonnage was reserved for the crown as well as one-tenth of everything secured by barter or otherwise. Mines had long been considered crown property in Castile and were so classified in the New World, with only one-third of the profits going to the actual producers.

25. Ernesto Schäfer, *El Consejo Real y Supremo de las Indias. Su historia, organización, y labor administrativa hasta la terminación de la Casa de Austria*, 2 vols. (Seville, 1935, I, 4–5.

However, the policy changed again in 1501 when the government ruled that no one could travel to the Americas without a royal license, and not long after it was decided to restrict exit and re-entry to the city of Seville alone.

This arrangement seems strange to modern concepts, yet the government had its reasons. Restricting all American trade to a single port had decided administrative advantages and as yet there was no previous experience to show the evil effects of such a policy. Furthermore, if one city was to be singled out, Seville possessed obvious attractions. It was the largest and wealthiest city of Castile and the natural business center of the kingdom. It also had a sizable community for foreign merchants, who had enjoyed various royal privileges since the days of Ferdinand III. Furthermore, although some distance from the open sea, it had a port in San Lúcar de Barrameda below the city at the mouth of the Guadalquivir River. The only possible rival for this selection was Cádiz, the ancient Phoenician city near the Strait. Its merchants, in urging their rival claims, pointed out its excellent harbor on the open sea (so excellent indeed that Drake was able to raid it with ease in 1587) and the size and industry of its business community. In 1508 the government yielded a bit and permitted vessels to register either at Cádiz or San Lúcar. Finally in 1535 a *juez oficial* was appointed for Cádiz and henceforth ships from America, even with gold and silver aboard, might unload here provided that their cargoes and registers were then transported intact to Seville. However, in spite of these concessions, Seville remained the principal center of the American trade until the eighteenth century, when everything was administered from Cádiz.

When Columbus returned in the spring of 1493 from the first voyage, the sovereigns decided to appoint someone to assume responsibility for the involved task of preparing the fleet for the second voyage. Their choice, or possibly Isabella's alone, fell on Juan Rodríguez de Fonseca, who had been born, like Columbus and the queen, in 1451. After entering the clergy, Fonseca was soon called to the attention of the queen and eventually became a kind of *protégé* of hers and of Talavera who took him to Granada. Later he became the archdeacon of Seville and was functioning in this capacity when he was asked to take over the business of the Indies. Because of Isabella's fondness for using ecclesiastics in government and her belief in his honesty and ability, Fonseca rose rapidly, becoming in steady succession bishop of Badajoz (1495), Córdoba (1500), Palencia (1505), and Burgos (1514). He was also a member of the Council of Castile and carried out certain important missions: he went to England with the Infanta Catherine (1501) and was sent to escort Philip of Habsburg and Joanna from the Low Countries after the death of Isabella (1505). It may be questioned, in this case at least, whether Isabella's confidence was justified. For all his ability, Fonseca was difficult to deal with, and often careless in his conduct of business. A contemporary, Dr. Antonio Guevara, presents a chilling estimate of his character and personality, calling him a firm Christian but a disagreeable bishop.[26] His quarrels with Columbus were famous, but it is perhaps questionable whether or not he had much to do with the admiral's later decline in influence. Fonseca could carry out policy, but he could not make it. The rulers kept a firm hand on all their subordinates and theirs, not the malice of Fonseca, were the decisions that led to the shelving of Columbus, administratively speaking. Perhaps, as Schäfer suggests, they were too busy in the years following the second voyage to pay too much attention to him. This was the period of the second French war, of the succession problems, of the renewed negotiations with England following the death of Catherine's first husband, Prince Arthur, and the complicated discussions with Philip the Handsome. And lastly Columbus was an inept administrator, and did not need Fonseca's help in getting things thoroughly confused.[27]

Fonseca began to function more and more as a colonial secretary with the help of his colleagues in the council of Castile. After Isabella's death in 1504 there were two years of confusion when everything drifted while Ferdinand was in angry retirement in Aragon and Italy. But when he returned to the western kingdom on 1508, order was imposed on the administrative chaos and things began to move as before. Between 1508 and Ferdinand's death early in 1516, colonial affairs were managed by Fonseca and Lope de Conchillos with the exception of judicial business which was definitely under the Council of Castile. As yet there was no council for the Indies and when documents refer to one, invariably they mean the Council of Castile.[28] During the interregnum between Ferdinand's death and the arrival of his grandson Charles, duke of Burgundy (1516–1517), Fonseca and Conchillos were eliminated from colonial affairs. The arrival of Las Casas with his bitter criticism of the treatment of the natives, and the new policies of the regent, Cisneros, aided by Adrian of Utrecht, all foreshadowed the coming of a new regime. Until the arrival of Charles from the Low Countries the enterprise of the Indies came under Cisneros, or Japata, or Carajal; sometimes the name of secretary Jorje de Baracaldo appears on the documents. As in the case following the death of Isabella, only time would tell what the new government would keep of the old system, or what innovations would be introduced.

After 1495 Castile decided to abandon its plan to create a royal monopoly out of colonial trade. It had already discovered that the

26. Schäfer, I, 2–3.
27. Ibid., I, 31–32.
28. Ibid., I, 26–27.

task of colonizing and civilizing a vast, unknown area was going to be too great for the crown to bear alone; help from private business was needed, and so trade was thrown open to all subjects of the crown. But although the government had opened up the trade, it still intended to compete with its subjects and consequently felt the need of some kind of regulatory institution to look after its business and manage the profits. This appears to have been the thought that lay behind the creation of the *Casa de Contratación*,[29] justly considered one of the most famous institutions of the Spanish empire. As in so many other cases, the influence of Portugal was significant. After Vasco da Gama's discovery of the sea route to India, King Manuel had decided to confine the new communications with the Far East to fleets chartered by the crown. He also established a *Casa da India* which should supervise the sailing and outfitting of ships, and provide a place where cargoes from the East could be stored, or sold. Among other things the government fixed prices on colonial goods to make sure of its own profits.[30]

After the Castilian government retreated from its liberal trade policy in 1501, the establishment of a supervisory organization was a logical step. The sovereigns may have requested suggestions; for a letter exists, probably written by Francisco Pinelo in the middle of 1502 according to Schäfer, outlining some of the major functions.[31] The rulers responded on January 20, 1503, by establishing the *Casa de Gontratación* in the city of Seville, and in describing its functions they depended a good deal on the earlier letter. Briefly, it consisted of three chief officials, each with his staff of assistants. The treasurer's principal duty was the receiving of the American treasure, a task which constantly increased throughout the century. The *factor* was in charge of supply. If colonial officials wished to purchase anything, the factor handled the buying and shipping. He was also supposed to fit out and service the armadas used in the voyages, to supervise their supplies, and maintain arsenals. Later as business expanded, these tasks became too great for one office and they were subdivided among many officials. After the discovery of the quicksilver method for the extraction of silver from ore in 1556, which greatly increased silver production, the factor was placed in charge of the packing and exporting of the mercury of Huancavelica in Peru. All in all, his was perhaps the most important and difficult job in the Casa. The *contador*

29. The name of this institution is often translated Board or House of Trade, giving, in my opinion, an entirely inadequate idea of its function. Since we have no institution which is exactly comparable today, I have decided to retain the original name. See also Haring, pp. 22–26.

30. Ibid.

31. Schäfer, I, 9–10.

was a kind of auditor-bookkeeper who kept the extensive records not only of the business transactions, but also a kind of registry of all persons permitted by the government to go out to the colonies. Isabella had no intention of letting just any one emigrate to America. Each individual had to show proofs of orthodoxy, and other documents which were carefully noted down (a boon to future historians), before he might board his ship. Needless to say heretics, rebels, and other enemies of society were not to have the chance to infect the Indians, the pure children of nature.

The Casa began to function on February 25, 1503, with the aforementioned Francisco Pinelo as factor, Dr. Sancho de Matienzo, a canon of Seville, as treasurer (evidently a churchman was considered safer for a post exposed to such temptations), and Jimeno de Bribiesca, an official of Fonseca's, as *contador*. It had been originally intended to make the Casa the center of a network of trade houses in the Americas closely connected with the mother-house, for Nicolás de Ovando was ordered to do this; but the idea was never developed and the casas in the colonies became little more than customs houses.[32] Nevertheless the Casa was soon busy enough to become involved in sharp jurisdictional disputes with competing organizations since the royal orders were not always precise enough in defining judisdictions and functions. Many of these disputes involved the authorities of the city of Seville, where the Casa was located. Several times there was the possibility of moving the Casa to Cádiz (which actually happened in 1717), but the fear of such a transfer always pacified the city officials and usually led to a solution of the difficulties.

The initial instructions for the Casa were issued, as we have seen, in 1503; a second series (now lost) were drawn up in 1504 just before Isabella's death. Administration of all sorts was in the doldrums until Ferdinand's return from Italy, but picked up again thereafter. On June 25, 1510, the king issued new ordinances for the Casa from Monzón and amplified them by additional regulations the following May. In these new orders there was less said about crown business and a good deal more attention was paid to the inspection, registration, and regulation of the goods of private traders. By this time certain more unusual duties had been added to the supervision of trade and persons. Officials of the Casa had to inspect vessels as to fitness, tonnage, and loading. Overloading, frequently a cause of marine disasters, was severely punished. Also the possibility of gold smuggling was carefully watched. Another important responsibility was the supervision of property of Spaniards dying at sea or in the Americas; the officials of the Casa were required to protect it and transmit it to the heirs.

32. Haring, pp. 26–27.

From this time on, as Haring puts it, it was not "a business house run for the private profit of the Crown, but a department of government, a ministry of commerce, a school of navigation, and a clearing house for colonial trade."[33]

Almost from its inception the Casa had considerable legal powers —virtually a necessity in the enforcement of colonial regulations—such as right to sit as a court to punish infractions of the ordinances. In 1511 it received a more precise definition of its legal duties; and some time later, when Charles I was defining the responsibilities of the Council of the Indies, he gave a still clearer shape to the work of the Casa. By a final statement in 1539, it could hear civil suits in all cases involving the treasury, trade, or colonial regulations, an appeal to the Council of the Indies being permitted in each case. It also was to enjoy complete criminal jurisdiction and competence over acts committed on voyages to or from the colonies without appeal except in cases where the penalty involved death or mutilation. Here an automatic review by the Council of the Indies was required.

Perhaps the most famous institution of the *Casa de Contratación* was its renowned Hydrographic Bureau. This really begins, in a humble way, with the appointment of Amerigo Vespucci as *piloto mayor* by Ferdinand in 1508. Recently recalled to Castile by the death of his son-in-law Philip the Handsome, the king had summoned Vespucci, Juan de Solis, Vicente Yáñez Pinzón, and Juan de la Cosa to consult with him on colonial matters, especially the task of finding a northwest passage through the barrier of the Americas. It was eventually decided that one of the four should remain at the Casa for the purpose of teaching and examining pilots and making corrections in maps. This was the reason for Amerigo's appointment. He was well known to the king, having previously resided in Seville as a commercial agent for the Medici. He had made some voyages, probably going out with Ojeda in 1499, later traveled to Portugal as an agent of the king, and sailed along the coast of Brazil. His surprising reputation came mainly from his letters to Piero de Medici and Pietro Soderini which were widely circulated in Europe. These letters were also included in an appendix to Martin Waldseemüller's *Cosmographia Introductio*, published in 1507, which proposed that the name America be given to the new continent. In this curious manner the name of a relatively minor figure was applied to the New World while the name of its discoverer was relegated to just one of the later republics and scores of cities. Such was the first *piloto mayor* of the Casa who served until his death in 1512. The office was well paid, fifty-thousand maravedís annually in addition to twenty-five thousand

33. Ibid., p. 32.

for expenses, and soon became famous by reason of the distinguished men who followed Vespucci. Juan de Sólís was next appointed to the office and served until his departure in 1515 on the expedition from which he did not return. His brother, Francisco Coto, then took over and was followed in 1518 by Sebastian Cabot (or Caboto). By this time eight pilots were established in the Hydrographic Bureau. Eventually a professor of cosmography took over the task of training navigators and the *piloto mayor* only examined them. The training thus obtained became famous and was greatly admired in Europe.

7

The statement that "Isabella to the day of her death regarded the welfare of the natives as a major responsibility" is not an overstatement of the facts.[34] Nor is it strictly accurate to say, as does Leslie Byrd Simpson, that she cared only for their souls and nothing for the welfare of their bodies; there are far too many references in her orders to treat them well and humanely for this judgment to be accepted in full.[35] Since both rulers looked to the church to carry out their Christianizing and civilizing mission to the Indians, any investigation of the treatment of the Indians in the Spanish empire must begin with that institution.

It is not known if a priest or monk accompanied Columbus on the first voyage, although in view of his almost mystic faith and sense of dedication, this omission, if it occurred, does not seem in character. However, in the large fleet of the second voyage there were perhaps a dozen under Fray Vernal Buil, and from this time on the church became deeply involved in colonial problems. A bull of November 16, 1501, gave the queen the right to collect tithes in the New World; it is true they were to be used for ecclesiastical purposes but under the control of the crown. The next step was taken in July, 1508, when a bull of Julius II extended the *patronato real* to the church in the New World; that is, the crown henceforth controlled the extending of dioceses, building of churches, powers of patronage, and nomination to all church officers and preferments. In short, the crown became the secular head of the church in the New World and so remained until the Spanish-American republics achieved their independence.

In 1504 the government obtained the right to create two bishoprics

34. Clarence H. Haring, *The Spanish Empire in America* (New York, 1947), p. 43; henceforth cited as Haring, *The Spanish Empire*.

35. Lesley Byrd Simpson, *The Encomienda in New Spain: Forced Native Labor in the Spanish Colonies, 1492–1550*, in University of California publications in history, Vol. XIX (Berkeley: University of California Press 1929), p. 33.

and an archbishopric in Santo Domingo, but this was never carried out; instead Ferdinand got the old ones cancelled in 1511 and in their place established two dioceses in the former island, and one in Puerto Rico. The first mainland see was set up at Darien in 1513 and all were suffragan to the archdiocese of Seville until 1545. In addition, an office of patriarch of the Indies, in imitation of the Portuguese, was created in 1513 with Fonseca as the first incumbent, but for the most part it was mainly a ceremonial office and had no real influence on the Church overseas. By the end of the colonial period there were ten archdioceses and thirty-eight dioceses in Spanish America. In the early period most of the clergy performing the church functions were friars; the Franciscans were there before 1500 and the Dominicans came out in 1510. It was this last group that soon became involved with the crown, colonists, and natives in a great crisis over the treatment of the latter.

Basically, it was a problem of an adequate labor supply. The fact was that neither the Indians nor the Spaniards enjoyed working in the Caribbean climate. But whereas the natives had early worked out a balance between their simple needs and the minimum labor necessary to meet them, the Spaniards with their much more sophisticated wants such as gold, silver, and a diversified diet required a great deal of hard work, which neither race wished to perform. From the second voyage on, with large numbers of settlers coming out to Santo Domingo, someone was going to have to produce food and other commodities for the colony and the colonists were determined that it must be the Indian. After all, he should do something to pay his teachers for the blessings of eternal salvation, or so at least it appeared to the Spanish.

Some sort of forced labor was obviously going to be introduced if the colony were to survive, but it took a little time to get the system organized and working. Preliminary steps toward it occurred after the rebellion of 1495–1496 when Columbus imposed a tribute on the Indians, but permitted it to be paid in labor when necessary. This may be regarded as the entering wedge, which soon widened. In 1499 after a revolt against Bartholomew Columbus, the admiral's brother, it was decided to pardon the mutineers to get them back into the colony. Their leader, Roldán, submitted only on condition that he and his friends be given allotments of land plus the services of the Indians living on it. This arrangement or *repartimiento* was well known in Spain where, during the Reconquest, it had been employed in territory recently conquered from the Moslems.[36] The

---

36. The terms *repartimiento* and *encomienda* are hard to distinguish accurately. Some writers prefer to write them together with a hyphen. In this study they refer to assignment of lands to the colonists with a *corvée* of Indian labor to work them.

king or some powerful military leader would conduct a *repartimiento* or re-division of lands, assigning allotments to his victorious associates. Along with these allotments went the necessary hands to work them.

Complaints, however, continued to come back from the colonies about the treatment of Indians and when the Catholic Kings sent out Nicolás de Ovando in 1502 he had strict orders not to use forced labor except in mines or public works and then with moderation and adequate pay. Apparently Ovando tried honestly to fulfill his orders, but eventually it became clear to him that without enforced labor the colony would die. As a result of his reports, the crown, through the orders of March and December 1503, decided on a compromise. It would legalize the forced labor of the Indians, but at the same time would try to protect them from exploitation. Once again the settlers were enjoined to treat them well and pay decent wages. Wherever possible, they were to be gathered together into villages under a protector; each village was to have a school, a teacher, and a priest. Intermarriage between colonials and natives was to be encouraged and they were to be treated as free persons "which they are." At the same time the government was willing to go so far as to instruct Ovando to put the villages as close to the mines as possible—for obvious reasons.

The way in which Ovando carried out his instructions was exactly what one would expect from a *comendator* of Alcánatara, and resulted in the famous *encomienda* system in the colonies. In the peninsula, the *encomienda* was one of a number of very similar devices, known as *prestimonio, mandación, encomienda, feudo, tenencia, tierra* and the like, for dealing with land tenure and service. Originally the *encomienda* was a grant by the crown to a member of the royal family, nobles, or ecclesiastics for purposes of administration, emigration, defense, rewards, or all of these together. The grant might be vacant territory, or it might include cities, towns, castles, and monasteries, with the grantee receiving powers of government and the right to receive revenues and services from the people living on the *encomienda*. The grant was supposed to be temporary, but those made for life probably had a tendency to become hereditary. Later, the church gave *encomiendas* as did also the military orders. By the fifteenth century most of the royal and ecclesiastical *encomiendas* had been suppressed, but those of the military orders remained, and, as previously mentioned, Ovando was well acquainted with the system.[37] The system he introduced was essentially the same as the one in the peninsula except that political authority no longer accompanied

37. For a thorough discussion of this problem, see Robert S. Chamberlain, "Castilian Backgrounds of the Repartimiento-Encomienda" in *Carnegie Institute of Washington*, No. 509, June 30, 1929, pp. 35–37.

the grant of an *encomienda*. Thus as political feudalism was dead or dying in western Europe, a form of social and economic feudalism was established in the colonies, where it flourished for the next two hundred and fifty years, leaving ineradicable scars on the structure of native and colonial society. It is perfectly clear that the crown did not intend the natives to be enslaved or even enserfed. But torn between their desires to civilize the Indians, and at the same time to get all the wealth possible out of the colonies, the Castilian government adopted this compromise in the hopes that it would offer some protection to the natives, closing its eyes to the obvious possibility that greed for wealth, and distance from Castile, would permit the system to degenerate to a terrible degree. And for this Ferdinand was partly to blame with his policy, as Simpson aptly puts it, of "get money, by fair means if possible, but get it!"[38]

Fortunately, for the Indians' sake, there were some who were ready to denounce compromise and expediency, and recall the crown to a sense of its responsibilities. The Dominicans came to Santo Domingo in 1510 and were shocked at the exploitation they observed. On Advent Sunday of 1511, Fray Antonio de Montesinos mounted his pulpit and denounced the startled congregation for their abuse and neglect of the Indian. The town was in an uproar and the colonists demanded a retraction from the monk. Those anticipating a retraction went eagerly to his second sermon when they were treated to an even more violent denunciation. Fray Antonio even threatened them with a denial of the sacraments if they continued in their evil ways. The outraged citizens retaliated by selecting a monk from the rival order of the Franciscans and sent him back to Spain to complain to Ferdinand about Montesinos. The king, extremely sensitive as always to anything that might involve his subjects' discussing the rights of the crown, ordered both sides to stop talking, but at the same time he did appoint a commission of laymen and clergy to look into the trouble. The result was the famous Laws of Burgos promulgated on December 27, 1512.

This was an attempt to preserve the compromise, to define it more precisely, but to retain the labor *corvées*. It went much farther in the latter direction than in the former. One-third of the Indians still had to work in the mines, and all Indians were liable for nine months labor out of the twelve for their new masters. Against these demands it is doubtful if the Indians considered the free gift of Latin instruction for the sons of chiefs as much by way of compensation. Conditions continued to deteriorate. The natives were simply dying out under the impact of a culture they did not understand and living conditions

38. Lesley Byrd Simpson, *The Encomienda in New Spain. The Beginning of Spanish Mexico* (Berkeley: University of California Press, 1950), p. 16.

they could not tolerate. Faced with a declining labor supply, the colonists complained to Ferdinand who, as early as 1509, had given them permission to "kidnap" Indians from nearby islands. After 1514 absenteeism was greatly increased when Lope de Conchillos carried through a new division of Indians for himself and his friends. Through this, many colonists lost all or part of their workers, who were reassigned to governmental officials living in Spain. Absenteeism was not forbidden until the New Laws of 1542 and even then was hard to stamp out.

Montesinos had been eliminated, but a new figure of far greater force and vigor appeared to carry on his work. For the next half century Fray Bartolomé de Las Casas dominated the field of Hispano-Indian relations. His father had come to the Caribbean with the fleet of the second voyage, and he himself arrived in 1502 with Ovando. Eventually he took holy orders and said his first mass at Santo Domingo in 1510. The next year he went to Cuba with Velázquez and received an *encomienda*. About this time he became convinced that the system inflicted a terrible injustice on the Indians and resolved to combat it. From this time on until the end of his life in 1566 he defended the rights of the natives in every way possible, and soon won his indisputable right to the title "Apostle of the Indians."

Like Montesinos, Las Casas denounced the evils he observed from the colonial pulpit, but like his predecessor to no avail. In 1515 he returned to Spain to plead his cause before Ferdinand. Unfortunately, most of the colonial officials were hostile and the king was a sick man who died early the next year before anything could be done. The regency government was more sympathetic and, in Cardinal Cisneros, Las Casas found a man who thrived on opposition. Las Casas was given the title of "Protector of the Indians" and was sent back to America with a commission of three Hieronymite friars. They were to investigate the entire problem and recommend a future policy to the regime. As might be expected, their coming in December of 1516 caused great alarm amongst the settlers. However, they seemed to have behaved cautiously and eventually the commission, if not Las Casas, realized the nature of the problem: the natives must be worked if there was to be a colony. As a solution they urged that the government stimulate emigration in every possible way, but did not suggest abolishing the *encomienda* system. Disgusted, Las Casas again sailed to Spain in 1517 to appeal to the young King Charles. The rest of his life properly belongs to that reign.

## 8

In the course of European history, there have been three great imperial experiments: the Roman, the Spanish, and the British. Of these the Roman was the longest in duration yet more compact geographically and easier to traverse. The British covered more ground than the Spanish yet, in the nineteenth century at least, had the advantage of the revolution in transportation and communications to assist it. In terms of human achievement, the Spanish was the greatest of the three. Coming at a time when transportation was clumsy and slow, the empire nevertheless covered an enormous area; at a time when governments were relatively weak and ineffective, the empire was highly organized and strong enough to remain virtually intact for three hundred years; at a time when most governments looked upon the aborigenes as enemies, Spain alone considered them a responsibility.

It is, of course, easy to make a very damaging case against Spain for her treatment of the Indians. It is also easy to make as bad a case or worse against the Portuguese, Dutch, British, and Americans for the same thing. The point is that empires are always founded on blood and cruelty; and, this being the case, the Spaniards are probably less guilty than the other imperial powers who have agitated the surface of the earth. Except in the Caribbean, the Indians were not exterminated, nor were they driven from their lands to become unwanted and somewhat embarrassing wards of the government as has happened in the United States in comparatively recent times. The native civilizations were driven underground, perhaps, but not destroyed, and in our own mid-twentieth century they have had a surprising renaissance as the work of painters like Orozco and Rivera reveals. As a result a new civilization, based on a fusion of both Spanish and native elements, made its appearance and is properly called "Hispanic-American". This has been effectively pointed out by the American philosopher F. S. C. Northrop. Although he was speaking particularly of Mexico, his words have a wider application:

> Fortunately, its [the Christian] destruction of Indian values was not complete. Certain fragments of the native insight, especially in the aesthetic sphere, persisted. To these were added certain superior, more humane religious practices of worship and the ecclesiastical, architectural forms which the Christian Spaniards brought. The product was a second culture in Mexico, termed the Spanish colonial, which, in copying Europe, added Indian elements that make it something precious and unique.[39]

As we have already seen, the latter part of the fifteenth century was less favorable to the growth of the political unit represented by the Mediterranean city-state. Larger political units found conditions more favorable to their growth, provided two components were present: a powerful unifying force which would provide the *mystique* or sense of mission and dedication necessary to form such empires and hold them together; and the economic resources to pay the costs.

39. F. S. C. Northrop, *The Meeting of East and West, an Inquiry Concerning World Understanding* (New York, 1946), p. 22.

The long and complex religious history of the Iberian peninsula helps provide the first, and the creation of the empire the second. For, whatever long range economic damage the colonies inflicted on the mother country ("Cursed Spain with barren gold and made the Andes fiefs of St. Peter")[40] the immediate results were to provide that nation with the economic resources to fulfill the role of a great world power, —the first in modern European history.

40. George Santayana, "Ode III" in *American Poetry, 1671–1928,* edited by Conrad Aiken (New York: Modern Library, 1929) p. 211.

*CHAPTER VI*

# The European Expansion of

# the Catholic Kings

Aside from its part in the Breton War (1485–1491) the dual monarchy of Ferdinand and Isabella seemed destined to play a minor role in European affairs. The reasons for this lack of involvement are clear enough. The 1470's were spent by both sovereigns in establishing their royal titles, which, in the case of Isabella, led to wars with Portugal. The 1480's were mainly occupied with the great struggle against Granada, and the early years of the next decade saw the first voyages of Columbus and Isabella's interest in pursuing the Moslems across the Strait into the north African littoral. Castile and, to a lesser extent, Aragon were forced to concentrate their attention on Iberian and colonial problems, and whatever interests Ferdinand might have had in pursuing traditional Aragonese foreign policies, he was forced to subordinate them to the needs of Castile.

During the decade of 1494–1504, which marked the last phase of Isabella's reign, a great change occurred. The sudden rupture of the precarious balance of power in Italy gave Ferdinand the opportunity to return to the traditional policies of his state—resistance to French expansion anywhere but particularly in Italy, which had been the object of the Aragonese ambitions since the Sicilian Vespers. Castilian aims and interests seemed suddenly forgotten. For whatever reasons —growing concern over the mental state of the Infanta Joanna, the deaths of some of her children, her own failing health—it seems clear that the great queen's influence over her husband was weaker during their last decade together than at any other time during the marriage.

Certainly the traditional friendship between the House of Trastámara and France came to an end. This friendship had been born during the Hundred Years' War when a subsidiary theatre of the war had been opened in Spain by the Black Prince.[1] During the last phase of the war, the anarchy in Castile under John II and Henry IV prevented that state from contributing anything to the French cause while at the same time its weakness tempted Louis XI to interfere in the Castilian succession crisis. Moreover, the French acquisition of Guienne removed an English buffer state which conveniently separated France from Castile. Henceforth both states faced each other directly across the Pyrenean frontier; any advance in this region was bound to be at the expense of the other power.

As Franco-Castilian friendship was rapidly cooling, the two-hundred year hostility between France and Aragon continued without abatement. When John II became involved in the long rebellion of Catalonia, René of Anjou, last of the line of ancient enemies of Aragon, intervened on the side of the rebels. Later, when John, needing money as always, pawned the trans-Pyrenean provinces of Cerdagne and Roussillon, Louis XI took advantage of this arrangement to occupy the two principalities permanently. On the death of old King René in 1480, and his nephew in 1481, Louis inherited not only the Angevine lands, giving him control of Provence, but also their somewhat fantastic claims to overseas territories such as Naples.

It was these hostile claims and old rivalries that led Ferdinand to take an anti-French policy in the Breton War, his first overt act against France. Basically, the Breton War was a feudal struggle between the duke of Brittany and his suzerain, the king of France, over the inheritance of the duke's daughter Anne, the heiress of the duchy. Charles VIII, or, rather, his astute advisors, were determined to bring Brittany into the French crown by force, by marriage, or a combination of both. This relatively local issue briefly flared up into a major European concern because of the politics of the great powers. Aragon, England, and the Empire—all traditional opponents of France—saw in the contest an excellent opportunity to embarrass an old enemy; and all were prepared to take advantage of the war in one way or another. For Ferdinand, however, the timing was bad; he was still deeply involved in the Granadine War and could not afford a distant diversion. The other two powers were not so entangled and both had a background of friendship with Brittany. Emperor Maximilian had had close relations with Brittany since 1486 and had become the betrothed of Princess Anne. Henry Tudor, king of Eng-

1. During the civil war in Castile between Pedro I and his half-brother Henry of Trastámara, the Black Prince had intervened on the side of the king while the French supported Henry, who won the crown in 1469. See above, p. 101.

land since 1485, had spent some twelve years in Brittany as a royal exile. Both, obviously, might be counted on to do much of the actual work of intervention.

Henry VII moved first. In 1488 he proposed a treaty of friendship and commerce with the dual monarchy, later to be more firmly cemented by a marriage between Arthur, Prince of Wales, and Ferdinand's daughter, Catherine of Aragon. Such a treaty was actually signed at Medina del Campo on March 27, 1489; the price Henry had to pay for the Infanta Catherine was his promise to break with France, and enter the Breton War in alliance with Maximilian. But it was one thing to promise and another thing to act. Maximilian was always the most uncertain of allies, and Henry hesitated to challenge the power of France. As a sign of his good faith, Ferdinand sent one thousand men to Brittany, who quickly became occupied in a siege, and it was only the French who acted with any decision. They pressed the invasion of Brittany so forcefully that in 1491 Anne agreed to marry Charles VIII; and Margaret, Maximilian's daughter by his first wife, who had herself been betrothed to Charles, was hurriedly sent home. Only then, with all the basic issues settled in favor of France, did Henry VII invade France in accordance with his commitments in the Treaty of Medina del Campo. It proved quite easy to buy him off for 745,000 crowns (Treaty of Étaples, November 3, 1492) which is probably all that he wanted in the first place. If Ferdinand had hoped, as various historians assert, to use the Breton War as a lever with which to pry Cerdagne and Roussillon out of the hands of the French, he had failed dismally.

From Ferdinand's point of view, it must have seemed that France blocked him at every point of expansion except in the New World, and here he was excluded by Castile. Should he return to his father's policies in Navarre, he must inevitably stand up against the French. If he sought the return of Cerdagne and Roussillon, he must first drive out the occupying French troops. And if he attempted any further expansion in Italy, there were the hostile claims of the House of Anjou which had now passed to the French crown. We hear much about the Habsburg encirclement of France in the next century, but we are apt to forget that Ferdinand could just as well speak of a Valois encirclement of Aragon had the term been invented in his day. In such a situation it was unavoidable that the Catholic King should be fundamentally anti-French.

With the advantages of hindsight, it is clear that his subsequent policies had the most profound and adverse consequences for Spain, and, indeed, for all Europe. But is it not expecting too much to believe that he should have foreseen this? How could he, or anyone else have known in 1494 or 1495 that the marriage alliances that were a major part of his anti-French policy would result in the advent of a foreign dynasty with enormous commitments in northern and central Europe and the ultimate destruction of his work? It hardly seems fair to condemn his policy as being too hostile to France as Mariéjol and others have done. Given the circumstances and the past traditions of his country, it could hardly have been anything else. As Mariéjol himself was to admit:

> It is not sufficient to say, by way of explaining the policy of the Catholic Kings, that they found France too strong. There is much more than that: the interests and greatness of Spain pushed them against a people that they found blocking their path at every point of expansion.[2]

What is not clear is just what Ferdinand could have done to counter the results of the Breton War, had not Charles VIII played into his hands by the monumental blunder of his expedition to Naples.

2

By the middle of the fifteenth century, the Italian states, always turbulent and quarrelsome, had achieved a precarious balance. Four things made this possible: (1) the check to Venetian expansion on the mainland; (2) the rule of Ferrante in Naples; (3) the Medici in Florence; and (4) the Sforza in Milan.

Ferrante had succeeded Alfonso V in 1458. Although a bastard and thoroughly unpopular, he showed real ability. A baronial revolt against him was promptly suppressed with great cruelty and the famous aristocratic family of San Severino was crushed. In spite of great papal hostility, he maintained himself in power and, through commercial monopolies, managed to increase his revenues. His relations with his uncle, John II of Aragon, and later his cousin Ferdinand, remained excellent. In 1476 he took as his second wife Joanna, Ferdinand's sister. In Italian affairs he drew closer to Milan, likewise threatened by French dynastic claims, and later bestowed his granddaughter on Gian Galeazzo, the young Sforza duke of Milan.

Ferrante's strong rule in Naples was roughly paralleled by the rule of the Sforzas in Milan. The powerful city and duchy, which dominated most of the routes leading from the Alpine passes into the peninsula, had long been ruled by the famous Visconti family, so richly endowed with homicidal tendencies. This line became extinct in 1447; and, after Milan's three unhappy years as a municipal republic, the old *condottiere* Francisco Sforza succeeded in seizing control, which his family maintained to the end of the century. When his son was assassinated in 1476 leaving an eight-year-old heir, the mother, Bona of Savoy, ruled until 1479. In that year Ludovico, nick-

2. Mariéjol, p. 66.

named "the Moor" because of his complexion, excluded his young nephew and took over the government himself. He thus became head of one of the richest states in Italy (the estimated annual revenue was 700,000 ducats) and soon established a brilliant court to which Leonardo da Vinci contributed his genius.

Since 1434, Florence had been controlled by the Medici family, who had solved the problem of establishing absolute rule over a population famous for its love of liberty by becoming something like "city bosses" who, without holding major offices, manipulated power behind the scenes, managing municipal affairs according to their own wishes. They would not have succeeded for so long had their policies not been marked by wisdom, moderation, and extreme common sense. While they satisfied public opinion by magnificent shows and extensive building, and won the support of the smaller merchants through their economic measures, in foreign affairs they worked with Milan and Naples to prevent aggression in the peninsula and so eliminate excuses for foreign intervention.

The two principal sources of danger to the peace of Italy from within came from Venice and the papacy. The former, breaking its rule of non-involvement in territorial affairs, had embarked on a program of aggression and mainland expansion early in the fifteenth century; this involved the republic in wars with Milan and other Italian neighbors, and also the Empire. A kind of balance was established in 1454 by the Treaty of Lodi, which stabilized the inter-city relationships. Venetian expansion was checked, and the war between Venice and Milan over the Sforza succession was ended when the Republic recognized the new dynasty. In this last phase, Milan had been supported by Florence; and after the death of Alfonso V, the threats from the papacy and the reassertion of Angevine claims to the throne of Naples forced Ferrante to establish closer relations between Naples and Milan. Thus a kind of triplice composed of Milan, Florence, and Naples, powers whose chief interest was in keeping the peace of Italy, came into being.

It was the papacy that provided the chief test of the new combination. Under Sixtus IV (1471–1484), one of the worst of the Renaissance popes, the Vatican embarked on a career of nepotism and open aggression that threatened to throw Italy into utter confusion. Although the popes were the traditional enemies of the Aragonese rulers in Naples and Sicily, Sixtus reached an understanding with Ferrante and turned his attention to despoiling the rich city of Florence. When the Florentines resisted the diplomatic pressure he brought against them, he turned to murder and conspiracy. The story of the Pazzi conspiracy is too well known to require retelling here; suffice it to say that the Pope's attempt to use the Pazzi family to exterminate the Medici and take over the government failed utterly. However, Florence was in a position of extreme danger until the young Lorenzo managed to re-establish good relations with Naples. The triplice thus survived this threat to its existence and to the peace of the peninsula.

Sixtus next planned the dismemberment of the duchy of Ferrara with the support of Venice. In May of 1482, the two powers attacked the duchy, the pope even going so far as to offer support for Angevine claims against Naples in return for French aid against Ferrara. The duke, who was the son-in-law of Ferrante, promptly turned to Naples for support; and Ferrante, in his turn, appealed to Aragon. The Ferrara War, viewed in the light of the Turkish threat to Italy, which was acute at this time, or the later French invasion, was a small affair. It is significant, however, because once again the triplice held together to resist aggression and also because they were quickly backed by Aragon. Although they were in the early stages of the Granadine War, Ferdinand and Isabella used all possible pressure to compel both Venice and the papacy to desist. With Sixtus IV they were successful; he withdrew from the war before the end of the year. With Venice, it was a different matter. The Very Serene Republic was not accustomed to taking dictation from another power, and in spite of the Turkish danger (Otranto had fallen to the Turks in 1480) was determined to have its way. It required the sending of a fleet to Italian waters, the threat of a commercial war, and the expulsion of Venetian nationals from the territories of the Catholic Kings before Venice yielded and reestablished the *status quo*. Perhaps the most significant outcome of the whole affair was that, as Merriman points out, Ferdinand had prepared the way for later interventions in Italian affairs.

In the last analysis, however, it was the danger of external invasion that was the greatest threat to Italy and there was ample precedent for it. Since the days of the *Römerzug* of the medieval emperors, or the Norman adventurers, foreigners had occupied Italy repeatedly by violence and force. France and Aragon had now replaced the German emperors, and each had sufficient claims to provide a veil of diplomacy to cover up the brutal fact. While Aragon was concerned with the south, France not only had the Angevine claims; but, since one of the Visconti had married the first duke of Orleans, it could be claimed that Visconti rights over Milan had passed to France during the Sforza usurpation. In addition, a new power which had no legal rights at all, but only the power of preponderant force, now threatened the entire peninsula: this was the Turks. The expansion of the Ottoman power was nothing new in the fifteenth century; however, with the fall of Constantinople in 1453 it was beginning to get uncomfortably close. Throughout the remainder of the reign of

Mohammed II (died, 1481), Venice was hard pressed by land and by sea. Much of the Balkans was occupied and the seizure of Otranto in 1480 meant that the Italian mainland was now directly threatened. Although the death of the sultan shortly afterwards brought about a relaxation of the pressure and his successor Bayazid was involved in the eastern part of his domains, the Ottoman Empire remained an aggressive power and no one could say when Italy might not be again directly menaced. That the Catholic Kings were extremely sensitive to the rise of Turkish power there can be no doubt. Turkish support of their fellow Moslems in Granada was always a real possibility, and if the Granadine War had been fought during the youth of Mohammed II, it might have had a different conclusion. Characteristically, it was Castile that contributed the seventy ships that joined the expedition that expelled the Turks from Otranto in 1481.

In view of the increasing inability of the Mediterranean city state to compete with the new type of political organization making its appearance in that area, it does not seem likely that anything could have maintained the Italian balance of power for very long. This new type of state, large, with solid economic resources, and animated by a tremendous *esprit de corps*, at the time was represented by the Ottoman Empire, the dual monarchy of Ferdinand and Isabella, and France. In the first two, this sustaining spirit came from a militant religious faith, and some of this was present in France where Charles VIII thought in ultimate terms of a crusade to recover Jerusalem after first obtaining a foothold in Italy. Any one of these three powers might have been considered as ready for major aggression in Italy; the fact that France was actually the one that initiated the descent on the peninsula must be taken as a matter of chance. Certainly, Ferdinand never ignored the possibility that the Turks might get there ahead of him. This danger is twice mentioned by him in his initial instructions to Juan de Lanuza, his viceroy in Sicily in 1495.

However inevitable the disruption of Italy by outside forces, its advent was definitely hastened by the decay of the triplice of Florence, Milan, and Naples in the last decades of the century. After Ludovico *il Moro* had excluded the young duke from the ducal throne, his wife, Isabella of Aragon, repeatedly complained to her father and grandfather in Naples of this usurpation, and relations between Milan and Naples rapidly deteriorated. As long as Lorenzo de' Medici lived, Florence might be expected to mediate these differences, but with his death in 1492 a restraining hand was removed. His successor Piero, stupid and unstable, was no man to pilot the republic through an international crisis which many could see approaching. Meanwhile, Ludovico, threatened by a hostile Naples, still awaiting imperial confirmation of his new power, and aware that the French house of Orleans had a claim on his duchy, felt his insecurity so greatly that he decided on an extreme course of great risk. He decided to urge Charles VIII, the young, impressionable king of France, to assert the claims to the throne of Naples that he had inherited from the Angevine line. In this way he would forestall hostile action from the Orleanist faction at the French court and likewise prevent Ferrante of Naples from coming to the aid of his granddaughter. Charles was highly receptive to the suggestion.

### 3

In 1492, the king of France was an ugly, misshapen youth of twenty-two; his outward appearance reflected his mental attainments. Until that year, the government had been managed by his older sister, Anne of Beaujeu, with the help of advisors from the previous reign. To these realistic minds, England was still the center of French diplomacy and the Angevine claims to Naples were so much smoke. At this point, the young king decided to assert himself and take over the government with the help of "new men" such as Briconnet and De Vese, as Commines, who was one of the older group, scornfully describes them. These advisors were much more willing to consider adventures in foreign policy than Anne and her more cautious supporters. Charles' fuzzy wits seem to have been nourished, if at all, by romances of chivalry, and he much preferred being a hero to a politician although Nature, unfortunately, had designed him for neither. He seems to have dreamed of a crusade to recover Jerusalem—as who had not in the Middle Ages—and probably looked on the conquest of Naples as the logical first step. The fact that France and Aragon had engaged in an almost colonial rivalry over Italy for the last two hundred years probably had much less influence over him than his own mental bias and the opportunities of the moment. The historical background provided a useful claim that could be brought forward when convenient, but the determining factors in 1492–1494 were Charles' personality, the disintegration of the triplice, the fears of Ludovico, and the ambitions of new advisors at the French court. And at the last moment, chance made its contribution: Ferrante of Naples died in January, 1494, and was succeeded by his son Alfonso, a much less capable ruler.[3]

However, before these last events took place, Charles VIII, his mind now made up, began to set his house in order before making

3. A part of the subsequent troubles of the kingdom of Naples came from the rapid succession of rulers. Alfonso succeeded Ferrante in January, 1494, and abdicated the following year in favor of his son, Ferrantino. Ferrantino died on October 6, 1496 and was succeeded by his uncle Federigo. Thus between 1493 and 1496, Naples endured four changes of rulers.

the journey to Naples. This consisted mainly in trying to placate his neighbors by throwing away some of the dearly bought achievements of his father. The Treaty of Étaples purchased the neutrality of Henry VII for 745,000 gold crowns. Ferdinand did much better. To win his neutrality and friendship, Charles returned Cerdagne and Roussillon without any monetary compensation (Treaty of Barcelona, January 19, 1493). To placate Emperor Maximilian, whose trouble-making proclivities were his chief asset as ruler, Charles by the Treaty of Senlis returned the dowry of the archduchess Margaret, his one-time betrothed, which consisted of Artois and Franche-Comté. With his daughter and her dowry back in Maximilian's possession, the way was now paved for the future pair of marriages between the houses of Habsburg and Trastámara so fraught with consequences for the history of Europe. Whatever effect the Treaty of Senlis might have had was quickly nullified when Maximilian, long a widower, married into the Sforza family in March, 1494. He had become emperor the year before on the death of his father. It was now clear that Charles VIII would not be allowed to play Italian politics by himself.

Meanwhile, all the powers watched the French invasion of Italy which had finally got under way in August, 1494. It appeared to be a succession of triumphs for the king of France, or rather for the "avenging angels of the Lord," as Savonarola put it. Without any opposition of importance, the French passed from north to central Italy and, as the new year began, prepared to cross the Neapolitan frontier. At this point, Ferdinand of Aragon was ready to show his hand. The time was ripe for action and he was in an unusually strong position. The Granadine War was over and the Iberian states were at peace. The war had left in his hand a highly developed instrument —the *tercio*—and in Gonsalvo de Cordoba, a general of genius.[4] Intervention in Italian affairs was almost traditional for a king of Aragon, and, after Alfonso V, especially for the Trastámaras. While Ferdinand had maintained correct and even friendly relations with his Neapolitan relatives, there seems little doubt that he had long hoped to supplant them. Furthermore, Naples in the late fifteenth century was quite a different state from the impoverished and feeble Spanish dependency of the seventeenth century. In Ferdinand's time she was the largest of the Italian states, occupied a strategic location,

4. The *tercio* grew out of the military reforms of Gonzalo de Córdoba at the time of the Granadine War, and after 1534 was the standard regimental unit. Taking its name from a threefold division into 1500 pikemen, 1000 swordsmen, and 500 arquebusiers, the *tercio* was the backbone of the famous Spanish infantry for the next 150 years. In battle they fought in squares which were considered extremely effective in defense and very hard to break. See Lynch, *Spain under the Habsburgs*, I, 77–78.

and was in a position to make sizable agricultural and financial contributions. Furthermore, since Ferdinand was already king of Sicily, the union of Naples with this crown was logically the next step.

And yet Ferdinand behaved with great caution; his timing, as the twentieth century would put it, was admirable. The first steps to check Charles VIII were made to the Vatican. Before the invasion, envoys were sent from the Catholic Kings to the new pope, Alexander VI (so recently Cardinal Rodrigo Borja of Valencia), to keep him if possible on the side of Naples. Failing this, Ferdinand sent ambassadors to Charles while he was still on French soil, urging him to concentrate his energies on a crusade against the Turk. When Charles is supposed to have pointed out that by the Treaty of Barcelona Ferdinand was to regard the enemies of France as his own, the envoys warned him that this did not apply to the Holy See and, since Naples was a fief of the papacy, it also did not apply to that power. This warning failed to stop Charles and the invasion went on as planned. Meanwhile, Ferdinand's diplomacy was working overtime.

In the light of hindsight, the steps he took seem so logical and obvious that it is surprising that even the fatuous king of France did not foresee them. But apparently that lover of knighthood could not believe that a man who was both king and knight could possibly violate his oath, and so continued to trust in the Treaty of Barcelona, as doubtless Ferdinand intended that he should. In the interim, while the invasion rolled on, Ferdinand's envoys went to Venice, to England, to Milan, and to the Emperor. The main line of policy was to form a league of various states to drive the French from Italy with the strong support of the Iberian powers, but other issues were taken up as well. Thus relations between Venice and Maximilian, usually bad, were greatly improved so as to permit their joint operations against the French. At the same time, Ferdinand revived a matrimonial scheme of 1492 when he sent Francisco de Rojas to Maximilian with instructions to conclude a double marriage between his heir, the Infante John, and the archduchess Margaret; and his daughter the unstable Joanna with the archduke Philip, joint heir of Maximilian and Mary of Burgundy. Although the formal signing of the League of Venice, as historians have agreed to call it, was considerably delayed, and Henry VII did not come in until it was all over, the king of Aragon had succeeded in mobilizing formidable opposition to Charles VIII. By the time Ferdinand was ready to break with France, and since Charles was drawing near to Naples a break could no longer be delayed, he felt he could count on the support of the papacy, Venice, the empire, and Milan in his efforts to drive the French from Italy. Meanwhile, with the abdication of King Alfonso, and the near approach of the French, the government of Naples was so weakened that in the future it would be largely dependent on the support and good will of Aragon. The final step in his preparations was the appointment of Juan de Lanuza, hereditary *Justicia* of Aragon, as viceroy of Sicily with Gonsalvo de Córdoba later added as commander of the military forces. In December of 1494 a fleet and some thirty-five-hundred soldiers were sent to Sicily, which was to be the advanced headquarters of the resistance movement.

Ferdinand broke with Charles while the latter was at Velletri near the Neapolitan frontier during January-February of 1495. There are various accounts of what happened, but it seems clear that Ferdinand warned Charles for the last time to desist, declared the Treaty of Barcelona had been violated since Charles had injured the Holy See, and made a last minute offer of mediation in the war. This was rejected, but after the interview at Velletri Charles VIII, slow as he was, can have had no further doubts of Ferdinand's hostility. The French pressed on into Naples, Charles was formally crowned king shortly afterwards, and the League of Venice was officially signed by all parties on March 31. Whereupon Ferdinand sent an additional twenty-one-hundred men under Gonsalvo de Córdoba to Sicily to assist the young king in recovering his kingdom.

The spectacle of Charles' invasion of Italy now passed from knightly drama to farce, involving the sordid effects of a major outbreak of syphilis among all parties. The French entered Naples on February 22, 1495, and Charles was crowned king shortly afterwards. Unfortunately, the opportunities of a city long known for its pleasures proved to be too much for an army a long way from wives and home, although the virulent syphilis epidemic proved to be only one of a host of troubles that now beset the French. Local supporters of the invaders were alienated—less by French social behavior than by the speed with which they absorbed lands and offices. Supplies were, not surprisingly, hard to come by and local insurrections made their expected appearances. Ferdinand's troops were in Sicily and the final touches were hastily put to the League of Venice. The formal documents of the member states were officially signed on March 31, 1495. Unless Charles VIII was willing to run the risk of being cut off in Italy, withdrawal was the only course.

The French withdrew, but it turned out to be a very near thing. Charles dallied in Naples while the forces of the League were mobilizing against him. He did not depart until May 21 and left some half of his army behind to hold the city. The League caught up with him on July 6 and tried to bar his route to the Alpine passes. The Battle of Fornovo cost the French their baggage train, but Italian casualties were heavy and the king and his troops were able to continue their retreat without further hindrance. By the end of October,

Charles was back in France, and thinking of doing it all over again some time in the future, since he had promises of additional help from Milan. However, his brief Italian kingdom quickly collapsed. His viceroy could not hold the kingdom in the face of the determined attacks of King Ferrantino and Gonsalvo de Córdoba. Although the Spanish contingent was relatively small, it represented the new type of army that had been developed during the Granadine War and was led by one of the outstanding military leaders of the age. The French won an initial success at Seminara, and then were systematically defeated in all the other engagements. By the spring of 1496 Ferrantino was back in his capital and Gonsalvo was able to clear the Papal States of the remaining French garrisons. On another front the Spanish were also successful; a small army under Enríque de Guzman made various forays into the trans-Pyrenean provinces of France, bringing back considerable booty until a regional truce halted such operations.

So far both Ferdinand and the League had been remarkably successful. However, subsequent efforts to follow up the initial victory were not so happy. It was decided to move against Florence, still a French ally, by assisting the Pisans in resisting a Florentine attack. However, Maximilian who went to Italy for this purpose failed completely and was forced to withdraw, discredited and bankrupt. The League itself began to show signs of disintegration; Milan had abandoned it before the end of 1495. As a reward for her contributions, Venice forced Naples to cede to her the four Apulian ports of Monopoli, Trani, Brindisi, and Otranto, a loss which disturbed Ferdinand of Aragon. Furthermore, the unexpected death of the new king of Naples on October 7, 1496, by bringing a new and untried ruler to power in that key state, added to the confusion and prepared the way for further policy changes among the powers.

As Merriman puts it,

The significance of these events was not lost on Ferdinand the Catholic. He had got rid of the French. He had no more use for his allies—indeed one of them, Venice, was actually in possession of a portion of the territory which he coveted for himself. The throne of Naples was at present occupied by a prince whom it promised to be easy to despoil. Now, if ever, was his chance to win the crown which Alfonso the Magnanimous had withheld from his father.[5]

The time was propitious for a new understanding with France, no longer a danger to him and not yet recovered from the disastrous expedition to Naples. Moreover, the Trastámara-Habsburg marriages of 1496–1497 and the revival of negotiations for a Spanish match for Arthur, Prince of Wales, clearly indicated that France might find her-

5. Merriman, II, 294.

self surrounded by a network of hostile marriage alliances controlled by the king of Aragon. Charles VIII was also anxious for a better understanding with his recent enemy.

After a suspension of hostilities, lengthy negotiations took place throughout 1497. Eventually an agreement was signed at Alcalá de Henares on November 24 which provided an entirely new approach to the problem of Naples—an approach which was to dominate the diplomacy of the next few years. Both powers now abandoned major aspects of their previous policies: France surrendered her claims to the totality of the Neapolitan state, and Aragon abandoned any pretense of defending it. In short, the new arrangement signed at Alcalá provided for a joint operation against Naples by both states and then partition; Aragon was to have Calabria and France was to get the rest. Further suggestions by Charles VIII for the eventual conquest of all Italy were rejected by the Catholic King. Thus, "all the preparations for the game that Ferdinand was to play in Naples between 1500 and 1504, at first with the aid, and then at the expense, of Louis XII of France, were made before the death of Charles VIII, which occurred as the result of an accident on April 7, 1498."[6]

4

The new king, Louis XII, soon left no doubt that French policy had changed. Italy was still the major interest, but the focus had shifted from Naples to Milan. Louis, as head of the Orleanist branch of the Valois family, had inherited the old family claims on Milan and intended to push them. According to rumor, he had tried to convince Charles of the importance of an attack on Milan at the time of the 1494 invasion. Failing this, he had bided his time, and his time had now come.

Milan and Venice tried to stir the League to action. Maximilian and Henry VII of England were approached; they offered advice and a little money, and Maximilian came to Italy for the League's operation against Florence. But, as we have seen, this attack failed and the emperor withdrew north of the Alps. He continued to be sympathetic to schemes to resist the French, but he had no money. Ludovico *il Moro* approached some of the smaller northern Italian states; Mantua, Ferrara, and Bologna were contacted, but were afraid to act. However, Milan was a wealthy state, and Ludovico was able to hire mercenaries and strengthen the key fortress of Alessandria.

Meanwhile, the diplomatic preparations of Louis XII were formidable. At his coronation he had taken the titles of duke of Milan and king of Naples. Maximilian refused to recognize them, but Louis had

6. Ibid., p. 297.

won the support of the emperor's son, Philip the Handsome, heir to the Burgundian lands through his mother Mary of Burgundy, and now, through his marriage to Joanna, son-in-law of Ferdinand of Aragon. This prince now began to play an independent role of his own in the diplomacy of the time, frequently to the annoyance of both his father and father-in-law. As virtually an independent sovereign in the Netherlands, and possessed of extensive ambitions, he was a factor of great though temporary importance in three significant areas: in the Netherlands, in France where his holdings made him one of the chief peers of the realm, and in Castile where his marriage to a daughter of Isabella opened up a strong possibility of a royal inheritance. Timely concessions by the French in Artois now won his support to the plans of Louis XII.

Other powers were approached and won over. The Swiss agreed to supply troops for the invading army in return for a subsidy. Florence secretly promised support and the papacy was brought in by the promise of a duchy for Cesare Borgia, the pope's son, and the hand of Charlotte d'Albret, the king's cousin. After long negotiations, Venice was induced to break with the League and provide 100,000 ducats in return for a share of Milanese territory.

The campaign began in August of 1499. Louis had some seventeen thousand infantry, including six thousand Swiss mercenaries. On the 29th Alessandria fell and four days later Ludovico evacuated Milan. On October 6 Louis XII made his triumphal entry into the capital of the duchy and appointed Gian Giacomo Trivulzio, a Milanese exile, as his viceroy. The following year, Trivulzio was forced to abandon the city when Ludovico returned to Milan, although the French still held out at various strong points in the duchy. However, he was not strong enough to maintain it and a defeat at Novara by the French on April 8 1500, ended his hopes forever; the remainder of his life was spent as a prisoner in France. Milan was once more French.

It was now time to turn to Louis' other dream—the conquest of Naples. Milan was in his hands, giving him control of most of the northern passes; as long as he held it, he could not be cut off from France. Venice was friendly and so was the Spanish pope, Alexander VI. Should he return to the early policy of Charles VIII and claim Naples solely for himself; or accept Charles' later policy of "joint operation and partition"? It is clear that Ferdinand was anxious that he should accept the latter; otherwise his Italian policies during 1499 –1500 make little sense. It can harldy be assumed that he was really concerned with aiding Venice against the Turks nor for that reason alone would he have assembled a large fleet and army under Gonsalvo de Córdoba. Even the successful operation against Cephalonia is rather pointless unless one assumes that Ferdinand wanted large armed forces close to the theatre of war in the event that he and Louis XII agreed to conduct joint operations against Naples. Negotiations between the two sovereigns were carried on with great activity during the summer and fall of 1500 while Federigo of Naples' appeals to Aragon for help were ignored. Louis showed himself willing to compromise and what was substantially the original agreement between Ferdinand and Charles of 1497 was written into the new treaty signed at Granada on November 11, 1500. After the usual complaints against the king of Naples to justify what was simply an act of naked aggression, the two rulers agreed on a joint operation to be followed by a partition of the kingdom, Aragon receiving not only Calabria but Apùlia as well (a considerable increase over the earlier agreement), with France taking the rest, including the city of Naples.

The joint operations began in the summer of 1501 with the French moving down from the north and the Spanish advancing from their Sicilian base into the areas assigned to them. Against such a preponderance of force, Federigo could do nothing. Eventually, he agreed to accept an honorable exile in France. Only at Taranto was there any serious resistance where Federigo's son, the duke of Calabria, successfully held up the Great Captain until March 1, 1502.

The peace that followed turned out to be a brief interlude, heralding a much more intense struggle between France and Aragon. Probably Ferdinand had never intended on any permanent peace with France until all of Naples was in his hands. So far Louis had assisted him in destroying the Neapolitan Trastámaras, and thus, in a sense, had done his work for him. The remaining step was to eliminate the French, operating so far from their main bases, and take over all Naples for himself. To create a rupture between the occupying powers did not prove to be difficult. Either through accident or design, the Treaty of Granada was vague concerning the possession of the Capitanata, an important bit of territory lying between the French Abruzzi and the Spanish Apulia. It was valuable because of its food supplies, especially to the inhabitants of the barren hills of Apulia, and because of the tolls which were levied on cattle passing through it from summer to winter pastures. The French claimed it was part of their share of the kingdom and although Ferdinand ordered Gonsalvo to spin out the discussions as long as possible, the French occupied the Capitanata and war thereupon broke out between the two allies.

At first, the advantages seemed to lie with the French. Gonsalvo was blockaded at Barletta, but managed to hold out because he controlled the sea and received supplies from Spain and Sicily. In the meantime, diplomacy attempted to find a solution to the quarrel. We have already seen that Philip and Maximilian concluded treaties with France at Lyons which provided for the marriage of Charles of Luxembourg (as he was then known), the infant son of Philip and Joanna of Castile, with Claude of France, daughter of Louis XII. When Joanna and Philip journeyed to Castile to receive public recognition as the heirs of Isabella they did not hesitate to traverse France en route to their destination. On his return to the Netherlands, Philip crossed France again in March, 1503, and seems to have had some sort of authority to treat with Louis to bring the Italian war to a conclusion if possible. Since Gonsalvo was still contained at Barletta, Ferdinand was probably insuring himself against a possible defeat by getting a negotiated settlement. At any rate, Philip met Louis at Lyons and on April 5, 1503, they signed a treaty ending, so they both apparently thought, the Neapolitan war. The marriage of Charles of Luxembourg with Claude of France was reaffirmed and a settlement was reached over the Capitanata which was to be governed by third parties in the name of the young couple. As far as the rest of Naples was concerned, each ruler was to retain the share assigned to him by the Treaty of Granada. Louis, apparently believing in the authority of Philip to negotiate for Ferdinand, immediately sent word to his forces in Italy of the peace. But at the same time Gonsalvo de Córdoba received the long awaited reinforcements from home and prepared to break out of Barletta. When reminded by the Duc de Nemours that peace had been declared, Gonsalvo stated that he could only suspend hostilities on receipt of a direct order from Ferdinand, which, needless to say, had not come. Gonsalvo advanced from Barletta and on April 28 thoroughly defeated the weakened and demoralized French at Cerignola. Two weeks later the Aragonese entered Naples and the French retired to Gaeta. Louis violently denounced the treachery of Ferdinand, but the Catholic King could well afford to ignore it. The French decided to make one last effort. Three armies were to be raised and directed against Spanish Navarre, Roussillon, and Naples. Luck seemed to be with them when Alexander VI died at this time and the election of Pius III presaged a more neutral papacy. French allies in northern Italy contributed troops and during the fall of 1503 a French army advanced south of Rome under the command of the marquis of Mantua. Eventually both armies faced each other across the Garigliano River for several weeks where they existed in various stages of near-starvation. Not until the last days of December did the stalemate end; then the Great Captain succeeded in crossing the Garigliano and fell upon the unprepared French, who were completely defeated. It was the end of the French struggle for Naples.

5

Ferdinand owed his victory over France to three things. First, was his own brilliant conduct of the diplomacy of the Italian Wars. Here his skill and resourcefulness, especially in duplicity, completely outclassed the French and aroused the admiration of contemporaries. "Nothing causes a prince to be so much esteemed as great enterprises and giving proof of prowess," wrote Machiavelli. "We have in our own day Ferdinand, King of Aragon. . . . He may almost be termed a new prince, because from a weak king he has become for fame and glory the first king of Christendom, and if you regard his actions you will find them all very great and some of them extraordinary."[6]

Second, Ferdinand owed his success to the power of the kingdom of Castile, whose resources were placed solidly behind him. This was especially true in the case of the new army. As we have seen, this had been developed in the Granadine War and had reached, especially in the *tercio,* a high degree of mobility and flexibility. Effective leadership had also emerged during the ten-year conquest of the last Moslem state in the peninsula, and this had reached a climax in the person of the Great Captain. Although nominally a subject of Queen Isabella, Gonsalvo de Córdoba, through the fact of the dual monarchy, was equally available for the service of Ferdinand. Without the powerful weapon of the new army and its distinguished leadership, the relatively petty ruler of Aragon could never have successfully challenged the power of France in Italy.

And last, Ferdinand owed his success to the blunders of Charles VIII and Louis XII. Charles, poor dreamer, was obviously no contender in the kind of *realpolitik* so brilliantly practiced by the king of Aragon. However, Louis was considerably superior to his predecessor, and had firmly established himself in the north before advancing to the south. Here, as Machiavelli was to point out, was his major blunder:

> He, now coveting the kingdom of Naples, divided it with the king of Spain; and where he alone was the arbiter of Italy, he now brought in a companion, so that the ambitious of that province who were dissatisfied with him might have some one else to appeal to; and where he might have left in that kingdom a king tributary to himself, he dispossessed him in order to bring in another who was capable of driving him out. . . . If France, therefore, with her own forces could have taken Naples, she ought to have done so; if she could not, she ought not to have shared it.[8]

Thus Louis was in the unfortunate position of doing part of the work

7. Machiavelli, *The Prince* (Modern Library Edition), pp. 81–82.
8. Ibid., p. 13.

of conquest for the king of Aragon and then promptly being dispensed with after all his pains.

The conquest of Naples both climaxed and completed the traditional Aragonese interests in the Mediterranean and in Italy. Furthermore, it brought together the southern part of the peninsula with the island of Sicily in a natural union under the crown of Aragon and later Spain. It also added sizable agricultural resources, and additional revenues. In addition it placed the Spanish power solidly in the central Mediterranean where it could strike out either to the west or to the east. A large galley fleet came to be based on Neapolitan and Sicilian harbors. At the same time Spain became the dominant secular power in Italy until the War of the Spanish Succession and exercised a powerful influence both on the papacy and the remaining independent states.

But these advantages were very nearly counterbalanced by serious disadvantages. Becoming the dominant power in Italy meant that Spain became involved in the morass of local Italian politics. Able to influence the papacy through her proximity to the Papal States, Spain also was forced to intervene frequently in ecclesiastical and papal affairs. Maintaining their position in Italy and preventing attacks on it became a continuing distraction to Spanish governments as Spanish power was more and more thinly spread over an ever increasing area—a distraction that was costly in men, money, and time.

As Spanish influence moved eastward toward the Mediterranean center, it came much closer to the rising power of the Turks moving in the opposite direction from Constantinople. Even if the Habsburg connection had not forced Spain to assume the lead in resisting Islam, the possession of Naples and Sicily would have had the same effect. Ferdinand and Isabella had been willing to assume the *Iberian* leadership in the crusade against Islam, but had they ever intended to go beyond this? Once placed in the central Mediterranean, their successors could hardly avoid the task of containing the Turk as he moved west. Probably little of this was clear to the Catholic Kings in the epochal year of 1504. Uppermost in their minds must have been the great victory of Ferdinand in Naples, but it was already beginning to be overshadowed by the tragic problem of the succession. Would, or could, a foreign king and an insane queen retain the achievements of the Catholic Kings and even continue them, or was the dual monarchy to founder and Spain to return to the anarchy existing before 1469?

# CHAPTER VII

# The Succession Crisis

FERDINAND AND ISABELLA REARED FIVE CHILDREN BEYOND THE AGE of childhood, but they lost at least five others who died in miscarriages or were still-born. Of these five who survived the perils of birth and childhood, only one had anything resembling a happy life, two died in youth, and two more lived long, terrible, tragic lives.

The eldest, Isabella, was born on October 1, 1470, at Dueñas at a time when her parents were struggling to make good Isabella's position in Castile, and Ferdinand's father was still engaged in putting down the Catalan revolt. A pale, delicate girl who may have been tubercular, she seems to have been deeply religious. Her nickname of *madre* within the family circle tells us something about her personality. On the basis of the scanty evidence available, one has the feeling that she was more suited to a convent than a court, but of course for a royal princess whose marriage would be an important move in Ferdinand's diplomatic game this choice was to be denied her.

The Infante John, heir to all the crowns of the peninsula except Navarre and Portugal, was born in the Alcázar of Seville on June 30, 1478. As the first male child, his birth was received with enthusiasm and many celebrations. At the christening a few days later, the papal nuncio and the Venetian ambassador assisted as godfathers and the duchess of Medina Sidonia as godmother. Contemporaries seem to have seen him very differently. Thus during the years of his infancy and childhood John is variously described as fair, dark, athletic, delicate, musical, and stuttering, *ad confusionem*. The German, Hieronimum Munzer, who may have been more objective, indicates a possible speech defect and Peter Martyr reports that he was fed eggs and other bland foods. All of which does seem to suggest that he was a frail child, a conclusion which his early death strongly supports. As the only son, he had a place above and apart from the other children and, even as a lad, he presided over a small court of his own, which has been described in the *Libro de la Cámara Real del Príncipe don Juan*.

Joanna, whose tragic life and terrible fate make her the best known of the children, was born on November 6, 1479, at the house of the Count of Cifuentes in Toledo where Isabella had gone to await the arrival of the cortes which she had summoned to that city. The new baby arrived during extremely favorable times for her parents. Ferdinand had just succeeded his father in Aragon, the war with Portugal was over, thus eliminating the last challenge to Isabella's right to wear the crown of Castile, and the great Cortes of Toledo was about to begin its work of reorganizing the financial structure of the kingdom. Again, there is confusion amongst contemporary accounts as to her appearance. Some found her plain; others describe her as a beauty. There is more agreement about her personality, which appears to have been strong. She seems to have been intelligent, with a sharp, ironical wit. Like her grandfather, John II of Castile, she was devoted to music; an inventory of her personal effects lists a clavichord, a small organ, and a guitar.[1] But apparently there were other indications which, had the age possessed any knowledge of psychiatry, would have been considered alarming. She was moody, aloof, and secretive. Such affection as she had seems to have been concentrated on her father. Certainly in later life she had serious differences with her mother and these may have reached back into childhood. In all of this, there was nothing that could be labeled insanity and even after her eccentricities (to use the mildest term) had become notorious, there were those who steadfastly refused to believe her insane.

Maria is the least striking of the children and the most difficult to visualize. She was born in Córdoba on June 29, 1482 during the early years of the Granadine War. Her birth was a difficult one and thirty-five hours later the queen gave birth to a second daughter, born dead. Maria seems something of a nonentity. Unlike her rather overwhelming parents and some of her sisters, she was a placid child and her life was destined to be uneventful. She was eventually married to a king of Portugal, who gave her a place in royal processions

1. Townsend Miller, *The Castles and the Crown: Spain*, 1451–1555 (New York), 1963, pp. 160–164. This writer has an excellent summary of all the children based on contemporary accounts, for which this author is greatly indebted.

immediately behind his pet rhinoceros, which suggests something less than a passionate love.[2] Perhaps she appreciated being spared the turbulence that surged around her sisters, Joanna and Catherine. At any rate, Maria leaves practically no imprint on the history of her times.

Catherine, fourth daughter and last child, was born at Alcalá de Henares during a lull in the Granadine War. The court was moving northward after having spent some time at Córdoba which, as we have seen, was a kind of advanced headquarters for the Catholic Kings during the prosecution of the war. A short distance north of Madrid Isabella was overtaken by labor pains, and made a hasty stop at a castle belonging to the archbishop of Toledo. Here, on December 16, 1485, the Infanta Catherine was born. Of all the children she most resembled her mother, and like her developed immense reserves of moral courage and determination when later on she was confronted with grave crises in her personal and public life.[3]

Isabella's own education had been rather sketchy and Ferdinand's was even less so. Yet both sovereigns had a real appreciation for learning and were determined that their children should receive the education demanded of them by their rank. Isabella in particular was "aware of the new stir in the world, of the eagerness with which the humanists were seeking the secrets of the past, of the deference Italians paid to the new learning. . . ."[4] Even after attaining royal rank, Isabella had begun the study of Latin under Beatriz de Galindo, and later this lady was prevailed upon to remain at court to continue her work with the children. Diego de Deza was the chief tutor of the heir, but others were added including such well known humanists as the Geraldini brothers, Antonio and Alejandro, and the Sicilian Tomás Marineo whom Ferdinand had brought to his court in 1484. The Infante John received the most detailed education, but the queen insisted on a thorough training for her daughters because, as Garrett Mattingly well puts it, ". . . a reigning queen—the only reigning queen in the first century of the Renaissance—could not admit that women's minds were incapable of profiting by classical instruction."[5] Of course they were taught some philosophy and theology, a sizable dose of languages and, very important for persons of their rank, history, genealogy, falconry, and the complex lore of the chase. The girls, moreover, as befitting future queens who would preside over royal households, were taught weaving, sewing, and baking. All in all, they

2. Ibid., p. 160.
3. Ibid.
4. Garrett Mattingly, *Catherine of Aragon*, London, 1942, p. 17.
5. Ibid.

were probably the best educated royal children in Christian Europe in the late fifteenth century.

And yet there was one thing they greatly lacked, and that might be called a home, and home life. Beyond most courts in this age, the Castilian court was peripatetic. All courts traveled to a degree, but in the most advanced states there was a clearly defined capital where the court was located during most of the year. Such places were Paris, Lisbon, London, Copenhagen, Rome, Naples, and Warsaw. Nothing like this existed in Castile. Both Aragon and Castile were *collections* of kingdoms held together by the fact that the same persons ruled in all of them. In the words of a contemporary Castilian jurist "these kingdoms have to be ruled and governed as if the king who keeps them together were the king of each of them."[6] It was this necessity which kept both the Catholic Kings constantly in motion, moving from one regional center to another, to see and to be seen, to hold court, to meet and frequently to pacify the local nobles, settle aristocratic feuds, and the like. Amid such peregrinations, the birth, rearing, and also the death of children had to be fitted in as best could be. As Townsend Miller aptly observes:

All the children were born in different places. Propelled from one end of her kingdom to another, moving incessantly on the large round of her unremitting tasks, the Queen was obliged to give birth in whatever town, and in whatever lodging the pangs happened to assail her. And if their birth places were varied, the scenes of the children's youth were even more kaleidoscopic; of necessity they grew up in the churning wake of their busy parents—on dusty roads, in strange alcazars, in military encampments. Not only did the nation have no capital; the royal family had no home.[7]

2

For Ferdinand, as for any of the rulers of his age, children represented pawns to be used in cementing treaties, diplomatic alignments, and frequently consummating abrupt changes in policy. Thus his mind was busy with matrimonial plans before his eldest daughter was out of childhood, and such plans continued even after Queen Isabella's death. That these plans which seemed so much a part of Ferdinand's astonishingly successful diplomacy would eventually bring down destruction upon Spanish power and undo all the work of the Catholic Kings would doubtless have seemed inconceivable to Ferdinand at the time of their conception. They were dictated by the needs of his foreign policy which, as we have seen, was mainly

6. H. G. Loenigsberger, *The Government of Sicily under Philip II of Spain* (New York, 1951), p. 12.

7. Miller, pp. 157–58.

an extension of the traditional Aragonese ambitions in Italy and resistance to France. Indeed, had it not been for a series of unexpected deaths in and about the royal family, it might have been the Trastámaras rather than the Habsburgs who would have been famous in history for using marriage as a means of conquest.[8]

The first marriage was arranged at the time of the peace settlement with Portugal in 1479. The Infanta Isabella, by now nine years old, was to marry Prince Alfonso, son of the heir to the Portuguese crown. Thus the Catholic Kings returned to the traditional Castilian policy of intermarriage with the House of Aviz, doubtless hoping chance might some day unite the two crowns on the same head—as indeed happened in 1581. After some uncertainties and a good deal of diplomatic haggling, the marriage finally took place at the end of 1490. By this time Alfonso's father had become King John II and the prince was now the official heir to the crown. But the marriage was ill-omened from the start. In the midst of elaborate preparations at Évora, the plague broke out and the inhabitants fled to the suburbs. When it was safe to return, preparations were resumed and the marriage was celebrated with elaborate merry-making that lasted from November 23 to Christmas. The following June, 1491, in a race with a friend, Prince Alfonso's horse threw him and then fell on top of him. The next day he died. The young Isabella returned to Castile where she became absorbed in religious activities and would not hear of any more talk of marriage. For the first time death had frustrated the matrimonial diplomacy of the Catholic Kings; it was not to be the last.

Meanwhile, the longest and most involved negotiations of all were about to begin for the hand of the baby of the family, Catherine. The first proposals emanated from the Court of Saint James. The House of Tudor was a new and as yet unstable dynasty whose legal rights to the crown of England were highly dubious. Anxious to strengthen his shaky throne, Henry VII sought to marry into a strong ruling family. Through their achievements at home, the Trastámaras had become famous abroad and consequently Henry VII approached them with a marriage proposal involving his son Arthur, Prince of Wales, and an infanta. Ferdinand was willing—for a price. Although the Granadine War was still in progress, he was already contemplating an aggressive policy against France. Henry might have the Infanta Catherine for his son if he would agree to break with France and join with the Catholic Kings in an attempt to recover the Pyrenean provinces of Cerdagne and Roussillon which had been seized by

8. According to an old jingle, "Let others make war, do thou happy Austria marry, for Venus bestows on thee the realms that Mars gives to others."

Louis XI some years before. To obtain the infanta, Henry agreed and the treaty of Medina del Campo, March 27, 1489, wrote these provisions into an Anglo-Spanish alliance.

The new alliance was tested in the forthcoming Breton War and did not prove very valuable, as we have seen.[9] Furthermore, when Charles VIII returned Cerdagne and Roussillon without compensation in order to buy the neutrality of the Catholic Kings during his expedition to Naples, Ferdinand had achieved a part of his policy and England was no longer so necessary to him. The marriage projects with England consequently lapsed.

By now Ferdinand had other interests. Charles VIII had invaded Naples and Ferdinand had joined in a European coalition to force him out. Charles had barely escaped from Italy and did not live long enough to make a second journey. Characteristically, Ferdinand had by now two policies to deal with any situation which might develop. Before the death of Charles VIII he had already reached an understanding with France which involved the partition rather than the conquest of Naples. But at the same time he had established the foundations of a potential coalition *against* France by the double marriages with the House of Habsburg.

Maximilian and Ferdinand had been sounding each other out about a marriage connection since 1488. In that year Maximilian had sent an embassy to Spain to discuss a possible marriage between the Archduke Philip, heir to the Low Countries and the Habsburg lands, with the Infanta Joanna. The initial reactions were favorable, but the negotiations went very slowly, with much exchange of correspondence and negotiators. Ferdinand and Isabella sent Bishop Juan de Fonseca, so often employed by them on delicate missions, to Flanders and in 1492 Philip's mayordomo came to Castile. Then a delay followed while Ferdinand was negotiating the involved problem of Cerdagne and Roussillon with France, and obviously not in a position to offend Charles VIII by a marriage alliance with Charles' old enemy. However, with the two provinces in his hands, and with the rapid development of Aragonese policy in Italy, Ferdinand was ready to draw closer to Maximilian and the marriage negotiations were resumed with the new idea of a second marriage between the Infante John and Philip's sister, the archduchess Margaret, once previously betrothed and wedded by proxy to Charles himself. Is it possible that at this early date the Catholic Kings were aware of the dangers that might threaten their work if their sole male heir, Prince John, were to die without issue? Was it to protect their crowns against a foreign succession that they now brought John's name into the

9. See Chapter VI, *passim.*

negotiations which had hitherto dealt only with Margaret? The marriage contract states that their mutual purpose is to arrange and correlate Spanish and Austrian interests in Italy, but Ferdinand and Isabella may well have become alarmed at the prospect of a frail, unmarried heir with sisters already married to foreign princes who might at some future time stand in the line of inheritance.

For whatever reasons, the negotiations were now carried through rapidly. Joanna's proxy wedding took place at Valladolid early in 1496 with the Bastard of Burgundy standing for the archduke Philip. The marriage contracts called for an early departure of the bride, accompanied by a large fleet that would take her to the Low Countries for the final ceremonies. The fleet would then escort the archduchess Margaret back to Spain for her wedding with the Infante John. All this called for a great show and Ferdinand and Isabella were prepared to make their daughter's wedding journey as splendid as possible. The fleet assembled is estimated at 110 to 130 vessels, mostly rented for the occasion, and carrying possibly as many as twenty thousand persons. According to Miller, a memorandum at Simancas lists such fascinating items as 85,000 pounds of hung beef, 150,000 herring, 1000 hens and 10,000 eggs, with 400 barrels of wine to wash it all down.[10] The attendants were selected with the greatest care; only those of the bluest or royal blood were permitted on board. Ferdinand's cousin, the Admiral Don Fadrique Enríquez, was in command of the expedition and had his own 450 attendants and followers. The fleet was ready to sail by August 20, 1496, but adverse winds held them up for two more days during which time the queen slept on board in her daughter's cabin.

Unfortunately, the delays did not improve the weather; and the fleet, once it put to sea, found very rough going. Storms forced them to anchor at the open roadstead of Portland in England where the local gentry entertained the new archduchess for two days. Then, with more favorable winds, they put to sea again and reached the Flemish coast. To avoid the danger of shipwreck, Joanna was taken off the large carrack in which she had sailed, and established on a much smaller vessel with lighter draft. This was a wise move as shortly afterwards one of the large vessels did go on the rocks and Joanna lost her trousseau and much of the clothing of her ladies. And the final blow took place when they reached port for Philip was not there. In fact, he was presiding over the Reichstag at Lindau on Lake Constance several hundred miles away. Upon receiving the news of his wife's arrival, the archduke and a small suite traveled with all speed

10. Miller, p. 168.

to join her while Joanna made a slow progress through the rich cities of Flanders until she reached the monastery of Lierre, where her future sister-in-law, the archduchess Margaret, found her ill with a cold. She was quickly aroused, however, by the arrival of Philip who routed out a chaplain and insisted on being married forthwith. A brief and private ceremony was hastily gone through and the young couple promptly went to bed. Next day there was a public ceremony with all the necessary pageantry. Such was the beginning of Joanna's violent and stormy marriage to Philip of Habsburg.

It was now necessary to prepare Margaret for her marriage to the Infante John as the fleet was anxious to return to Spain. Consequently, the first proxy ceremony was solemnly staged at Malines on November 5, 1496 with the Spanish ambassador Francisco de Rojas acting for the infante. The bride's father, the emperor Maximilian, gave her cloth of gold for her wedding gown and the two gold rings he had given her mother, Mary of Burgundy, so many years ago at their own wedding. It was now possible to depart, but bad weather again held them up and the fleet did not leave Flushing until January 22. This departure almost ruined everything, for they immediately ran into a terrible storm that drove them to seek harbor at Southampton. After waiting three weeks for better sailing conditions, on their first try out there was a major collision and the entire fleet returned to port. After a week's delay a second attempt was more successful and the fleet succeeded in putting to sea only to run into another terrible storm in which it was feared that the flagship would go under. Eventually, in a thoroughly battered condition—passengers as well as ships—they landed at Santander where they were not expected, and only some days later was the archduchess able to meet her future husband and King Ferdinand.

After these mishaps it is pleasant to relate that the ceremonies took place without further difficulties. Isabella received her new daughter-in-law at Burgos with great splendor, being attended by ninety ladies in cloth of gold. A quiet family Easter Sunday was spent at the convent of the Holy Trinity, and here Margaret and John fell in love—or so the chroniclers tell us. On Monday there was a private marriage ceremony in the small convent chapel, followed by the welcome seclusion of a week's honeymoon. Finally on April 3, 1497, in the full blaze of publicity, a formal marriage was performed by the archbishop of Toledo, followed by many public ceremonies and celebrations. By summer the infante was able to report the welcome news that Margaret was pregnant; only those close to the royal family knew that the physicians were beginning to be worried over the health of the heir. A schedule of too many public appearances and the duties of matrimony were more than the frail strength of John could sustain. The doctors even proposed to the queen that the young couple should be separated for a time; for reasons not at all clear, Isabella refused.

With Margaret now pregnant, it seemed possible for the Catholic Kings to return to the idea of a closer tie with Portugal, already tried once before and interrupted by the death of Alfonso. His father had died in 1495 and had been succeeded by Emmanuel the Fortunate who well remembered his late cousin's bride. Although the Catholic Kings spoke of the possibility of a marriage with their fourth child, Maria, Emmanuel asked for the hand of the Infanta Isabella. At this point there seems to have been a delay which both Zurita and Peter Martyr explain on the basis of Isabella's reluctance to marry again. However, Merriman thinks that the real reason was the desire of the parents not to send Isabella to Portugal until John's marriage had been consummated and a child was expected. As we have seen, both conditions were fulfilled by the summer of 1497, and Emmanuel was promised the Infanta provided he agreed to expel all Jews from Portuguese territory before the wedding took place. Thus Ferdinand and Isabella extended their solution of the religious problem of Spain to the entire peninsula. The expulsion was decreed and arrangements were made for the wedding ceremony for the coming fall of 1497. The sovereigns escorted their oldest child to Alcántara on the Portuguese-Castilian frontier and prepared to celebrate this latest marriage. At this moment, without preliminary warning, the succession crisis suddenly erupted.

3

The wedding celebrations at Alcántara were suddenly interrupted by terrible news from Salamanca. On arriving at that city, the Infante John had suddenly been attacked by fever and his life was in grave danger. Ferdinand left at once for his son's bedside and by hard riding was able to be present at the end. On October 4, at the age of nineteen and after five months of marriage, the Infante John died. The shock, both personal and political, was profound. A somewhat dubious contemporary account tells us that Ferdinand tried to prepare Isabella for the blow by reporting that the heir was improving but that he himself had fallen sick. The survival of the House of Trastámara in the male line now depended on Margaret and the child she was carrying. But the shock of John's death had been too much; Margaret was delivered of a still-born daughter, born prematurely. It was now clear that no male descendant of Ferdinand and Isabella would reign in Spain.

The repercussions of John's death were felt in distant places. In the Low Countries Philip of Habsburg proclaimed himself heir to the Catholic Kings, to their bitter resentment. Later he was forced by their indignant protests to disavow this hasty act. But it was clear that the question of the succession, which John's death had left open, must be settled as soon as possible. Since a woman could reign in Castile, there was no question about the rights of the oldest daughter. Consequently, Isabella and Emmanuel were summoned from Portugal to receive the allegiance of the Cortes of Castile. After meeting the Cortes at Toledo where they received its homage, the new heiress and her husband passed on to Saragossa to confront the Cortes of Aragon. Here they ran into trouble. Aragon adhered to the mythical Salic Law and would not allow a woman to rule. Pleas and pressures only produced the stubborn reply that the law could not be broken by anyone regardless of rank. However, a compromise solution was finally discovered: sons of royal females could be accepted. Since Isabella was expecting a child, the Cortes settled down with the court to await the blessed event. On August 23, 1498, the young queen of Portugal died in giving birth to the Infante Miguel. Isabella was prostrated, but the various Cortes must recognize the young prince as the heir to all the Iberian crowns and grief had to stand aside. Between September of 1498 and March of 1499 the Cortes of Aragon, Castile, and Portugal swore allegiance to the baby who not only foreshadowed the final unity of the peninsula, but also represented an Iberian dynasty. Therefore, with Miguel there rested the last hope of preventing the succession of an alien ruler. As the child seemed healthy, King Emmanuel decided to leave it with Queen Isabella when he returned to Portugal.

Marriage plans had been under discussion for some time for the English match, and the Spanish ambassador in London reported that Henry VII was ready to sign the treaty when, in 1500, a series of births and deaths changed everything again. On February 24 Joanna presented Philip with his first son. The baby, named Charles after the last Burgundian duke, stood to inherit the Low Countries and the Austrian lands and was separated from the Spanish inheritance only by the Infante Miguel. And then on July 20 Miguel, the "child of union" as one historian has called him, died.

> What history would have been like had Dom Miguel lived is a fascinating question. The Netherlands would have escaped an unnatural domination, and the Habsburgs, undistracted by their southern inheritance, might have welded Germany into a national state in harmony with the tendency of the time. Brought together earlier and under happier auspices, Spain and Portugal might have fused into a single nation for which geography seems to have meant them, and that nation, unburdened by the responsibilities in other parts of Europe under which Spain finally foundered, might have enjoyed centuries of healthy, vigorous growth. Such were the issues which might hang on a single royal baby's

life. Ferdinand and Isabella could not see so far, but they could see that their whole position in Europe was altered by the fact that their sceptres would ultimately fall to the alien, German, house of Austria.[11]

Ferdinand and Isabella rallied as well as they could. Some pieces of their hopes and plans could still be secured. The connection with Portugal must be maintained and so they agreed to the marriage of King Emmanuel with Maria, their last unattached child. In view of the fact that Spain and the Netherlands were to be more closely associated than ever before, the attitude of England assumed a greater importance. Consequently, the marriage of Catherine to Arthur, Prince of Wales, was finally concluded, and the infanta, the last of the children to leave, was started on her journey to England on May 21, 1501.

Philip and Joanna, the rulers of the Netherlands, now assumed a position of commanding importance. Not only because their son, Charles of Luxembourg as he was now offically titled, would very likely inherit the various Iberian crowns, but because Joanna would succeed to Castile when Isabella died, and Philip was the legal heir to the Austrian duchies and would stand a good chance of election as Holy Roman emperor when his father Maximilian should die. Moreover, the wealth and geographical location of the Low Countries made them practically a great power and, if for no other reason, their ruler was a major figure on the European stage. With war about to break out again over Naples, for which France and Aragon now nominally allied were actually rivals, Philip's support or hostility was something to be reckoned with. As a result, he became the center of an intense struggle to control him which involved members of his family and the neighboring powers.

History has dealt harshly with Philip. Since he did not live long enough to provide a great deal of historical evidence as to his abilities or policies, many interpretations of him have been made, usually unfavorable. Historians who write of his marriage are likely to be sympathetic with the troubles of Joanna, and are apt to forget what it must have been like to live with a passionate and highly neurotic wife. Spaniards remember his unashamed looting of Castile for his Burgundian friends and his flirtation with Louis XII. Granted that Philip was a rather dull young man who was averse to hard work, it does not seem too hard to work up a little sympathy for him.

His marriage had not gone well. As early as 1498, Isabella had become alarmed both at rumors regarding Joanna's eccentricities and also at the lack of letters. Consequently during July of that year, the queen dispatched Tomás de Matienzo, sub-prior of the Convent of

11. Mattingly, p. 24.

Santa Cruz in Segovia, on a special mission to Brussels. He was there for several months, and seems to have spoken quite bluntly to the infanta. There was a brief interruption of his reports to Isabella to allow for the birth of Elinor, Joanna's first child, and then more followed in addition to letters from Fray Andreas, confessor to the princess. All indicate an inner disturbance and unhappiness. Matienzo uses such words as *turbación* (confusion) and *torbellino* (whirlwind, restlessness) to describe the state of mind of Joanna.[12]

Although his wife was to bear him five more children, husband and wife were not brought together by these births. Joanna's eccentricities and pecularities were to increase until they brought her to the verge of mental collapse. Moreover, she and her Spanish attendants probably found much to dislike in a land whose lush greenness was so utterly different from the sunbaked plains of Castile, and in a people whose easy-going ways had little in common with the intensity and the *gravitas* of Castilians. There seems little doubt that she was passionately in love with Philip and that his infidelities caused her violent anguish and jealousy. Doubtless there were terrible scenes and constant recriminations. Much of this can be found in her documents. Still, princely infidelity was the rule rather than the exception, and even Isabella's household was not exempt. Ferdinand had fathered at least five bastards whom he openly acknowledged, and one of them became archbishop of Saragossa. The surprising thing is not so much that it happened to Joanna, but that she reacted the way she did. Her mother had learned to put up with it; apparently she could not.

One contender in the struggle for control of Philip, therefore, was his wife. But he was pulled in other directions. He was sovereign of the Low Countries and responsible, to a certain extent, to his council. He was also the son of Emperor Maximilian and a son-in-law of Ferdinand. His advisors were nervous about these potent relations and tried to steer a course closer to France as a counterpoise to the Austrian-Spanish combination. This displeased both his father and his father-in-law. By virtue of his marriage he was a prince of Castile and in the course of time would probably become king-consort of a land where his wife would be queen and where women could rule. This promised additional difficulties and complexities.

From that viewpoint of the Catholic Kings, the most important thing was to try to turn Philip into a Spaniard as soon as possible. His son, the future Emperor Charles V, was eventually to acccomplish this, but it took years and there were many difficulties to be overcome. Ferdinand and Isabella were probably defeated before they began,

12. Miller, pp. 192, 195.

but obviously the effort must be made. At least, everything must be done to strengthen Joanna's position and to attempt to give Philip the Spanish view of international affairs. Philip and Joanna were urged to come to Spain as soon as possible in order to receive the necessary recognition by the Castilian Cortes. On the other hand, the Flemish council, not anxious to have Philip out of its influence, urged delay. The pressure on the unhappy archduke increased. The Catholic Kings suggested that if he could not appear in person before the Cortes he should let Joanna come by herself to represent him. It had even been intimated that their son, Charles of Luxembourg, should be brought up in Spain. Pulled in various directions, the archduke and his wife continued to hesitate. As Fuensalida, the new ambassador from Spain, reported to his sovereigns, "Some say they will come at the end of October...some say the end of November. I believe nothing for nobody tells the truth....*They have no more desire to go to Spain than to hell.*"[13]

The date for an official state visit was finally set, but there was doubtless dismay in Spain when it was learned that they planned to journey overland and travel through France as guests of Louis XII, who was obviously making his bid for control of Philip. It must be remembered that the partition of Naples had begun and was soon to be followed by open war between France and Aragon. So distressed were the Catholic Kings by this impending visit of their daughter and son-in-law to France that they hastily dispatched the faithful Fonseca on a special mission to Flanders to explain the situation to Joanna. His reports were not encouraging. The infanta was anxious to help her parents, but he found her almost completely isolated at the Burgundian court with even some of her Spanish attendants now won over to the Burgundian side. Juan de Moxica and Juan Manuel, in particular, had become staunch supporters of Philip and bitter enemies of Ferdinand.

The trip began in state with the journey from Flanders to Paris, which was reached on November 25, 1501. Everything possible was done to emphasize Phillip's position as a peer of France, and, it must be added, as a vassal of France. He presided over a session of the Parlement of Paris in his quality of peer, and then on December 7 he and Joanna were received by Louis at Blois. The visit was not a happy one for the archduchess. Efforts were made to induce her to take part in ceremonies which might be interpreted as an act of homage to the king of France; otherwise, she was kept as far from Louis and Philip as possible. Without consulting her, a treaty was drawn up providing for the marriage of her son, Charles, with Claude

13. Miller, pp. 201–204. Italics mine.

of France, a daughter of Louis XII. It must have been a great relief for her when they resumed their journey toward Spain.

After traveling through torrents of rain and snow, they passed into Spain at Fuenterrabia on January 26, 1502, and finally reached Madrid during Holy Week, going by way of Burgos, Medina del Campo, and Segovia. En route to Toledo where the sovereigns awaited them, Philip came down with measles and it was not until May 7 that they made their official entry into Toledo and were formally received by the Catholic Kings. The next day the four dined privately at a family dinner with Joanna serving as interpreter since Philip had not learned Spanish. Then, before the official festivities had gotten under way, everything had to be cancelled because of the death of Prince Arthur, the news of which had just reached Spain. Joanna was pregnant again and Philip was restless and unhappy. By the time the Castilian Cortes officially recognized them (May 22), it was clear that the visit was not turning out the way Ferdinand and Isabella had hoped it would.

The Aragonese Cortes made trouble, as might have been expected. They would recognize Philip only as long as Joanna lived. Furthermore, they insisted on the very important point that, if Isabella died and Ferdinand remarried, a child by this second marriage would inherit Aragon. This proviso does not seem to have been sufficiently emphasized by historians considering the motives for Ferdinand's later marriage to Germaine de Foix. He now knew that if he had a son Aragon was virtually promised to the child. That such a succession would destroy the dual monarchy is obvious, but it seems likely that Iberian unity never meant as much to Ferdinand as it did to Isabella. After the swearing was completed in this manner, Ferdinand departed leaving Philip to preside over the Cortes, which had been asked to consider the problem of raising funds for the war against France which was then in progress. Since Philip was one of the principal vassals of the French crown, and had recently been received in the warmest manner by Louis XII, it can hardly have been a happy situation. Ferdinand must have chuckled at the thought of the predicament in which he had left his son-in-law, who was now beginning to assume more of the position of a rival rather than that of an ally and a member of the family.

Efforts to keep Philip happy and induce him to prolong his visit proved fruitless. He was by now determined to leave Castile and, when told that Joanna's condition prevented her from traveling, he left without her on December 19, 1502. He did offer to attempt to settle the differences between Ferdinand and Louis and enroute through France he signed the Treaty of Lyons in Ferdinand's name. This treaty was so unfavorable to his father-in-law that Ferdinand did not hesitate to repudiate it as soon as he had studied the text.

This, as we have seen, gave the Great Captain an opportunity to break the truce by attacking and defeating the French. Meanwhile, in spite of his haste to leave Castile, Philip showed no hurry to get to Flanders. After the fiasco of Lyons he wandered into Switzerland, and then visited in Bavaria, all in all taking almost a year to get home.

In Castile Joanna was passing through the last stages of her confinement in a state of abstraction and brooding. The word *transportada* now begins to appear in the doctors' reports. On March 10, 1503 she gave birth to the future Emperor Ferdinand, but this failed to dispel her melancholia. Relations with Queen Isabella grew worse and both women seemed to have an extremely bad effect on each other. Isabella's doctor wrote about this time that "the queen is better but in great tribulation and fatigue with this princess, God pardon her."[14] It was finally decided to separate the mother and daughter; Isabella went to Segovia while Joanna was sent to the formidable castle of La Mota near Medina del Campo. Was she really a prisoner? Was this done for her health or as a means of exerting pressure on Philip? Probably we shall never know, but the possibilities remain.

At La Mota things rapidly grew worse. In November, 1503, Philip wrote to Spain asking that his wife and new son be returned to him. Rumors reached Segovia that the infanta was preparing to depart. Isabella therefore sent the ever-faithful Fonseca to find out what was going on and to "reason" with Joanna if necessary. On his arrival, he found the courtyard filled with her equipage and she in the act of leaving. A dreadful scene followed. Failing to "reason" with the distraught princess, Fonseca finally ordered the drawbridge raised and forcibly prevented her departure. On her part, she refused to leave the courtyard and spent the night at the gate. Next day, since she absolutely refused to return to her quarters, temporary lodging was found for her in a small guardhouse nearby the gate. Isabella then sent first Cardinal Cisneros, then Admiral Enríquez, and when they failed, she herself traveled the distance from Segovia to Medina; finally Joanna was persuaded, or forced, to return to her apartments.

However, it was obvious that she could not be detained indefinitely and Philip was demanding his wife. It was equally clear that Ferdinand and Isabella had lost the struggle to control Philip and relations between mother and daughter were at their worst. On April 11, 1504, Peter Martyr wrote that at long last Joanna lay in Philip's arms. Exhausted with their ordeal, the Catholic Kings went to Olmedo—a curious choice in view of its recollections for them—to spend Holy Week. While they were there, terrible news arrived from Brussels. Joanna, jealous of a lady who had attracted Philip's roving

14. Martin Hume, *The Queens of Old Spain* (Edinburgh, 1906), p. 131.

eye, had attacked her rival with a pair of scissors and had seriously
wounded her in the face. The relations of the archduke and his wife
were becoming an international scandal of the worst sort.

Under these repeated blows, the health of Isabella rapidly deteriorated. From Olmedo she went to Medina del Campo and there in
July she received the famous diary of Juan de Moxica.[15] This was a
detailed account of Joanna's behavior which Philip now had sent to
Isabella presumably in defense of his own position and as illustrative
of his problems with his wife. The effect it had on the sick queen
can be imagined. Both sovereigns now took to their beds and although
Ferdinand recovered, it was clear that the queen was dying. As rumors
of her condition spread over Europe, Louis, Maximilian, and Philip
agreed to oppose Ferdinand if he should claim the throne of Castile
on Isabella's death. In Spain, old friends, visitors, and foreign envoys
journeyed to Medina to say goodbye.

Although dying, Isabella worked on until the end. Three days
before her death she dictated a codicil of three articles to her will.
The first article raised a question about the legality of the *alcabala*
and requested the cortes to investigate it; the second article urged
the new administration to proceed to a new recodification of the laws;
and the third dealt with fair and generous treatment for the Indians
of the New World. On November 26, 1504, a little before noon, the
great queen died. Peter Martyr wrote to Talavera, formerly the
queen's confessor:

> My right hand fails for grief.... The Queen has breathed her last. The
> earth has lost its noblest ornament. For never have I read of another
> woman formed by God and Nature, in a mold like hers.... [16]

She was undoubtedly the greatest woman of her time, and one of
the great queens of history. With her passing, everything seems to
darken. The drama of the succession crisis becomes more and more
sordid; the chief actors, especially Ferdinand, lose whatever decency
they possess, and the tragedy of Joanna becomes constantly more
pitiful against a background of growing anarchy in the land.

### 4

With the death of Isabella, the struggle for control of Philip assumed
a new and more intense form. Ferdinand and Philip were now the
chief rivals supported by mutually hostile factions, and Joanna was
the victim of their conflict. Isabella's will provided the opening phase.
This document began with the usual recommendation to her successors to govern in accordance with the Christian religion and to follow

---

15. Unfortunately, this diary has completely disappeared. Perhaps Ferdinand or Isabella had something to do with this.

16. Miller, p. 234.

strictly the laws of Castile. Appointments to high office were to go only to natives of the kingdom. There was even a reference to Gibraltar; it should always be kept Spanish.

Joanna was recognized as queen-proprietress of the kingdom—provided she was able to rule—a significant point. If she were unable or unwilling, Ferdinand was to act as regent until his grandson Charles of Luxembourg was of age to claim his kingdom. Probably too much has been made of the elimination of Ferdinand from the succession. The laws of Castile were perfectly clear on the subject;

Joanna was the legal heiress and Ferdinand had no rights. Furthermore, Philip was an alien whom they signally failed to win over. It was difficult to see what else Isabella could have done, the situation being as it was. Moreover, it must have been clear to the queen, after the experience of thirty years of rule, that many of the nobility would not accept Ferdinand as king, and the events of the immediate future bore this out. Perhaps her only mistake in drawing up the will as she did was to believe that the two men most concerned, Ferdinand and Philip, would accept Joanna as queen. And yet one was the father, and the other the husband. If they would not grant Joanna her rightful place, who would? On the other hand, if Joanna were insane, Ferdinand was obviously the better choice for the regency than the foreigner Philip.

Was Joanna insane? The question was debated then by contemporaries and by historians ever since. Later on Henry VII was to question the Spanish ambassador bluntly on this subject:

Tell me, ambassador, is the Queen such as they say she is? If what they say is true, God defend that I should marry her for three such kingdoms such as hers, but there are those who say it is your king who keeps her shut up and spreads this rumor about her. Indeed I have had reports from Spain that she listens and replies rationally and seems quite normal. When I saw her two years ago, her husband and some of her council were giving it out that she was mad, but at that time I saw her speak and act rationally and with great grace and dignity. I thought her sane then and I think her so now. On your honor, is she not such as her husband would desire?[17]

This was plain speaking indeed, and Fuensalida, the ambassador being questioned, could not reply. The fairest statement that can be made about Joanna's sanity seems to be that she was sane when she married Philip and became insane after his death. This is not to say that she was completely normal at any time. She was probably unstable, neurotic, and certainly strongly attracted physically to Philip. Under the terrible pressures to which she was subjected by her own

17. Calendar of State Papers, Span. IV, ii, f. 592 as quoted by Mattingly, p. 82.

nature as well as by Ferdinand and Philip, she became increasingly unstable and, eventually, mad. Yet her progress toward complete disintegration was neither consistent nor steady, and this explains the different impressions about her state of mind which were gathered by observers. During her better days she was capable of perfectly rational behavior, at least as late as the time of the *Comunero* revolt, and much was made of this, especially by those who were anxious to establish her sanity for political reasons. Unfortunately, neither her father nor her husband were in this category and from the conflicting reports of doctors and ambassadors they could build up almost any kind of case against her that they chose. From Ferdinand's point of view, both Joanna and Philip stood between him and the control of Castile which supplied him with the resources he needed for his Italian wars. Therefore, one or the other or both must be eliminated in some way and the regency of Castile confirmed in his possession. To Philip, Joanna as Isabella's sole, legal successor stood in the way of his control of Castile which he must have to combat the power of Ferdinand, whom he was now regarding as his major enemy. Therefore, both men, for entirely different reasons, had an interest in finding Joanna mad.

For the moment, Ferdinand could do little after Isabella's death beyond what the laws required. He summoned the Castilian Cortes to Toro and in their pesence, and that of Cardinal Cisneros, had Isabella's will read. Moxica's diary was also produced and for the first time Joanna's mental incapacity was revealed to the deputies. As a result, they naturally confirmed Ferdinand in the regency. Philip, advised not only by his Flemish council, but also by Juan Manuel, Moxica, and others of a pro-Burgundian Spanish group that now clearly showed its hand, ordered Ferdinand to retire to Aragon, and dissolved the Cortes until he and Joanna could reach Spain. Meanwhile he sent agents to Castile well supplied with funds to win the support of the nobility. In this he was quite successful. For a good price, many of the grandees who hated Ferdinand were willing to turn against him. The duke of Medina Sidonia, one of the great landowners of the south, is supposed to have offered Philip two thousand horse, eight thousand infantry, and a loan of fifty thousand ducats if he would land in Andalusia and appoint the duke its captaingeneral. Ferdinand endeavored to win Joanna's support, but either through force or threats she was induced to send letters to Castile which were disseminated among the aristocracy telling them that she and Philip would soon be in Spain.

It is clear that during his years as king-consort of Castile Ferdinand had made many enemies, and it is probable that the dual monarchy rested on more shaky foundations than historians have been willing to admit. The events of the next few years were to make this fact evident. Many of the Castilian grandees feared "the old Catalan" as a strong king and hoped to see him replaced by a weaker one they could control. They were represented in Flanders by Juan Manuel, whose sister Maria was maid of honor to Joanna and who was related to the Córdobas, the Silvas, and the Mendozas among the great families of Castile. It was Juan who served as the principal agent between Philip's Burgundian friends and advisors and the potentially rebellious Castilian nobility. Until the succession of Charles, a constant traffic existed between Spain and the Low Countries which involved adventurers, agents, and diplomatic representatives, all concerned with what Elliott appropriately calls "the squalid drama" of the succession.[18]

However, there were other ties beyond political opportunism that naturally bound the two regions together, and the chief of these was economic. The growth of the wool trade made the two regions economically interdependent. Nearly one-half of Spain's export trade was with the Low Countries by the middle of the sixteenth century, and one-third of the exports from the Netherlands went to Spain. After the discovery of the New World, American produce and silver were added to the commodities which were shipped to Flanders.

In the months following Isabella's death, Ferdinand's position in Castile steadily deteriorated. With Philip's visit impending, the Catholic King suddenly astonished his rivals by an abrupt change in policy. He approached France for a French bride. He offered as the asking price a promise of Naples to any child which he might have as a result of the marriage, or, failing any issue, he promised to return the French half of Naples to Louis XII. In return, he asked for the hand of Germaine de Foix, niece of the French king. Louis agreed, the marriage treaty was drawn up, signed, and the proxy wedding of Ferdinand and Germaine took place at Blois in October, 1505.

Much has been made of this wedding and the implications involved. Modern historians have accused Ferdinand of deliberately destroying his life work, the joint creation with Isabella of the dual monarchy. It may well be doubted that anyone in the fifteenth century could have understood this interpretation. As we have seen, the kingdoms of Castile and Aragon, each in itself a congeries of earlier kingdoms, were never completely fused together by the famous marriage. Each remained separate, and distinct, although common policies were followed in both states by the Catholic Kings. During the wars with Portugal and Granada, Isabella could hardly be expected to lead

18. Elliott, *Imperial Spain*, pp. 127, 133.

armies in the field and this role was naturally fulfilled by Ferdinand in his quality of king-consort of Castile. This undoubtedly gave him a certain preeminence, which, as the events now being discussed clearly prove, was deeply resented by many of the Castilian grandees. Yet this status of Ferdinand's was largely due to his connection with Isabella and it snapped at her death. Castilian law, in recognizing the right of a queen to rule, certainly excluded Ferdinand from everything but regency rights in the event of Joanna's incapacity. Moreover, the action of the Cortes of Aragon in leaving the way open to the succession of a child of Ferdinand by a second wife virtually invited him to marry again. The growing hostility of the Archduke Philip and the intensification of Joanna's neurosis—to use the safest word —made the acquisition of a powerful ally more important than ever. Should Philip succeed in dominating the Castilian scene and consolidating the nobility behind him, the possibility of war between Philip and Ferdinand was not in the least unlikely. Therefore, it seems unfair to blame Ferdinand for his apparent treason to the cause of Iberian unity. *Mater Hispania*, although not entirely forgotten during the Middle Ages ("Spain is one under all her Spains"), was more of a literary than a political concept. During the famous marriage it was more apparent than real, more a matter of convenience than legislation. In 1469 nor later in 1504 did any one really think in terms of Iberian unity in an administrative sense. The division of the peninsula into separate kingdoms was considered as unalterable.

Yet in spite of the new understanding with Louis, Ferdinand's position was still insecure and for this reason he was willing to agree to a temporary understanding with Philip. The result was the Treaty of Salamanca in November of 1505, which recognized a tripartite rule of Philip, Joanna, and Ferdinand. This was so obviously a temporary expedient that it may be called a farce. Philip now knew that he must come to Spain at once; and as soon as Joanna had recovered from the birth of her fifth child, the pair set out on January 8, 1506.

Since the understanding between Ferdinand and Louis, the trip across France was out of the question and they traveled by sea. This time, Philip had determined to come with sufficient force to settle matters in his favor. Some two thousand soldiers were packed into about forty ships. The fleet got as far as the Bay of Biscay without serious trouble and then on the fourteenth they ran into a terrific storm which almost sank the flagship and caused serious damage to the whole fleet. On the seventeenth they were virtually thrown up on the English coast. A long visit followed with Henry VII, lasting until April 21.

After the usual difficulties were overcome—the local inhabitants first took them for pirates—they received a warm welcome. There were parties, hunts, and constant parleys from which Joanna, to her intense anger, was omitted. Wild marriage plans were discussed, never to be fulfilled, and there was an exchange of orders, the Fleece for the Garter. A commercial treaty between Henry and Philip was drawn up which was so unfavorable for the Low Countries that it was nicknamed the *Intercursus malus*. Clearly, Henry VII was calling the tune and Philip was following it in order to win support for his Castilian policy. Meanwhile, Joanna was kept out of all this and was not even allowed to see her sister Catherine. They met briefly on February 10 when Joanna came to court and made a striking impression on Henry, as we have already seen. Then every one separated and the archduke and his wife headed south toward the ships by separate ways. They met again at Exeter, where they were delayed for some time while the fleet was being prepared; and here Joanna conceived her sixth and last child, the child of her captivity. At long last, they sailed on April 22, 1506.

Should Philip land in Andalusia and summon the rebellious nobles to a war against Ferdinand? Some of the nobility hoped that he would; but either because of a change of plans, or the dictates of the weather, the fleet put in at La Coruña on the extreme northwest tip of Castile. Ferdinand may have planned on armed resistance, but the rush of nobles, including his cousin the admiral, to meet Philip and Joanna must have caused him to forget this idea for the time being. Joanna refused to perform any acts of sovereignty until she had met with her father, which probably influenced Ferdinand to seek an interview with his son-in-law. Philip tried to avoid such a confrontation and demanded Ferdinand's immediate withdrawal, but the old king was too much for him. As Philip moved south, the king followed him and on June 19, when they were only six miles apart, the archduke had to consent to an interview, which was held the next day in an oak grove near the village of Villafáfila. Never was Ferdinand's uncanny skill shown to greater advantage. Philip turned up in full armor at the head of his troops, likewise prepared for battle. They were met by the king of Aragon in civilian dress ambling on a mule in the midst of a small suite quite unarmed. At the outset Philip was made to look like a fool. The two men rode off for a private conference, out of which the Treaty of Villafáfila emerged some days later. There were really two treaties: by the first one Ferdinand agreed to withdraw from Castile, handing the government over "to his beloved children," yet retaining the grandmasterships of the military orders, and one-half the revenue from the Indies; by the second, both parties agreed that Joanna would be excluded from the sovereignty of Castile. After the signing of the treaties, and the withdrawal of the archduke, Ferdinand then made a secret declaration before witnesses that since the treaties had been extorted from him by a threat of force, he had consented to them, but he now denounced them and stated that nothing could set aside Joanna's rights to the crown of Castile. Thus setting the scene for a future break with Philip, the old man departed for Aragon and thence to Naples—doubtless in a high good humor. He had certainly justified Machiavelli's flattering estimate of his skill in diplomacy.

5

Philip now appeared to have achieved his major aim: Ferdinand was eliminated. There remained only Joanna to deal with, but unexpected difficulties arose. When she learned of the agreement of Villafáfila, there was a violent reaction. She attempted to escape from Philip and his Flemings and had to be prevented by force. At this point the first serious rift appeared between the archduke and his Spanish supporters. When Philip wished to have his wife declared incompetent by reason of insanity, they would not hear of it. On July 12, 1506, when the Cortes of Valladolid met to give its oath of fealty, they gave it, not to Philip, but to Philip *and* Joanna jointly. When Philip proposed to the cortes that Joanna be declared incompetent and he the sole ruler, Admiral don Fadrique Enriquez spoke out boldly in her behalf and the cortes refused to act on Philip's demand.

The rift widened during the next few weeks when Philip, following the same disastrous course his son was to follow eleven years later, began to reward his Flemish friends with the choicest Castilian appointments and offices. This was resented, and it was in the midst of increasing tension that the court came to Burgos on September 7. On the evening of the 17th, after a strenuous game of *pelota,* the archduke became ill, but this did not prevent him from spending the next day at the hunt. On the 19th a violent chill announced a major virus infection, and the following days the patient rapidly ran a course from pains and blood-spitting to a violent diarrhea. From the onset of the infection Joanna had not left his bedside. Forgotten were the violent scenes and the bitter disputes. With the same passionate intensity that led her to insist on her proprietary rights to the crown of Castile, she was now determined to reclaim Philip from the edge of death. She, of course, failed and by Thursday the archduke was in a coma. On Friday, September 25, 1506, a little after noon, he died.

During the next few months, the realm appeared to descend into a chaos highly reminiscent of the terrible times of John II and Henry IV. At court two bitter factions emerged: one, a mixture of Flemings and certain Spaniards, such as the dukes of Infantado and Najera, the marquis of Villena, and some of the Andalusian nobles, were fighting to retain what they had gained from the generosity of Philip. These men wanted the distant and pliable Emperor Maximilian declared regent for his grandson, Charles of Luxembourg. A second group, led by the formidable Cardinal Cisneros and the duke of Alva, wanted to call Ferdinand back to resume the regency as the only guarantee against a return to feudal anarchy. In fact, Cisneros had already written the king, who was en route to Naples, urging his return. However, Ferdinand had learned of the death of the archduke before the letter reached him. He contented himself with continuing his march while sending off a message full of platitudes to Cisneros. He knew well what he was doing.

Meanwhile, the effort to take even the first steps to keep the government in operation broke against the stubbornness of Joanna's grief. Utterly locked in her own private world, she refused to sign anything, convoke the Cortes, or perform any official function until she had seen her father. In her crumbling world, doubtless he came to represent what was left of order, stability, and affection. She would do nothing, she repeated on numerous occasions, until he returned and she had talked with him, and she maintained this resolve even against the appeals of the entire Council of Castile.

Finally, on December 20, she took two decisive steps: she annulled all appointments made since the death of her mother and she announced her intention of accompanying the body of her husband to its assigned burial place in Granada. But travel was difficult because of the weather, the condition of the roads, and her own advanced state of pregnancy. She covered the seven miles from Burgos to Cavia and then stopped. When she resumed her journey, she was able to get to Torquemada, thirty-one miles from Cavia, and again stopped, exhausted. Here Catherine, her last child, was born February 14, 1507. Government officials followed her on this heart-rending trip and Cisneros himself arrived with 1,000 troops for her protection. Daily funeral services were held about the coffin, and on at least four occasions she had the casket opened and looked on the dead face which, according to a contemporary, by this time looked like nothing human.

In April she felt strong enough to venture south again and made about four miles to Hornillos. Here she stopped while spring turned into summer and then came the glorious news that Ferdinand was coming home. The king had been in Naples since 1506, ousting many of the Castilians who had previously received offices in that kingdom. However, he had followed carefully the course of events in Castile through letters from Cisneros and his own agents. Not until his representatives had won over all but the completely unreconcilable among the grandees did he venture back to Spain. He sailed from

Naples on June 4, 1507, and stopped for a state visit at Savona with Louis XII, old enemy and new uncle-in-law. Here it is possible that the two kings made the initial arrangements for the coming attack on Venice. By July 20, Ferdinand was at Valencia and in August he crossed over into Castile. Joanna had already set out to meet him and at Tórtoles father and daughter embraced in a moving scene that brought all, even Ferdinand, to tears.

It does not seem impossible to believe that even at this late date Joanna's reason could have been saved. At least, if any man could have done so, it was her father. But, aside from humanitarian reasons, for what purpose? To be used by the rebellious feudal elements against Ferdinand? This, far more than anything Ferdinand had done, would have destroyed the work of Isabella. It must have been clear to the king that whatever happened Joanna must not become a weapon in the hands of a faction—exactly as she was to become in 1520–1521. Perhaps he toyed with the idea of getting her out of the country and this may have been behind his reopening the idea of her marriage to the widower Henry VII of England. However, her violent resistance to this idea forced him to drop it.

The only alternative to this, as Ferdinand must have seen it, was to have her locked up in some secure place. Consequently, on the eve of an expedition to Andalusia to subdue a rebellious noble, the king suggested to Joanna that he conduct her to the Castle of Tordesillas. She objected passionately and a long tussle followed. Perhaps at this point her mind at last completely gave way. The Bishop of Málaga, perhaps not a completely disinterested witness, reported that her personal habits had become dreadful. Eventually Ferdinand's patience gave way. At 3 A.M. on the morning of February 14, 1509, Joanna was awakened and told she must dress at once for her journey to Tordesillas. In spite of her protests, she was bundled out in an icy dawn and taken to the castle, never to leave it for forty-six years. To ease what was virtually her imprisonment, she was allowed to take her youngest child, Catherine, with her. The following year, the Cortes named Ferdinand what he had been, *de facto*, ever since his return, regent of Castile.

6

The approximately nine years of Ferdinand's rule in Castile (1507 –January, 1516) constitute a kind of unit in themselves. They were marked by his successful elimination of any rival to his power, either from the dissatisfied feudality or his own daughter, and by the failure of his hopes for an heir. They were also marked by the acquisition of a few strong points along the African coast—Mers el Kebir, Peñón de la Gomera, Oran, Bugia, Tripoli, and Algiers—and Ferdinand's highly successful adventures in Italian and Pyrenean diplomacy. In this last field, the "old Catalan" brought off some of his most remarkable successes.

Any chance of Joanna's claims to the throne being used by the nobility as a weapon against Ferdinand was ended by one of the king's cruelest acts. This was the unexpected visit in full state, by Ferdinand and most of the Castilian nobility, to Joanna in November, 1510. Without prior warning to the infanta, the nobles were suddenly brought into her room and were treated to a full view of this tragic woman in her filth and dishevelment. This seems to have effectively ended all talk of Joanna's rights to the crown as long as Ferdinand was living, although the issue was to arise again when a second foreign king arrived to take over Castile in 1517.

In the tangle of international claims over Italy, Ferdinand was an old hand and as usual he successfully out-guessed and out-maneuvered his rivals. During the years following his return to Spain, he participated in most of the leagues formed to partition parts of Italy; and since he knew exactly what he wanted, and usually limited his objectives to what was actually possible, he made decisive gains. Thus he joined with Henry VII, Louis XII, Emperor Maximilian, and Pope Julius II in the famous League of Cambrai (1508) which was organized by the pope with the pious intention of despoiling Venice of some of her mainland possessions, parts of which had once been papal territory. According to Merriman and others, Ferdinand hoped through this venture to regain the Adriatic ports of Monopoli, Trani, Brindisi, and Otranto, which the Venetians had seized in 1504. However, Miller thinks that his real purpose was to get his allies to recognize his regency rights to Castile should Joanna die.[19] This was done in the Treaty of Blois, which was confirmed at Madrid in October, 1510. Next month Ferdinand staged his official visit to Joanna at Tordesillas, as we have seen, and so consolidated both internationally and internally his firm hold on Castile.

Against such a concentration of forces represented by the League, Venice could not contend. Julius got back the papal territory he coveted, Ferdinand received his Adriatic ports, and France easily occupied Bergamo, Brescia, Crema, and Cremona. Verona, Vicenza, and Padua surrendered to emissaries of the emperor. Meanwhile, the republic strengthened its inner line of defense and endeavored to reach an understanding with Julius, who, in truth, had never contemplated the total destruction of Venice. Although his terms were severe, the republic accepted them and the pope lifted the ban of

19. Miller, p. 290.

excommunication from the republic in February, 1510. The League of Cambrai now began to fall apart.

Doubtless this was not displeasing to the king of Aragon. The pressures that had forced him into the arms of Louis XII in 1505 no longer existed. Philip was dead and he was now in firm control of Castile. Furthermore, the prospect of an heir through his marriage to Germaine de Foix had also been settled. After consulting all the available doctors and quacks, after dosing himself with all the unpleasant messes they prescribed, Ferdinand's efforts were rewarded and Germaine became pregnant. Almost as much depended on the successful delivery of this child—the "child of disunion"—as on the survival of the Infante Miguel some years earlier. A male heir would naturally inherit Aragon, as the Cortes had made clear, and since Ferdinand's hatred for Philip seems to have been transferred to his son Charles, it would not be unlikely that the king hoped that his child, especially if male, might expect some consideration in Castile which had already had one unpleasant, if brief, experience with a foreign ruler. But the stars in their courses were on the side of Charles, and the baby, when born, lived just long enough to be baptized with the name of John, and then departed to join Miguel and the others who had once stood in the way of Charles of Luxembourg. Although still unreconciled in his heart, the old king outwardly gave in and tacitly accepted his grandson as his successor. At least, one thing was now clarified: there was no longer need of his alliance with France.

There were at least two reasons why he wished to get out of it: first, he wished to escape from the promises he had made to Louis concerning the division of Naples, and second, he was probably formulating his plans for the last acquisition he was to make, namely, Navarre. Consequently, he terminated his connection with France by joining a new combination known somewhat improbably to history as the Holy League because it included the pope. This league consisted of the pope, Maximilian, Ferdinand, Venice—now restored to good standing—and the Swiss. Conveniently, Julius now absolved Ferdinand from his obligations to France. The purpose of the league was to drive the French from Italy. To this end Ferdinand sent Gonsalvo de Córdoba to invade northern Italy with Spanish troops. The French strongly resisted and sent the youthful Gaston de Foix, brother of Germaine, and one of the rising stars of the age, as commander of a French army. After a few brilliant successes early in 1512, he joined battle with the Spanish forces outside of Ravenna on April 11, and although the French won the engagement and later took Ravenna, Gaston was killed. This ended the French successes. A rapid adjustment of Italian affairs then followed. The Swiss entered

Milan and restored the Sforzas; the Spaniards took Florence and restored the Medici. Genoa hastily joined the side of the victors. According to Mariéjol, the Holy League established the Spanish domination of Italy.[19] It might be argued that this domination had already been considerably achieved. What the Holy League did do was to make possible Ferdinand's successful invasion of Navarre.

His connections with this kingdom were a family affair. As we have seen, Navarre had been ruled by Ferdinand's father and later by his sister. After that it had passed to Count Gaston Phoebus of Foix whose sister, Catherine, had married Jean d'Albret. With the death of Gaston at Ravenna, Ferdinand put forward the rights of his wife, Gaston's sister, against Jean d'Albret, who took the title of king of Navarre. He also managed to bring the new English king, Henry VIII, who was also his son-in-law, into the Holy League by promising him the duchy of Guienne.[20] Actually, the English contributed little to the campaign beyond a certain nuisance value in keeping the French occupied. Taking advantage of his war with France, Ferdinand now demanded the right of uncontested passage through Navarre. This was refused and on July 21, 1512, the duke of Alba entered the kingdom. Pamplona fell three days later and by the end of September the rest of the kingdom had been occupied. The pope considerately excommunicated the king of Navarre and just before his death in 1513 recognized the king of Aragon as the rightful ruler.

Ferdinand has frequently been praised in modern accounts because he annexed Navarre to the crown of Castile. This was not his original intention. After he accomplished the occupation of Spanish Navarre, he joined it to the crown of Aragon. But three years later he broke the connection with Aragon and associated Navarre with Castile. Zurita suggests that this was done because Ferdinand was afraid the association of Navarre with his stubborn subjects of Aragon might encourage the Navarrese to demand more autonomy than he was willing to give them. Nevertheless, they retained a good deal; they still met in their own cortes, and had their *diputación* or committee of estates to meet when the cortes were not in session. Also Ferdinand established a separate council for Navarre instead of merely extending the jurisdiction of the Council of Castile. A truce, signed by Orthez in 1513 with Louis XII, gave temporary recognition to Ferdinand's occupation

19. Mariéjol, p. 80.

20. After the death of Prince Arthur in 1502, long negotiations between Ferdinand and Henry followed concerning the marriage of Catherine to Henry, the new heir. After the Spanish victories in Italy in 1503, things moved faster and a new marriage treaty was ratified in June, 1503. Henry was to marry Catherine in 1506 when he would be fifteen. Actually, the marriage did not take place until Henry was king, in the summer of 1509.

of the kingdom, although a much smaller area north of the Pyrenees remained technically independent. After Ferdinand's death, France later accepted this division as permanent.

Ferdinand's last two years were filled with uncertainties and tentative plans that did not materialize. If he seems unlike his earlier, more decisive self, this was probably due to the deterioration of old age. He discussed the idea with Louis XII of marriage between Renée of France with his favorite grandson, the Infante Ferdinand, who had been brought up in Spain, but this fell through when Louis brought about a *rapprochement* with England and himself married the sister of Henry VIII. The aged groom found the nuptial celebrations and other duties too much for him and shortly died. The new king of France, Francis I, was full of youthful ardor and determined to win glory for himself on the battlefield. Still technically at war with the Holy League, he began to assemble a strong army in August of 1515. He had the Venetians as allies and the skill of the great artillery expert, Pedro Navarro, who had formerly served under Ferdinand and who was an expert at sieges. The League mobilized its forces; Pope Leo X lent troops, and a Spanish contingent was rushed up from Naples. The Swiss were entrusted with the defense of Milan, the key to north Italy, but were weakened by the unpopularity of the regime of Massimiliano Sforza and the existence of a pro-French party both in Milan and the cantons. Francis chose to strike first at Milan and, after a surprise crossing of the Alps at the Col d'Argentière, he engaged the Swiss on September 14–15, 1515, and won the decisive battle of Marignano.

The Holy League was shattered. Leo X made peace, and Francis I became duke of Milan. The Swiss withdrew from international affairs and Maximilian returned Verona to Venice, which by now had regained its strong position on the Lombard plain. The new status of France was reflected in the famous Concordat of 1515, which the papacy was forced to sign with the victor. The balance of power had now shifted in favor of France and once again Italian affairs were in turmoil. The advantage of hindsight tells us that these changes were not to issue in a new order of things, and that Charles V was to recover in 1524 all that seemed lost in 1515; but of course Ferdinand could not know this, and Francis' victory at Marignano must have struck him a telling blow. Unfortunately, his government in Castile was too unpopular and his own health too precarious to permit him to react.

Already, some of the most important of the Castilian aristocrats, such as Gonsalvo de Córdoba, the marques de Priego, and others, were planning to desert the old king and take service with Charles of Luxembourg, the future heir. Ferdinand, siezed with a strange restlessness, wandered over northern Spain, seldon staying long in any place. He had already had one heart attack and it was clear that the end was not far off. He still seems to have hoped that some place could be found for his grandson Ferdinand in the administration of the Spanish kingdoms, but Charles and his Flemish advisors were determined not to have this. Death overtook the king in the mountains of Estremadura in the little village of Madregalejo, January 23, 1516. According to a rumor, his advisors kept him from a last minute attempt to alter the succession in favor of the Infante Ferdinand. By his will, Charles' rights were fully recognized; pending his arrival in Spain, Cardinal Cisneros was to be regent for Castile and Ferdinand's bastard son, Alonso de Aragon, was to be regent for Aragon, Catalonia, and Valencia.

For the last time Cisneros was called upon to hold together a realm that seemed to be falling apart. Violent conflicts broke out between hostile nobles, such as the quarrel between the duke of Infantado and the count of La Coruña. Political factions quickly sprang up: some planned to discredit Cisneros in the eyes of the coming king. Others still pinned their hopes on the İnfante Ferdinand and one group even plotted to overthrow Cisneros, sieze the infante, and proclaim him king. On his part, the cardinal and his supporters were striving to establish some form of control over Charles and to nullify, if possible, the influence of his Flemish counsellors. But they also had to deal with opposition from another quarter: many of Ferdinand's Aragonese supporters, including a considerable number of *conversos*, now hastened off to Brussels to counteract the influence of Castile and to protect their own positions. The possibility that the new administration would be managed by a combination of Flemings, Aragonese, and *conversos* doubtless caused Cisneros worry.[21]

Yet the cardinal managed to hold everything together until Charles arrived. When the young, unprepossessing grandson of the Catholic Kings first stepped on Spanish soil and found himself in a land whose customs, language, and institutions were unknown to him, the heritage of Ferdinand and Isabella was his to deal with as he chose. Whether he would continue their work, or prepare the seeds of its destruction was still in the unknown future.

21. Elliott, *Imperial Spain,* pp. 132–34.

# Epilogue: The Advent of the Habsburgs

THE HOUSE OF HABSBURG ARRIVED SUDDENLY, AND ALMOST unexpectedly, on the international scene. Although a member of the family succeeded in winning the imperial crown as early as 1274, this was more of a testimony to Habsburg weakness than a tribute to dynastic strength. While the family increased its holdings within Germany, it did little for the Holy Roman Empire itself; and during the long and virtually lifeless rule of the Emperor Frederick III (1440 –1493), the imperial structure reached its nadir. Except for his astonishingly successful marriage projects, the next emperor, Maximilian I, did little better. His efforts to reform the Empire internally were successfully frustrated by the local interests of the princes, and it was only in these princely states that any political consolidation took place in the fifteenth century. Although the German princes had less control over Maximilian's foreign policies, they did not support them and most of the emperor's schemes foundered for lack of funds and the military power that money could buy. Only in the matrimonial aspects of his foreign policy was Maximilian successful in preparing the way for the enormous accumulation of territory and crowns that descended on the head of his grandson, Charles of Luxemburg, between 1506 and 1516. In the short space of a decade, the House of Habsburg had acquired the potential for becoming a power of the first rank.

Along with this went a major reorientation of Habsburg interests. The various duchies of Austria had seldom showed any interest in western Europe. They were basically Danubian and southeastern. But with the acquisition of the Burgundian lands, the Habsburgs suddenly found themselves deeply involved with the commercial and diplomatic relations of the West. The family itself was profoundly changed. It must be remembered that both Charles and his father were born and raised in Flanders. Thus their cultural background was Franco-Burgundian and quite different from that of Maximilian or Frederick III. If Charles was regarded as a foreigner in Castile, he was scarcely less so in Germany. The language he had heard from birth through adolesence had been French, and even as late as the Diet of Worms (1521) he had barely managed a few words in German as an addition to the official statements made in his name by his chancellor.[1]

Thus both the dynasty and the territory it controlled were something quite new and different in 1517 from what they had been in the past. And just where did the Spanish kingdoms fit into the new structure? This was a question the Spanish were asking themselves and they were not happy with the answers. To many of Charles' Spanish contemporaries his advent was regarded as a disaster. Probably Isabella and certainly Ferdinand saw it in the same light. Later, of course, opinions changed. For one thing, Charles himself changed. He neither remained Burgundian nor became a German; he was Hispanized. The process had begun when he selected the Portuguese Infanta Isabella as his bride and spent his honeymoon in Seville. Unable to speak the Spanish language in 1517, he was able to master it so as to address the pope and the College of Cardinals on April 2, 1536. And lastly, it was to Spain that he returned for his retirement and his death.

The question, however, still remains to confront the historian. Did the advent of the Habsburgs mark a sharp break with the Spanish past? Was it, indeed, a disaster which eventually and ineluctably led to the moribund Spain of Charles II? Did the Habsburgs destroy or further the work of Ferdinand and Isabella? Unfortunately, no easy answer can be given, but some facts must be recognized if any estimate of the Habsburg influence on Spain is to be attempted.

For all that Charles' first contacts with his Spanish subjects were disastrous and led directly to the anti-foreign movements of 1520–1522, he did not introduce any novelties in the structure or administration of his Spanish kingdoms. The conciliar system developed by the Catholic Kings remained basically unchanged, although some additional councils were added later. However, all remained within the general pattern of the previous reign. Even the Inquisition, although Charles was under strong pressure to change it, emerged with

1. Karl Brandi, *The Emperor Charles V. The Growth and Destiny of a Man and of a World Empire.* Translated from the German by C. V. Wedgwood (New York, 1939), p. 128.
2. Ibid., p. 131.

its prerogatives intact. The precious *fueros* of the eastern kingdoms were untouched, although Charles obviously did not like them; and Castile, as in the time of Ferdinand, continued to be the chief peninsular source of revenue for the diplomacy of the emperor.

In matters of foreign policy a considerable case can be made for continuity of interests and goals from the Trastámaras to the Habsburgs. Of course, certain new problems appear, such as the relations between the duchy of Burgundy and the crown of France; but Charles, like Ferdinand, is still fighting Italian wars with France, still attempting to maintain good relations with England, and still trying to check the advance of Islam westward in the Mediterranean. The colonial expansion begun by the Catholic Kings is continued under Charles with outstanding success and over a much greater area; here, in this field of endeavor as in the others, there are no fundamental changes.

So far, it would seem that rather than representing a break with the past, and the beginning of something new, the Habsburg administration actually continued to its logical conclusion the work of Ferdinand and Isabella, especially in the suppression of feudal anarchy which seemed about to return after the death of Isabella and again after the death of Ferdinand. Yet, in the long run, such was not to be the case. I believe that the Habsburg dynasty did destroy the greatness of Spain and did eventually reduce the nation to the level of a third-rate power, but not in the way this statement is usually understood. It seems clear from the preceding pages that most of the institutions and policies of the reign of Charles I can be found in embryo in the times of the Catholic Kings. Most of them, save one major issue: the German problem.

Two facts need to be kept in mind: one, the election of Charles as emperor; and two, the inauguration of the Reformation by Martin Luther. Since both events occurred at approximately the same time, this created a conjuncture that was to be ominous for the future of Spain. For it was through the Habsburg connection that Spain eventually became the leader of the Counter-Reformation and it was this burden that ruined her economy, involved her in hopeless wars far from home, destroyed her military and naval establishments, and terminated the work of Ferdinand and Isabella.

> Ye know that I am born of the most Christian Emperors of the noble German Nation, of the Catholic Kings of Spain, the Archdukes of Austria, the Dukes of Burgundy, who were all to the death true sons of the Roman Church, defenders of the Catholic Faith....Thus I am determined to hold fast by all which has happened since the Council of Constance. For it is certain that a single monk must err if he stands against the opinion of all Christendom.... Therefore I am determined to set my kingdoms and dominions, my friends, my body, my blood, my life, my soul upon it. For it were great shame to us, and to you, ye members

of the noble German Nation, if in our time, through our negligence, we were to let even the appearance of heresy and denigration of true religion enter the hearts of men.[2]

In these memorable, but seldom quoted words, Emperor Charles V addressed the Diet of Worms after the outlawing of Luther. This pronouncement may be called the declaration of war by the Counter-Reformation against the Protestants. From this moment on, the House of Habsburg had a mission: the preservation of Christian unity against the threat of the new Protestant heresies. Of course, the Turk would have to be included among the enemies of the true faith and somehow both Charles and Philip managed to find time, although not very much, to attempt to contain him. But this responsibility never had the overriding importance of the obligation that Charles assumed at the Diet of Worms. After all, the Turk was, in a sense, outside the Christian world and trying to break in; the Protestant heretics were within and trying to corrupt the body politic in heart and soul. Or so the Habsburgs saw it.

It is not surprising that in a remarkably short time the Spaniards saw it the same way. Everything in the religious history of the Iberian peninsula had prepared them for this championship of the Catholic faith. The long struggle with Islam, the efforts to keep the faith pure from Morisco or Jewish taint, the Inquisition—all these factors meant that Spain was going to be extremely responsive to the issues presented by the challenge of the Reformation. And who could more effectively channel these responses into total support for the Church than the young Spanish ruler who had just assumed responsibility for the defense of the faith. Thus Spain came to assume the leadership of that vast Catholic reaction to Protestantism which we know as the Counter-Reformation. At first, this was undoubtedly a great source of strength. It imparted a kind of messianic intensity to Spanish projects that enabled this Spaniards to overcome the twin handicaps of time and space which afflicted the administration of so vast an empire. In short, the great Habsburg conglomeration rested on an ideology, the ideals of militant Catholicism (of which the Basque Iñigo de Loyola was to be so significant an exponent) and this provided for a time the impetus necessary to hold it together.

Yet only for a time. Eventually the Spanish commitment to the Counter-Reformation placed burdens on the Iberian states that none of them—particularly Castile with its still rather primitive economy—could long support. Even the splitting of the dynasty, after the abdication of Charles V (1555), into Austrian and Spanish branches did not relieve the burdens on the Spanish side of the family. The king of Spain, as head of the senior branch, was still regarded as the

2. Ibid., p. 131.

head of the family, and expected to support the particular plans and projects of Vienna even when they did not fit in very well with the policies devised in the Escorial. Long before the end of the reign of Philip II it was becoming clear that Spain was carrying greater burdens than it could bear. Even a monarch as dedicated to the cause of the Counter-Reformation as Philip realized this during the last few years of his reign and attempted to lighten the burdens of his feeble successor. Under Philip III it would have still been possible to withdraw from the extensive commitments in the Netherlands and central Europe; the truce with the Dutch (1609) seemed a step in the right direction. Yet in the long run, the advocates of the old policies of an aggressive foreign policy prevailed; and as Philip III died (1621), Spain was already involved in support of the designs of Ferdinand II of Austria and preparing to renew the Dutch war on the expiration of the Twelve Years Truce. The not unexpected result of all these obligations which Madrid had assumed was the collapse of 1640, when revolts broke out simultaneously in Portugal and Catalonia. From this time on until the end of the Spanish Habsburgs in 1700, the disintegration of the Spanish world power was apparent to all.

Faced with the enormous gap between wishful thinking and a harsh reality, between the ideals of the Counter-Reformation and actual conditions in Spain, with their sacred king a feeble degenerate, Spaniards took refuge in either fantasy or an intense pessimism. The choice, it seemed, was between Don Quixote or Sancho Panza and neither appeared to offer much hope for the future. The national mood of the seventeenth century seemed well expressed in the sonnet by Francisco de Quevedo, called, appropriately enough, *Death Warnings.*

> I saw the ramparts of my native land,
> One time so strong, now dropping in decay.
> Their miseries robbed the light of day for me.
> That has worn out and rotted what was grand.
> I went into the fields; there I could see
> The sun drink up the waters newly thawed;
> And on the hills the moaning cattle pawed,
> Their miseries robbed the light of day for me.
>
> I went into my house; I saw how spotted,
> Decaying things made that old home their prize;
> My withered walking-staff had come to bend,
> I felt the age had won; my sword was rotted;
> And there was nothing on which to set my eyes
> That was not a reminder of the end.[3]

3. Mark Van Doren and Garibaldi M. Lapolia, eds., *The World's Best Poems* (New York, 1932), pp. 256–57. The translation of the sonnet is by John Masefield.

Taking over the massive achievement handed down to them by Ferdinand and Isabella, the Habsburgs were able to create a world power, the first of modern history, which reached its climax before the end of the sixteenth century and rapidly declined thereafter. It was, essentially, a transitional state which emerged after the feudal anarchy of the fifteenth century had weakened the late medieval monarchies in France, England, and Castile; and after the Mediterranean commercial city-state had proved too weak to survive in the tumult of international conflicts. The new imperium, too extended and too diffuse for the backward means of transportation and communication in the fifteenth and sixteenth centuries, survived for as long as it did because the militant Catholicism, first of the revived *Reconquista* in Spain, and later of the Counter-Reformation, provided an *élan*, a drive, that enabled Spaniards to overcome temporarily these problems of time and space. The militant nationalism of the nineteenth century in its successful drive toward national unity in Germany and Italy provides us with a somewhat comparable parallel. The influx of gold and silver bullion from the New World, although disastrous to Spain in the long run, did provide the economic bases for the Spanish predominance of the sixteenth century. Unfortunately, men cannot live on the heights for any great length of time, and eventually these flights of the human will and spirit are followed by a decided slump in morale. When this is accompanied by a major economic breakdown, the damage may be irreparable. This appears to have happened in the case of Spain.

Fortunately, Ferdinand and Isabella did not live to see this and, in spite of their concern over the succession of a foreign dynasty, could not suspect what lay in store for their states in the seventeenth century. And even the knowledge of what was going to happen to their work cannot dim our appreciation of their achievement. In terms of their time and place, what they accomplished was immense and, in spite of obvious flaws, gives them the right to be included among the great statebuilders of history.

# Bibliographical Essay

The following bibliographical comments are not intended to furnish the general reader or student with a complete bibliography of Spanish history. However, it is hoped that they will prove helpful for the reader who wishes to go beyond the information contained in this study or in the footnote citations. Although many of the works that will be cited in the following paragraphs have their own bibliographical information, no student of Spanish history should neglect the three indispensable bibliographical guides to historical literature dealing with Spain and Spanish America: B. Sánchez Alonso, *Fuentes de la historia española e hispanoamericana* (3rd ed., 3 vols., Madrid, 1952); *Indice histórico español: Bibliografía histórica de España e Hispanoamérica* (10 vols., Barcelona, 1953 to date); and the *Handbook of Latin American Studies* (Harvard University Press, 1936–50, University of Florida Press, 1952– ).

In the field of broad, general surveys of Spanish history one should probably begin with the works of Rafael Altamira y Crevea (1866–1951). His *Historia de España y de la civilización española* (3rd ed., 4 vols., Barcelona, 1913) was a pioneering work for its time, and is still valuable in spite of the fact that some parts have been superseded by more recent research. A condensed version rendered into English and extended to 1926 is by Charles E. Chapman, *A History of Spain* (New York, 1927). A more elaborate and detailed multi-volume project for Spanish history was successfully carried out somewhat later by Antonio Ballesteros y Beretta in his *Historia de España y su influencia en la historia universal* (2nd ed., 12 vols., Barcelona, 1943–8). A rather unusual approach to Spanish history in that it is less influenced by Castilian development is the *Historia de España* (8 vols., Barcelona, 1952–9) by Ferrán Soldevila. It also contains valuable bibliographical listings. Harold V. Livermore's *A History of Spain* (London, 1958) is a useful one volume manual of Spanish history and is particularly good for the medieval and Habsburg periods of Iberian history. He is also the author of *A History of Portugal* (Cambridge, 1947).

The fact that Spanish history is divided into several rather clearly marked divisions—Roman, Visigothic, Moslem, Christian, for example—creates its own special problems for historians. Are these periods sharply ruled off from each other, or is there something fundamental in the Spanish character, something that can be identified as *"hispanidad"*, that remains intact and provides a kind of continuity across all the divisions of Spanish history? The question was answered strongly in the affirmative by Ramon Menéndez Pidal (1869–1969) when he published in 1929 *La España del Cid* (2 vols., Madrid, 1929). He held, and was still holding in 1959, that a culture may be transmitted by tradition and literature in spite of drastic military defeats or foreign occupations. Opposing this point of view are the important works of Américo Castro (1885–    ) and Claudio Sánchez Albornoz (1893–    ). In 1954 Castro published *La realidad histórica de España* which was a reworking of an earlier study, *España en su historia: cristianos, moros y judios* (Buenos Aires, 1948). Here, he insisted that there was no organic connection between Roman and Visigothic Spain on the one hand, and the Spain of the Reconquest on the other. The Islamic invasion destroyed the old social structure and what followed was a new blend of Moslem, Hebrew and Christian elements. In this view he is supported to a degree by Jaime Vicens Vives (1910–60). Opposition to Castro's thesis was also elaborated in Sánchez Albornoz' *España: un enigma histórico* (2 vols., Buenos Aires, 1956). No one today who is interested in the foundations of Spanish history can ignore these works. Nor can the modest volume of Vicens Vives on the major issues of that history also be ignored. This is not the place to discuss the extraordinary contributions of this brilliant historian to the history of his country. Let us concentrate instead on his *Aproximación a la historia de España*. (Barcelona, 1952).[1] It is astonishing that in less than 200 pages of text, Dr. Vicens Vives has managed to summarize not only the major themes and controversies of Spanish history, but a considerable amount of bibliographical material as well. For anyone who wishes to understand what Spanish historians consider significant in the history of their country, this book is extremely helpful.

General works that still cover a wide sweep of Spanish history but with a special orientation are typified by Vicens Vives' *An Economic History of Spain* (with the collaboration of Jorge Nadal Oller) translated by Frances M. López–Morillas (3rd ed., Princeton, New Jersey, 1969). Beginning with the economy of prehistoric Spain, this work covers with remarkable success practically all aspects of Spanish economic activity to the end of the nineteenth century. Naturally, the authors' special interests affect the distribution of emphasis; Professor Vicens Vives has done significant work in the economic and social structure of Catalonia in the fifteenth century while Professor Oller has concentrated on the economy of sixteenth and seventeenth century Spain, areas which receive careful scrutiny. The bibliography is also very valuable. By contrast, Roger B. Merriman's four volumes on *The Rise of the Spanish Empire in the Old World and the New* (New York, 1918–34, reprinted in 1962) concentrate mainly on political history, yet they are invaluable for the four major topics covered by each volume respectively: I—the Spanish middle ages; II—the era of the Catholic Kings; III—Charles I and V; and IV—Philip II.

1. Translated into English by Joan Connelly Ullman with the title of *Approaches to the History of Spain* (Berkeley: University of California Press, 1967).

Prehistoric, Roman, and Visigothic Spain have each attracted the attention of distinguished specialists whose works can be found listed in the various bibliographies mentioned above. Pedro Bosch Gimpera (1891–    ) and Luis Pericot Garcia (1899–    ) have written extensively on the importance of the African influence in Spanish prehistory—a view frequently rejected by the younger prehistorians. For additional reading on Roman Spain the student should consult the works of Julio Caro Baroja (1914–    ), especially *España primitiva y romana* (Madrid, 1957) E. S. Bouchier[2] and Manuel de Torres, "La peninsula hispánica, provincia romana," in *Historia de España* (edited by R. Menéndez Pidal, vol. II: *La España romana*, Madrid, 1935). Monographic studies on the Visigothic state carried out in recent years by Spanish medievalists have tended to denigrate its influence on later epochs of Spanish history. It is now believed that the Visigoths were, in the words of Vicens Vives, "only a superstructure of power"[3] and the theory of Sánchez Albornoz that they later fused with Basques and Cantabrians to constitute the Castilian population is now seriously questioned.[4] Most Spanish authorities are in agreement that a great deal of additional research needs to be done before the elucidation of many of the problems of Spanish Visigothic history can take place. Ramón de Abadal y Vinyals (1888–    ) has made many contributions to our understanding of the history of the Visigothic kingdom as has José Antonio Maravall, especially the later's *El Concepto de España en la Edad Media* (Madrid, 1954). One should also consult Alvaro d'Ors, *Estudios visigóticos* (Rome–Madrid, 1960). A valuable although rather limited study has been published by E. A. Thompson entitled *The Goths in Spain* (Oxford, 1969). The title indicates the limitations. As Thompson points out in his preface, there is a difference between writing a history of the Goths in Spain, which he has done, and writing a history of Spain during the Visigothic era, which he has not done. By concentrating exclusively on the Gothic occupation, Thompson is able to by-pass some of the complex questions that have exercised the attention of Spanish historians.

Questions concerning continuity versus discontinuity in Spanish history come to a head in the study and interpretation of the Moslem occupation. Thus Stanley Lane–Poole (1854–1931) held in his nineteenth century classic, *The Moors in Spain* (London, 1888) that they were responsible for the greatness of Spain whose decline began with their expulsion, while Sánchez Albornoz feels that the Moslem period was a temporary episode. Castro, on the other hand, while rejecting the thesis of Menéndez Pidal as we have seen, is convinced that Christian Spain is a creation of *both* Moslem and Christian cultures and their interaction. One of the earliest but still useful studies of Spanish Islam is the work by Reinhart Dozy, *Historie des Musulmans d'Espagne* (Leiden, 1861, translated into English as *Spanish Islam*, London, 1913). This history must be supplemented by the works of Évariste Lévi-Provencal (1894–1956). Although his *Historie de l'Espagne musulmane* (2nd ed., Paris–Leyden, 1850) only comes down to 1031, it is a major work as is his shorter *La civilisation arabe en Espagne, vue générale* (3rd ed., Paris, 1961). A valuable popular work is *Historia de la España musulmana* (4th ed., rev., Barcelona, 1945) by A. Gonzalez Palencia. Also brief and easily comprehensible is *A History of Islamic Spain* by W. Montgomery Watt and

2. See Part I, Chapter I, this study.
3. Vicens Vives, *Approaches to the History of Spain*, p. 158.
4. Ibid., pp. 158–59.

Piere Cachia (Anchor Books, New York, 1965); the authors are both professors of Arabic at the University of Edinburgh. For an account more directly oriented toward cultural aspects, the student should consult the outstanding work by Henri Terrasse; *Islam d'Espagne, une rencontre de l'Orient et de l'Occident* (Paris, 1958). The well-known Arab scholar Philip K. Hitti has an extended section on Spanish Islam in his *History of the Arabs* (London, 1937).

The outstanding work on Spanish feudalism is *En torno a los oigines del feudalismo* by Sánchez Albornoz (3 vols., 2nd rev. ed., Buenos Aires, 1945); and one should also consult this author's "The Frontier and Castilian Liberties"[5] although some of the interpretations are now seriously questioned. The origins of the Christian states of the peninsula are thoroughly treated in a political fashion by Merriman in the first volume of his *Rise of the Spanish Empire* . . . and there are a great number of monographs and local histories by Spanish historians such as Abadal's *Els primer contes catalans* (Barcelona, 1958) and the excellent survey of Catalan history, sometimes ignored by Castilian historians themselves, by Fernando Soldevila Zubiburu (1894– ): *Història de Catalunya* (3 vols., Barcelona, 1935). Any detailed reading in Aragonese history should certainly begin with *Aragón en el pasado* (Saragossa, 1960), by José Maria Lacarra. Since much of the Reconquest involves economic, social, and demographic factors, these will be found treated extensively in Vicens Vives and Oller's *An Economic History of Spain,* especially in Parts I and II, sections 11–14, 20. The excellent, classified bibliography will provide the reader with many additional titles dealing with these topics.

Concerning the Jews in Spain, most of the general works cited deal with this important subject in varying detail. Furthermore, most of the studies of the Inquisition, to be mentioned below, go into it still further. But these references do not replace the very significant work by Abraham A. Neuman, *The Jews in Spain. Their Social, Political and Cultural Life during the Middle Ages* (2 vols., Philadelphia, 1944) or the equally important *Los judíos en España moderna y contemporánea* by Julio Caro Baroja (3 vols., Madrid, 1962). Although somewhat older, Fritz Baer's *Die Juden im christlichen Spanien* (2 vols., Berlin, 1929) is still significant. For a general, popular account of the whole Jewish history, including Spanish Jewry, one should consult Abram Leon Sachar, *A History of the Jews* (New York, 1945).

Accounts of the reign of the Catholic Kings are legion and can be found in all the general histories of the period. Beginning with a few of the broader surveys and then passing to the more specialized, one might mention *The New Cambridge Modern History,* vol. I, *The Renaissance* (Cambridge, 1957) which contains a satisfactory survey of the work of Ferdinand and Isabella by J. M. Batista i Roca. Although his work deals primarily with the sixteenth and seventeenth centuries, there is an excellent evaluation of the work of the Catholic Kings in the first chapter of John Lynch's *Spain under the Habsburgs* (2 vols., Oxford, 1964–69). About one half of J. H. Elliott, *Imperial Spain, 1469–1716* (New York, 1964) is devoted to a detailed examination of the achievements and failures of the two rulers, although the coverage is uneven. Economic, social, and cultural matters are fully treated, often with striking originality, but foreign policy is not as well done.

For works concerned exclusively with all or a part of the joint rule of Ferdinand and Isabella, the reader is referred to Merriman's second volume,

5. See Chapter IV, this study.

*The Catholic Kings,* already frequently mentioned in this study. Although very old, but still valuable, there is the well-known *History of the Reign of Ferdinand and Isabella the Catholic* (2 vols., New York, 1838) by William H. Prescott, which is based on much work in the archives. An admirable French study by Jean Hippolyte Mariéjol which appeared in 1892 is now available edited and translated by Benjamin Keen, *The Spain of Ferdinand and Isabella* (New Brunswick, New Jersey, 1961). The English edition contains such useful aids to scholarship as an excellent editor's preface, a glossary of persons, and an able bibliographical essay on recent publications dealing with this period in Spanish history. There is also an interesting popular account with special emphasis on family affairs by Townsend Miller, *The Castles and the Crown: Spain, 1451–1555* (New York, 1963).

Spanish accounts of the two rulers are apt to be overly eulogistic and uncritical. Slightly more objective, yet conventional in interpretation, is the account by Manuel Ballesteros Gaibrois entitled *La obra de Isabel la católica* (Segovia, 1953). However, when the Transtámara family background is involved, one name is outstanding: Vicens Vives. In three major works, this distinguished historian has added enormously, not only to our knowledge of the sovereigns and their family background, but to the whole of the Spanish fifteenth century: *Juan II de Aragón: Monarquía y revolución en la España del siglo XV* (Barcelona, 1953); *Els Trastàmares* (Barcelona, 1956); and *Historia crítica de la vida y reinado de Fernando II de Aragón* (Saragossa, 1952). Also very interesting for the light it throws on the relations between Isabella and her half-brother Henry IV is the revisionist study by Orestes Ferrara, *L'Avènement d'Isabella la Catholique* (Paris, 1958). While it is admittedly difficult to make out Henry as an able ruler, Ferrara is on strong ground when he argues that our generally bad opinion of this king comes from biased, contemporary accounts written by the supporters of Isabella who had good political reasons for blackening Henry's character.

Economic history during the reign of the Catholic Kings is well summarized in Part IV, Section 23 of Vicens Vives *An Economic History of Spain.* However, this necessarily brief account should be supplemented by other studies. Although Fernand Braudel's great work, *La Méditerranée et le monde méditerranéen à l'époque de Philippe II* (Paris, 1940) deals mainly with the later period, it is a work of striking originality and contains information and interpretations that are extremely important for an understanding of Spain during the administration of the two sovereigns. In much the same category are the important studies of Earl J. Hamilton, especially his *American Treasure and the Price Revolution in Spain, 1501–1650* (Cambridge, Mass., 1934), in which he attributes the rapid rise of prices in Spain to the influx of American gold and silver. Elliott offers a convenient summary of recent criticism of Hamilton's theories in his *Imperial Spain.* The important roles of grazing and agriculture are studied in Julius Klein, *The Mesta: a Study in Spanish Economic History* (Cambridge, Mass., 1920), still considered the standard work on this institution; and E. Ibarra y Rodríguez, *El Problema cerealista en España durante el reinado de los reyes católicos* (Madrid, 1944).

The New World has its own vast literature and the necessary guides for those who wish to penetrate it. This renders it unnecessary to provide an extensive bibliography here. However, certain works should be mentioned for those who wish to go beyond the references contained in this study.[6] In addition to the highly suggestive works by Braudel and Hamilton, one

6. See Part II, Chapter V, this study.

of the best studies of the Castilian preparation for colonial expansion can be found in Richard Konetzka *Das Spanische Weltreich: Grundlagen und Entstehung,* which has been translated into Spanish as *El imperio español. Orígenes y Fundamentos* (Madrid, 1946). A most stimulating perspective on the influence of India and the Far East in the expansion of Europe, with special reference to Portugal and the spice trade, is contained in *Asia in Making of Europe,* vol. I, *The Century of Discovery* (Chicago, 1965) by Donald F. Lach. J. H. Parry has written valuable studies of the expansion of Europe in which there are sections devoted to Spain's role in this movement, but one should especially consult his *The Spanish Seaborne Empire* (New York, 1966) which is a part of the series entitled *The History of Human Society,* edited by J. H. Plumb. H. and P. Chaunau have assembled a vast mine of material in their *Séville et l'Antlantique* (8 vols., Paris, 1955– ) while for standard, one volume treatments of the Spanish colonial world one should consult two valuable studies by Clarence Henry Haring: *Trade and Navigation between Spain and the Indies in the time of the Habsburgs* (Cambridge, Mass., 1918); and *The Spanish Empire in America* (New York, 1947). For Columbus the outstanding work is by the unique sailor-historian, Admiral Samuel Eliot Morison, *Admiral of the Ocean Sea* (2 vols., Boston, 1942; also combined into a one volume edition issued the same year). Las Casas and the Indian problem in general have been studied by several distinguished historians, but outstanding in this field is the research of Lewis Hanke. Three of his works are especially noteworthy: *The Spanish Struggle for Justice in the Conquest of America* (Philadelphia, 1948); *Bartolomé de Las Casas. An Interpretation of his Life and Writings* (The Hague, 1951); and *Aristotle and the American Indians* (New York, 1959).

The American scholar, Henry C. Lea, is still the most important name in the bibliography of the Inquisition and related issues. His *History of the Inquisition of Spain* (4 vols., New York, 1906–06) remains indispensable for any thorough investigation of the subject, and, in the words of Benjamin Keen, "efforts on the part of apologists for the Inquisition to diminish the book's stature by diligent search for flaws have so far yielded trifling results."[7] Still, research on the Inquisition has not ceased since Lea and those who wish to bring the subject up to date should consult the excellent one volume study of Henry Kamen, *The Spanish Inquisition* (New York, 1965). Less satisfactory but still useful are A. S. Turberville, *The Spanish Inquisition* (New York, 1932), and Cecil Roth, *The Spanish Inquisition* (London, 1937). For an excellent treatment of the Morisco problem, see Julio Caro Baroja, *Los Moriscos del reino de Granada* (Madrid, 1957). Several works on the Jews in Spain have already been mentioned; in this context, one should add Roth's *A History of the Marranos* (New York, 1932), reprinted by Meridian Books, 1959), and A. Domínguez Ortiz, "Los Conversos de orígen judío después de la expulsión," *Estudios de la historia social de España,* Vol. III (1955).

Foreign affairs are, of course, discussed extensively in all the works heretofore mentioned that treat of the era of the Catholic Kings. This is also true of the succession problem. Altamira, Mariéjol, Merriman, and Lynch are helpful here. In addition, see R. Trevor Davies, *The Golden Century of Spain,* 1501–1621 (London, 1937), and the introductory chapters of Karl Brandi, *The Emperor Charles V, The Growth and Destiny of a Man and of a World-Empire* (translated by C. V. Wedgwood, New York, 1939). Although the study

7. Mariéjol, *The Spain of Ferdinand and Isabella,* p. 366.

by José M. Doussinague, *La política internacional de Fernando el Católico* (Madrid, 1944) is overly biased in favor of its major figure, it is still very much worth consulting. Special aspects of Ferdinand's foreign policy are examined in A. de la Torre, "Los reyes católicos y Granada," *Hispania*, Vol. XV (1944) pp. 244–307, Vol. XVI (1944) pp. 339–82, and in P. Prieto y Llovera, *Política aragonesa en Africa hasta la muerte de Fernando el Católico* (Madrid, 1952).

# INDEX